About the Author

Joining the London Fire Brigade as a cadet at the tender age of sixteen, **DAVID PIKE** was destined to become very much an operational firefighter. Awarded the Queen's Commendation for Brave Conduct as a young fireman, he rose steadily through the ranks during his thirty-plus years' service within the LFB. He commanded one of London's busiest and most challenging fire stations, Brixton. Heavily committed to raising monies for fire service charities, he rowed himself into *The Guinness Book of Records* whilst attracting many thousands of pounds through his, and his companions', endeavours. He retired in senior rank from the Brigade in 1996. David now lives in Devon.

David C. Pike

FIRE-FLOATS AND FIREBOATS

A history of London's firefighting boats

AUSTIN MACAULEY
PUBLISHERS LTD.

A CIP catalogue record for this title is available from the British Library.

ISBN 978-1-78693-588-5 (paperback)
ISBN 978-1-78693-589-2 (eBook)

www.austinmacauley.com

First Published (2016)

Austin Macauley Publishers Ltd.
25 Canada Square
Canary Wharf
London
E14 5LQ

Dedication

In memory of the late

Brian William 'Bill' Butler, MBE, OStJ, QFSM

and

Gordon White

Retirees of the London Fire Brigade

Acknowledgements

Tim Jones

Paul Wood

Darren Tulley

Sarah Kelly

Bill Hickin

Ian Pettit

Tom Gilmore – Mary Evans Picture Library

Illustrated London News (for access to their archive)

Fire Protection Association

The Bodleian Library

Walter Stephenson, Austin Macauley Publishers

Contents

Foreword 9

Introduction.. 11

Chapter 1
A Short History of London and the Thames.............13

Chapter 2
Early Firefighting 22

Chapter 3
Towards the London Fire Engine Establishment 31

Chapter 4
Metropolitan Fire Brigade, 1866-1904 72

Chapter 5
London Fire Brigade, 1904–1939 120

Chapter 6
The War Years and the River Thames Formation.. 177

Chapter 7
The 'Massey Shaw' Fire-Float.................................. 232

Chapter 8
The Post-War Period, 1948-2000 287

Chapter 9
Firefighters Rowing Boats on the Thames 377

Chapter 10
A New Millennium... 400

Appendix I
A River Fireman's tale – The last 'shout' 445

Appendix II
The Massey Shaw Education Trust 483

Appendix III
Roll of Honour: WWII and the Blitz on London ... 487

Foreword

IT HAS BEEN MY pride and privilege to have been closely associated with the London Fire Brigade over many years, both as the Leader of the former Greater London Council and as the first elected Mayor of London of the London Assembly. Contained in their statutory functions was the role of the Fire Authority for Greater London: approving policy for the London Fire Brigade. One of my last most pleasurable duties as Leader of the Greater London Council (GLC) was to approve and welcome in a new generation of the River Thames's fireboats, the 'London Phoenix', the capital's first combined fire and rescue vessel that my GLC Fire Brigade Committee had approved.

London's Fire-floats and Fireboats is David Pike's history of the Thames's river fire engines. Its pages provide a wonderful narration into the development and growth of London's waterborne firefighters. It is a story that continues right up until the present day. In recounting both the highs and lows of London's river fire service this book delivers a notable retelling of this remarkable tale. It is a significant contribution to the river firefighter's story, a story which weaves its tapestry as it draws on the many people, the events and the numerous vessels that have added to the chronicles of the River Thames's unique culture, its traditions and, at times, its colourful and varied customs.

As the Thames has inevitably changed over time, so has the range and extent of its fireboat service. Today the service continues to play an important role in making the capital's river a safer place on which to conduct trade, for people to travel on and to enjoy. With the profits from David's insightful accounts going to the Massey Shaw Education Trust, a charity whose aim is the advancement of public education in the history of marine vessels, particularly involving the preservation and public display of the 'Massey Shaw 'fireboat, I am pleased to be able to add my personal support to this book.

Ken Livingstone

Introduction

A fireboat was designed to be a floating pump that would never run out of water. This is a history of London's fire-floats and fireboats and the stories of the people who worked them.

FOR OVER THREE HUNDRED years there has been a connection between generations of London's firefighters and the River Thames. It is thought that the capital's very first firefighting 'float' was owned by the Sun Fire Office Insurance Company. Whilst no record of the actual vessel exists it is highly probable that it comprised either a large rowing boat or an oar-propelled barge that carried a manual pump operated by volunteers recruited from the riverside at the time of a fire. The Insurance Company firemen directed their leather hoses onto the blaze whilst the volunteers worked the pump.

Given that London boasted one of the greatest commercial ports in the world it might come as a bit of a surprise that London's fire-floats and fireboats only played a supporting role in the history of its fire brigades. The first Sun fireboat came into service around 1765; others followed, but it was over seventy years before a larger 'floating engine' came into service in 1837. It would have looked quite an impressive craft with its sixteen rowers to propel it through the water and ninety pumpers to operate its manual pumps.

As London's fire brigades developed over time so did its water-borne firefighting capability. London's firefighting river service has remained in constant service right up to the present day. This is its story. It is a tale of highs and lows. London's major river has changed together with its docklands, the riverside and its river traffic. This book chronicles how London's river fire service responded to those changes. It considers the development and growth of London and that of London's fire brigades. This book highlights many of the central characters who brought firefighting onto the River Thames and of the generations of rank and file river service firefighters whose stories deserve to be told.

CHAPTER 1

A Short History of London and the Thames

THE RIVER THAMES ONCE provided a route for settlers and invaders alike. It was once considered, by some, that London barely existed before the arrival of the Romans, but this is almost certainly not the case. London as a major town, at least by the standards of the time, must have existed before the arrival of the Romans. None of the experts disagree that there was something like a village or a town before London became a walled city; this would be true of virtually all the largely populated areas of Iron Age Britain and its Celtic culture, which was the last phase of prehistoric Britain before the Roman occupation.

The River Thames may have taken its name from the Sanskrit *Temas*, or the Celtic *Temasis*, meaning 'dark' as its waters are often dark and cloudy; another school of thought is that it is was named after its Roman origins as *Tam* means 'wide' and *Isis* means 'water'.

By AD 140 London, or Londinium, had become the Roman capital of Britain. The River Thames afforded easy access to the sea, and now bridged, London had become a walled city with a population of approximately sixty thousand people. The Romans first organised firefighting in the parts of Britain they controlled, certainly their major centres, even though fighting fires was often limited to nothing better than buckets of water or simple syringes that squirted water at the fire. Once the Romans left in the fifth century AD, firefighting took a backward step for centuries as the districts and the centres of population fell into decline.

Roman London, like the rest of Britain, was menaced by the Franks, Picts, Scots and Saxons. When the Normans finally invaded in 1066 they built the Tower where the Roman wall met the river so that they could defend the city from the east. The City of London became a powerful centre for crafts with the medieval Guilds and Livery companies. It would much later be the City Fathers who insisted on a fire brigade to protect their investments and property.

The Thames provided a means of transportation both for goods and people. But the water was beginning to get increasingly polluted. In 1236, water was being brought to the rich in the City of London by lead pipes from Tyburn Spring, now the site of Marble Arch. By the 16th century London was prosperous as a result of exploration and discovery abroad, in which the Thames continued to play a very important role. London was the largest port in the country. In many respects, it resembled a seaside town. On its north bank it spread from Westminster to the Tower with the river serving as a means of communication, of drainage and water supply. The Thames supported a thriving fish population, including salmon, bream, dace, gudgeon, flounders and sea trout.

The tragedies of the Great Plague in 1665, followed a year later by the Great Fire in 1666, changed the city. The expansion to the west of the city started as some of those displaced in east London did not return after the fire, preferring to settle in the leafier open squares in Kensington and the villages of Chelsea and Fulham. By the end of the 17th century, London had been transformed from a timber-built medieval port into a city made of bricks and mortar. But for the poor of London, misery continued, especially when it came to the water supply. Their choice remained between a polluted Thames and a frozen Thames. Between 1564 and 1814, the river froze six times as the weather grew colder and glaciers in northern Europe advanced. Georgian London was now the capital of the then British Empire and a world trading centre.

In mid-19th century London, out of the 70,000 houses in the city, 17,000 had their own wells, while the rest relied on standpipes – one for every 20 to 30 houses – which supplied water for

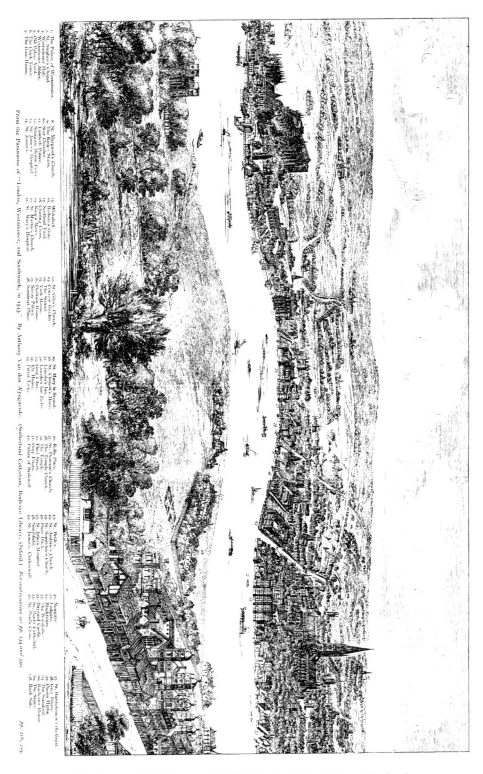

London and the Thames. 1543. (The Bodleian Library. Oxford)

one hour only, three days a week. Few houses had bathrooms and even when Queen Victoria moved into Buckingham Palace, she found no bathrooms. A series of cholera outbreaks in the 1840s and 1850s paved the way for a system of sewers built with the main outfall at Becton and Crossness, away from the central areas and leading to a dramatic drop in death rates (from 130 per 1000 down to 37 per 1000). The first filtration plant for the Thames was built in 1869.

A view of London's riverbank in Lambeth. It was later developed to become the Albert Embankment when construction started in 1863. In 1937 Lambeth's river station was erected here and remains here today.
(Illustrated London News)

As a further precaution, the Victoria, Albert and Chelsea embankments were built to speed the river and to reduce the levels of putrid mud from its banks. The Victorians built more sewers. By the end of the nineteenth century, London was the largest city in history and physically very much what we know today. The building of the embankments and the Beckon sewers improved the quality of the river water. But during the twentieth century, it gradually deteriorated again and by the 1950s, it was little more than an open sewer, containing no oxygen. The production of hydrogen sulphide gave off the smell of rotten eggs. The problem was further aggravated by fluctuating tides as it can take up to 80 days for water to be flushed out to the sea in periods of low rainfall.

The development of the motor vehicle and subsequent growth in road transportation, plus the decline of the British Empire in the years following 1914, reduced the economic prominence of the River Thames. In 1928 a disastrous flood of the river affected much of riverside London. It occurred on 7th January during the hours of darkness. Fourteen people were drowned in London and thousands were made homeless when flood waters poured over the top of the Thames Embankment and part of the Chelsea Embankment collapsed. This was the last major flood to affect central London. However, the North Sea flood of 1953 came within millimetres of overtopping the Embankment and did flood Bermondsey and some other low-lying parts of the city. Another flood later affected the lower Thames in 1959. It was the circumstances of the disastrous North Sea flood of 1953 that ultimately led to the implementation of new flood-control measures for London. These included raising the height of the Thames embankment walls, flood prevention measures in the London Underground's riverside stations and tunnels and culminated in the construction of the Thames Barrier in the 1970s which became operational in 1982.

The damage caused by the flood of 1928 took several years to repair. Millbank, the most seriously affected area, was largely rebuilt from scratch; the run-down dwellings and warehouses that had characterised the area were so badly damaged that they had to be demolished. They were replaced with modern office blocks and apartment buildings. The current headquarters of MI5, located in Thames House and designed by Sir Frank Baines, the principal architect of the Government's Office of Works, was one of the new buildings constructed in the area in 1929–1930. A new Lambeth Bridge was constructed to replace its dilapidated predecessor and Horseferry Road was widened to afford access to the new bridge.

During World War II, the protection of certain Thames-side facilities, particularly docks and water treatment plants, was crucial to the munitions and water supply of the country. The river's defences included the Maunsell forts in the estuary, and the use of barrage balloons to counter German bombers using the reflectivity and shapes of the river to navigate during the Blitz.

In post-war Britain, while the Port of London remained one of the UK's three main ports, trade was already moving downstream from central London. The face of London's docks and its related trades were changing. There was also a marked decline of heavy industry and tanneries in the inner city areas of south, east and west London. The reduced use of oil pollutants, and improved sewage treatment, led to much better water quality for the Thames compared with the late 19th and early- to mid-20th centuries, this meant aquatic life would return to many of its formerly 'dead' stretches.

The 20th century saw a huge decline in the use of the River Thames for trade, especially in the Port of London area. It was a combination of factors that included the reluctance of dockers to see changes to their working practices and the introduction of container ships needing deep-water anchorage that led to the closure of the London docks. The Isle of Dogs (Millwall) and the Royal Docks were never to be the same again. In Essex the development of containerisation saw new docks built at Tilbury to handle the lorries and containers coming in from all over the World. Now the emphasis on trade and the part London's Thames once played shifted downriver from London itself.

Trade also declined on the upper reaches of the river. More goods were being moved by land. Riverside power stations were taken out of commission and some found a new life, like Bankside as the New Tate Modern. The last years of the 20th century and the start of the new millennium have seen an unprecedented surge of building programmes which have changed the character of the London riverside areas from industrial use to residential use. To own an apartment by the riverside with river views is now a treasured, and expensive, aspiration.

New infrastructure programmes were changing the very profile of the river. The Docklands Light Railway (DLR) route takes in the Isle of Dogs Docklands area, which has changed out of all recognition over the past 25 years. The initial system comprised two routes, from Tower Gateway and Stratford to Island Gardens.

Most was elevated on disused railway viaducts or new concrete viaducts, with use of disused surface railway formation between east London's Poplar and Stratford. These fully automated new trains are controlled by computer and have no driver. The DLR line was formally opened by Queen Elizabeth II on 30 July 1987

The Docklands area also found new life with the construction of the London City Airport, which is linked by the Docklands Light Railway to the City of London. The City airport also opened in 1987; by 1988, the first full year of operation, the airport handled 133,000 passengers. By 2005, London City Airport DLR station opened on a branch of the Docklands Light Railway, thus providing rail access to the airport for the first time, with fast rail links to Canary Wharf and the City of London. By 2006 more than 2.3 million passengers had used London City Airport.

The Thames riverside today sees luxury flats nestled alongside huge skyscrapers and glass walls alongside its riverbanks and embankments, together with shops, restaurants and smart wine

Residential apartments in the former St John's London wharf in Wapping, East London. (Author)

bars. Where once stevedores were busy wrestling with heavy, smelly cargoes, today smartly-dressed City workers, bankers and investment managers scurry to meetings, passing designer coffee shops and crossing over footbridges and walkways built across the new waterways. Londoners and tourists have replaced stacked goods as they converge on the myriad of shops which have mush-roomed in the lower levels of converted warehouse buildings.

Leisure activities have also grown on the river and in the docks themselves. Exhibition centres situated in the docks host interna-tional events. Water sports clubs and societies have been formed and grow, making use of the docks for sailing, canoeing and other activities. Many hotels have sprung up in former docks, catering for business meetings, weddings and weekend breaks. In recent years greater use has also been made of the River Thames by the introduction of a regular commuter service by boat between piers in Docklands and the centre of London.

Tourism plays a great part in the use of the River Thames today, with boat trips up and down the Thames in London, a river trip accompanied by a running commentary from one of the experi-enced boat pilots on the history in front of you is a 'must-do' for most tourists visiting London. The Tate Modern is a Thameside success story. This former huge Bankside power station belched out noxious fumes for more than 50 years before closing down. It was completely refurbished in 2000 and reopened as a show-case venue for the latest in modern art. Connected to the north bank of the Thames at St Paul's Cathedral by the Millennium pedestrian bridge, it is yet another example of the River Thames, and its buildings, re-inventing themselves. Another major change in the river has been its water quality. During the first half of the 20th century the quality of water in the River Thames dangerous declined. A report in the 1950s stated that there was no fish life between Kew and Gravesend. A determined effort was made from 1960s onwards to clean up the Thames in London: the result is that the Thames is now one of the cleanest rivers in the world.

For over three hundred years 'fireboats', in one form or another, have played a part in the River Thames story. These firefighting craft have ranged from little more than a rowing boat carrying a manually operated fire pump, to fire-floats with steam fire engines towed by fire tugs, up to purpose-built and iconic fireboats like the 'Massey Shaw'. As the river and its environment changed so did the fire cover provided on the Thames.

The London Fire Brigade today has multifunctional craft, still capable of fighting fires they now have a strong search and rescue role, frequently working in close co-operation with the police and RNLI. This is a story of some of those who worked on these craft through the ages and the development of London's fireboats.

London Fire Brigade's latest fire and rescue craft. (Paul Wood)

CHAPTER 2

Early Firefighting

IN HIS 19TH CENTURY book *Stories of the Fire Brigade* Frank Mundell began by writing: 'Fire is a good servant but a bad master.' That truism remains with us today. We may think we have obtained fire's mastery but woe betide those who forget the nature of the servant. It was just such a fear that saw the creation of elementary fire brigades in the Mediterranean empires of early civilisations. The business of extinguishing fire occupied the minds of both the Greeks and Romans. Rudimentary fire engines, sophisticated for their time, which contained pumps with air vessels and valves to improve performance, were constructed, but they were later lost for centuries after the demise of these civilisations. Academics and historians continue the debate over the gradual collapse of Roman power, which is generally believed to be as the consequence of a series of contingent events. No general causes can be assigned that made it inevitable. Whatever the reasons, any form of organised firefighting was lost for the following generations right across Europe.

It is worth taking a moment to recall what the Romans achieved, however. The Romans were seen as establishing properly organised fire-fighting Legions. Their influence extended right across the Roman Empire in all its major cities, including that of Londinium. Rome itself had a colossal organised fire brigade; initially comprised of slaves, it later recruited freedmen. Archaeological digs in various Roman sites have discovered an assortment of fire-fighting relics and in one case an actual fire station.

After a particularly disastrous fire in AD 6 Emperor Augustus completely reorganised the Roman fire-fighting force. He established a corps of *VIGILES*, something that lasted for the next five hundred years. They wore *two hats* initially: one as fire-fighters, the other as policemen. As the decades became centuries so the standing of the Roman fire service grew in both its stature and ability. What started as a fire brigade of slaves became firefighters enlisted from freedmen, then from those of educated and noble Roman birth. By AD 207 a noble, Rustius Rufinius, was made Chief Officer. Whilst the **Vigiles** never served as soldiers they held parity with the Imperial troops and were proceeded ceremonially by a banner of their Emperor, Rustius.

At their height Rome had a fire brigade split into fourteen districts, each with a main barracks-like fire station with a substation located on its boundary. A Tribune was in charge of each district and the fourteen districts were under the command of a Superintendent. The equipment was the most comprehensive of the age. A fairly elaborate fire pump of a type used by the Romans was excavated in Silchester in Hampshire is now housed in the British Museum although nothing has ever been located from Londinium itself.

Britain had to wait another six centuries before another invasion, by the Normans this time, and before William the First (also known as William the Conqueror) gave us our first 'fire safety' decree. Over nine hundred years ago he issued an edict that all fires and lights must be put out at the ringing of the Curfew Bell at eight o'clock at night. Whilst some of the English thought it an unjust law, others considered it only a revival and enforcement of an old Saxon law. Whichever was the case, both saw prevention better than cure given that the vast majority of buildings in the towns were made of timber, so when a single building caught fire, the entire town was in danger of being destroyed.

Among the earliest accounts of a systematic attempt to preserve life and property from fire appears to have been brought about by Richard the First around 1188. Among the rules for households within the City walls, and drawn up by the Mayor of London, was *'that all those who dwell in great houses within the ward, have a ladder ready to help their neighbours in case of fire.'* It was also ordered that *'those within such houses have before their doors a full barrel of water for quenching such a fire.'*

Despite such laws London was almost lost to fire in 1212. This disaster was known as the 'Great Fire of London' until the later, more famous one in 1666. Still no fire brigade was formed in the aftermath of London's near destruction and fires continued to be fought by volunteers in the vicinity of the blaze. During the 1500s the Lord Mayor of London issued a pamphlet, prepared by a City engineer, on how to fight fires.

It is known that the Romans had used bucket chains, buckets passed hand-to hand, to deliver water to the fire. This and then 'squirts' were used in the Middle Ages to apply jets of water to fires. The squirt worked rather like a bicycle pump. The nozzle was dipped into water and about two 'quarts' (about two litres) was sucked up by pulling out the plunger. The charged squirt was then directed at the fire and the plunger pushed home to eject the water.

Lithograph of early firefighting. (Fire Protection Association)

Elsewhere in Europe and in the American colonies firefighting equipment was equally rudimentary. Before the Great Fire of London in 1666, bucket chains, hooks and squirts were the main equipment of fire protection. They were looked after, in theory, by a parish officer. However, any organised firefighting had all but disappeared. There were primitive fire engines comprising a cistern, which was filled by buckets, and a manual force pump which produced intermittent squirts of water.

Fire hooks in use, 1500s. (Jackson's London Fire Brigades)

At 1 a.m. on Sunday 2 September 1666 fire was discovered at a baker's on Pudding Lane in the heart of the City of London. The baker, Mr Farynor, had forgotten to douse his embers the previous evening and sparks had ignited his nearby woodpile. For four days the Great Fire of London raged, consuming 436 acres, including 80 per cent of the City and some 50 livery halls, 87 churches and 13,200 homes. Out of the ashes of this disaster would rise a new type of business, namely competing, 'for-profit' fire insurance companies, each one of which also owned a fire brigade.

Engraved for Harrison's New History of London, &c.

A View of LONDON as it appeared before the dreadful Fire in 1666.

References

1 St. Pauls
2 St. Dunstans
3 Temple
4 St. Brides
5 St. Andrews
6 Baynards Castle
7 St. Sepulchres
8 Bow Church
9 Guild-hall
10 St. Michaels
11 St. Laurence Poultney
12 Old Swan
13 London Bridge
14 St. Dunstans East
15 Billingsgate
16 Custom house
17 Tower
18 Dr. Wharf
19 St. Olaves
20 St. Mary overs
21 Winchester house
22 The Globe
23 The Bear Garden
24 Hampstead
25 Highgate
26 Hackney

In the immediate aftermath of the fire the Lord Mayor and the City Aldermen attributed the great fire to the *'hands of God'*. They made no immediate effort to establish any form of public firefighting. Their energy was, however, put into the rebuilding of the city. The government of Charles the Second immediately passed the Rebuilding Act of 1667 requiring that only certain types of houses were rebuilt. The provisions were designed to lessen the likelihood of fire.

1666. Great Fire of London. (Fire Protection Association)

Some expressed concern over the lack of formal fire brigades as many suggestions to employ firemen were laid before the City. One such was suggested by one Andrew Yarranton. Yarranton is mainly remembered as a navigation engineer today; however, in his pamphlet *England's Improvement by Sea & Land*, he proposed that sentinels, or special fire commissioners, be assigned for fire protection. The sentinel, it was suggested, should be placed on the *'top of the highest steeple whereby he may look all over the town'* and *'if he observes any smoke or fire he presently sounds a trumpet and hangs out a bloody flag towards that quarter of the City where the fire is.'* Yarranton further proposed that upon hearing the sounding trumpet, *'immediately all the people which are for the quenching of fires with the Commissioners and engineers, or as many as there are in the town run to the place.'* Yarranton's plan was never implemented. Instead, the government passed another Act, this time requiring that fire-fighting equipment be kept in each district of the city, parishes were given equipment, and water supply was improved. The government's limited response to the Great Fire focused mostly on fire prevention measures.

1666: The Great Fire of London. (Fire Protection Association)

Whilst the London fire did stimulate the development of a two-person operated piston pump on wheels, others in the New World had already taken a far more serious view. For example, the Governor of New Amsterdam (the future New York City), a certain Peter Stuyvesant, in 1648 was the first in the New World to appoint fire inspectors with the authority to impose fines for 'violations' of the Cities fire rules. The City of Boston imported the first fire engine to reach America in 1679, thirty-three years after the Great Fire of London.

Early manual fire engine – dated about 1678.

The 'Squirt' in use during the 1600s. (Jackson's London Fire Brigades)

Squirt. (LFB Museum)

CHAPTER 3

Towards the London Fire Engine Establishment

THE 'GREAT FIRE' ENCOURAGED prominent London citizens and merchants to initiate a system of fire insurance. Nicholas Barbon, a physician, and in partnership with others, set up the first London fire insurance office. He conceived the idea of founding an insurance company to protect owners of homes and buildings against losses by fire. His was the first joint-stock company for fire insurance in London and perhaps the world. It was renamed the Phoenix Office in 1705. Initially it insured just buildings, not the furniture, fittings, or goods. Barbon soon realised the folly of standing by while insured buildings burned.

He recognized that the service of an insurer should reach beyond the mere provision of indemnity in case of loss. He instituted the practice of maintaining a number of 'watermen in livery with badges' who would assist in extinguishing fires. It was his office which originated the use of fire marks where properties it insured could be identified when fires occurred. By 1680 he had formed the first private fire brigade to protect his interests and from then on the insurance offices and their fire brigades offered the best protection London had enjoyed for centuries. Public provision for fire protection was made in 1707 when parishes in London were required to provide and maintain a large engine, a hand engine and a leather hose.

Watchman and Beadle, 1600s. (Players cigarette card series)

Mr Barbon was elected a Member of Parliament in 1690 and again in 1695. He rightly deserves the title 'father of fire insurance', because his office was the first private enterprise fire insurance company in the world. His signature appears on early policies issued by his company.

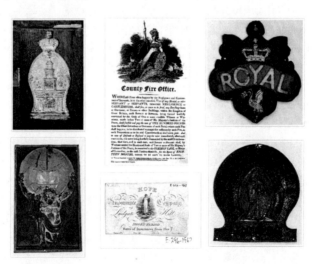

Insurance Company badges and certificate. (Author)

The practice of providing a plaque, or fire mark, to affix to each insured building by a particular company was common. The original purpose of the fire mark, introduced by the Friendly Society, was to denote a house as 'secure'. The fire mark designs showed which houses were insured and by which company. Further, fire marks were to be used as a directive to brigades: if the fire mark was from their company, services were to be provided. However, the entire system of using fire marks broke down. First, the practice of insurance companies removing their fire marks after a policy had expired eventually stopped, with some insurance companies letting the fire marks remain on buildings as a form of advertisement. Second, many individuals were in the practice of insuring their property and valuables separately, with different insurance companies. This would mean that two fire marks, or possibly more, would be affixed to one building. This meant it was impossible for individual insurance brigades to use the fire marks as reliable directives.

The insurance companies had good reason to develop their fire brigades in the first place. They were a means to reduce the financial losses from fire and the subsequent pay-outs. Fires spread, so to allow a building to burn simply because it did not display the appropriate fire mark could result in that fire reaching another house or building that was insured. It is counter-intuitive to suggest that the same individuals who created fire protection would have allowed buildings to burn.

Mr Richard Newsham was an English inventor. In 1721 he took out a patent on the first American fire engine manual pump. In

(Player's cigarette card series)

1725 he took out a similar patent in England. His fire engine had two single-acting pistons and an air vessel placed in a tank which formed the frame of the machine. The pump was worked by men using the long cross handles. The water cistern held around 140 gallons (630 litres) of water pumping up to 80 gallons (360 litres) a minute. In 1737 Newsham made a manual fire pump for the Parish of Bray in Berkshire. He died in 1743.

During the mid-1700s the UK government was in need of money to fight the Colonists in the American War of Independence. As governments do, they imposed a tax, this time on the insurance companies. The insurance companies in turn passed the tax onto their policy holders by raising the insurance premium. This increase in cost to policy holders is thought to have discouraged some potential clients from taking out protection. Though the tax was not all bad for the insurance companies, it was nevertheless generally disliked, so it was later repealed in 1869.

The population of London stood around 600,000 in 1700. It would rise to 950,000 by 1800. Fashionable suburbs had spread north along Tottenham Court Road and to the North West near the village of Paddington. Other London villages included Islington and Chelsea. To the east were the villages of Stepney, Limehouse and Wapping, whilst in the south there were Bermondsey, Rotherhithe, and Walworth and Kennington villages. Several hospitals were also founded in London in the 18th century including Westminster (1720), Guys (1724), St Georges (1733), London (1740) and Middlesex (1745).

Many new buildings were being erected in Georgian London. Buckingham Palace was built in 1703 for the Duke of Buckingham. (It was altered in the 19th century by John Nash (1752-1835) and the first monarch to live there was Queen Victoria in 1837.) Marlborough House was built in 1711. The British Museum was founded in 1753. Also in 1753 Mansion House was built as a residence for the Lord Mayor of London. In 1757 the houses on London Bridge were demolished. New bridges were built: Westminster in 1749 and Blackfriars in 1770.

London was growing and changing. Whilst an Act of Parliament of 1761 set up a body of men called the 'Board of Commissioners', who had power to pave and clean the London streets, London's fire brigade's remained under the control of the insurance companies. However, parishes, volunteers and individuals who owned private equipment also contributed to the protection of London. The government had required parishes to maintain certain fire-fighting equipment, including one small and one large engine. Various records suggest that these London parishes did not keep their equipment in good working condition. Churchwardens were placed in charge of the local fire plugs (a means of connecting to the water supply and an early form of a simple fire hydrant). According to a report by the Hand in Hand insurance company they ran an advertisement 'prosecuting' the churchwardens for 'failing in their duty'. The Government were unwilling to enforce the very guidelines it had laid down. If these mandates did anything, they contributed to confusion at fires as parishes were often unable to operate their engines and water was sometimes unavailable at fires because the church wardens had been remiss in their duty to supply fire plugs.

Insurance Company firemen. (Fire Protection Association)

Volunteers provided additional assistance during this period, particularly in areas not covered sufficiently by the private insurance brigades. Some individuals owned and operated their own fire-fighting equipment as well. This practice was in part due to early insurance policies written to protect only houses, and in part due to the length of time it took to call the insurance companies brigades. Often it was the manufacturers and high-risk companies who pursued this form of self-protection.

Different insurance fire company firemen racing to a London blaze.
(Fire Protection Association)

Fires at this time were often scenes of chaos and disorganisation. Contributing to the confusion were rewards laid down by Parliament, among them varying payments for the first three engines to arrive complete with necessary equipment. Further, the 'watermen' could not always recognise their office directors – watermen or wherrymen were an essential part of early London, who using a small boat called a wherry or skiff would ferry passengers along and across the river – and there was no unified control system. The chaos that ensued at fires is described in *A Record of the Guardian Assurance Company Limited*:

> 'Great rivalry existed among Fire Insurance Companies in their attendance at fires. Their firemen were not exclusively employed for this service, being, as a rule, drawn from the ranks of the Thames watermen, and to get them together when a fire broke out was often a slow process. As these men wore the livery of whatever Fire Office they were attached to, their presence was a constant means of advertisement for their particular offices.

THE ALBION MILLS on FIRE. 1

1
Wednesday March the Second day,
At Six in the Morning (people say,)
In Seventeen Hundred Ninety One,
The Fire at the Albion Mills began,
      Ri toll, tall de roll,

2
This noble building burnt so fast,
Black Friars Bridge could not be past,
Nor could they get the Engines nigh,
These Mills did burn so furiously,

3
At length the roof did all fall in,
And then the Engines did begin,
But tho' with vigour they did play,
The Albion Mills were burnt that day,

4
The folks were all fill'd with amaze,
Beholding such surprising Blaze,
The answer to those who did enquire,
Was, the Albion Mills are all on fire.

London, Publish'd, March 10th 1791. by C. Sheppard No. 19 Lambart Hill, Doctors Commons.

5
And now the folks begin to chat,
How the owners they did this and that,
But very few did sorrow show,
That the Albion Mills were burnt so low,

6
Says one they had it in their power,
For to reduce the price of flour,
Instead of letting the bread raise,
But now the Mills are all on blaze,

7
In lighters there was saved wheat,
But scorched and scarcely fit to eat,
Some Hundred Hogs saved disrant ways,
While the Albion Mills were in a blaze,

8
Now pray God bless us one and all,
And send the price of bread may fall,
That the poor with plenty may abound,
Tho' the Albion Mills burnt to the ground.

Often the brigades quarrelled among themselves about the rewards earned for prompt attendance at fires, and the absence of any central control on such occasions frequently resulted in their duties being performed in a confused and inefficient manner. At the best their exertions were largely confined to saving the property which happened to be insured in their own offices.'

The excerpt depicts the disarray that occurred at fires. It also makes clear that the chaos may not be attributed solely to the private insurance companies. The government's rewards for prompt arrival contributed to it; so did the lack of any central control. This would have been a function of not only the private brigades operating independently, but also the presence of parishes and whoever else may have rushed to the scene. As explained below, the insurance companies developed a partial solution to this problem. Finally, it is not surprising that some confusion existed at fires; firefighting was, after all, a new trade.

The saving of life from fire was a secondary activity of all the insurance brigades. As a consequence the Fire Escape Society was formed in 1828 in recognition of the high loss of life in fires. Six-wheeled escape ladders were provided, each under the control

Fire on Southwark Bridge. Copy by J Bluck from an original by Rowland and Pugin, published in 1808.

of a conductor whose responsibility was to 'run' the escape to a fire with such help from members of the public as he could muster. The organisation was not well supported and eight years later it was succeeded by the Royal Society for the Protection of Life from Fire.

James Braidwood.

In spite of London being the country's leading city, and probably the largest in the world, in 1824 Edinburgh would bring into being the first municipal fire brigade in Great Britain. It was led by a Scotsman, James Braidwood. Appointed as the 'Master of Fire Engines' at just twenty-four years of age, he took command two months prior to the Great Fire of Edinburgh. His force had neither been fully trained nor equipped, yet it fought bravely, losing two of its number to the flames. Despite help from the army garrison the fire burned out of control until it was largely extinguished by heavy rain. The situation was not helped by a confusion of public officials who often issued contradictory orders, wasting the efforts of the Scottish fireman. An enquiry praised the new force and a law was quickly passed which gave the 'Fire Master' ultimate control of such emergency operations. Braidwood was seen to establish principles of fire-fighting that are still applied today. His early training as a surveyor gave him exceptional knowledge of the behaviour of building materials and housing conditions in the Old Town of Edinburgh. He had recruited to the fire brigade expert tradesmen – slaters, carpenters, masons and plumbers – who could apply their various fields of expertise to firefighting. He also recruited experienced mariners for an occupation that required heavy manual work in hauling engines and trundling wheeled escape ladders up and down Edinburgh's steep streets, as well as nimble footwork when negotiating rooftops and moving through partially destroyed buildings. His many original ideas of practical organisation and methodology, published in 1830, were adopted throughout Britain. He was, however, resistant to the introduction of steam-driven engines.

In 1829 the Metropolitan Police Force was established under the Metropolitan Police Act that was seen through Parliament by Sir Robert Peel, the then Home Secretary.

The Victorian age was one of innovation. New craft were coming onto the Thames with the beginning of a new century. The steamship, sometimes referred to as a steamer, was slowly making its presence felt. The steamship was a seafaring vessel, propelled by one or more steam engines that drove (turned) propellers or paddlewheels. The first steamships came into practical usage during the early 1800s; however, there were some exceptions that came before. Steamships were given the prefix designations of 'PS' for paddle steamer or 'SS' for screw steamer (using a propeller or screw). As paddle steamers slowly became less common, SS' is assumed by many to stand for 'steam ship'. The designation still stands today.

Steamboat services on the Thames are recorded as starting around 1815. For nearly 25 years the main use of steam vessels was to carry passengers. This was before the emergence of the railways in the south of England. During this time at least 80 steamers are recorded in the Thames. The *Steamboat Act* of 1819 became the first statute to regulate the safety of this new technology for the public.

The first steam tug on the Thames was the *Majestic* in 1816. The use of tugs to guide sailing boats bringing passengers and cargo up the London River increased the efficiency of waterborne operations enormously. The paddle wheel showed off its maximum advantage. Paddle tugs could apply full power quickly in either direction and by having separate engines for each paddle wheel could virtually turn on the spot. The Port of London Authority (PLA) was handling 12,000 coastal vessels within its jurisdiction and over 3,000 overseas vessels annually by the start of the nineteenth century. The PLA quickly became dependent on steamers. Previously gangs of men in rowboats drew the sailing vessels to port against wind and tide. By 1830, the use of steam tugs became part of the battleground between the competing dock companies as the London and St Katharine dock companies used steamships to tow vessels up-river past the West India Docks.

Paddlewheels as the main motive source became standard on these early vessels. It was an effective means of propulsion under ideal conditions but otherwise had serious drawbacks. The paddlewheel performed best when it operated at a certain depth; however, when the depth of the ship changed from added weight it further submerged the paddle wheel causing a substantial decrease in performance

A year after the London Fire Engine Establishment came into being, the Woolwich Steam Packet Co. and the London Steamboat Co. were established in 1834. They provided services from central London to Woolwich, which were later extended downriver to the Kent and Essex boarders along the Thames Estuary. They would later amalgamate in 1876 to form the London Steamboat Company. They became the dominant force in the Thames estuary excursion business at that time. However in 1878 the greatest disaster in the history of British coastal cruising occurred when PS

Princess Alice sank after a collision near Woolwich with the loss of almost 700 lives.

London saw the arrival of the first fire-float as early as 1765, built for the Sun Fire Insurance Company. It was followed by other fire-floats as more insurance companies wanted to add a floating engine to their companies' firefighting capabilities. Now these fire-floats added to the general mix and divergence of the river craft on the Thames. However, they still remained a manual pump carried either in a barge, towed to the scene of a fire, or in an oar powered craft. One such craft was reported to have sunk at its moorings in 1830. It was replaced with a craft fifty feet long, powered by eight pairs of oars and had three manual pumps fitted to it. It required ninety pumpers in addition to the crew.

Even with the arrival of steam the insurance fire brigades for London maintained the status quo. Steam power had, in fact, been first applied to work a fire-engine in 1830. The steam fire-engine had been originally introduced by the firm of Messrs Braithwaite and Ericsson of New Road, London. Real innovation in fire-fighting had so far remained somewhat static. All that changed in 1831 when a company in Liverpool purchased a three-barrel steam-powered fire pump. It was believed to be the first steam fire engine to be bought in the world. This one engine did the work of many manuals, but conservatism in the London's insurance companies was strong and the various boards basically did not like them. They were considered to be heavy to pull about and took a long time to get up steam.

However, the introduction of the steam fire pump was not the only matter that concentrated the minds of the boards of the insurance companies. They were increasingly expressing their concerns over shouldering the cost of fire protection in London. They argued they were relieving the government of this important duty. Among their concerns were not only the failing conditions of the parochial engines, but the possibility of an insured property and an uninsured property catching fire at the same time. The government chose to ignore their concerns.

London Fire Engine Establishment

London in the year the London Fire Engine Establishment was created.

It had taken the insurance companies a whole year to come together to form one London-wide fire brigade. The Brigade came into force in January 1833. This amalgamation of the former insurance brigades helped to remove some of the chaos that had up to then been occurring at fires.

The London Fire Engine Establishment's (LFEE) Superintendent was to be James Braidwood. He had been enticed to come to London to lead this new brigade at a salary of £400 p.a. Most of the London insurance companies saw the benefit of mutual co-operation, and were impressed by the successful working of the fire brigade force in Edinburgh. Braidwood was their natural choice to command the London Fire-Engine Establishment. Initially the companies to combine were the Alliance, Atlas, Globe, Imperial, London Assurance, Protector, Royal Exchange, Sun, Union, and Westminster. They were later joined by the British, Guardian, Hand-in-Hand, Norwich Union, and Phoenix. Only two fire-offices from London chose not to be involved with the LFEE.

The insurance brigades had amalgamated under the LFEE banner with the Brigade managed by a Committee comprising of a director from each of the contributing fire offices. This Insurance Companies Committee, who paid for LFEE in agreed proportions, divided London into four fire districts. They were:

1st, eastward of Aldersgate Street and St Paul's.

2nd, westward to Tottenham Court Road and St. Martin's Lane.

3rd, all westward of the 2nd district.

4th, south of the river.

In each of four districts the Committee established fire engine stations with about three stations to each district. At each station were one, two, or three engines, according to the importance of the station. The most easterly station was at Ratcliff, and the most western near Portman Square. At these stations were the total brigade complement of thirty-five engines and the brigade's force of around ninety men under the sole direction of the Brigade's Superintendent Braidwood. There was no deputy. The brigade's two fire floats were still the oar-propelled craft with manual pumps. One, pumped by 90 men, was located by Southwark Bridge (Upper Float); the other, pumped by 45 men, was stationed off King's Stair in Rotherhithe (Lower Float), on the south side of the Thames.

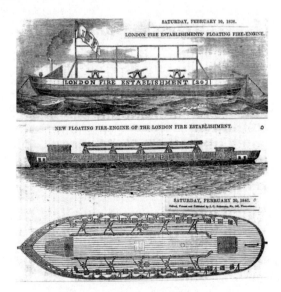

(Illustrated London News)

44

The LFEE firemen were clothed in a matching uniform. They were recruited with reference to their *'expertness and courage at fires'*. A nominated number of the firemen were required to be ready at all hours of the day and night. Their engines available to depart at a minute's notice in case of a fire. It was, as a rule, stipulated that when a fire occurred in any one district, all the men and engines of that district would attend to the address given, together with two-thirds of the men and engines from each of the two adjoining districts, with one-third from the one most removed from it. However this arrangement was modified according to the extent and size of a fire, or the number of fires which may be burning across London at one time.

CHANDOS-STREET FIRE-ENGINE STATION.

(Mary Evans)

Braidwood brought his new ideas and original techniques to his new London Brigade. He encouraged the idea of getting into a building to fight a fire and not the insurance brigade's previous practice of the 'long shot', a hose played at a distance from the outside of the building. He also insisted that no fireman should ever enter a building alone, and that there should always be a comrade to assist in case of an accident or if the colleague collapsed due to the heat or fumes.

Some writers have not been overly kind, or fair, to Braidwood, commentating on his alleged delay in the introduction steam fire engines on fire floats. It was noted by some that despite the growth of the newly invented steam pumps Braidwood was a traditionalist when it came to maintaining the manual fire engines he used. For many years the introduction of steam pumps into the LFEE was delayed. In fact Braidwood was sympathetic to the purchase of a steam fire engine mounted on a float and submitted a favourable report seeking the Committee's approval for its purchase. It was the Committee who rejected the proposal arguing, once again, that they considered it expensive and felt the steam pumps delivered greater pressure than the manuals, therefore the firemen's jets would cause too much water damage and deter the firemen from getting close to the fires.

The manually operated fire engines of the early nineteenth century were themselves both heavy and cumbersome. They were also expensive to operate, with up to twenty men, ten on each side, to work the pump handles up and down. Braidwood did expand the float engines on the Thames. They were long, wide oar-powered boats; many pumpers were required to operate the pumps the fire-floats carried. There was the additional problem of not only paying the pumpers but ferrying relays of pumpers from the shore to the floats. At a fire in Tooley Street in 1837 the LFEE manual fire-float had required three hundred and thirty-three pumpers to work the pumps during the course of the fire.

The first high profile test of Braidwood's new brigade came when his force was less than two years old. On Wednesday 16th October 1834 the Palaces of Westminster caught fire. By the late Georgian period, the buildings of the Palace of Westminster had become an accident waiting to happen. The rambling complex of medieval and early modern apartments making up the Houses of Parliament was by then largely unfit for purpose. Complaints from MPs about the state of their accommodation had been rumbling on since the 1790s, and reached a peak when they found themselves packed into the hot, airless and cramped Commons chamber during the passage of the Great Reform bill.

Throughout the day, a chimney fire had smouldered under the floor of the House of Lords chamber, caused by the unsupervised and ill-advised burning of two large cartloads of wooden tally sticks (a form of medieval tax receipt created by the Exchequer). At a few minutes after six that evening, a doorkeeper's wife returning from an errand finally spotted the flames licking the scarlet curtains in the Lords' chamber where they were emerging through the floor from the collapsed furnace flues. There was panic within the Palace but initially no one seems to have raised the alarm outside. A huge fireball exploded out of the building at around 6.30 p.m., lighting up the evening sky over London, and immediately attracting hundreds of thousands of people.

J. W. M. Turner, Burning of the Houses of Parliament, 16th October 1834.

The fire turned into the most significant blaze in the city since 1666, burning fiercely for the rest of the night. It was fought by parish and insurance company fire engines, and the private London Fire Engine Establishment, led by Superintendent James

Braidwood. Braidwood ordered twelve engines and had sixty-four of his LFEE men leading the battle to quell the flames. Hundreds of volunteers, from the King's sons and Cabinet ministers downwards, manned the pumps on the night, and were paid in beer for their efforts. Astonishingly, no one died in this disaster.

By the middle of the evening it was clear that the fire was uncontrollable in most of the Palace. Westminster Hall then became the focus for Braidwood's efforts and those of his men and hundreds of volunteers. The thick stone Norman walls provided an excellent barrier against the spread of fire, but the late fourteenth-century oak roof timbers were in great peril. The efforts of all, from the highest to the lowest, plus a lucky change of wind direction at midnight, and the arrival of the London Fire Engine Establishment's great, floating barge-mounted fire engine, finally started to quell the fire in the early hours, and ultimately saved Westminster Hall. The fire crews finally left five days later, having put out the last of the fires which kept bursting out from the ruins.

The damage to the wrecked and uninsured Palace was estimated at two million pounds. No-one, however was prosecuted, though the public inquiry which followed found various people guilty of negligence and foolishness. Braidwood was praised for his leadership and the standing of his LFEE force greatly improved. Yet despite the fire Braidwood still refused to consider steam fire engines. Plans for a floating steam fire engine were submitted by Braithwaite (the inventor of the land steam fire engine) in 1835. They were rejected.

However, a large riverside fire occurred some months later and Braidwood had a mini revolt with the pumpers he had on board one of the oar powered fire-floats. They demanded more beer, the payment for the pumpers, and stopped pumping several times. As a result Braidwood finally had a steam pump fitted to the float. Initially it was driven using the jets of water as its propulsion system but this did not prove successful. Instead, a tug was used to tow the float to the fire. The savings made by not having to pay pumpers meant building a new steam fire-float a financially viable option. London finally had its first waterborne steam fire engine.

The steam fire engine was a British invention, the earliest example being manufactured by Braithwaite and Ericsson of

London in 1829. It had a 10 horsepower steam engine with two horizontal cylinders and pump, and weighed 2,286kg: steam could be raised in only 13 minutes. Although never sold, the machine was taken and tested at several London fires and performed well on each occasion. At its first large fire, the Argyll Rooms in Soho, on 5th February 1830, Braithwaite's steamer worked constantly for five hours without breaking down and threw water right over the building. Despite this power, and the huge saving in manpower when compared to the manual engines the new engine was met with a fair degree of prejudice and scepticism by the firefighting profession, not least by the insurance companies' board.

Whilst details of large fires were regularly reported, information provided to Londoners about the workings of the LFEE were sparse. It was often supposed that there were watch-towers on the roofs of the insurance offices or of fire engine-houses, where watchmen were posted at night to watch for the outbreak of fire and raise the alarm. However, if it was ever acted on by the insurance companies it was not the practice in the LFEE stations. There was an arrangement made by the Metropolitan Police commissioners that a policeman, on discovering a fire, reported it instantly to the nearest LFEE station. For doing so he was given a gratuity of ten shillings. This, and a smaller gratuity awarded to other individuals who 'call an engine,' did provide an early warning and information about the outbreak of a fire.

Also recorded in those formative years of the LFEE was the problem of false alarms, or as recorded at the time: *'the lovers of mischief so far show their silliness as to give "false alarms".'* An average of sixty to seventy false alarms were received each year. Some of these 'false alarms' would by today's standards be considered of 'good intent'. Even the LFEE firemen themselves were caught out occasionally. Once they were tantalized by an atmospheric phenomenon (the Northern Lights, or *aurora borealis*). Two such events occurred in London, the first of which resulted in twelve engines and seventy-four firemen looking for the blaze reflected in the sky from late evening until six o'clock the following morning. Some of the engines even reached Hampstead, and others Kilburn before it was realised that the glare was the effect of the Northern Lights. On the other occasion, a crimson glare of light was spotted at the north-east part of the London horizon around eight o'clock in the evening. It appeared to be the result of a fierce conflagration. As if to confirm the suspicion the resemblance was increased by what looked like clouds of smoke rising up after the glare and breaking and rolling away beneath it. Thirteen LFEE engines and many firemen went in search of this supposed fire. They did not detect their error till they had reached far to the north-east of the capital. (Subsequent accounts showed that the military and fire-patrols in Dublin, Leyden, Utrecht, Strasbourg, Troyes, Rennes, and Nantes, had been similarly deceived by the atmospheric phenomena on the very same night.) What was noticed by London's public, or at least reported to them in the then press, was *'when it is really a conflagration to which the attention of the brigade is called, there is an admirable coolness and system displayed in the whole proceedings.'*

London Fire Engine Establishment firemen fighting a fire whilst the public pumps the engine. (Fire Protection Association)

Some slight improvement was made in securing water supplies of firefighting. The Water Companies, by clauses in Acts of Parliament, became regulated and were required to *'furnish water freely in case of fire; and the hose or suction pipe of every engine is speedily placed in connexion with the temporary pool of water derived from the street-plug.'* However, even Acts of Parliament didn't stop the problems of securing water supplies. In January 1838 the Royal Exchange and the adjoining court office of the Lord Mayor were entirely destroyed by fire. The presence of eight fire engines and sixty-three of Braidwood's men was ineffective as the fire-plugs had frozen up. Then, when at last water was obtained, the manual pumps froze up too.

The fire-plugs were upright vents that stood up from the water main below the ground. At a fire it was the job of one fireman to knock out the plug and insert a tapered standpipe, which was inserted into the mains vent against the pressure of the water main. Water then gushed into a canvas dam from which suction hose drew water. It was never an easy task, resulting in the loss of much water and a drenching in the bargain for the unfortunate fireman allocated the task. Valve hydrants had not yet been invented.

Regardless of the Parliamentary regulations, water supply was frequently inadequate. Water in some cases was supplied by unregulated private companies who were not required by law to provide a continuous supply. Many locations would have their water turned on just to fill cisterns and reservoir tanks and then have the water turned off again. If a fire broke out at such premises the LFEE would have to await the arrival of the turn-cock so the water could be turned on before firefighting operations commenced. Frequently it was too little, too late. Even with the water supplied it still had to be projected onto the fire via the manual pumps. For this the firemen had to obtain the aid of bystanders, for the number of firemen allocated to each engine was wholly insufficient to work it and fight the fire. The captain of each engine was empowered by the insurance companies to pay the rate of one shilling for the first hour, and sixpence per hour afterwards, together with a supply of creature comforts (which translated to beer), for the services of as many pumpers as were needed. It required twenty or thirty men to work each engine; and at large fires more than five hundred pumpers were engaged.

While the pumpers were engaged with the manual engines, the firemen were directing their jets of water on the *'destructive element which they have to combat.'* Braidwood's firemen were clothed in a neat and compact uniform and wore a stout leather fire helmet. But like the firemen who would follow in their footsteps for the next one hundred years they faced the fiercest heat, were alternately drenched with water from their hoses and half-scorched by the flaming materials. *'Over and under, through and around the burning house, they directed their energies, braving alike the fire itself and the dangers attendant on falling ruins. It is lamentable to think that men, while thus engaged in a work of humanity, should lose their own lives; but such is the case, although, on account of the judicious arrangements of the corps, not very frequently.'* So wrote a commentator of the period of the lot of a LFEE fireman.

There was only the most basic of breathing apparatus for Braidwood's firemen, or any other firemen come to that. One of the most serious dangers they faced arose from the suffocating effects of the vast volumes of toxic smoke emanating from the fires they fought. It both blinded and choked those battling the flames. It was a rare event that the calamity of being 'burnt to death' befell these fireman. The real cause of death was mostly suffocation from smoke, the burning and charring of an unfortunate soul occurring after they had already succumbed to the smoke. In theory at least, to rescue anyone trapped in a fire they had what was described as *'a very ingeniously-constructed smoke-proof dress'*. The dress was based on that of the diver at the time. It consisted of a leather jacket and a head-covering which was fastened at the waist and wrists. It made for a tolerably smoke-proof hooded jacket.

Two glass windows were fitted into the hood, and an air pipe attached to the girdle allowed fresh air to be pumped into the enclosed jacket supporting the respiration of the wearer. It was promoted as: *'thus equipped, the fireman may dare the densest smoke, although the dress is not so formed as to resist flame.'* However, the practicalities of getting the equipment to work and records of its use indicate that the theory was rarely, if ever, put into practice.

The London Fire Engine Establishment at work at a City of London blaze.
(Fire Protection Association)

The London Fire Engine Establishment's fire-float at work on the Thames.
(Fire Protection Association)

Throughout its tenure the LFEE remained a private body over-seen by the insurance companies, although it was seen as the public fire service for the whole of the then London area. In an LFEE advert, published on 1st January 1833, it announced their goal was to provide better fire protection to the inhabitants of the 'Metropolis'. James Braidwood led a force that consisted of 80 'watermen' (firemen) and operated from 19 fire stations. Braid-wood had instituted formal training programs for his firemen, and required that they have working knowledge of the district that they were appointed to. The LFEE was considered to be an efficient organisation and Braidwood a formidable leader of his men. However, the large insurance offices did not consider the protection the Brigade provided adequate for the City of London, and preferred fire protection to be publicly funded. London was rapidly expanding and so was the cost of protecting the metropolis from fire. In 1833, the cost of firefighting was £7,988; by 1865 the cost would rise to £26,005.

One large fire followed another. Major fires put pressure on the insurance company profits. Fires at high-profile locations also caused the insurance companies to continue to pursue their claim with the government for a change to funding the fire brigade. One such fire occurred in October 1841. The Tower of London Armoury, containing some 280,000 items of arms and armour, much of great historical interest, was destroyed by fire. The government had provided buckets, hand pumps and small manual pumps to the Tower but they were woefully inadequate and subsequently it was found they had been neglected and were in a dilapidated condition.

Today banner news headlines of sensational news stories are the norm. It is not such a recent innovation. Even back in 1841 this style of news reporting was being produced by both weekly journals and especially daily newspapers. This is the flavour of the *'Latest Particulars of the Awful Fire and Total Destruction of the Tower of London on the Night of Saturday 30th October 1841'*, by J T Wood, printer and publisher of Fore Street, Cripplegate, London.

In Mr Wood's view, this was *'the most alarming and destructive fire that has occurred within the memory of the present age.' 'In the midst of the general confusion,'* says Wood, *'we could but remark on the absolute sublimity of an element let loose, roaming at discretion, from building to building the fire seemed to rejoice to madness, emitting light and heat which astonished [...]'*

THE TOWER OF LONDON,

(Fire Protection Association)

The fire was, in fact, first noticed at about half past ten on the evening of the 30th October, by a sentinel on duty near the Jewel Office. He raised the alarm by firing his musket and the entire battalion of the Scots Fusilier Guards turned out. Flames soon burst out from windows of the Round Tower. Colonel Auckland Eden, the Officer Commanding, directed the troops to turn out the nine Tower manual engines. These were soon supplemented by the LFEE fire brigade engines. The Round Tower was rapidly consumed and the fire had spread to the Armoury roof. Braidwood's firemen carried their hoses from two of the brigade engines into the Armoury and trained them on the ceiling and walls, but they had to leave hurriedly when the ceiling began to give way.

The Armoury was 345 feet in length, and one of the largest in Europe. It contained a great variety of trophies and artefacts, many of which had seen service in important battles of English history, much of which was lost. By 11.30 p.m. flames were issuing from all parts of the Armoury, and the fire had now reached the Clock Tower. Great crowds of Londoners had assembled to witness the blaze and had to be kept at bay by several hundred policemen. The heat was so intense that it was impossible to stand on the broad walk between the Armoury and the White Tower. The glare of the fire was so bright that the Minories had the appearance of daylight.

Tower of London fire, 1841. (Author)

Aftermath of the Tower of London fire 1841. (Author)

Efforts of the firemen and soldiers to put out the fire were hampered by the fact that the water tanks under the Tower contained very little water. Also, the Thames was at low tide, so that when eventually Braidwood's floating engines arrived and moored off the Traitor's Gate, his men had over 700 feet of hose to lay out and could do little but supply water to the fire engines nearer the fire.

At about two o'clock, a rumour spread about that a large magazine was attached to the Armoury and some of the crowd dispersed hurriedly, fearing an explosion. This was apparently occasioned by the loud roaring of the flames, which went on until about 2.45 a.m. on the 31st October, when the fire began to abate and the firefighters were able to get nearer to the ruins.

By about four o'clock in the morning of the 31st October, the fire was out in most places although the ruins smouldered for days. There was one fatal casualty, a fireman who was killed by falling masonry. Almost everything was destroyed.

Immediate steps were taken by the Government to find the cause of the fire and to examine the conduct of officers and troops but there is no reason to think that the fire was other than accidental. Probably it was caused by the armourer's forge in the Round Tower, or the flues of the stoves there.

(**Illustrated London News**)

The LFEE was purely in the business of saving *property* from fire, not the saving of *life*. In 1836 The Royal Society for the Protection of Life from Fire was formed. It followed in the footsteps of the Fire Escape Society (1828), an organisation set up by philanthropists in reaction to the high death rate in domestic properties. The Royal Society for the Protection of Life from Fire provided escapes at fires working alongside the fire brigade to protect the citizens of London from fire.

As before, parishes, volunteers and individuals owning and operating equipment continued to exist. Parishes, while perhaps providing some assistance at fires, generally had not improved the condition of their equipment. Volunteers continued to supplement the private brigades' coverage, providing a great assistance to Braidwood and his force that were responsible only for the insured properties located primarily in the centre of London. Individuals owning their own fire equipment continued to provide additional protection.

Manual fire engine typical of the London Fire Engine Establishment. (Mary Evans)

This period is characterised by the unification of the previously independent fire brigades. Although the formation of a single brigade did improve the fire service in London and reduce the costs experienced by the brigade, there were problems with the business model employed. Insurance companies were responsible only for insured property. Uninsured property would suffer if ever it should catch fire at the same time as an insured property. Despite having concerns about the fire service which had been brought to its attention, the government declined to become involved.

In 1852 Shand Mason & Co. undertook the conversion of the LFEE fire-float, moored at Southwark, to steam power to drive the pumps. Two years later the same company built a purpose-design steam float. It was fitted with a water power (jets) propulsion system, the idea being that the energy from jets of water striking the Thames moved the float through the water. Holes were cut into the sides of the float and the fixed jets directed through these openings. Control of the jets, positioned around the float, made it highly manoeuvrable. However it failed to move more than 8 mph, and when trying to move against the Thames tidal flow its speed was negligible. It was nevertheless a formidable pumping machine. When used at the Tooley Street fire in 1861 it was pumping for some 400 hours, a duration that no London fire-float or fireboat has ever surpassed since that one incident.

London was still expanding and the cost of fire-fighting was growing. The insurance companies struggled to continue to provide the service. It was clearly not becoming a profitable endeavour. They were paid to provide insurance, not to fight fires, and the cost of offering fire protection was proving to outweigh the benefit to share-holders and company profits. Furthermore, because insurance companies were paid to provide insurance, an incentive existed for the offices to protect insured homes. A problem could certainly arise if both an uninsured property and insured property caught fire at the same time – the insurance companies would focus first on the insured property and the uninsured would follow. No incentive existed for insurance companies to correct this problem because they were not paid to fight fires. The government however felt the services provided were adequate and turned its attention elsewhere, for now.

The Tooley Street fire would bring Braidwood's reign to a tragic end. James Braidwood had proved himself to be a well-respected leader of his men. He was popular with the public too. He was a quiet man, in fact he was described as a gentle character with a devoted wife and family when he was not waging battle against many of the major fires to confront the City of London and area of the LFEE brigade. He was also loyal to his employers, the insurance companies. He kept his eye on the ball throughout his career in London; a frequent visitor to his fire stations, he also attended tests and trials of the new fire engines and fire equipment. However he was also a cautious man, taking time to consider these new developments before making changes to previous practices.

The twenty-second of June 1861 may well have been an average day for Braidwood. What he was engaged in prior to the outbreak of fire in Tooley Street remains a matter of conjecture, and is of little concern given what followed. It had been a hot summer day in London. Scovell's warehouse was located on the river's edge in Southwark, adjacent to London Bridge. The hot day may have been the reason some of the substantial iron, fire-proof, doors had been opened and allowed air to flow between the storage areas on various floors. What is known is that the doors should, in fact, have remained closed. The warehouse contained vast quantities of hemp, cotton, sacks of sugar, wooden casks of tallow, bales of jute, boxes of tea and spices.

Later reports would suggest the fire, like most fires, started small: bales of damp cotton giving rise to very higher temperatures until the threshold arrived where spontaneous combustion occurred. As the flames rose and spread, so the fire consumed ever more goods. With the iron doors not containing the blaze it soon spread beyond its point of origin.

The alarm was finally raised around five o'clock in the afternoon. It became immediately apparent that the fire had a firm hold on Scovell's wharf and was spreading to the adjoining Cotton's wharf, and it would eventually consume both Hay's and Chamberlain's wharves too. Braidwood was quickly on the scene from Watling Street and had twenty-seven horse drawn engines, one steam engine, his two fire-floats and one hundred and seventeen firemen and officers, plus fifteen drivers fighting this conflagration on the south side of the River Thames. The fire had such a hold that water from the firemen's hose evaporated before it even reached the boundary of the fire. Burning tallow, oil and paint flowed onto the river, almost consuming one of the fire-floats. The winds and thermals caused by the fire, aided by the Thames currents, sucked small boats into the flames.

Braidwood was not fighting the flames unaided. Captain Hodges had brought his private fire brigade to assist Braidwood in his endeavours, his two steamers working alongside the LFEE's solitary steamer. Hodges' firemen was joined by other private brigades before parish manual pumps were rushed to the Thames-side conflagration too. Sadly these parish pumps did little to help the situation; poor training and even poorer leadership of their crews only added to the confusion and nuisance their arrival caused.

The Tooley Street fire, 1861. (Fire Protection Association)

Captain Frederick Hodges owned a gin distillery in Lambeth. He also owned, and led, one of London's most famous private fire brigades, stationed at his south London distillery from the 1850s to the 1860s. His was the first fire brigade to use an engine with steam as opposed to manual pump power. He had started his brigade on the 1st May 1851. It was common practice that the larger factories had a private fire brigade (in later times called 'works fire brigades'), Hodges' neighbours, Burdett's Distillery and the Price's Candle factory, being two such examples. He had equipped his brigade with 'two powerful engines' in 1854, supplied by Shand Mason & Co. in nearby Blackfriars.

Things were not going Braidwood's way. It would get tragically worse. Even the Thames was working against him. The ebbing tide meant his fire-floats were kept a considerable distance from the all-engulfing blaze due to the exposed foreshore and its mud flats. The firemen and the pilots of his fire-floats nevertheless still had their hands and faces blistered and burned by the enormous quantities of radiated heat as they directed their jets from their vantage points. Braidwood was considered to be at his calmest at times of greatest danger. He also cared about his fireman.

It was seven in the evening when one of his men reported the fire-floats were scorching and was seeking Braidwood's instructions. Braidwood made his way to the river bank by way of a narrow alley off Tooley Street to see what the situation was for himself. On the way he paused to give aid to one of his men who had gashed his hand. Braidwood removed his red silk Paisley neck scarf to use as a bandage to bind the man's bleeding hand. As he moved on towards the river, accompanied by Peter Scott, one of his officers, a warehouse wall many storeys high suddenly bulged and cracked before giving way completely. It fell with a deafening noise, killing both Braidwood and Scott instantly. The efforts by his men to save the two were fruitless, but they tried anyway until beaten into a retreat by the relentless fire. Given the contents of the warehouses it is hardly surprising that explosions occurred; these projected flaming materials far and wide, setting fire to other warehouses and buildings. Braidwood's death was said to have created confusion and disorganisation at the fire since there was no one appointed to lead in his absence.

The fire burned for another two days, totally out of control. Tides ebbed and flowed. On the high tides the fire-floats could move closer to the blaze, but whatever progress they made was mitigated when the tide went back out and they had to move back towards mid-stream to direct their hoses. For over a quarter of a mile the south bank of the Thames was ablaze. Braidwood's body, and that of his companion, lay under the hot brickwork for three days before they could be recovered. Whilst no other firemen perished in the fire it claimed the lives of four men on the river attempting to collect tallow. Their craft was surrounded by a river of flames flowing from the fire. Paints, oils, waxes and the very tallow they were trying to collect had ignited and streamed out onto the water's surface, their boat was engulfed and the men died in the flames.

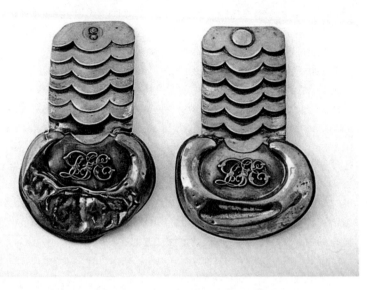

The crushed shoulder epaulets of James Braidwood, recovered from his body after the Tooley Street fire. (Stephen Jacob)

James Braidwood was buried at Abney Park Cemetery on 29 June 1861. He was buried alongside his stepson, who was also a firefighter and had been killed in a fire five years prior. The funeral procession was a mile and a half long and shops were closed with crowds lining the route. As a mark of respect, every church in the city rang its bells. The buttons and epaulets from his tunic were removed and were distributed to the firefighters of the LFEE.

The death of Braidwood left the LFEE bereft of any natural successor from its own ranks. The insurance company had not appointed a deputy. It seemed that they had considered Braidwood immortal. They once again looked outside the capital for a suitable replacement. They found one in the guise of a certain Captain Eyre Massey Shaw, late of the North Cork Rifles. It was a commission that Shaw had resigned from the year before the Tooley Street fire, when in 1860 he was appointed Chief Constable of Belfast. His job description also covered that of Superintendent of the Belfast fire brigade, which Shaw discovered in a very unsatisfactory state of affairs. He immediately set about putting the brigade and its firemen on a more organised and professional footing. His success coming to the attention of the various London insurance companies, now urgently seeking a new Superintendent to lead the LFEE.

The Tooley Street fire cost the insurance companies dearly. The loss of property alone was estimated to be in the region of £1,500,000 to £2,000,000. To pay the pumpers they paid out a further £1,100. Rumours spread around the City of London that the companies would collapse, but they settled the claims and continued, albeit unhappily. The Tooley Street fire finally convinced the authorities that something 'definite and decisive' had to be done. It would take almost four years of negotiations between the government, the Metropolitan Board of Works and the insurance companies before anything was done.

Shaw took the job. Born in 1830, he was thirty-one when he arrived at Watling Street, the LFEE headquarters station, to take charge of the Brigade in the latter part of 1861. Shaw had had a mixed background. He was the son of a General. With a view to entering the Church he had studied at Trinity College, Dublin, only then to enter the army. He was a man who loved the water and was considered to be a competent sailor. Donning the mantle of the LFEE's new Superintendent he inherited the eighteen land stations of the LFEE and its two fire-floats. His brigade covered the ten square miles of central London and the City of London, an area that formed the greatest risk for the insurance companies.

A useful indicator of the workload of the fire brigade is provided by Shaw himself in his annual report for 1861.

'Fires in 1861.
Totally destroyed 53.
Considerably damaged 332. Slightly damaged 798.
Total 1381
Two to six miles from nearest station 20.
Hazardous trades 25.
Number of buildings destroyed 113.
At great fire, e.g. Tooley Street. 33.
At London, six miles from station 7.

Fires at private houses 196
Totally destroyed 2
Considerably damaged 25
Slightly damaged 169
Fires at lodgings 115
Slightly damaged 105
Fires at churches 5
Fires at hospitals 1
Fires at places of entertainment 2
Fires at unoccupied premises 11
Slightly damaged 9
Fires in wagons on road 2
Trifling fires, about 400
Chimney [Of these no record is kept.]
False alarms 19
Chimney alarms 137

The Fire Brigade, with 120 skilled workmen, 36 engines, 18 stations and 2 floating engines is maintained at an expense of close upon £25,000 a year by the various fire-insurance offices who contribute in a rateable proportion on their business. The management is vested in a committee, which contains one representative from each office.'
   (From *Cruchley's London in 1865: A Handbook for Strangers.*)

The following year the companies contacted the Home Secretary (Sir George Grey), arguing that a city the size of London should not have its fire brigade funded by private or commercial means and devoid of any municipal or government support whatsoever. Playing for time the Cabinet set up a Select Committee to look into the matter, not that they were not aware of exactly what the problems were! Shaw gave evidence to the Select Committee in 1862 and was later requested to submit schemes for a new London Fire Brigade. It was a daunting review for anyone to undertake, but especially so for someone fresh to London. This new brigade was to cover the whole one hundred and seventeen square miles of London and not report to the insurance companies, as Shaw currently did, but to the Metropolitan Board of Works (MBW), London's municipal authority.

In 1862 when John Drummond, Esq. Managing Director of the Sun insurance company, and Chairman of the Committee for Managing Fire Extinctions, was questioned by the Select Committee on the *'principles on which the London Fire Brigade has been formed'* he replied *'solely for the protection of the offices; it is an association of nearly all the offices in London.'* The insurance companies were becoming acutely aware of the financial strain of fire protection, and sought every opportunity to rid themselves of their burden.

There was a growing interest in steam fire engines and three examples were publicly tested at the International Exhibition of 1862 in London's Hyde Park. The next year was marked by the famous three-day competitive steam fire engine trials at the Crystal Palace. Ten engines (including three from the USA) were subjected to exhaustive tests, at the end of which Messrs Merryweather's 'Sutherland' model was declared the best, and won the £250 prize. Second was Shand Mason's steamer 'Shand', of a similar double-horizontal cylinder design.

On land or on the river, Shaw realised that steam power was the way ahead for his Brigade.

Shaw's first proposals were detailed and thorough. He proposed the increased usage of steam engines for both land engines and especially the fire-floats. However, in the end it all came down to a question of money, government money. His proposals sought to increase London's fire-floats by 100%. New stations and new equipment were all costed. Shaw's plans were submitted via the MWB and viewed by Grey who had but one comment, *'Out of the question.'* So started an exchange of correspondence and detailed reports that engaged Shaw's considerable organisational talents until January 1865.

As importantly in 1862 Shaw had commenced connecting the stations of the London Fire Engine Establishment by telegraph as a trial. This was to be its first large-scale private network, and was completed by December 1863. Its seventeen stations were connected by this new electric telegraph.

The stations were spread across the metropolis at:

107 Broad Street, Ratcliff;

Wellclose Square, Ratcliff;
23 Bishopsgate Street Without;
64 Whitecross Street, Finsbury;
66-69 Watling Street, Cheapside;
27½ Farringdon Street, Blackfriars;
254 High Holborn;
44 Chandos Street, St Martin's Lane;
George Yard, Crown Street, St Giles's;
76 Wells Street, Oxford Street;
33 King Street, Baker Street;
39 King Street, Golden Square;
Horseferry Road, Westminster;
84 Waterloo Bridge Road;
2 Southwark Bridge Road;
165 Tooley Street, London Bridge;
and the floating station at Lucas Street, Rotherhithe.

Their fire engines responded to all calls by the public, not just those for insured property. The London District Telegraph Company contracted to install and maintain the circuits: Siemens, Halske & Company provided their magneto-dial instruments. The headquarters station in Watling Street was initially put in circuit with each of the so-called foreman's stations, with two or more appliances. Subsequently the remaining district stations with single engines were connected to the foreman's stations, with switching so arranged at the latter that Watling Street could communicate directly to every station, *even the most remote* at Ratcliff, Baker Street, Westminster and Rotherhithe. The system was *of the simplest possible kind, each line complete in itself with a dial instrument at each end*. The cost benefits were considered to be excellent, replacing foot messengers, allowing a concentrated response to large fires whilst reducing the number of engines called out to minor incidents and to false alarms. Also by special arrangement the British Museum was connected by the District Company to the London Fire Engine Establishment's station at Holborn.

The insurance companies continued to apply pressure on the government regarding funding and continuing fire losses. In a letter to the government, they noted that: *without any public authority whatever it [the LFEE] has for nearly 30 years extinguished the fires which have occurred in the metropolis and surrounding districts without inquiry and without charge.'* The insurance companies had pleaded for reconsideration of the state of the fire service: *'In the opinion of the Committee such an increase in the number of fires and in the expenditure incurred, rendered a reconsideration of the whole subject imperatively necessary, more particularly as they were satisfied that a system for the extinction of fires which might formerly have been adequate for the metropolis, has now become very insufficient for its present greatly extended limits.'*

The London Fire Engine Establishment used its first steam fire engine in 1860. (Illustrated London News)

The insurance companies finally sent a note to the Home Office in 1864, giving notice that they had decided to discontinue with the LFEE. The writing was on the wall for the LFEE: the question for the Home Secretary was what to do next. He had already charged Captain Shaw, via the insurance companies' controlling board, to come forward with ideas. In his first scheme on the list of Shaw's priorities was a floating steam engine capable of delivering

4,000 gallons per minute. Submitting his first scheme in December 1864 Shaw concluded that his proposals provided real value for money. His estimated annual costing of £70,000 for the new brigade would be protecting property valued at some nine-hundred million pounds. His suggested increase from two to four fire-float stations had them located at Westminster Bridge (new), the existing Southwark Bridge and Rotherhithe plus Limekiln Dock (new). His estimates for the four fire-floats were £12,000 (£3,000 each).

The reply from the Home Secretary, sent to Shaw via the insurance company board, ran only to a few lines. Shaw was to go back to the drawing board and keep his expenditure to £50,000 per annum.

Shaw adjusted his estimates and proposals but refrained from any reduction to his suggested river fire cover. He signed off his second scheme from the Fire Engine Station-Watling Street in January 1865. His scheme was costed at £52,000 per annum.

Shaw was said to be furious with the penny-pinching reply to his scheme when it arrived. However, he set about adjusting his costings. With the loss of one of the additional fire-floats and tweaking the summary of expenditure he was within the £50,000 ceiling. The Home Secretary signed off on Shaw's proposals and set about preparing a Bill to bring forward 'establishing a fire brigade for the metropolis'. In the reply sent on behalf of Grey, by T. G. Baring MP, it was acknowledged:

'The present strength of fire engine upon the river is altogether inadequate, consisting of one efficient one inefficient engine. It is proposed to establish four efficient floating steam engines on the river, thus organize a force capable of grappling with those conflagrations which are so disastrous when they occur, and to which so much public property is exposed.'

Finally, after a very long time, with several schemes submitted by Shaw, the Government passed into law the Metropolitan Fire Brigade's Act in 1865. At the end of its last year, prior to being taken over by the MBW in 1865, the LFEE had at its seventeen stations and one hundred and thirty-one black-clad firemen, with two floating steam pumps, two large horse-drawn steam pumps, six small horse-drawn steam pumps and thirty-three small horse-drawn manual pumps.

The budget for renting the private telegraphs was £500 per annum. In addition there were the 85 fire escape stations, each with a wheeled ladder and a 'conductor', operated by the charitable institution the Society for the Protection of Life from Fire, which the MWB was also to absorb.

Leather helmet introduced by James Braidwood for the London Fire Engine Establishment.

The Metropolitan Fire Brigade (MFB) came into being on the 1st January 1865. Its first Chief Officer was Captain Shaw.

CHAPTER 4

Metropolitan Fire Brigade, 1866-1904

W ITH THE CREATION OF the Metropolitan Fire Brigade (MFB) the insurance companies and parishes were officially relieved of their fire-fighting duties. Both were required, however, to contribute monetarily to the new public brigade. Insurance companies were mandated to pay at a rate of £35 per million gross insured. Those previously providing brigades were now required to pay for the service. In addition, the companies remained actively and voluntarily involved in monitoring the efficiency of the new institution. Whilst some of the downstream docks maintained a floating engine within the docks only the London Fire Engine Establishment had had fire-floats operating on the Thames. These were transferred to the new brigade.

In addition to assuming firefighting duty, the MFB also took on the services previously provided by the Royal Society for the Protection of Life from Fire. This transfer was driven by the Society which had experienced a drop in income. Additionally, the parishes, which were now paying for fire protection, believed the saving of life from fire should be included as part of their payment. The MFB eventually succumbed and took over this duty. The Metropolitan Board of Works (MBW) was set up in 1855 to deal with many of the services common to the whole of the metropolitan London area.

The transfer of firefighting from the private to the public sector was not without its problems. The financial situation was dire. The budget set for the brigade was tight, and borrowing power of the MBW was restricted. The MBW did receive funds from both the parishes and the insurance companies, as well as the government, yet its financial troubles endured. The brigade had difficulty taking over mortgages of former LFEE stations from the insurance companies, not to mention the need to build new stations where no coverage had been in place previously.

The working conditions for Shaw's firemen worsened under the MBW. Firemen were forced to work longer hours, and in uncomfortable settings. Both pay and funds provided in the event of a loss were slashed. The LFEE had paid families of those lost £10 to cover funeral expenses, but the Board now only paid £5. The MBW faced a serious manpower issue, fuelled by the small budget and the growing metropolis.

The contract with the Fire Engine Establishment was continued when it was taken into state control in 1865. By 1 January 1869, the new 'Metropolitan Fire Brigade' had 49 stations, with 47 private telegraph circuits consisting of 71 miles of wire, and 90 fire escape stations. In that year the Company billed the brigade through the Metropolitan Board of Works for £1,052 in line and instrument rental.

On losing their fire engines to the state the fire insurance companies formed the 'London Salvage Corps' on 22nd December 1865. The corps were tasked with rescuing insured goods and protecting them from damage by water, rather than fighting fire; duties that the 'old order' had also undertaken but which the state refused to take on. The corps became operational in March 1866 under William Swanton, who was formerly a senior officer of the Western Division of the Fire Engine Establishment and its acting deputy superintendent. It took premises for its vehicles and 64 men, mostly former firefighters at 31 Watling Street in the City of London, close to the Fire Brigade headquarters, and at four other stations: on the Commercial Road, in Hackney; Southwark Bridge Road, Southwark; Shaftesbury Avenue, in the West End; and Upper Street, Islington. During the spring of 1866 these were connected via private telegraph wires by the District Company.

Although they co-operated closely there was some competition between the Fire Brigade and the Salvage Corps. The Corps proved somewhat quicker in responding to telegraphed alarms and used its old skills to extinguish small fires before the Brigade turned up.

Shaw's first day at his desk as the Chief of the MFB was a truly memorable one. In truth little had changed other than the name of the brigade but the Metropolitan Fire Brigade was delivered its first ordeal by fire. A fire had started at St Katharine Dock, Lower East Smithfield, and a message reporting the fire was passed to Shaw. The fire was growing in strength and had already consumed the jute store where it had started. Flames were spreading rapidly by the time Shaw had sped through the City to Smithfield from Watling Street. Shaw ordered immediate reinforcements and more steam fire engines than ever before were engaged for the first time fighting this major fire, engines that included Shaw's fire-floats. Not wishing to see a repeat of the Tooley Street fire other steam fire engines where brought into action too. Three steamers came from a fire engine manufacturer whose engines were destined for

Fire at St Katharine Dock. London, 1st January 1866.
(Fire Protection Association)

foreign buyers; one steamer came from a volunteer brigade and another from a different fire engine maker. It proved a major test for the steam engines and some were found to be wanting. One suffered a broken crank shaft, another a burst in the boiler, and others had to be repaired in situ. The steam engines on fire-floats had no such problems.

With an insurance loss of £200,000 Shaw faced criticism that his men were not up to the task – something that Shaw strenuously denied, though he knew that he had a task ahead of him to deliver the force he had outlined in his plans. New stations were needed and these provided slightly better accommodation for his men and their families. The firemen were still on duty twenty-four hours a day with only short breaks from duty.

Shaw monitored and observed the rapidly improving steam fire engines that were to steadily replace the outdated, old style manual pumps, although they would still be around for the next twenty years or so. Shaw was also more innovative than Braidwood, who had not welcomed the introduction of the telegraphic communications. Shaw saw the system expanded to all his stations.

Historical records show that the new public authority encountered many problems in the early days of providing London's fire service, the largest of which was financial. The Board did not have the funds to improve protection, or perhaps even offer the same level of service that had been provided by the insurance companies. Compensation for firemen was cut, and there were problems with manpower. Even after firefighting was transferred to a wealthier branch of government, worker-related issues continued. While this transfer to a public authority certainly aided the ailing insurance companies, it is arguable whether firefighting improved in the initial years. Improvements to the fire-floats were slow in coming, not least because of the procrastination on the part of the MBW and its Fire Brigade Committee. London's fires were multiplying as fast as its population grew, despite the fact that fire-proof construction of buildings was adopted more than ever. London headed the UK fire list with fourteen hundred fires annually.

Some of Captain Shaw's problems were far more mundane, not least some of the shenanigans that his firemen managed to get up to. Those serving on the fire-floats were no exception. Fireman

Fourth Class John Harris was discovered having allowed a prostitute to be in Watch Box at Hungerford Pier on the evening of the 28th September 1871. The charge was considered proved but before Captain Shaw could adjudicate on the case and the man face dismissal he resigned before the case was heard.

Writing from his '*Chief Station*' in Watling Street Captain Shaw submitted a report to the MBW Fire Brigade Committee on the 11th July 1874. He was writing to them on the matter of: '*Floating Fire Engines*'. In his opening paragraph Shaw wrote: '*I have to report that I have been for some time considering whether it would be possible to devise some means of reducing the very heavy cost of the coal and coke consumed in keeping up steam constantly in the two largest Fire Floats, and I have come to the conclusion, that some considerable saving may be effected without incurring any serious risk to the water-side property of the metropolis.*'

Shaw continued: '*Before proceeding further, I think it right to state that these two floats, although not quite perfect in detail, are the most powerful movable Fire Engines in the world, and that they are, in my opinion, absolutely necessary for the protection of the vast wealth of the river-side of the metropolis. Any remarks, therefore, or suggestions, which I make in this report, are not intended in any way to disparage the undoubted effieacy* [sic] *of these vessels for the purposes for which they are used.*'

Shaw went on to make a strong case for the placement of steam fire engines, less their wheels and carriage, onto a frame with rollers that could be placed upon a series of barges, each barge being about forty-five feet long, sixteen feet wide and with an exceptionally shallow draft of six to nine inches. The barges would be transported to the scene of a fire by the means of a small steam tug. Shaw's plan was to place the barges at strategic points along the Thames and that they would be dispatched during the early stages of a fire, before the arrival of the larger fire-floats. His case being that rather than keeping the larger fire-floats in a constant state of readiness, their fire would be prepared but not light until the craft are actually required. His estimate showed it was cheaper to keep fires going on the four proposed small fire tugs, with the cost amounting to £160 per year compared to the average cost of £1,400 for the two big floats. He gave the Fire Brigade assurances that arrangements could be made for the two large floats to get their steam up within forty minutes, plus his judgement that in the meantime the engines on the barges would be got to work on the fire and keep it in check. He suggested that some of the engines mounted on the barges might, in some cases, even succeed in extinguishing the fire before the arrival of the major floats.

The new Metropolitan Fire Brigade headquarters, Southwark, opened 1878. (Mary Evans)

It took the Fire Brigade Committee three years to consider Shaw's report and come to a decision. Rather than agreeing Shaw's scheme in full they authorised the purchase of just one raft (barge), one steam engine and one tug boat.

In contrast in the early days of the MFB the Metropolitan Board of Works committee had agreed to purchase land, south of the River, for a new fire brigade headquarters. The site was located in Southwark Bridge Road. There was much consternation by the City Fathers and the insurance companies that the fire brigade headquarters would be moved outside of the City limits. However, the site was purchased and the building works commenced. In the words of the Boards Annual Report for June 1877, they commented:

'The Board have now agreed to purchase a piece of freehold ground with a range of buildings thereon, known as Winchester House in Southwark Bridge Road, for the sum of £35,000. The area of the ground is about one and three-quarter acres, amply sufficient for all requirements. The strength of the Brigade is at present as follows:

48 fire engine stations;
107 fire escape stations;
4 floating stations;
56 telegraph lines.'

By the 1st June 1878 the move to the new MFB Headquarters had taken place. The former fire station in Southwark was closed but the firemen, and their families, from the floating station at Southwark Bridge were still housed there.

The Portland stone relief that once adorned the MFB's HQ entrance arch at Southwark. (Author)

The other fire-float stations were located at Millbank, near Lambeth Bridge (from 1869-1884), Rotherhithe at Cherry Garden Pier (1833-1871 then from 1871-1894), plus the fire-float repair depot at Charing Cross.

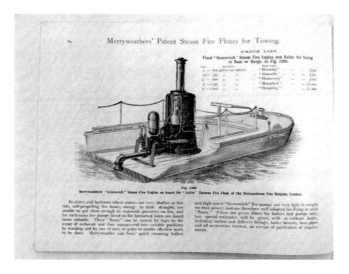

(Merryweathers – Greenwich)

It was during the reign of Queen Victoria that Britain emerged as the most powerful trading nation in the world. Many of the social and economic effects delivered in that revolution are still being felt today. From the latter part of the 1700s the process of industrialisation had established a foundation for the growth and expansion that followed. At the heart of this was the successful development and application of steam technology. By 1845 over two thousand miles of railway had been opened up. Some millions of passengers were now travelling by rail as the railways offered new opportunities. Trains were immediately popular, a popularity encouraged by acts of parliament that ensured that they conformed to standards of speed and comfort and offered rates that were affordable by all. It also guaranteed the expansion of London.

The building of the capitals road network was another major achievement of the Victorian period, changing forever both social patterns and the landscape of London. New embankments were created, sweeping away much of the old and rotting riverside frontages. Six new bridges were built in the previous century but only two, Blackfriars and Westminster, served central London. After 1800 Londoners got four more bridges to service the centre particularly the newly built up areas south of the River Thames: Southwark Bridge in 1819, Lambeth Bridge in 1862, Vauxhall

Bridge in 1816 and Tower Bridge in 1894. Also, new tunnels under the river at Deptford and Surrey Docks (Rotherhithe) and Greenwich (Blackwall) were opened; on the Victoria Embankment (1870) redevelopment had reclaimed some 37 acres of land from the Thames between the Houses of Parliament to Blackfriars Bridge by building a new river wall 500 feet out into the Thames. The Albert Embankment was another, where in 1937 a new fire brigade headquarters and river station would be opened.

The technology of the telegraph had rapidly expanded, making possible mass communication on both national and global scales. With instruments in every fire station, Shaw had used the telegraph communication on a scale hitherto inconceivable. Other improvements were delivered too, first via the Board of the MWB and then the later London Country Council. It saw both innovation and expansion passed onto London's fire brigade. By the time of the opening of his new headquarters Shaw had ensured his brigade had increased in both size and efficiency. Forty-eight steam engines were purchased and still more fire stations were being built. Its four floating stations had three floating steam fire engines and one iron barge to carry a land steam fire engine. The

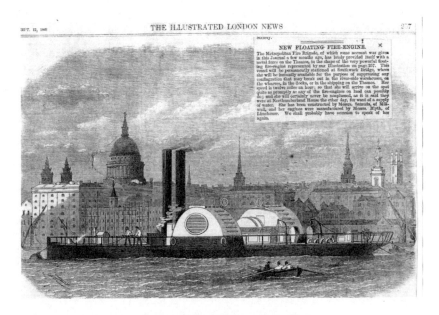

(Illustrated London News)

Metropolitan Fire Brigade's growth was very much part of the Victorian success story.

'Paddle steamer on the Thames' by Ben More, 1884.

However, despite the many pluses of the Victorian era this was still Victorian London, the capital city of England and the seat of the largest empire in the world. For most of this period London was still filthy and dangerous; cholera and tuberculosis were endemic. There is a recorded case of two firemen contracting 'small-pox' after dealing with a fire on an isolation hospital ship moored on the Thames. The average life expectancy in Dickens' London was 40.2 years for men, 42.2 for women. London's firemen, or their families, were not excluded from the statistics. More than 70 per cent of the population were under 35. Crime was reported as out of control. Population growth had been partly to blame, a growth from one million to seven million in the 100 years up to 1900. There was the indifferent attitude of the rich to the poor, and London's firemen were certainly not considered wealthy. Living in London was as potentially life-threatening to London's firemen as fighting its fires. As for the river firemen, falling into the polluted and contaminated Thames was something they tried to avoid at all costs. Not all succeeded.

(Illustrated London News)

Mr Jack White was a London reporter. He covered the work of the Metropolitan, then later the London, Brigade for more than fifty years, writing about his experiences from 1878 until 1930. His was an era when newspapers went to press later than their modern counterparts, therefore he could attend an evening fire of note and rush off a column or two and still get it to Fleet Street for the morning's editions. His was a frequent face seen on the fire-ground and even riding on the fire-floats occasionally.

Jack White was a companion of Captain Shaw, whom he described as a tall elegant man with a *'rather longish goatee beard, which was going rather grey'*. When White first met the 'great' man his view was that Shaw was a fair man but someone who would not tolerate fools. He considered Shaw as a 'stern disciplinarian but a thoroughly just man.' Captain Shaw never forgave nor forgot to punish a *'neglect of duty'*. If Shaw suspected a neglect of duty he would leave no stone unturned until the truth was out. Such was the case of Rotherhithe's fire-float, moored at Cherry Garden pier, and its crew's penchant for a bit of a sing-song over a glass of beer which would incur the 'Captain's' wrath.

It had got back to Shaw that this crew were in the habit of not keeping watch properly. In fact they were in the habit of leaving their fire-float unattended whilst they went for drinks in a nearby hostelry in the company of their officer.

One evening Shaw went to see for himself, taking his carriage from Winchester House to Southwark Bridge where he boarded the Southwark fire-float and directed them to head down-river to the Rotherhithe station. Shaw always knew the state and times of the Thames tides. On arrival he instructed the float's pilot to pull alongside and hail their crew. There was no response!

Shaw did not bother to look for the crew; instead he instructed Southwark's crew to take the miscreants' fire-float in tow. He continued further downstream to a point where he could leave the vessel high and dry on the mud, carefully securing the craft so it could not drift away. Shaw then dashed back to Southwark Bridge and onward to his headquarters where he telegraphed the District Superintendent asking the bemused man where his missing fire-float was.

The Superintendent went straight to the Rotherhithe mooring where he found a perplexed crew wondering what had happened to their fire-float, a fire-float that they were meant to be in charge of. Shaw had given precise instructions to the Superintendent to discover the whereabouts of the fire-float and he had no intention of drawing a veil over his men's blatant misdemeanours. He instituted an immediate search. A shipmate of the Rotherhithe float's pilot eventually came forward telling them where he had seen the beached craft. It was re-floated and returned to the Cherry Garden moorings.

There followed a formal court of inquiry. The officer was found to have lost all sense of discipline. He also lost his job. The crew lost both privileges and, more painfully, a stoppage of pay.

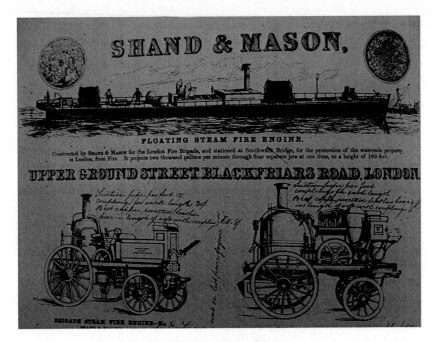

(Fire Protection Association)

In 1888, as a result of the Local Government Act, the area of the City of London and the metropolis was constituted the 'Administrative County of London' and the London County Council (LCC) was established as its central authority. The London County Council came into force the following year. It had been created following a succession of scandals involving the MBW, and was also prompted by a general desire to create a competent government for the city, more capable of strategising and delivering public services effectively. Although the Conservative government of the day, led by Robert Cecil – the Marquis of Salisbury – would have preferred not to create a single body covering the whole of London, his electoral pact with Liberal Unionists led him to this policy. It was established as a provisional council on 31 January 1889 and came into power on 21 March 1889. The LCC initially used the Spring Gardens headquarters inherited from the Metropolitan Board of Works. The LCC now controlled the Metropolitan Fire Brigade, a fact that Captain Shaw would increasingly find difficult to accept given the increasing bureaucratic control he experienced.

This was a period when London's firemen were riding the crest of a wave. It would not always be so, but they were generally seen and reported upon in a very favourable light, poorly paid yet putting their life on the line when it mattered. Fire disaster did occur in London and innocent lives were lost, including that of the firemen themselves. However, concern and criticism were directed at the lack of equipment or funding as the root cause, not the endeavours of Shaw's men. Getting a flavour of what Londoner's saw was frequently found in the editions of the *Strand* magazine. One such example is provided here:

The First Arrival. MFB firemen shout "Hi Hi Hi" to clear the way.

The Metropolitan Fire Brigade – Its home and its work

"Fire!" This startling cry aroused me one night as I was putting the finishing touches to some literary work. Rushing, pen in hand, to the window, I could just perceive a dull red glare in the northern sky, which, even as I gazed, became more vivid and threw some chimneys near at hand into strong relief. A fire undoubtedly, and not far distant!

The street, usually so quiet at night, had suddenly awakened. The alarm which had reached me had aroused my neighbours on each side of the way, and every house was "well alight" in a short space of time. Doors were flung open, windows raised, white forms were visible at the casements, and curiosity was rife. Many men and some venturesome women quitted their houses, and proceeded in the direction of the glare, which was momentarily increasing, the glow on the clouds waxing and waning accordingly as the flames shot up or temporarily died down.

"Where is it?" People ask in a quick, panting way, as they hurry along. No one can say for certain. But just as we think it must be in Westminster, we come in sight of a huge column of smoke, and turning a corner are within view of the emporium – a tall, six-storied block, stored with inflammable commodities, and blazing fiercely. – Next door, or rather the next warehouse, is not yet affected.

The scene is weird and striking; the intense glare, the shooting flames which dart viciously out and upwards, the white and red faces of the crowd kept back by the busy police, the puff and clank of the engines, the rushing and hissing of the water, the roar of the fire, and the columns of smoke which in heavy sulky masses hung gloating over the blazing building. The bright helmets of the firemen are glinting everywhere, close to the already tottering wall, on the summit of the adjacent buildings, which are already smoking. Lost on ladders, amid smoke, they pour a torrent of water on the burning and seething premises.

Above all the monotonous "puff, puff" of the steamer is heard, and a buzz of admiration ascends from the attentive, silent crowd. Suddenly arises a yell – a wild, unearthly cry, which almost makes one's blood run cold even in that atmosphere. A tremor seizes us as a female form appears at an upper window, framed in flame, curtained with smoke and noxious fumes. "Save her! Save her."

The crowd sways and surges; women scream; strong men clench their hands and swear – Heaven only knows why. But before the police have herded back the people the escape is on the spot, two men are on it, one outstrips his mate, and darting up the ladder, leaps into the open window. He is swallowed up in a moment, lost to our sight. Will he ever return out of that fiery furnace? Yes, here he is, bearing a senseless female form, which he passes out to his mate, who is calmly watching his progress, though the ladder is in imminent danger. Quick! The flames approach!

The man on the ladder does not wait as his mate again disappears and emerges with a child about fourteen. Carrying this burthen easily, he descends the ladder. The first man is already flying down the escape, holding the woman's dress round her feet. The others, rescuer and rescued, follow. The ladder is withdrawn, burning. A mighty cheer arises 'mid the smoke. Two lives saved! The fire is being mastered. More engines gallop up. "The Captain" is on the spot, too. The Brigade is victorious.

In the early morning hour, as I strolled home deep in thought, I determined to see these men who nightly risk their lives and stalwart limbs for the benefit and preservation of helpless fire-scorched people. Who are these men who go literally through fire and water to assist and save their fellow creatures, strangers to them – unknown, yet in that they require help and succour ? I determined there and then to see these brave fellows in their daily work, or leisure in their homes, amid all the surroundings of noble calling. I went accompanied by an artistic friend, to whose efforts the illustrations which accompany this record are due.

Emerging from Queen-street, we find ourselves upon Southwark Bridge, and we at once plunge into a flood of memories of old friends who come, invisibly, to accompany us on our pilgrimage to old Winchester House, now the headquarters of the Metropolitan Fire Brigade, in the Southwark Bridge Road. The whole neighbourhood is redolent of Dickens. From a spot close by the head office we can see the buildings which have been erected on the site of the King's Bench Prison, where Mr Micawber waited for something to turn up, and where Copperfield lost his box and money. We are courteously and pleasantly received in the office of the Metropolitan Fire Brigade.

Our credentials being in order there is no difficulty experienced in our reception. Nothing can exceed the civility and politeness of the officials, and of the rank and file of the Brigade. Fine, active, cheerful fellows, all sailors, these firemen are a credit to their organisation and to London. The Superintendent hands us over to a bright young fellow, who is waiting his promotion – we hope he has reached it, if not a death vacancy and he takes us in charge kindly.

Standing in the very entrance, we had already remarked two engines. The folding, automatic doors are closed in front of these machines. One, a steamer, is being nursed by means of a gas tube to keep the fire-box warm. If the fire-call rings there is no time to begin to get up steam. The well-heated interior soon acts in response to the quickly lighted fire as the engine starts, and by the time our steamer reaches its destination steam is generated. A spare steamer is close at hand.

Very bright and clean is the machine, which in a way puts its useful ally, the "manual", in the shade though at present the latter kind are more numerous, in the proportion of seventy-eight to forty-eight. Turning from the engines we notice a row of burnished helmets hanging over tunics and below these, great knee-boots, which are so familiar to the citizen. When the alarm is rung, these are donned rapidly but we opine the gates will occupy sometime in the opening.

Our guide smiles, and points out two ropes hanging immediately over the driving seat of each engine. "When the engine is ready the coachman pulls the rope, and the gates open of their own accord, you may say. See here!"

He turns to the office entrance, where two ropes are hanging side by side. A pull on each, and the doors leading to the backyard open and unfold themselves. The catch drops deftly into an aperture made to receive it, and the portals are thus kept open. About a second and a half is occupied in this manoeuvre. We consider it unfortunate that we shall not see a "turn out," as alarms by day are not usual. The Superintendent looks quizzical, but says nothing then. He gives instructions to our guide to show us all we want to see, and in this spirit we examine the instrument room close at hand.

Here are fixed a number of telephonic apparatus, labelled with the names of the stations: – Manchester Square, Clerkenwell, Whitechapel, and so on, five in number, known by the Brigade as Superintendents' Stations, A, B, C, D, E Districts. By these means immediate communication can be obtained with any portion of the Metropolis, and the condition and requirements of the fires reported. There is also a frame in the outer office which bears a number of electric bells, which can summon the head of any department, or demand the presence of any officer instantly.

It is extraordinary to see the quiet way in which the work is performed, the ease and freedom of the men, and the strict observance of discipline withal. Very few men are visible as we pass on to the repairing shops. Here the engines are repaired and inspected. There are eleven steamers in the shed, some available for service, and so designated. If an outlying station require a steamer in substitution for its own, here is one ready. The boilers are examined every six months, and tested by water-pressure up to 180 lbs. on the square inch, in order to sustain safely the steam pressure up to 120 lbs when it blows off.

Passing down the shed we notice the men – all Brigade men – employed at their various tasks in the forge or carpenters' shop. Thus it will be perceived that the headquarters enclose many different artisans, and is self-contained. The men were lifting a boiler when we were present, and our artist "caught them in the act."

Close to the entrance is a high "shoot" in which hang pendant numerous ropes and many lengths of drying hose. The impression experienced when standing underneath, and gazing upwards, is something like the feeling one would have while gazing up at the tops of the trees in a pine wood. There is a sense of vastness in this narrow lofty brick enclosure, which is some 70 ft. high. The hose is doubled in its length of 100 ft., and then it drains dry, for the moisture is apt to conceal itself in the rubber lining, and in the nozzles and head-screws of the hoses.

No precaution is neglected, no point is missed. Vigilant eyes are everywhere; bright responsive faces and ready hands are continually in evidence, but unobtrusively. Turning from the repairing shops we proceed to the stables, where we find things in the normal condition of preparedness. – "Be ready" is evidently the watchword of the Brigade. Ready, aye ready neatness and cleanliness are here scrupulously regarded. Tidiness is the feature of the stables. A pair of horses on either side are standing, faces outward, in their stalls. Four handsome, well-groomed, lithe animals they look; and as we *enter they regard us with considerable curiosity, a view which we reciprocate.*

Round each horse's neck is suspended his collar. A weight let into the woodwork of the stall holds the harness by means of a lanyard and swivel. When the alarm rings the collar is dropped, and in "half a second" the animals, traces and splinter bar hanging on their sleek backs and sides, are trotted out and harnessed. Again we express our regret that no kind householder will set fire to his tenement, that no nice children will play with matches or candle this fine morning, and let us "see everything," like Charles Middlewick. Once more our guide smiles, and passes on through the forage and harness-rooms, where we also find a coachman's room for reading, and waiting on duty.

It is now nearly mid-day, and we turn to see the fire-drill of the recruits, who, clad in lops, practise all the necessary and requisite work which alone can render them fit for the business. They are thus employed from nine o'clock to mid-day, and from two till four p.m. During these five hours the squads are exercised in the art of putting the ladders and escapes on the wagons which convey them to the scene of the fire. The recruit must learn how to raise the heavy machine by his own efforts, by means of a rope rove through a ring-bolt. We had an opportunity to see the recruits raising the machine together to get it off the wagon. The men are practised in leaping up when the vehicle is starting off at a great pace after the wheels are manned to give an impetus to the vehicle which carries such a burden. But the "rescue drill" is still more interesting, and this exhibited the strength and dexterity of the firemen in a surprising manner. It is striking to notice re different ways in which the rescue of the male and female sexes is accomplished. The sure-footed fireman rapidly ascends the ladder and leaps upon the parapet. The escape is furnished with a ladder which projects beyond the net. At the bottom a canvas sheet or hammock is suspended so that the rescued shall not suffer from contusions, which formerly were frequent in consequence of the rapid descent.

One fireman passes into a garret window and emerges with a man. He makes no pause on the parapet, where already, heedless of glare and smoke and the risk of a fall, he has raised on his shoulders the heavy, apparently inanimate, form, and grasping the man round one leg, his arm inside the thigh, he carries him steadily, like a sack of coals, down the ladder as far as the opening of the bag-net of the escape. Here he halts, and puts the man into the net, perhaps head downwards, he himself following in the same position. The man rescued is then let down easily, the fireman using his elbows and knees as "breaks" to arrest their progress. So the individual is assisted down, and not permitted to go unattended.

The rescue of a female is accomplished in a slightly different manner. She is also carried to the ladder, but the rescuer grasps both her legs below the knees, and when he reaches the net he places her head downwards and grasps her dress tightly round her ankles, holding her thus in a straight position. Thus her dress is undisturbed, and she is received in the folds of the friendly canvas underneath, in safety.

There is also a "jumping drill" from the windows into a sheet held by the other men. This course of instruction is not so popular, for it seems somewhat of a trial to leap in cold blood into a sheet some twenty feet below. The feat of lifting a grown man (weighing perhaps sixteen stone) from the parapet to the right knee, then, by grasping the waist, getting the limp arm around his neck, and then, holding the leg, to rise up and walk on a narrow ledge amid all the terrible surroundings of a fire, requires much nerve and strength. Frequently we hear of deaths and injuries to men of the Brigade, but no landsman can attain proficiency in even double the time that sailors do – the latter are so accustomed to giddy heights, and to precarious footing.

Moreover, the belt, to which a swivel hook is attached, is a safeguard of which Jack takes every advantage. This equipment enables him to hang on to a ladder and swing about like a monkey, having both hands free to save or assist a victim of the fire or one of his mates. There is a death-roll of about five men annually, on the average, and many are injured, if not fatally yet very seriously, by falling walls and such accidents. Drenched and soaked, the men have a terrible time of it at a fire, and they richly deserve the leisure they obtain.

The fireman's brass helmet was introduced into the Metropolitan Fire Brigade by Captain Massey Shaw.

This leisure is, however, not so pleasant as might be imagined, for the fireman is always on duty; and, no matter how he is occupied, he may be wanted on the engine, and must go.

Having inspected the American ladder in its shed, we glanced at the stores and pattern rooms, and at the firemen's quarters. Here the men live with their wives and families, if they are married, and in single blessedness, if Love the Pilgrim has not come their way. Old Winchester House, festooned with creepers, was never put to more worthy use than in sheltering these retiring heroes, who daily risk their lives uncomplainingly. Somewhat different now the scenes from those when the stately palace of Cardinal Beaufort extended to the river, and the spacious park was stocked with game and venison. As our conductor seeks a certain key we muse on the old time, the feasts and pageants held here, the wedding banquet of James and Jane Somerset, when the old walls and precincts rang with merry cheer. Turning, we can almost fancy we perceive the restless Wyatt quitting the postern-gate, leaving fragments of the mutilated books of Winchester's proud bishop. These past scenes vanish as our guide returns and beckons us to other sights.

Of these, by far the most melancholy interest is awakened by the relics of those brave firemen who have died, or have been seriously injured, on duty. In a cupboard, in a long, rather low apartment, in the square or inner quadrangle of the building, are a number of helmets; bruised, battered, broken, burnt; the fragments of crests twisted by fire, dulled by water and dust and smoke. Here is a saddening record indeed. The visitor experiences much the same sensations as those with which he gazes at the bodies at the Great Saint Bernard, only in this instance the cause of death is fire and heat, in the other snow and vapour, wind and storm; but all "fulfilling His word," Whose fiat has gone forth, "To dust shalt thou return."

Aye, it is a sad moment when on a canvas pad we see all that remains of the brave Fireman JACOBS, who perished at the confla-gration in Wandsworth in September, 1889. It was on the 12th of that month that the premises occupied by Messrs. Burroughs and Wellcorne, manufacturing chemists, took fire. Engineer Howard and two third-class firemen, Jacobs and Ashby, ran the hose up the staircase at the end of the building. The two latter men remained, but their retreat was suddenly cut off and exit was sought by the window. The united ladder-lengths would not reach the upper story, and a builder's ladder came only within a few feet of the casement at which the brave men were standing calling for a line.

Ashby, whose helmet is still preserved, was fortunately able to squeeze himself through the bars, drop on the high ladder, and descend. He was terribly burned.

But Jacobs being a stout man – his portrait is hanging on the wall in the office waiting-room in Southwark – could not squeeze through, and he was burned to a cinder, almost. What remained of him was laid to rest with all Brigade honours, but in this museum are his blackened tunic-front, his hatchet and spanner, the nozzle of the hose he held in his death-grip. That is all! But his memory is green, and not a man who mentions but points with pride to his picture. "Did you tell him about Jacobs?" is a question which testifies to the estimation in which this brave man is held; and he is but a sample of the rest.

For he is not alone represented: Take the helmets one by one at random. Whose was this? Joseph Ford's? Yes, read on, and you will learn that he saved six lives at a fire in Gray's Inn-road, and that he was in the act of saving a seventh when he lost his life. Poor fellow Stanley Guernsey; T Ashford; Fm Hoad and Berg too, the heros [sic] of the Alhambra fire in 1882. But the record is too long. Requiescant in pace. They have done their duty some have survived to do it again, and we may be satisfied... Come away, lock the cupboard, good Number 109. May it be long ere thy helmet is placed with sad memento within this press?

Descending the stairs we reach the office once again. Here we meet our Superintendent. All is quiet. Some men are reading, others writing reports, mayhap a few are in their shirt-sleeves working, polishing the reserve engine: a calm reigns. We glance up at the automatic fire-alarm which, when just heated, rings the call, and "it will warm up also with your hand." See? Yes! But suppose it should ring, suppose— Ting, ting, ting, ting-g-g-g!

What's this? The call? I am at the office door in a second. Well it is that I proceed no farther. As I pause in doubt and surprise, the heavy rear doors swing open by themselves as boldly and almost as noiselessly as the Iron Gate which opened for St. Peter. A clattering of hoofs, a running to and fro for a couple of seconds four horses trot in, led by the coachman in the twinkling of an eye the animals are hitched to the ready engines the firemen dressed, helmeted, and booted are seated on the machines; a momentary pause to learn their destination ere the coachman pulls the ropes suspended over head the street doors fold back, automatically, the prancing, rearing steeds impatient, foaming, strain at the traces; the passers-by scatter helter-skelter as the horses plunge into the street and then dash round the corner to their stables once again. "A false alarm?" "Yes, sir. We thought you'd like to see a turn out, and that is how it's done!"

A false alarm! Was it true? Yes the men are good-temperedly doffing boots and helmets, and quietly resuming their late avocations. They do not mind. Less than twenty seconds have elapsed, and from a quiet hall the engine-room has been transformed into a bustling fire station. Men, horses, engines all ready and away! No one knew whither he was going. The call was sufficient for all of them. No questions put save one, "Where is it?" Thither the brave fellows would have hurried, ready to do and die, if necessary.

It is almost impossible to describe the effect which this sudden transformation scene produces; the change is so rapid, the effect is so dramatic, so novel to a stranger. We hear of the engines turning out, but to the writer, who was not in the secret, the result was most exciting, and the remembrance will be lasting. The wily artist had placed himself outside, and secured a view, an instantaneous picture of the start but the writer was in the dark, and taken by surprise. The wonderful rapidity, order, discipline, and exactness of the parts secure a most effective tableau.

After such an experience one naturally desires to see the mainspring of all this machinery, the hub round which the wheel revolves – Captain Eyre M. Shaw, C.B. But the chief officer has slipped out, leaving us permission to interview his empty chair, and the apartments which he daily occupies when on duty in Southwark.

This unpretending room upstairs is plainly but comfortably furnished – though no carpet covers the floor, oilcloth being cooler. Business is writ large on every side. On one wall is a large map of the fire stations of the immense area presided over by Captain Shaw. Here are separately indicated the floating engines, the escapes, ladders, call points, police stations and private communications.

The chair which "the Captain" has temporarily vacated bristles with speaking tubes. On the walls beside the fire-place are portraits of men who have died on duty; the chimney-piece is decorated with nozzles, hose nozzle of various sizes. Upon the table are reports, a map of Paris, and many documents, amid which a novel shines, as indicating touch with the outside world. There is a bookcase full of carefully arranged pamphlets, and on the opposite wall an illuminated address of thanks from the Fire Brigade Association to Captain Shaw, which concludes with the expression of a hope "That his useful life may long be spared to fill the high position in the service he now adorns."

With this we cordially concur, and we echo the "heartfelt wishes" of his obliged and faithful servants as we retire secure in our possession of a picture of the apartment. There are many interesting items in connection with the Brigade which we find time to chronicle. For instance we learn that the busiest time is, as one would expect, between September and December. The calls during the year 1889 amounted to 3131. Of these 594 were false alarms, 199 were only chimneys on fire, and of the remainder 153 only resulted in serious damage, 2185 in slight damage. These are exclusive of ordinary chimney fires and small cases, but in all those above referred to engines and men were turned out. The grand total of fires amounted to 4705, or on an average 13 fires, or supposed fires, a day. This is an increase of 350 on those of 1888, and we find that the increment has been growing for a decade. However, considering the increase in the number of houses, there is no cause for alarm. Lives were lost at thirty-eight fires in 1889.

The personnel of the Brigade consists of only seven hundred and seven of all ranks. The men keep watches of twelve hours, and do an immense amount of work besides. This force has the control of 158 engines, steam and manual of all sorts; 31½ miles of hose, and 80 carts to carry it besides fire-floats, steam tugs, barges, and escapes long ladders, trolleys, vans, and 131 horses. These are to attend to 365 call points, 72 telephones to stations, 55 alarm circuits, besides telephones to police stations and public and private building and houses, and the pay is 3s. 6d. per day, increasing!

From these, not altogether dry, bones of facts we may build up a monument to the great energy and intense esprit de corps of

Captain Shaw and his Brigade. In their hands we place ourselves every night. While the Metropolis sleeps the untiring Brigade watches over its safety at the head-quarters or at the outer stations, at the street stations, boxes, or escape stations, the men are continually vigilant; and are most efficiently seconded by the police. But for the latter force the efforts of the firemen would often be crippled, and their heroic attempts perhaps rendered fruitless by the pressure of the excited spectators.

We have now seen the manner in which the Metropolitan Fire Brigade is managed, and how it works the splendid services it accomplishes, for which few rewards are forthcoming. It is true that a man may attain to the post of superintendent, and to a house, with a salary of £245 a year, but he has to serve a long probation. For consider that he has to learn his drill and the general working of the Brigade. Every man must be competent to perform all the duties. During this course of instruction he is not permitted to attend a fire such experience being found unsuitable to beginners. In a couple of months, if he has been a sailor, the recruit is fit to go out, and he is sent to some station, where, as fireman of the fourth class, he performs the duties required.

By degrees, from death or accident, or other causes, those above him are removed, or promoted, and he ascends the ladder to the first class, where, having passed an examination, he gets a temporary appointment as assistant officer on probation. If then satisfactory, he is confirmed in his position as officer, proceeds to head-quarters, and superintends a section of the establishment as inspector of the shops, and finally as drill instructor.

After this service, he is probably put under the superintendent at a station as "engineer-in-charge," as he is termed. He has, naturally, every detail of drill and "business" at his fingers' ends. The wisdom of such an arrangement is manifest. As the engineer-in-charge has been lately through the work of drill instructor, he knows exactly what is to be done, and every other officer in similar position also knows it. Thus uniformity of practice is insured.

There are many other points on which information is most courteously given at head-quarters. But time presses. We accordingly take leave of our pleasant guide, and the most polite of

*superintendents, and, crossing the Iron Bridge once more, plunge
into the teeming thoroughfares of the City, satisfied.'*
(The Strand, *1891. As quoted in Gareth Cotterell's* London
Scene.*)*

The Victorian fireman remained very much a revered character.
Many a writer penned a piece or two for the weeklies and other
journals reporting the daring deeds or commented on the activities of the Metropolitan Fire Brigade. This, an adapted version, is
from 'Walks around London' that was published in 1895 at a cost
of 3d.

**Metropolitan Fire Brigade firemen working from their fire-float and
steamers fighting a Thameside blaze, 1860s.
(Fire Protection Association)**

*'THE RIVER FIREMAN. It is late in the evening, and the river
by Southwark seems more than usually crowded with barges and
other vessels passing along. There is a constant hum of watermen's
and lightermen's voices and the clammer of rigging and ropes from
the wharf sides, and the whirring of moving wheels, or the noisier*

rattling over the quayside cobbles as some delivery driver more eager than the rest rushes along. The embankment air is filled with these and the usual sounds of a busy river-scape at the close of day, when from the water's edge there comes the hoarse roar of shouts. A sound which we know at once to herald the departure of a fire-float of the Metropolitan Fire Brigade. In the distance we see the pilot leading the firemen and the officer towards their craft. Smoke soon billowing from the funnel of the tug as it gets up steam and pulls away, taking with it the fire preparing the steam fire engine on the attached float. Its whistle sounds to warn the pilots and captains of other river vessels to draw away and to give a clear space for the tug and float pass quickly on its way.

Unlike the horse drawn engines that dash by these river firemen are at a more sedate pace, controlled in part by the flow of the Thames. But when going with the tide they pass quickly enough, in fact you catch a glimpse of them, and they were gone. We could just see the pilot encouraging his engines, watching the river as they bounded on their way. There are a shower of sparks flying from the fire engines funnel as the engineer put more coal on the engine fire, and the roar of voices cheering and shouting "Fire! Fire!" dies away in the distance, and they are gone.

A volume of smoke just beginning to be tinged with the red reflection of the flames shows where the fire has broken out down-stream. We want to see these men at work, so we hasten along to the scene of the fire. Here we are at last. The lower part of the ware-house is already burning fiercely. The flames are rapidly spreading upwards, till from every loophole and barred window smoke is beginning to pour forth. There are some workers left inside who cannot get out, because the stairs are burning. But help is at hand, for the crowd in the street is opening and cheering as the tall fire-escape is rapidly pushed through by eager and willing hands. Quickly, quietly, and without any confusion, the fireman sets his ladders up and leans them against the window-sill of the smoking room. All the while the river fireman draw closer to the blaze. How still and quiet everyone is as the fireman nimbly runs up the ladder. He opens the window and jumps into the room. When he comes out again he is carrying the frightened woman whom he has found. What a deafening cheer the crowd give for the brave fellow but they are all brave fellows. There is not one among them who would not do the same if he had the opportunity.

But see there go some others in at the smoking doorway to hunt through the house, to find out where the seat of the fire is, and to see that all the people have been rescued. And if you could follow them, you would see them, when entering the rooms, stopping to close the doors behind them, and to shut all the windows, because where there is a draught there the fire burns quickest and fiercest. You would see them rushing up over the blazing stairs and through volumes of smoke, and searching into every nook and corner with their lamps. When their lamps begin to burn dimly, or go out in the heavy smoke, then they hasten away from that spot, lest they should become overpowered with the impure air and be suffocated.

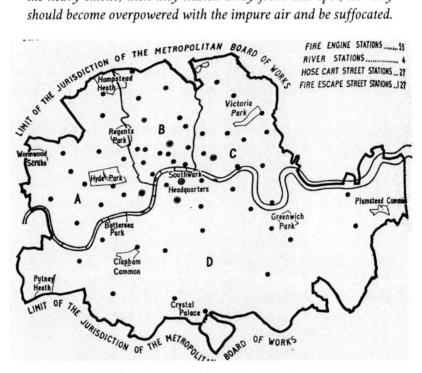

London's fire station locations in the MFB. (Mary Evans)

The river firemen arrived and has got an unquenchable supply of water. Fire is reflected in the river as in a glass. The firemen have unrolled their leathern hose, and the ground seems to be covered with gigantic worms. The nozzle to one length of hose is being screwed on by yonder river fireman, and as he raises it and points it, the stream of water rushes through and against the burning mass, and a cheer bursts from the excited crowd; and again and again they cheer, as other firemen, some from the tug and others from the float point their hose and throw stream after stream of water upon the fire.

(You will, I am sure, say, "What a noble body of men they are!" and will wish them "God speed" on all their journeys, when I tell you that in one year, out of 160 people whose lives were in danger, the London Fire Brigade rescued 127.) There are three river stations and fifty-eight land stations, where 39 steam fire engines and 115 manual engines are kept ready to be sent out at a moment's notice to any fire. There are 137 fire-escapes and 575 firemen. In one year the firemen were called to many fires, and altogether the boats and engines ran 25,754 journeys, or a distance of 58,377 miles. At the fires they pumped 21,000,000 gallons of water on the flames.'

As the London County Council grew in stature and more competent in its wide-ranging London powers it also grew increasingly bureaucratic. Shaw found himself more and more at odds with his political masters and the Fire Brigade Committee of the LCC. On 26 June 1891 Shaw tendered his resignation. It took the LCC by surprise, but for its own reasons the Committee were slow to express its 'regret' at Shaw's decision, although it did eventually do so. But too late for Shaw. He wrote back immediately upon receiving their letter dated 22 July requesting that he reconsider his decision to retire. His mind was made up, he was going. On the 31 October 1891 Captain Shaw became Sir Eyre Massey Shaw, bestowed a Knighthood by Queen Victoria.

A footnote on Shaw: Sir Eyre Massey Shaw died on the 26th August 1908. After the Metropolitan Fire Brigade he had been appointed a director of the metropolitan Electric Company. Shaw had not enjoyed the best of health post retirement from the Brigade, first having one leg amputated and at the age of 78 the other. When he retired from the MFB his brigade had dealt with 173,984 outbreaks of fire in the '*metropolis*'. He had dramatically seen the number of fire stations increase and the number of firemen rise as London's fire cover grew and spread. Shaw had not delivered the same degree of improvements on the river, for whilst the river stations had increased Shaw remained committed to tugs and fire-floats. It would take another decade before purpose-made fire-floats would be brought into service. However, Shaw left with the devotion of his men, in large part because of his solicitude towards them. One tale characterizes his concern for his firemen's welfare. A fireman, terribly injured, was taken to hospital at 11 p.m. and required immediate surgery. The first words the fireman uttered when regaining conscious were, "Has the governor come in to inquire about me?" The hospital staff doubted if he would as so late an hour. But the injured man knew better, and sure enough a few moments later Captain Shaw arrived in evening dress. He had hastened away from a social function to comfort the injured fireman, who although in great pain, struggled to salute his chief.

Captain James Sexton Simonds had been Shaw's deputy. He was appointed to take the helm of the Brigade. It was a relatively short reign as after five years it came to an ignominious, and premature, end when he was required to resign for unprofessional conduct. However in those years new stations opened at Wandsworth, East Dulwich, New Cross, Hackney and Brompton. Additional quarters were also to be provided at Cherry Gardens Pier for the fire-float crews.

On the 23rd January 1894 a number of engineers, navel men and fire officers of the Metropolitan Fire Brigade met at Messrs Merryweather and Sons' works in Greenwich Road to witness the trials of a new floating steam fire engine with its hydraulic propulsion system for the vessel. The craft was destined for the Chamber of Commerce of Alexandria, Egypt. It was the second fire-float for the Alexandria harbour, the first being supplied in 1876. That craft was provided with propelling engines and was altogether designed as a sea-going vessel. The new craft was for canal work only. Built of steel, it was sixty feet long and ten and a half feet wide. With its vertical boiler and working pressure of one hundred pounds, the engine was the standard two-cylinder Merryweather design. Its

Captain Eyre Massey Shaw. Chief Officer of the Metropolitan Fire Brigade.
(Fire Protection Association)

capacity was two thousand gallons per minute and the jet from the monitor could be thrown to a height of two hundred feet.

Driven by means of water propulsion, no propeller screw, it was designed to move at four to five miles an hour on the still canal waters. The metropolitan Brigade had already rejected propulsion designs due to the power of the Thames tidal flow, which on Spring tides could travel in excess of four miles an hour. Simonds chose to stick with the existing fire-floats for the Metropolitan Fire Brigade.

(Illustrated London News)

Following the scandalous departure of Simonds a replace-ment was sought. He came in the form of a naval man: Captain Lionel de Latour Wells. He had been a naval officer all his life and joined the Brigade at the age of thirty-seven. He also came highly recommended. Of the eighty-three contenders who had applied to become the next Chief Officer, Wells had recommendations from the likes of the Duke of Edinburgh, Lord Fisher (who would become the First Sea Lord) and Rear Admiral Lord Seymour. Captain Wells got the job.

Given his background one of his first priorities was the state of the Brigade's fire-floats. Wells was in fact the father of the new generation of fire-floats. Firefighting on water was about to be revolutionised. Prior to his arrival fire-floats had required a draught of nine feet of water. Wells pointed out, given his experi-ence on Royal Navy torpedo boats and as the second in command of Davenport's Torpedo School, that if the floats were properly designed the craft would only need two feet and therefore be able to operate close to the banks, particularly at low tides. A competent draughtsman, he drew up the boat's outline blueprints himself, plans that were based upon Royal Navy gunboats. The firm of Messrs Yarrow and Company studied his drawings, approved them and prepared the detailed design specifications. Yarrow's were new to the fire scene but that was about to change. Wells not only changed the design concept of the MFB's fire-floats but how the river service was organised and operated. The five river stations were remodelled, new working practices brought in. The Thames licensed watermen, who had formed the crews, had often lived some distance away from their craft. Now they were required to live 'on the job' as the land firemen did.

Yarrow's tube boiler meant when fitted to the new style fire-floats they could raise a head of steam from cold water in only fifteen minutes on a vessel almost one hundred feet long, eighteen feet wide and with a draught of only one foot seven inches. Previously the fire-floats had taken over twenty minutes before they had sufficient power to clear their moorings and get underway. That time had now been drastically reduced. Individual float crews were also amalgamated so that there was always a float crew

The style of Royal Naval (HMS Hood) gun-boat which Captain Wells modelled his fire-floats on.

on board and ready to respond. Under Wells' scheme, approved by the LCC's Fire Brigade Committee, there were to be four new river stations: Battersea, Blackfriars, Rotherhithe and Deptford (Royal Victualling Yard) with the firemen and officers of the Blackfriars float lodging at the new Whitefriars fire station in the adjacent Carmelite Street. It also maintained the Charing Cross float station and repair depot.

The 'Alpha' fire-float, a new generation in firefighting boats for the River Thames. (Mary Evans)

London's river fireman, and their land counterparts, not only had the extremes of heat of major blazes to contend with, there was also occasionally the cold. Such was the case in the 'Great Freeze' of 1895. The setting was a London docks fire and now the cold weather had really arrived. The docks and wharves were exposed to the cold gusts of wind coming off the river. Fighting a fire in the London's docks that winter was made almost impossible by the extreme conditions.

During the late frost, and after attending the fire in the Pool of London docks, involving the loss of some £60,000 or £80,000 in goods, the river firemen were proceeding homeward, at 9 o'clock in the morning and heading towards London Bridge. To those crossing the bridge they presented a most remarkable appearance. In a number of cases their helmets were frozen to their heads. Icicles, nearly six inches in length, hung from them and also from the firemen's coats. This was not hardly surprising considering the circumstances with which Wells' men had carried on their arduous labours. So intense was the cold, indeed, that when an engine stopped working for a few moments the water froze in the hose. As the water was thrown out of the nozzles the ice formed round the end of the metal until there were complete rings of ice several inches long on the end of the nozzles, through which the water passed. When two firemen held the same 'branch' they froze together where they stood, and yet such was the heat from the fire it was impossible for them to face it for any length of time.

The water as it ran out on to the ground froze instantly. The firemen soon became completely encased in sheets of ice, which froze on their uniforms, hair, and beards. Their ladders became perfect pictures, being covered with long lines of ice. The ruins of the fire gave it a picturesque appearance, with enormous icicles hanging from the roofs, while the walls were entirely covered with a pure white frost. The jetty cranes and lampposts had been converted into pillars of ice and were a constant source of danger owing to the possibility of the ice breaking away and falling with such force as to seriously injured, if not kill, those struck. The men did not move about on the fire-float as it cruised back to its station lest they slip on the ice that encased their craft and they fall into a watery winter's grave.

The appointment of Wells had done much to enhance the standing of the brigade and his changes generally always found favour with the LCC's Fire Brigade Committee. Not only was Wells open to new technical developments that might be introduced into the brigade, he also delivered changes to its working practices. In early 1898 he presented proposals to the Fire Committee that the previous policy of only employing sailors as Metropolitan firemen should cease. The Committee approved his idea and his request to increase the strength of the brigade by another twenty-five firemen. The Council also endorsed the Fire Brigade Committee's recommendation, as proposed by Wells, that each fire station would be equipped with at least a steam fire engine, a fire escape drawn by horses, a hose cart and a light manual escape ladder, and that the complement of each station would consist of one officer, nine firemen and two coachmen with four horses.

New fire stations were approved and the provision of eight new steam engines and twenty-nine horsed escapes at a cost of £6,185.0s.0d. Wells also had operational standards agreed. They included that it should be practicable to concentrate one hundred firemen in under fifteen minutes in any dangerous area for large fire occurrences. Additionally, on any call the firemen should be able to leave the station at once and reach the scene of the fire in less than five minutes. The changes that Wells had brought about saw the river service at its highest compliment, with five floating river stations, seventeen pilots, eighteen steam tugs, twelve barges and twelve skiffs.

The following September (1899) the brigade took possession of a substantial building that had already been erected at a cost of some £6,000 and located on the south side of Battersea Bridge. It was to provide accommodation for the firemen attached to the Battersea fire-float. The men had previously lodged at local private houses. The building was almost identical to the Cherry Garden Pier building built for the Rotherhithe fire-float firemen. The buildings had fifteen flats for the firemen's family accommodation. Additionally the stations housed a light-wheeled escape ladder and maintained a hose cart so firemen at the station could respond to urgent calls for assistance in the immediate vicinity of the station in the event of a fire.

That October the Charing Cross floating station, adjacent to Hungerford Bridge, was due for demolition. A new station was located and built at the other end of the Victoria Embankment by Blackfriars Bridge.

In 1901 a journalist, Mr Ernest A. Carr, writing in *Living London*, described the new fire vessels in action:

'*A message from the smaller MFB station down at Blackwall intimates that a brig proceeding upstream has caught fire, and has been run aground [...] The strong glare of light round the next bend marks the fire-floats' objective, and a very few minutes more bring them abreast of the flaming vessel. There followed two hours of unremitting labour, aiding the crew of the fire-floats at their toil. Their firemen taking wet lines*

aboard and fixing them to mooring posts and buoys, creeping down to
windward of the flames to receive the salvaged goods, and helping to fend
the brig off by means of stout ropes into deeper water, where the volumes
of water streaming in from the fire hose may submerge her."

Leading Members of the LCC were congratulating themselves
on their appointment of Wells. He brought much needed change
to the brigade. He also happened to be popular with his men, not
least because he brought a more human side to some of the Shaw
legacy for strictness regarding discipline. Firstly he considered
that after any man was awarded a punishment it was considered
done and over with. There was no subsequent continuing punitive
action though loss of seniority on the MFB's promotion boards.
Secondly, married firemen were allowed, for the first time, to be
able to take their meals in their quarters when on call. Wells also
brought other changes too: the power of the steam engine moved
from coal to oil.

Wells' honeymoon period lasted right through his first five years
with the MFB. London had experienced no devastating major
fires since his arrival in 1896. Certainly none that caused a public
outcry or 'Questions' to be raised in parliament. Then in 1902 a
fire occurred which did, and whilst it had virtually no impact on
the river service it is worthy of mention here.

At the close of business on 9th June 1902 a waste paper basket
caught fire. The blaze occurred in a five storey building in Queen
Victoria Street, in the City of London. The fire started in the workshop where artificial flowers were made, and part of the process
involved the use of rubber tape, rubber solution and celluloid.
(Problems of the flammability of celluloid had already seen an
increase in the number of fires where it was used, in part because
it did not necessarily require an ignition source to catch fire just
a rise in temperature.) The fire on the lower floor quickly established a firm hold, toxic and acrid smoke started to rise, and with
a wooden spiral staircase now ablaze, thirteen typists and packers
working for the General Electric Company on the upper floors
were trapped and in desperate need of rescue.

No one immediately summoned the fire brigade; it was some
ten minutes before they received the initial call. Watling Street

firemen were first on the scene. Women were screaming for help sixty feet up; the firemen raised their ladders which were between six and ten feet too short. The firemen were powerless to save those trapped. Although at the public inquest after the disaster the extraordinary efforts of some were made known. One such endeavour was from the Watling Street Station Officer who had run to an adjoining roof and hacked down a telegraph line to use as a rescue line. After lowering himself down he pulled two girls to safety. The 'long ladder' from the No 1 station at Southwark was ordered. This was a seventy-five foot escape ladder Shaw had introduced after a visit to the fire departments in the United States. The long ladder allowed the firemen to save two more girls. But tragically nine others, eight girls and a young man, perished. The report in the *Spectator* read thus:

'A great and fatal fire took place at a warehouse.

In Queen Victoria Street in broad daylight on Monday evening. The building, which is close to the Mansion House Station of the District Railway and only three hundred yards from the chief City fire-station, is used as workshops, offices, and stores by the General Electric Lighting Company. When the alarm was given at five o'clock a number of girls were at work on the fourth floor, which the Watling Street fire-escape proved too short to reach. Many of the girls leaped into a tarpaulin held out in the street, but when the fire had been got under control and the fourth floor entered, the bodies of eight girls and one boy were found in the ruins. The firemen appear to have worked with the utmost gallantry, and in particular two women were rescued by splendid efforts on the part of the men of the Salvage Corps. But the fact that the longest fire-escape available at the chief City fire-station was unable to reach the fourth floor of a London warehouse has created a very painful impression. We do not wish to make any criticism in regard to individuals till after the inquest, but it is clear that the life-saving apparatus available at short notice in the City, with its lofty buildings, is at present by no means adequate, and must be made so without delay if needed, the whole Fire Brigade does not however require reorganisation.'

There seemed to be a surprising, similar outcry from Londoners. Newspaper headlines said: 'Wells should go'. But the warnings
of Captain Shaw given some twenty years earlier had gone
unheeded. Architects were building ever taller London buildings,
giving little thought that the ladders employed by the fire brigade
would not reach the upper floors. The firemen, the London County

Council, and top of the list the Chief Officer were the scapegoats of this tragedy. Thankfully the jury of the City Inquest arrived at a more considered verdict than the angry wider public mood. Blame was laid with the General Electrical Company for what would today be deemed a failure in its duty of care; the Factory Inspector was also found to be negligent, as was the District Surveyor for not giving due consideration for the process being carried out. Yet despite the unqualified support of the jury given to both fire brigade and the salvage corps the press maintained its campaign against Wells, stating he was self-satisfied, inefficient and was responsible for a decline in moral and efficiency. None of this was the view of the LCC's Fire Brigade Committee, indeed it was not even true.

Captain Lionel de Latour Wells, Chief Officer, MFB

Hook ladders and escape ladders combined in drills at the MFB HQ in Southwark. (John Nadal)

Change did result however. The hook ladder was introduced and were, in the hands of London's firemen, responsible for the saving of many lives over the coming years. Plus at selected stations horses now stood, two hours at a time, hitched up to the engines ready to move.

Wells stood his ground for a year but resigned in 1903. His tenure was one of considerable success. He had expanded London's river fire service and placed it on a truly profession footing, something historians thought he achieved for the brigade as a whole. (With War declared in 1914 Wells returned to the Royal Navy as a Commodore where he served with distinction. He was subsequently knighted.)

His replacement was Rear Admiral James de Courcy Hamilton, who had retired from the Royal Navy. His was a remarkably under-achieving period as London's Chief Fire officer. It was said he knew nothing of firefighting when he arrived and little more when he left five years later to become a director for the Army and Navy Stores. Progress was made by the competence of his deputy Mr S. G. Gamble.

London County Council, **Note Extract from a book on the Fire Brigade, November 1903.** [*Jas. Truscott and Son, Ltd., Printers, London, E.C*]

It may here be mentioned that the London County Council has resolved to seek parliamentary authority to alter the title of the brigade to "London Fire Brigade," and the title of the chief officer of that force to that of "chief officer of the London Fire Brigade." The word "metropolitan" is used in connection with areas (e.g. metropolitan police, metropolitan water, and metropolitan gas), of which London forms part only, and which are of much greater extent than what comprises London. The title Metropolitan Fire Brigade is therefore misleading.

Under the Fire Brigade Act the Council may permit the brigade to proceed outside London for the purpose of extinguishing fire. In such cases the owner and occupier of the property on which the fire occurs are jointly and severally liable to pay a reasonable charge in respect of the attendance of the brigade.

The officer who receives a call to a fire outside the county is authorised to exercise his discretion in each particular case, but the practice is for the call to be immediately responded to. Assistance is thus not infrequently rendered outside London, particularly in the districts bordering on the eastern side of the county. No direct charge is made for services rendered by the brigade in connection with the saving of life or the extinction of fire (save in the case of chimney fires) within the county of London.

The scale of charges (except in the case of the Victoria and Albert docks) for the attendance of the brigade outside the County of London is as follows –

For the attendance of a floating fire engine –

First hour £6.

Each succeeding hour of part of an hour £1.

For the attendance of a tug –

First hour £5.

Each succeeding hour of part of an hour £1.

For the attendance of a manual engine, a land steam fire-engine or a horsed escape – £2

If the steam engine be got to work – First hour of part of an hour £1.

Each succeeding hour 10s.

The charges for the attendance of the brigade at the Victoria and Albert docks are as follows –

For the attendance of a floating fire engine – First hour £15.

Each succeeding hour of part of an hour £2.

For the attendance of a tug – First hour £10.

Each succeeding hour of part of an hour £2.

These sums include charges for firemen, horses, coal, assistance, use of apparatuses, etc. but out-of-pocket expenses are charged in addition.

For fire brigade purposes London is divided into six districts as follows –

Central or F district. (In which are the headquarters, Watling Street, Whitefriars, Tooley Street, Waterloo Road, and Scotland Yard stations):

The A district or west end:

The B district or the northern part of the City and the middle part of London north of the City:

The C district or east end:

The D district or south-east:

The E district or south-west: (The D & E being entirely on the south of the Thames.)

Each district is in the charge of a superintendent, who is assisted by a district officer, both of whom reside at the principal station of the district.

The A, B and C districts are supervised by a third officer of the brigade, who resides and has his office at the Euston Road station.

The D and E districts are, with the river-stations, supervised by the second officer of the brigade, who resides and has his office at the headquarters in Southwark Bridge Road.

North Woolwich, a detached part of the county of London, is, for fire brigade purposes, considered to be in the D district, notwithstanding that it is on the north side of the Thames. The superintendent and the district officer of the central district are accommodated temporarily at the Whitefriars station.

The senior superintendent of the brigade resides at the chief station, where he is, under the chief officer, responsible for the arrangements for instruction and mobilisation. The Chief Officer controls the whole organisation from headquarters, where he resides.

When the London County Council came into existence early in 1889 the fire brigade was admittedly not large enough properly to protect the whole of London. The provision in various suburban districts being notoriously inadequate to the requirements. This has been corrected, and for some years past the Council has been engaged, not only in enlarging and improving old stations, but in carrying out a scheme of additional protection laid down after careful consideration of the needs of London as a whole.

The scheme, which was approved on 8th February, 1898 [and somewhat enlarged in 1901] provides for the placing of horsed-escapes at existing firestations; for the establishment of some 22 additional stations provided with horsed-escapes; and for the discontinuance of nearly all the fire-escape and hose-cart stations in the public thoroughfares.'

Some of London's river fire stations had come and gone since the creation of the Metropolitan Fire Brigade. A summary of their locations are:

r

Battersea River Station. (Mary Evans)

Millbank float, off Millbank, near Lambeth Bridge. Demolished.	1869-1884
Pimlico float, Pimlico Old Pier, Grosvenor Road. Demolished.	1884-1898
Bankside float. Southwark Bridge.	1866-1889
Blackfriars. Victoria Embankment.	1900-
Limehouse Float. Off Limehouse Reach.	1871-1889
Shadwell float. Shadwell fish market.	1889-1898

Rotherhithe float. Off Kings Stairs.	1833-1871
Rotherthithe. Off Platform Wharf.	1871-1894
Rotherhithe. Cherry Garden Pier.	1893-
Battersea float. Battersea Bridge.	1898-
Charing Cross float and depot. Charing Cross Pier.	1889-1900

Battersea river station had a complement of one tug, two engines on rafts, one stores barge, plus one manual escape, one hose cart with one Station Officer, eleven firemen and three river pilots. In 1903 the Brigades river stations were located at:

(I) Battersea.

Blackfriars.

Cherry Garden Pier.

Deptford – Royal Victualling Yard.

Cherry Gardens River Station, Rotherhithe. (Mary Evans)

CHAPTER 5

London Fire Brigade, 1904–1939

THE LONDON FIRE BRIGADE was officially given that title on the 1st April 1904. To the vast majority of ordinary Londoners, however, it was the name by which it had been more popularly known for some considerable time. The Metropolitan Fire Brigade had been established by an Act of Parliament, so it took another Act of Parliament to have the former Brigade's name changed.

On land the first turntable ladder was introduced into the brigade in 1905. They were horse drawn, and when being driven through the streets they were no longer than the wheeled escape ladder but could reach to eighty-five feet when fully extended. These new ladders were self-supporting and did not need to lean against a building. With a monitor fitted to the top of the ladder its use as a water tower would soon make the turntable ladder an important addition to the brigade's appliance fleet. Some other engines had already made their presence felt. The self-propelled steam engine was first seen on London's streets in 1902. By 1904 twelve had been purchased and allocated to selected fire stations. Weighing in at five and a half tons, the steam-driven 'Fire King' had a top speed of twenty-five miles per hour on the flat. It slowed to a crawl when climbing a steep incline. The self-propelled fire engine did not immediately bring to an end the days of horse drawn fire engines, but it was the beginning of the end.

"'Hi! Hi! Hi!" on the Thames: The Floating Fire-Engine at Full Speed in the Pool', drawn by Fleming Williams. (Illustrated London News)

The concept of a shallow-draught fire-float design, introduced by the previous Chief Officer, Captain Wells, was followed up by his successor, Rear Admiral Hamilton. By 1906 the London County Council had approved the brigade's request to the purchase of a larger, more powerful, fire-float that was named 'Beta II'. The vessel was almost one hundred feet long, sixteen and half feet wide and had a draught of three feet. Its cost at £11,000 raised some eyebrows with the Members of the Fire Brigade Committee but the LCC approved the purchase. It was built by Forrest and Co.

This new fire-float was fitted with twin screw engines and two water tube boilers, which made the vessel capable of steaming along at the rate of ten to eleven miles an hour under normal conditions. The fire-float was fitted with four pumps, supplied by Shand Mason, each one of which was capable of discharging one thousand gallons per minute at a pressure of one hundred and forty pounds per square inch. When commissioned, the 'Beta II' was stationed at the Cherry Garden Pier in Rotherhithe on the South bank of the Thames.

Fire-float 'Beta II' at her Cherry Gardens moorings, Rotherhithe.
(Raymond Jewell)

Metropolitan Fire Brigade funeral procession of Sir Eyre Massey Shaw
passing the London Fire Brigade Headquarters in Southwark. (Mary Evans)

The 'Beta II' was followed by the 'Gamma II' two years later. Built by Thorneycroft and Co she was commissioned in 1911. The 'Gamma' was the brigade's first motorised engine fire-float.

Sir Eyre Massey Shaw died at Folkestone in Kent on the 25th August 1908. He was instrumental in bringing many innovative ideas into the Metropolitan Fire Brigade. He had retired in the early days of the LCC, after not seeing eye to eye with the LCC's Fire Brigade's Committee or its ways. In his thirty years' service he had increased the number of river stations and had established more efficient fire tugs and barges. His passing brought out London's public in force. The people lined the streets to pay their respects to one of London's characters and its heroes. He was buried in Highgate Cemetery on the 29th August.

LCC's County Hall

In April 1905 the LCC had finally agreed to seek powers to buy three adjoining plots of land on the eastern side of Westminster Bridge as a site for a single headquarters. The debate in the council chamber was somewhat heated, with one councillor objecting to the purchase as it was *'on the wrong side of the river [...] in a very squalid neighbourhood [...] and quite unworthy of the dignity of a body like the council.'* However, a leading member of the then council, a John Burns, countered that it *'would brighten up a dull place, sweeten a sour spot and for the first time bring the south of London into a dignified and beautiful frontage on the River Thames.'* It would take another seventeen years before the LCC's County Hall was built and formally opened by the King in 1922. It would then provide a permanent home for the LCC until 1965 when the Greater London Council was created. It would also be the permanent meeting place for the Fire Brigade Committee, the body who oversaw the funding and administration of London's fire brigade, including its river service.

COUNTY OF LONDON.
HIS STONE WAS LAID BY
HIS MAJESTY KING GEORGE
ON THE NINTH DAY OF MARCH.
MDCCCCXII. THE SECOND YEAR
OF HIS MAJESTY'S REIGN.
HER MAJESTY QUEEN MARY
BEING PRESENT ON THE
OCCASION.

As the London wide 'county' authority, the LCC discharged the administrative duties formerly carried out by the MBW's functions and greatly developed them. The LCC had taken control of the London Fire Brigade on the 21st March 1889. In addition to enhancing London's fire brigade, it had also carried through a number of major London street improvements, rebuilt six bridges over the Thames, and constructed vehicular and pedestrian tunnels at Blackwall, Rotherhithe, Greenwich and Woolwich, in addition to continuing the former Board's work in maintaining sewerage and drainage systems. Further duties were added to the LCC, most notably the responsibility for education in London, which was transferred to the LCC on the abolition of the School Board for London in 1904.

The increasing range and scale of the LCC's duties added considerably to the size of its staff and budget. In 1891 the total number of its employees was 3,700; by the mid-1930s the corresponding figure was 78,000, and its annual expenditure rose from less than £2 million in its early years to £37 million. The Fire Brigade's Committee of the LCC had already made significant changes to the way the fire brigade recruited its fireman. The practice of only recruiting former sailors was discontinued. New fire stations where being increasingly built by the LCC and new equipment purchases made. In the note book of the Clerk to the Council, he recorded the brigade's fire-float fleet's disposition in 1908 as:

'The Alpha lies at the river station by Blackfriars Bridge.

The Beta is kept at the Cherry Garden Pier, where also a tug is moored.

At Battersea there is a tug and two rafts.

At the Charing Cross fire-float repair depot there are two tugs and two rafts.

A stores barge is kept at each river station. The firemen are able to get away with their fire-floats in from six to ten minutes.'

The 'Alpha' fire-float, 1900s. (Mary Evans)

The increases in LCC staffing were also reflected in its fire brigade. (Although the conditions of its firemen remained a matter of serious concern for the men themselves.)

The authorised strength of the brigade at the 25th February 1908 stood at:

1 Chief Officer, at £1,000pa, plus house, coal and light allowance.
2 Divisional Officers, at £500-£600pa, plus house (or quarters), coal and light.
2 Assistant Divisional Officers, at £300pa, plus quarters, coal and light.
1 Senior Superintendent, at £270pa, ditto.
7 Superintendents, at £195pa, ditto.
8 District Officers, at £2. 16s. 0d per week, ditto.
91 Station Officers, at £2. 5s. 0d per week, ditto.
96 Sub Officers, at £1. 5s. 0d. (See below).
898 Firemen, at £1. 5s. 0d. (See below)
40 Firemen under instruction. £1. 4s. 0d per week. (See below)
1,146 Sub Total.
194 Coachmen. (Horse drawn fire engine drivers) £1. 4s. 0d per week.
12 River pilots. 6 shillings a day (twelve hour shift)
1352 Total strength.

Sub Officers received a special duty pay of 6d a day. The pay scales were agreed in February 1907. Married sub officers and a certain number of the senior married firemen were entitled to two rooms, for which they paid 2s 6d a week. All other married firemen who had completed three years' service were provided, where possible, with two rooms at 4s a week. If three rooms became available the Chief Officer could allot them to sub-officers or firemen and no extra charge was made for the third room. Single firemen paid one shilling a week for their accommodation. None of the allowances were pensionable.

Firemen under instruction at the headquarters station at Southwark lodged there and paid one shilling a week for the privilege. The coachmen were provided with quarters free of charge and the brigade's head coachmen and those after their fifteen years' service were provided with a coal and light allowance.

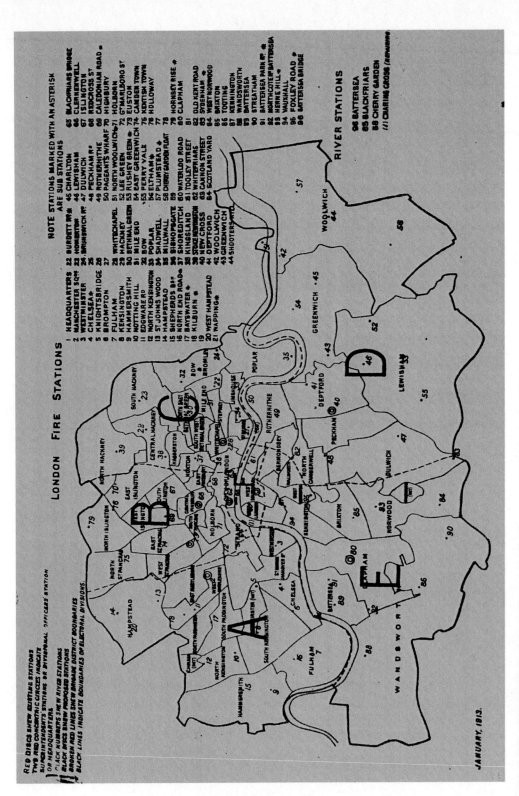

London's fire engine and fire-float stations, circa 1913.

By 1913 the LCC had ensured that the brigade's fire-floats had increased to four purpose-built vessels. The MFB's 'Alpha' had been added to by the 'Beta II' (1906), followed by the 'Delta II' and 'Gamma II'. These four fire-floats provided the backbone of the brigade's river service for over twenty years. Both the 'Alpha' and 'Beta' fire-floats were moored at Blackfriars; the 'Gamma' and 'Delta' fire-floats were stationed at Cherry Garden Pier and Battersea Bridge respectively.

Tragedy struck at the Battersea river station in 1916 when Fireman George Cobbold, aged twenty-nine, fell off the 'Delta II' into the River Thames and drowned. George Cobbold had been an Able Seaman in the Merchant Navy and had joined the London Fire Brigade in 1911. His first two years were spent at Vauxhall fire station and by 1913 he had been appointed a first class fireman with a pay increase from £1.5s 0d to £1. 8s 6d a week. He was moved first to Clapham, then Sydenham fire stations during 1913, subsequently being transferred to the Floating Station No 96 Battersea in February 1914. As a non-reservist Cobbold was not called back to the 'colours' on the outbreak of World War One in summer 1914, but continued to serve on the fire-float. He died on the 24th August.

The First World War, 1914-1918

World War One ('The Great War') was declared on the 28th July 1914. The first impact of the outbreak of that war was felt by the London Fire Brigade during the following month of August and the calling up of all reservists.

From its pre-war strength of 1,251 men some 280 army and navy reservists were called back to the colours. In addition another 120 others volunteered to fight and joined the armed forces. The brigade was 400 men short by October 1914. It had lost over one third of its operational strength. This sudden depletion adversely affected both the land and river fire stations' operational ability. The LCC and the brigade's senior officers were concerned about the impact that the departure of so many men would have in the event of enemy air raids. This was not a view shared by central Government who held to their belief that the risk of aerial attack was not considered to be a serious one. For nine months the Government's judgement appeared sound. Then the first air raid took place on the 18th May 1915 at about 11 a.m. The targets were North and East London. Four people were killed and thirteen were injured.

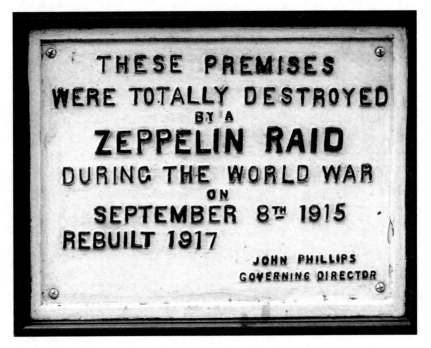

Sign from the Farringdon Road, London. (Author)

The third raid, carried out by zeppelins, occurred on the night of 8th September 1915. The shadow of a sleek cigar-shaped zeppelin passed over the dome of St Paul's Cathedral and unloaded a three-ton bomb, the largest ever dropped at the time, on the city's financial hub. The attack caused massive damage and killed 22 civilians, including six children. The raid would result in the death of a London fireman too: Fireman J. S. Green. Twenty-two motor fire pumps were required at the fires involving Wood Street and Silver Street, in the City of London. The fires, which were very destructive, caused half a million pounds' worth of damage. A report of Fireman Green's actions and demise was later issued by the LCC, who posthumously awarded Fireman Green the Silver Medal for Bravery – the firemen's VC.

'We regret to report that Fireman J. S. Green died on the 17th September 1915 from injuries sustained in performing his duty at the outbreak of a fire caused by bombs dropped from enemy aircraft on 8th September 1915. On the night in question Fireman Green was on duty with a turntable ladder, when a call was received to an outbreak of fire. On arrival at the scene of the fire it was found that an explosive bomb dropped in the roadway had caused a fire in a gas main, and that the flames from the main had set alight buildings on both sides of the road, and had cut off the means of escape from a building in which were eighteen persons. "Having assisted in the rescues of these persons, Green searched the building, and then got a hydrant to work in a neighbouring building which had been set on fire by incendiary bombs.

While Green was working on the ground floor of the latter building he was informed that there were two persons in the upper part of the premises. Green there upon ascended the staircase at imminent risk to his life. On reaching the upper floor he was enveloped in an outburst of flame, and being severely burned, he was compelled to throw himself into the street. His fall was broken by a projecting lamp bracket, and he was not seriously injured by the fall, but the burns he had received proved fatal.

We are much impressed by the zeal, promptitude and courage displayed by Fireman J. S. Green. Had he survived we should have recommended the award to him of the Council's Silver Medal for extraordinary bravery, and we think that in the circumstances the medal should be presented to his widow. Green was thirty three years of age, and had competed eight years' service in the Brigade. In addition to his widow, he leaves one child, a boy two months old.'

The largest single explosion, or rather a series of explosions, occurred in January 1918, but not as the result of enemy action. A small fire had occurred in an ammunition factory in Silvertown. The West Ham fire brigade had responded and was dealing with the incident. There followed a massive, catastrophic, explosion. It utterly destroyed the whole of the extensive factory. It killed a Sub Officer and fireman from the nearby Silvertown fire station, which was also severely damaged, and killed two young children of the firemen living there.

The ammunition factory explosion damaged and set fire to a gas holder at Blackwall containing nine million cubic feet of coal gas; the sparks, blowing across the Thames, started another major fire involving a tar manufacturer in nearby Greenwich. Despite the heavy LFB involvement in those two separate fires, with a fire-float in attendance at each, the brigade sent twenty-two motor pumps and its other two fire-floats to the Silvertown disaster to assist the small West Ham force. Fire appliances remained in attendance at the scene for a total of ten days.

The ninth air raid occurred on the 17th June 1917. It was considered the largest raid of the war to date. Fourteen aeroplanes attacked London. Over three-hundred buildings were affected and the raiders dropped seventy-six bombs. Seven serious fires were started. Adjacent to the river at Bermondsey's Battle Bridge Lane and adjoining Tooley Street the fire-floats helped stop the fires spreading along the riverside. Fire stations were not immune from the bombing either. At Whitechapel fire station, in East London's Commercial Road, Fireman A. Vidler was killed when a bomb struck the station.

Artist's impression of an MFB fire-float at work at a riverside wharf blaze.
(Fire Protection Association)

Following the daylight raid on the 17th June the resources of the brigade were severely strained. The LCC made urgent representations to the Government's War Cabinet and as a result instructions were issued by both the Admiralty and the War Office for the return to the brigade of members of the London Fire Brigade on active service.

An early daylight raid on the 18th December 1917, the twentieth in the total series of aerial raids, concentrated on the riverside areas of Westminster, Chelsea, Southwark, Bermondsey and Lambeth leaving four people dead. When a bomb fell on the Victoria Embankment, near the Blackfriars river station, two civilians were badly injured. The 'Alpha' fire-float was elsewhere at the time, already battling a riverside fire.

The highest single casualty rate involving a fire not caused by enemy action occurred on the 30th January 1918. Seven firemen lost their lives at a fire on the Albert Embankment, Lambeth. It was the highest death toll in the history of the brigade. The fire involved an animal feed warehouse; whilst damping down the fire an upper part of the building collapsed with fatal consequences. The firemen who died came from the Vauxhall, Kennington Road and Clapham fire stations.

The New Year saw no respite in the aerial bombing. The twenty-third raid happened on the 17th February 1918. It left one thousand premises damaged; the widespread firefighting operations had involved all the brigade's fire-floats on the Southwark and South London riverbanks. Fifteen people were also killed in the Euston Road when the Midland Grand Hotel was bombed. The last, and twenty-fifth, air raid happened on the 5th March 1918. Seven bombs were dropped resulting in the deaths of nineteen people, while thirty-nine were injured. This bombing raid concentrated on North London and whilst there was no involvement for the fire-floats, firemen rescued one woman using their hook ladders.

Compared with the air raids that were to follow in 1940/41, those in the years of 1915 to 1918 seem trivial. Of the 1,415 people killed in the United Kingdom, 670 perished in greater London. In the four years of the Great War conflict, in London and around the country, the casualty's figures on the home front caused by enemy action was exceptionally light when compared to the horrendous slaughter of the ten million killed, on all sides, in the trenches and along the various front lines. The total number of military and civilian casualties in that War reached thirty-seven million: over 17 million deaths and 20 million wounded, ranking it amongst the deadliest conflicts in human history. The total number of deaths includes seven million civilians.

London's firemen were summoned to a total of 224 fires and rescued 138 people as a direct result of enemy action from hostile aircraft and Zeppelin attacks. The King subsequently bestowed the award of the Medal of the Most Excellent Order of the British Empire to 47 men of the brigade for their conspicuous courage and devotion to duty in the rescue of individuals from buildings wrecked by hostile attacks.

The 'Dorcas': Woolwich, 1920

The 'Dorcas' was registered at the Port of Dover and was a two-masted, wooden, spritsail, sailing barge, built in 1898 by Messrs Gill and Son, of Rochester. She was eighty-five feet in length, eighteen and half feet in breadth with a draft of almost six feet, with gross tonnage of sixty-six tons. A single-decked vessel, the hold was separated from the forecastle and master's cabin, respectively, by wooden bulkheads. She had two hatches, the fore hatch being on the forward side of the mainmast and the main hatch to the rear.

The hatch covers did not fit tightly but left a gap about the size of a man's finger between the hatch and its cover. The forecastle was ventilated by a six-inch cowl ventilator; the cabin had a hinged skylight. Entrance to each was by hatch and stairway. There was no ventilator fitted to the hold. The wheel was on the foreside of the mizzen mast. In the forecastle there was a stove for burning coal or coke, and a lamp. In other respects the 'Dorcas' complied with the then Regulations of the Board of Trade. She was owned by the East Kent Brewery Company Ltd, having its principal place of business at Sandwich, in the County of Kent, Mr John Royle Linell being her registered manager.

After survey and general overhaul the 'Dorcas' left Sandwich, in Kent, around noon on the 12th August 1920. It had a crew of three under the command of the master, Mr William Hallett. It was carrying 450 empty steel barrels, which had contained petroleum spirit. Some 370 barrels were in the ship's hold, and the remainder stored upon the open deck. The voyage was uneventful. Early in the afternoon of the 13th August she arrived safely at the wharf of the Anglo-American Oil Company, Limited, located at Silvertown, where the unloading of the empty barrels commenced soon after her arrival. Having been discontinued for the night it was resumed the following day and completed about 8 o'clock that morning. Directly after the unloading was finished, the loading of full barrels of petroleum spirit started, this was continued until completed.

Altogether, 450 barrels, some of 40 gallons others of 50 gallons capacity, were put on board. Three hundred and seventy were stowed in the hold and about eighty placed on the deck. At or about 4.45 p.m. of the 14th August, the stowing of the hold having been completed, the main hatches were put on, covered with tarpaulins, and battened down. Then the fore-hatches were put on and covered with a tarpaulin, which was turned back at each end, with the intention of thus providing ventilation to the hold. The loading of the deck cargo was then started, and was finished about 6 p.m. The work of unloading and loading was carried out by the employees of the Anglo-American Oil Company Ltd, the shippers of the cargo, and was superintended by Mr Benjamin Jordan, their wharf foreman, under the general supervision of Mr Walter William Dixson, their assistant wharf superintendent, subject to any instructions which might be given by the master or mate of the vessel.

The barrels containing the petroleum spirit were made of steel. Each were well constructed with a strong chime. Most of them had the bunghole in the bilge, but some had it in one of the ends. All of them had the tap hole in the end. Each bunghole was closed by a screw bung, and each tap hole by a screw plug. They were properly marked in accordance with the Petroleum Act of 1871. They were slung, two at a time, by can-hooks, and lifted by a crane from the wharf to the vessel. Of the barrels which were carried on deck, some were stowed on their side and others on their end. Those in the hold were stowed so that they lay, fore and aft, in three tiers.

At 2.30 a.m. on the 15th August the 'Dorcas' cast off her moorings and proceeded down the River Thames under her own sail, with an ebb-tide, and with a fresh north-westerly breeze on her port quarter. After leaving the wharf, the mate lit the navigation lights in the forecastle and placed them in position. The swinging lamp in the cabin was also lighted. The mate, Mr William Harrison, took the wheel, and the master seated himself on the port side of the fore hatch. The cook, Jack Foord, who was in the forecastle, was called by the master a little after 3 a.m. and ordered to get breakfast ready. He was in the after cabin engaged in doing this when the explosion occurred about 3.15 a.m.

Prior to the explosion a tug passed the 'Dorcas' on the starboard side, bound up the river. It was later suggested that a spark from the funnel of this tug might have caused the explosion but this was discounted by the subsequent inquiry as the tug passed to leeward of the 'Dorcas'. At the time of the explosion, the 'Dorcas' was mid-stream, between the works of the Western Electric Company at North Woolwich and the Royal Dockyard, Woolwich. From the evidence of the mate the explosion appears to have occurred in the hold. The master, who was seated there on the hatch covers, was blown overboard. He was not seen alive again. A search was made by the Metropolitan river police and the mate. His body was later recovered by the police on the 19th of August from the foreshore of the river at Barking Reach. The mate was blown from the wheel, lost consciousness, and when he recovered found himself lying on the starboard quarter of the deck. The cook, who was laying the cloth on the table in the cabin, was injured about the head by broken glass. He scrambled on to the deck, and saw flames coming from the fore hatch. The mate, on recovering consciousness, noticed the fire coming aft, along the deck, from the hold. He hauled the boat alongside, which was towed behind the 'Dorcas', and helped the cook into it. They looked about for the master, but could see nothing of him, and they were eventually taken by the police water patrol to the Royal Dockyard, where they were landed. From the Dockyard they were afterwards removed to the Seamen's Hospital, where they received attention.

Fire-floats 'Alpha' and 'Gamma II' at work on the Thames.
(Jack White, Fifty Years of Firefighting in London)

The 'Dorcas' was now ablaze from stem to stern. She drifted down and across the river, under the influence of the tide and the wind, towards the south landing stage of the London County Council's Free Ferry at Woolwich, where the steam ferryboat 'Hutton' was lying. From the landing stage, after colliding with and setting fire to it and to the 'Hutton', she continued her drift down the river to the western end of the West Wharf of the Royal Arsenal, setting fire to the sailing barge 'Darrant', on the way, and to the dumb barges 'Alexandra', 'Shamrock', 'Elms', 'Alberta', 'Horne', 'Lizzie' and 'Halifax." Finally the 'Dorcas' was secured by grappling hook and chain to the wharf, where she continued to burn until she finally sank in the early morning of 15th August.

Woolwich fire station had opened in 1887, in the days of Captain Massey Shaw expanding his fire station building programme. When its two motorised fire engines turned out, the crews were confronted by a widespread disaster scene. Superintendent Major Morris was the first senior fire officer to arrive. He was greeted with the news that the 'Dorcas' was in mid-stream and setting fire to several barges. The fire-float was standing by but her crew were unable to get a wire-hawser aboard and take her in tow on account of the ferocious heat. This turned out to a very lucky escape for the fire-float crew and their craft.

Morris, who would in later years be appointed the Brigade's Chief Officer, was faced with a disaster scene that was continuing to engulf both riverside buildings and vessels moored on the foreshore. Morris sent back a message to Headquarters at once: *'Brigade Call for Woolwich Arsenal. It is a petrol barge well alight near the quay and threatening Woolwich Arsenal.'* The Brigade Call message brought twenty pumps, the emergency tender and the Chief Officer, Mr Arthur Dyer, rushing to the scene. The fire-float from Cherry Garden pier was already on station and a second fire-float from the Blackfriars river station was ordered additionally. With Chief Officer in charge he had motor fire engines and two fire-floats making every endeavour to subdue the fire. Their efforts were seriously hampered by several explosions. These were again identified as coming from the petrol barrels expanding and rupturing owing to the intensity of the heat.

Fire-float 'Alpha' attacking a Thames warehouse fire.
(Jack White, Fifty Years of Firefighting in London)

The fire was so severe that it damaged three of the land motor fire engines which were endeavouring to put it out. Two warehouses, a stationery store and some railway trucks in the vicinity of the wharf were also scorched by the radiated heat. Much of the escaped spirit had spread over the surface of the water, and this was greatly increased in quantity when the 'Dorcas' sank, so that a considerable area of the Thames by Woolwich Reach was in flames. It eventually burnt itself out.

There followed a Board of Trade inquiry. Despite the detailed evidence given and the opinion of expert witnesses the Inquiry found no evidence to justify a definite finding of the Court as to the precise cause of the accumulation in the hold of vapour of petroleum spirit.

While alongside the wharf at Silvertown, the precautions prescribed by the shippers were observed; but the Court was satisfied that, once they were afloat and away from the wharf, the crew almost entirely disregarded every usual precaution against fire or explosion. They smoked, struck matches, used naked lights, cooked food, as a matter of course, and as the master and mate had been in the habit of doing, without accident, for over 20 years. The evidence of the only two persons in a position to know what lights were on board at the moment of the explosion, is not as clear and definite as to be quite convincing; but it is not surprising that there should be such lack of clarity in their minds. In fact the crew were doing nothing different from what they had been accustomed to doing in the ordinary course of their lives on board, and the explosion would not be likely to help them to remember, accurately, matters of which they took no particular notice at the time.

The navigation lights had been lighted at least half an hour before the explosion and were certainly in their places; and a swinging oil lamp was burning in the cabin. But it is possible that the lamp in the forecastle may also have been alight, though the glass of it was broken, and there may have been a fire burning in the stove in the cabin, as well. Owing to the construction of the vessel, vapour could pass under the ceiling, or through the bulkheads, into the cabin or the forecastle. It is, therefore, conceivable that flammable vapour, in either of these places, may have been ignited and the flame thus communicated to an explosive mixture in the hold. In seeking the cause of the casualty, this possibility cannot be entirely disregarded.

If any member of the crew were smoking at any time, it is clear that none of the others would have taken any particular notice of it, or would have given the incident a thought, as anything out of the common. The two surviving members of the crew were agreed that the master was a regular smoker, and that he always carried matches. They also agreed that just before the explosion he was sitting on the fore hatch through which, as mentioned, the force of the explosion was directed. Both said that they did not see, and did not know, whether he was, in fact, smoking as he sat there. When his body was found, however, there was, in his pockets, a pouch of tobacco and the bowl of a pipe, without a stem and useless for smoking; but no serviceable pipe and no matches. A fair inference seems to be that, when the explosion occurred, the master had his matches and his pipe out of his pocket, and that they were blown away by the explosion. If any appreciable time had passed after he last struck a match, the matchbox, at least, would, probably, have been returned to his pocket. It is possible, therefore, that he did light his pipe, and that after lighting it he dropped the lighted match, accidentally, through an opening between the hatch covers of the fore hatch. In the opinion of the Court this was the most probable cause of the casualty and he brought about his own demise.

After the 'Dorcas' barge fire: the burnt pumps

The 'Dorcas' had been burning fiercely and drifting down the river, when she was very skilfully stopped and secured by a grapnel and chain thrown on board. This, however, is a difficult and dangerous operation in such circumstances, and it might well be an impossible one in another similar case. In view of such a contingency, the Court desires to draw particular attention to the appalling disaster that might occur if a barge, in the condition of the burning 'Dorcas', were to drift up stream and get amongst the crowded shipping, above Blackwall, before she could be stopped.

The Inquiry found that the cause of the loss of the S. 'Dorcas' and the loss of life was the explosion and fire. The primary cause was the non-existence of any adequate Regulations, or power to make any such Regulations, controlling the carriage of petroleum spirit outwards from the river Thames, or forbidding the use of unsuitable vessels for such carriage. In view of these very limited powers of making adequate bye-laws, the Court is of opinion that the law requires strengthening by making adequate provisions, or by giving to local authorities powers to make such provisions, for the shipping, loading and stowing of petroleum spirit at ports within the United Kingdom, for controlling the movements of vessels outwards and within any such port, as well as inwards, when carrying petroleum spirit, for regulating the construction of vessels carrying petroleum spirit within any such port, for the licensing of such vessels, and for the loading and unloading of petroleum spirit shipped at one part of a port and landed at another part of the same port.

Lower Oliver's Wharf fire: 1st November 1920

It was later determined that the fire had most likely been smouldering since Saturday night, after the wharf had closed for business on 31st October. It had been an exceptionally busy few weeks for the London Fire Brigade. Only eleven days earlier, on the 20th October, the brigade had tackled a massive blaze at the Southwark Hop Exchange, Southwark Street in the shadow of the Brigade's headquarters. So serious was the blaze that many appliances were mobilised within minutes of the first call. Forty motor-pumps, four turntable ladders and other special fire engines fought the blaze and with a couple of hours the fire was thought to have been brought sufficiently under control that only four engines remained at the scene. Then some hop dust exploded in the part of the building that had been saved. It very quickly involved the whole of the western end's six upper floors. Once again dozens of fire engines had to attend the scene and it took five hours to bring the blaze under control. It was not until the 11th November, three weeks after the outbreak of fire, that the brigade were able to leave the scene.

London's major fires attracted large crowds: in many cases thousands of spectators flocked to watch the London Fire Brigade at work and the drama unfold. For the crews of Shadwell fire station it was the start of a new month, the month of November. For three of their number it was the last day that they would ever see. Like most of all London's firemen they had welcomed major changes in their working conditions. The LCC had finally agreed to introduce into the brigade two watches (shifts) and its firemen had now only to work a seventy-two hour week. The news had not made much impact on the daily London newspaper coverage, but their demise would as the following day newspapers ran the headlines, 'London Fire Tragedy' and 'Disastrous Wharf fire at Wapping.'

Late into the evening on Sunday 1st November the fire engines at the former Metropolitan fire brigade stations of Shadwell, located in Glamis Road, E1 (adjacent to the Shadwell Basin) and Whitechapel, at 27 Commercial Road, turned out of their respective stations and responded to a fire call to 'Lower Oliver's Wharf' in Wapping. The nearest fire-float, the 'Beta II', prepared to leave her moorings at Cherry Garden Pier and proceed to the fire that they already had sight of on the north bank of the river as it stood adjacent to the St Johns' Wharf less than a mile distant. Within minutes the motor-engines arrived and the fire was already of such proportions that it necessitated the urgent attendance of other fire station crews to tackle a rapidly developing fire situation.

Lower Oliver's Wharf was built in the 1830s. The Victorian brick-built riverside wharf, a wide four-storey building in the narrow Wapping High Street, was one of many such warehouses located in a mix of five and six storey building that lined the river frontage. The wharf stored untreated rubber and some of the firemen quickly pitched their wheel escape ladder, whilst others used an extension ladder to gain access to the upper floors and from where hose might be directed. In the meantime others, under the direction of the Station Officer from Whitechapel, Station Officer Moore, entered the building to seek the seat of the fire. Within a very short time Moore detected the smell of escaping gas. He immediately instructed his men to withdraw.

It was too late for some. Even as the firemen were making their escape a tremendous explosion occurred. The firemen on the fire-float saw its devastating effects but were then unaware of its fatal consequences. The sound of the explosion reverberated across the wide expanse of the Thames, a signal to the local population on both banks of the river that something dire had just happened. On the riverside and the frontage on the narrow street the windows shattered and cases of burning rubber shot out into the night

In the East London street fleeing firemen were caught in the blast, many being injured by the falling brickwork, iron shutters and other falling/flying debris. The escape ladder was tossed across the street together with the pitched extension ladder, hurled away from the wharf by the sheer force of the explosion, two of the firemen on the escape ladder being thrown to the ground.

Shadwell firemen John Coleman, Albert Best and Harry J. Green, who was a notable boxer and swimmer, all received fatal injuries as a result of the explosion. District Officer Wood, who had arrived to take charge of the fire was caught in the blast and resultant collapse of part of the frontage of the building. He and six other firemen and officers, together with the dead, were removed to two nearby hospitals: the Wapping Infirmary and the London Hospital in Whitechapel.

In the immediate minutes following the explosion chaos reigned as firemen desperately fought to recover and render assistance to their fallen colleagues. Some only received relatively minor injuries whilst others suffered potentially life-threatening wounds. For the three Shadwell firemen it was already too late. As other firemen protected their comrades from the fire, salvagemen from the London Salvage Corps, Whitechapel station rushed forward to assist in the rescue efforts.

THREE FIREMEN KILLED BY EXPLOSION.

SERIOUS RIVERSIDE BLAZE.

Three firemen have died and several other men are lying seriously injured as the result of the explosion which, as reported in later editions of *The Times* yesterday, occurred at the fire at Lower Olivers Wharf, Wapping, late on Sunday night. The following is a list of the casualties :—

Killed.—Firemen J. Coleman, A. Best, and H. J. Green (all of Shadwell Fire Brigade).

Seriously injured.—District Officer Wood, Sub-Officer Leedon, Fireman W. E. Baxter, Fireman A. G. Triggs (all of Whitechapel), Fireman G. H. Leech (Shadwell), Fireman H. Hare.

Injured.—James Bell, turncock ; dock policeman Macfarlane ; Fireman G. T. Hawkins (Whitechapel) ; Fireman E. Hollingham.

The fire was discovered at about 11.30 on Sunday night in a four-storey rubber warehouse. The origin of the outbreak is unknown, but the flames are supposed to have been smouldering since Saturday night. The Shadwell and Whitechapel brigades were first on the scene, and on entering the building they detected a very pungent smell of gas. Before they had time to get to work a loud explosion occurred. The heavy iron shutters of the building, together with a quantity of brick-work and tons of unmanufactured rubber were hurled into the street, carrying with them a number of firemen who had entered the building and burying them in the debris outside. A fire-escape and a ladder outside were also hurled to the ground, two men on the ladder being thrown down. The injured men were taken to the Wapping Infirmary and to the London Hospital, most of them suffering from severe burns and shock, and some of the more serious cases from scalp wounds and other injuries.

The fire gave out tremendous heat, and at one time over 40 pumps and three water floats were playing on the flames. The warehouse was burnt to the ground, and Lusk's Wharf adjoining was also gutted, but the firemen saved the other surrounding premises, though an official report gives particulars of 11 buildings which were more or less severely damaged. The barge Ripon, of 100 tons, which had been moored alongside the wharf with a cargo of rubber, caught fire and sank. By 6 a.m. yesterday the fire was well in hand.

The damage is estimated at over £120,000.

DISASTROUS WHARF FIRE AT WAPPING

Part of the fallen wall under which three firemen were killed at Oliver's Wharf, Wapping Wall, London. Several policemen and others were injured by an explosion, which occurred shortly after midnight yetserday. Inset: Fireman Coleman (wearing cap) and Fireman Green, two of the victims. (Daily Mirror photograph.)

Opposite and above: Press coverage of the deaths of Fireman John Coleman and Harry Green at Wapping. Fireman Best later died from his injuries. (Bob Wilkinson)

With the 'Beta II' fire-float now attacking the fire from the riverside, Chief Officer Arthur Dyer was heading to the scene of the catastrophe. He was only in his second year as London's Chief Officer. He had joined the Brigade sixteen years earlier in 1904. By 1909 he had risen to the rank of District Officer. In those sixteen years fifteen London firemen had been killed at operational incidents, but these were the first three on his 'watch'. In the months prior to his appointment as Chief seven London firemen had perished on the Albert Embankment. Dyer was very much a fireman's officer, a man who led his men from the front. He himself was the recipient of the Brigade's Distinguished Conduct Medal for his actions at a South London burning oil-shop, when the lives of two children were saved by his and another's actions. The other fireman was awarded the Silver Medal by the London County Council, the fireman's equivalent of the VC. Now once again Dyer lead the crews of forty motor pumps and pump escapes and three of his four fire-floats to quell the blaze that had spread to the adjacent Lusk's Wharf and involved a one hundred ton barge, the 'Rippon', that had been laden with rubber.

Chief Officer Arthur Reginald Dyer, 1918-1933. (Mary Evans)

Lower Oliver's Wharf was burnt to the ground. Lusk's Wharf was gutted by fire and the barge, 'Rippon', sank. However, it was only by the combined efforts of both the land and river crews that the eleven other buildings that would have been involved if the subsequent fire spread were saved from more serious fire damage. The cost of the fire, in financial terms, was estimated to exceed £120,000. To London's firemen that cost paled into insignificance when compared to the lives of their three lost colleagues.

Dyer led the Brigade's funeral honour guard as the bodies were carried on three of the brigade's motor pumps. The firemen turned out in force to honour their dead. The coffins were borne by brass-helmeted firemen past the lines of land and river firemen as the three were carried shoulder high into St Paul's Church, Shadwell on Saturday 6th November. The bodies were later buried the same day at Firemen's Corner in Highgate Cemetery, North London.

The Concordia Wharf fire, Bermondsey. (Mary Evans)

The Concordia wharf fire in the 1920s did not result in fatalities. However, it was reported to be one of the most memorable fires of the decade; a decade that had more than its fair share. The wharf was used, once again, to store bales of crude rubber. When the Brigade responded to the first call at 1.40 p.m. it immediately became apparent that they had to tackle an exceptionally difficult fire. The upper part of the building, which was five storeys tall and covered an extensive area of the riverside, was entirely in flames. A strong wind, blowing from the river, was fanning the flames and the fire soon spread to adjacent buildings.

An adjacent timber yard was particularly at risk and the stacks nearest the fire caught alight on a number of occasions before the firemen's hoses were able to control the spread. Thirty of the brigade's motor pumps were directed by Chief Officer Dyer and the three fire-floats – 'Alpha II', 'Beta II' and 'Gamma' – fought the flames with what the news reports considered as 'zealous determination'. Within two hours the fire was surrounded and deemed to be under control. However, it would take another four days and the fire-floats taking turns to be in attendance before the fire was put out and sections of elevated dangerous walls demolished.

A new fire-float: 'Beta III'

In 1926 another fire-float joined the brigade's river fleet, the 'Beta III'. Her top speed was ten knots. Built by Merryweather and Sons, her hull was made of British steel and her deck laid in teak. She would serve London admirably.

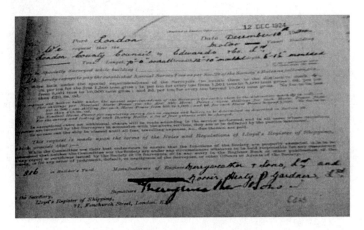

(Helen Symonds – betaiiifireboat)

(Helen Symonds – betaiiifireboat)

THE MECCANO MAGAZINE 561

New Fire-float for London Fire Brigade
Pumps Thousands of Gallons of Water Each Minute

A NEW fire-float, "*Beta III*," has been built by Messrs. Merryweather & Sons, the famous Greenwich firm of fire engineers, to suit the special requirements of the London Fire Brigade. The float is a twin screw vessel, 70 ft. in length, 13 ft. 6 in. in breadth and 3 ft. 9 in. extreme draft. The vessel, which has been built throughout under Lloyd's special survey, Class 100 A.1. for fire-floats, and also to Board of Trade requirements, has a hull of steel and a deck of teak.

The main engines consist of two separate internal combustion type, petrol - paraffin six - cylinder engines. They start up instantly on petrol and run on it for the first five minutes after starting. They are then turned over to paraffin, on which latter fuel they develop and maintain their full power without difficulty.

Consuming three quarters of a pint of paraffin per B.H.P. per hour, each engine is capable of developing 110 B.H.P. at 500 revs. per minute. The engines are arranged so that, by means of special clutches, their power may be used either for propelling the vessel or for driving the gun-metal turbine pumps.

The Powerful Pumps

Each of these pumps, of which there are two, is nominally rated to deliver 1,000 gallons per minute at a pressure of 90 lbs. per square inch. Actually, under test, each pump discharged 1,380 gallons per minute at this pressure. They were well up to specification, for even when delivering 1,000 gallons per minute the pumps exceeded the contract pressure by about thirty per cent. At a pressure of 50 lbs. per square inch each pump delivered over 2,400 gallons per minute.

A special arrangement of valves and piping permits the pumps to be driven either in parallel (for large quantities at ordinary pressure) or in series (for very high pressures up to 170 lbs. per square inch) as required. The contract figures have been considerably exceeded throughout, a result that is principally attributable to

the very high efficiency of the pumps, which are of a new design.

Details of Pumping Arrangements

The auxiliary machinery includes two combined dynamo and air compressor sets, driven by internal combustion engines. These compressors are employed for charging cylinders containing the compressed air used for effecting an instantaneous start with the main engines. The dynamos furnish the current for lighting the vessel, and also for operating a 20 in. Admiralty type searchlight fixed on deck. The suction arrangements include the ordinary suction feed to the pumps, through strainer boxes fitted on either side of the vessel. There are also four special salvage suction inlets on deck (two port and two starboard), arranged to take standard London Fire Brigade 4 in. suction hoses.

The delivery arrangements comprise a special delivery monitor arranged to take nozzles from 1½ to 3½ in diameter, and two deck discharge boxes each fitted with four valves and connections for delivery hose. The discharge pipes from the pumps are so arranged that either or both pumps may serve either the monitor and the deck boxes simultaneously, or the monitor alone, or either of the deck boxes separately, or both together. The vessel has been specially designed for easy manipulation in a restricted space, and is capable of turning in twice its own length under normal conditions. The speed, which is nominally 10 knots, was exceeded on an average of six runs over the measured mile.

The New Float Placed in Commission

The official trial of the vessel—apart from the speed test over the measured mile, which had taken place previously—was held under the supervision of Mr. A. R. Dyer, Chief Officer, assisted by Major Morris, Divisional Officer, and Captain Jackson, of the London Fire Brigade. Messrs. Merrywether & Sons Ltd *(Continued on page 590)*

" Beta III." the new Fire-float of the London Fire Brigade

(Helen Symonds – betaiiifireboat)

'Beta III' fire-float in the Pool of London. (Mary Evans)

In 1928 the *Daily Telegraph* published an account, in glowing terms, of the work of the London Fire Brigade at a massive warehouse blaze in Bermondsey. At the heart of this labyrinth of South London warehouses in the shadow of Tower Bridge the fire rapidly took a hold and engulfed the building, a six-floor store containing peanuts, coconuts, beans and cereals.

Fate was not on the side of the firemen tackling the blaze. They required the assistance of a fire-float to add its weight to support their attack on the inferno. There was a painful wait for the Thames tide to rise so that St Saviour's Dock was again navigable. Once positioned 'Beta III's' monitor, which resembled an artillery cannon, shot 1,500 gallons per minute into the conflagration limiting any further spread of fire. A scorching mass of peanuts, 'freshly roasted', showed red through the roof, but the flames soon subsided to a few sullen flickers. The *Telegraph* quoted an observer to the dramatic happening who said *'scores of burnt out rats scurried into the river to seek refuge from the flames.'* The surrounding streets of Bermondsey flowed with the resultant mix of the warehouse's contents and the firemen's water: it looked like a thin pea-soup.

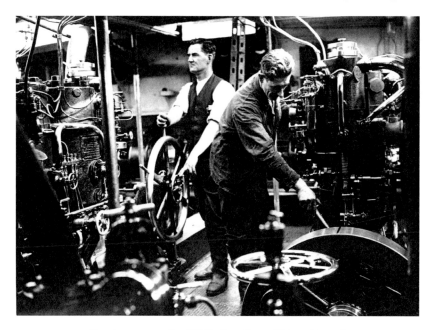

Engine room of a 1920s fire-float. (Mary Evans)

The Thames Flood, 1928

On the 7th January 1928 the Thames flooded much of central London. The flood had fatal consequences. It was the last time the centre of London has been under such widespread water. It was soon after midnight that the river burst its banks. Most Londoners were sleeping as the Thames floodwaters forced its way into the homes of the rich and famous as well as subsuming many of the city's narrowest slum streets, close to the river, under four feet of foul river water.

The Houses of Parliament, the Tate Gallery and the Tower of London were all swamped and basements and cellars filled to the brim and more. So too, tragically, were many of the crowded basement dwellings into which the city's poorest families were crammed. Fourteen people were drowned in the cold winter water and thousands were left homeless, their meagre possessions ruined.

The river poured over embankments at Southwark, Lambeth, Temple Pier and the Houses of Parliament, where Old Palace Yard and Westminster Hall were quickly flooded. The river firemen rushed to take charge of their fire-floats lest they be pulled from the moorings or the pontoons rise so high that the pontoon and the fire-floats were carried away on the flood water.

'It came like a waterfall over the parapet and into the space at the foot of Big Ben', wrote the Times' correspondent. The moat at the Tower of London was filled for the first time in 80 years. The Blackwall and Rotherhithe tunnels were under water. There was extensive flooding around Victoria Embankment Gardens, Charing Cross Station and where the fire-float 'Alpha' was kept at Blackfriars. 'The RNV training ship President floated at street level,' reported the Manchester Guardian.

The first sections of the riverbank walls to give way were at Millbank, adjacent to the Tate Gallery. Despite its proximity to the River Thames, many of the gallery's works were stored underground in the lower ground floor. Eighteen works of art were damaged beyond repair, another two hundred and twenty-six oil paintings were badly damaged and many others were slightly damaged.

The Thames Flood of January 1928. (London County Council)

However, the most serious devastation and death was in the working class areas that backed on to the river. What *The Times* described as the *'many little narrow streets, courts and alleys, reminiscent of Shakespeare and his times'* between Southwark and Blackfriars bridges were flooded, as was the Bankside area. Police went door-to-door urging residents to leave.

Many of them were taken away on carts. *'The water was rising so quickly that many who were roused from their sleep simply threw a blanket round their shoulders and made their escape in their night attire,'* *The Times* reported. Worst affected were the slums on the Westminster side of Lambeth Bridge, where 10 of the 14 victims lost their lives. The majority of the people who died were poor, people living in crowded basements. They had little, or no, time to escape death. At one of the subsequent inquests, a man named Alfred Harding identified the bodies of his four daughters – Florence Emily, 18, Lillian Maude, 16, Rosina, six, and Doris Irene, two.

A separate inquest heard how two domestic servants, Evelyn Hyde, 20, and Annie Masters Moreton, 22, drowned in similar circumstances in a room they shared in Hammersmith. The coroner, Mr H. R. Oswald, said they had been *'caught like animals in a trap drowned before they realised their position'.*

The flooding occurred as far west as Putney and Richmond. The high waters were caused by a depression in the North Sea which sent a storm surge up the tidal river. It was the highest levels the Thames had witnessed for 50 years. What made the relief effort harder was that London had already suffered extensive flooding in the days leading up to 7 January. Chief Officer Dyer had committed his brigade to assist in the relief and rescue efforts. For some of the riverside stations of Bermondsey, Rotherhithe and Whitefriars they were themselves caught up in the need to evacuate the lower levels of their respective stations and keep their families on the upper floors. Heavy snow over the Christmas period had melted, swelling inland rivers and leaving much of east London under several feet of water.

Butler's Wharf 1931

The areas of Bermondsey and Rotherhithe were, up until the start of the Second World War, great centres of riverside trade and industry. The wharves along the River Thames and the Surrey Docks, on the Rotherhithe peninsula, handled a vast range of goods. Tooley Street became known as 'London's larder'. Londoners could discern what spices and consumable goods the various warehouses contained just by the smells wafting into the street. There were new huge cold stores being opened between Jamaica Road and the river, whilst the Surrey Docks were the centre of the timber trade. Rotherhithe was noted for its ship repair and barge building and maritime-related industries like rope-making flourished. A feature of this stretch of the London river scape was also the brigade's river fire-float station at Cherry Garden Pier and its fire-float.

Brigade's coldest fire: Butler's Wharf, Bermondsey. (Mary Evans)

The area also had a much more salacious notoriety because of the levels of considerable poverty and social deprivation. Much of the work available was casual and wages were often kept low.

The housing conditions frequently appalling with overcrowding, unsanitary conditions and absentee landlords. The brigade's river station accommodation for the fire-float firemen (and their families) was considered the envy of many surrounding the LCC built station house. What all suffered living in this locality was that the industrial activity made for constant poor air quality. (Bermondsey's Jacob's Island had been the setting for scenes in *Oliver Twist*. Dickens had described it as *'the filthiest, the strangest, and the most extraordinary of the many localities that are hidden in London'*.) The worst of the housing on Jacob's Island had been cleared in the previous century to make way for warehouses that now filled the area. However, that was not before a major cholera epidemic and the fire that had killed James Braidwood and had raged for two weeks or more in 1861.

The area was now the setting for the 'coldest fire' of the pre Second World War era in London. *'Moderate or fresh East or North East winds; bright intervals; snow showers; very cold'* – this was London's gloomy forecast for Saturday 7 March 1931. In London's Chelsea, athletes due to represent Oxford and Cambridge universities that afternoon at Stamford Bridge, read the forecast, looked to the sky, and prophesied slower times and shorter jumps. In Southwark Bridge Road, the location of the headquarters of the London Fire Brigade, firemen read the same forecast, looked at the same sky, and wondered why they chose a career that made them get up on such a morning.

Less than a couple of miles away, in a warehouse at Butler's Wharf near London Bridge, a fire was already in its infancy. Shortly after 10 o'clock that morning the Brigade was called for: the station bells went down at the recently opened Dockhead fire station, which had replaced the former Metropolitan Fire Brigade stations of Tooley Street and Rotherhithe's Gomm Road. Now the firemen, their breath condensing beneath brass helmets, scrambled aboard their motor machines and sped to the scene. The crew of the fire-float 'Beta II', which had only a short distance to travel, cast off from the Cherry Garden pier and proceeded up river towards the blaze. A pall of black smoke already hung over Shad Thames and as the fire-float drew nearer the acrid fumes of burning rubber stung their nostrils. The fire-float 'Alpha II' was also ploughing her way towards the wharf from the Blackfriars station and crowds gathered on both banks of the Thames to watch the spectacle.

On arrival the firemen immediately got to work. They attacked the blaze from the street and adjoining premises, they even used the moored cargo ship 'Teal' as a standing platform. The large monitors from both fire-floats added their considerable presence and the weight of water being pouring onto the blaze. In charge of these operations was the brigade's Chief Officer, Arthur Dyer, who had arrived swiftly from his Southwark headquarters. Also on hand were the men of the London Salvage Corps, from the Corps' Southwark and Watling Street stations, under the command of their Captain Miles.

The Brigade managed to confine the blaze to the single building but it was a long time before the last flame was quenched. All day it burned and when darkness fell so did the temperature, drastically. During the night searchlights were brought into action. Compared with other conflagrations this particular fire was not very large, but it was the unbelievably cold conditions that made the firemen's task so difficult. Water froze as it ran down the walls: sheets of ice spreading across the road made even the most limited of movements hazardous and everywhere hung monstrous icicles like the serpents of Medusa after her decapitation by Perseus.

The last words on the subject belong to another more qualified to speak, one of the river firemen: *'The temperature was so low that all branches had to be wrapped in sacking, or it would have been impossible to hold them without our hands freezing to them.'*

The arrival of the 'Massey Shaw' and the Colonial Wharf fire, 1935

Chief Officer Dyer retired in 1933 after a long and distinguished career in the Brigade. He was replaced by Major Cyril Clark Boville Morris who had entered the London Fire Brigade by 'direct entry' as an officer after his military service in the First World War. He arrived as a 'war hero', having been awarded the Military Cross whilst serving in Royal Army Service Corps. (The Military Cross was first instituted on 28 December 1914 as an award for gallantry or meritorious service for officers.) Major Morris had also been 'Mentioned in Despatches'. Rising to Senior Divisional Officer, he was awarded the Kings Police and Fire Brigade Medal in 1924. Major Morris had shown himself to be a natural leader of men; he was also an accomplished engineer. Once appointed Chief Officer he brought his considerable talents to bear in the reorganisation and re-equipping of the London Fire Brigade. Major Morris may well have been small in stature but he was big in ideas and getting them delivered.

The introduction of the hose-laying lorry that could lay, at speed, twin lines of two and three quarter inch hose was due to Morris. He also oversaw the introduction of the first dual purpose appliance in 1934. This sleek, open-topped fire engine made by Dennis of Surrey could carry either the fifty foot wheeled escape ladder or an extension ladder and hook ladders. It was equipped with a hose reel tubing and carried a 'first aid' firefighting water tank.

Outside of his control were the country's continued financial difficulties. The men had secured a trade union by this time, first called the 'Firemen's Trade Union' but then changed to the 'Fire Brigades Union' to avoid confusion with the Union of Ships' Stokers and Railway Firemen. Prior to Morris' appointment as Chief, London's firemen had been forced into a ten percent wage cut in line with that imposed on the police. Some of the firemen's' conditions had improved, however. Their Firemen's Pensions Act of 1925 had provided a pension of one half pay after twenty-five years' service, and two-thirds pay after thirty years' service. Additionally it also provided for the payment of a pension where retirement was necessitated by an injury received on duty or by ill-health. Although with the normal retirement age of a firemen at fifty-five years of age and average life expectancy in the 1930s for men being sixty, not very many retired firemen carried their hard earned pension into old age. For the firemen themselves the highest standards of physical fitness continued to be required. Of all the applications made for entry, normally only two percent were accepted. In the 1937 intake, from the two thousand seven-hundred and seventy-one applicants only fifty were enrolled.

The 'Massey Shaw' fire-float midstream of her Blackfriars moorings.
(Massey Shaw Educational Trust)

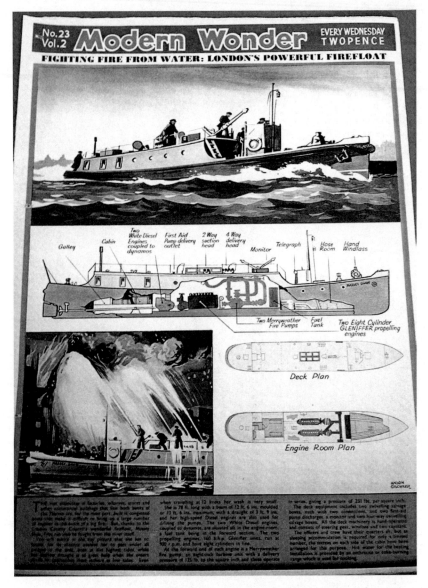

Modern Wonder was a largely factual magazine aimed at boys and young men. It began publication in 1937 but had to cease production in 1941 because of paper shortages caused by World War II.

In 1934 the political complexion of the LCC had changed. The Labour Party controlled the LCC for the first time and therefore it controlled the Fire Brigades Committee too. The building of a new fire brigade headquarters had already been agreed in principle and the new administration carried through with the plans. They also agreed much more, the building of a new fire-float and station at which it would be kept. The 'Massey Shaw' was launched in 1935 (see Chapter 7) and replaced the 'Delta' fire-float that had launched in 1913. The 'Massey Shaw' had a pumping capacity of three thousand gallon per minute compared to her sister craft's ('Beta III') two thousand gallons per minute.

Colonial Wharf

The Colonial Wharf fire at Wapping: sixty pumps and three of the Brigade's fire-floats attended this Thames-side inferno. (Mary Evans)

On the 25th September 1935 the fire-float 'Beta III' was moored alongside the Cherry Garden Pier in Rotherhithe. The pier, as today, is located in the now defunct 'Port of London', just downstream from Tower Bridge on the Thames' south bank. On the immediate opposite riverbank lay a range of imposing wharves and warehouses that included the Colonial Wharf. This nine-storey warehouse was full of crude rubber and other highly combustible products and it burned for four days, during which time a number of explosions took place. Sixty pumps, twenty special appliances and three fireboats, manned by some 600 firefighters, fought this huge blaze.

The fire had been discovered by an employee working on the fifth floor of the warehouse. The first call was given by exchange telephone direct to the Whitechapel Fire Station at 3.28 p.m. A second call was given by a passer-by on the south of the river at 3.35 p.m. to the firemen crewing the 'Beta III' at their Cherry Garden Floating 'D' Station. Fire engines from Whitechapel, Shadwell and the 'Beta III' immediately headed to the scene. Five minutes later a 'home call' message was sent back from the fire and other local stations were dispatched to the developing Wapping High Street blaze.

The first fire crews to arrive found the nine-storey warehouse alight on the sixth floor, although no fire was visible from where they had parked their fire engines in Wapping High Street. Owing to the height of the building – one hundred feet tall – the narrow internal staircases and the meandering means of approach, they experienced great difficulty in quickly finding the seat of the fire, and even an entrance door to the floor involved. (The fire was eventually reached from the fifth floor of an adjoining warehouse on the west side. It was a tortuous route via an iron doorway, just inside of which was a small cat-ladder leading up through a trap-door (about 18" by 2') to the floor where the fire was in progress.) At 3.48, and twenty minutes after the first call was made, a 'district call' was made. This brought in all the surrounding fire engines of the division. Fire engine's from the now forgotten City of London's fire stations of Red Cross Street, Whitefriars, Bishop's Gate and Cannon Street rushed towards the great pall of smoke rising from the eastern side of Tower Bridge. The 'Massey Shaw' fire-float was summoned, as were additional turntable ladders. The Chief Officer, Major Morris, left his Southwark Headquarters in his staff car heading towards the incident.

The fifth floor had been packed, almost to the ceiling, with two-hundredweight (one hundred kilogramme) bales of crude rubber, which were now alight. The whole floor was soon engulfed in fire and the firemen had to abandon their positions owing to the extreme heat and dense, choking smoke. More pumps and turntable ladders were ordered and the fire was attacked by jets from five turntable ladders positioned in Wapping High Street. At 4.41 Major Morris sent a 'Brigade call'. Sixty pumps attended the fire. Radial branches were used in Wapping High Street, on barges and from all available positions on the river-front to throw large jets of water at this now massive fire. Three of the brigade's four fire-floats were brought into action. The twin-funnelled 'Beta' had been the first to arrive. Its large capacity firefighting monitor was fitted near her prow and was projecting a powerful column of water, of many hundreds of gallons per minute, to the height of the Colonia Wharf. The 'Massey Shaw' had passed under Blackfriars, Southwark, London and Tower Bridge to arrive at the burning wharf, and now the 'Massey Shaw' and the 'Beta' were throwing five thousand gallons per minute into the inferno. The fire-float 'Delta', which had steamed down from Battersea Bridge, was feeding jets through lines of hose carried to the shore.

Although street hydrants were used to some extent, the brigade pumps mainly obtained their water from the nearby Hermitage Basin and Wapping Basin, and the Port of London Authority officials took special steps to ensure the locks were kept filled with water.

The fire at Colonial Wharf, High Street, Wapping, at 4.0 p.m. on 25th September, 1935

The fire burned fiercely; it had spread rapidly to the adjoining warehouse on the eastern side. A warehouse also stocked with crude rubber. Spreading to the top floor, the fire soon burned through the roof, on which was mounted a large crane. As the roof fell in, the crane collapsed and fell onto barges moored in the river below. Large parts of the walls of both warehouses collapsed. Three of the barges were sunk, but one was subsequently re-floated.

The fire was surrounded by 9.45 p.m. that day; however, it burned fiercely throughout the night, and seriously threatened the adjoining warehouses on both sides. Early the next morning, the front wall of the building partially collapsed into Wapping High Street. Shortly after 7 a.m. there was a violent explosion in Colonial Wharf which brought down its side wall and severely damaged the roof of the adjoining warehouse on the east side, but a barrage of jets prevented the fire from securing a hold on that warehouse. The fire continued to burn all day. As it spread downwards it again threatened the adjoining warehouse, but the monitor of the 'Massey Shaw' threw vast quantities of water onto that side of the fire. Further violent explosions occurred later, some of them so forceful that they blew two hundredweight bales of rubber out into the surrounding streets.

A further difficulty was also handicapping the brigade. In Wapping High Street the drains could not cope with the amount of water and molten rubber which had spread over the street. By the Thursday night sewer-men, trying to keep the drains clear, were up to their knees in a viscous, oily flood. Several hundred lengths of the Brigade's hose were submerged in this sticky liquid.

By early Friday morning the body of flame had diminished, and by 8.26 a.m. the fire was in hand. Nevertheless, the rubber continued to burn, and one explosion blew a heavy iron door out into Wapping High Street and flames several feet long shot out across the road. The fire was still not completely under control until Sunday, 29th September and the Brigade finally left their duty at 6.00 p.m. on Tuesday, 1st October.

The fire was reported upon widely, both at home and abroad. Pictures of the fire-floats at work accompanied many of the articles and news stories in the press. Published in the *Yorkshire*

Telegraph and Star was another fireman's view of the fire which had caught the public's imagination. His story is repeated below:.

'The Wapping Blaze
Impressions of Sheffield Fire Brigade Chief

"I had never seen such a spectacle in my life," – said Superinten-dent Breaks, Chief of the Sheffield Fire Brigade, describing to a 'Star' reporter to-day his impressions of the £250,000 Colonial Wharf blaze in Wapping.

Superintendent Breaks, who had been supplied with helmet, boots, and the necessary equipment for firefighting, drove to the building when the fire was at its height on the second day.

"Tongues of flame were lapping from the windows of the giant building, cascades of sparks rebounded from crashing roofs and

300 Firemen at London Blaze

Four thousand tons of rubber blazing in a seven-storey warehouse on the Thames side, at Wapping, London, last night made a grim spectacle as 300 firemen working from forty fire engines and river floats, water towers, and the roofs of neighbouring buildings poured thousands of gallons of water on the flames.

Dense fumes rolling in immense clouds from the burning rubber impeded the fire fighters, who had to wear breathing apparatus.

As they worked coping stones fell from a height of seventy feet and blocks of burning rubber, each weighing 2 cwt., crashed from the warehouse around them, some falling on to lighters on the wharfside, bouncing twenty feet or more into the air amid a shower of sparks.

Lighters on Fire.

Braving the peril of being hit firemen rushed to extinguish the flames as the tarpaulins of the lighters began to catch fire. Occupants of houses in the vicinity, including the historic Turks Head Inn, were ordered by the police to leave.

Then, prefaced by the crashing of a heavy crane from the top of the warehouse, part of the wall on the wharf side fell into the river.

In five hours the fire had relentlessly burnt its way downwards through seven floors to the ground floor and burned away the bottom of the wall.

As the eighty foot high pile of masonry, more than twenty feet long on the frontage to the river, began to totter, firemen who had been directing hoses on the flames from lighters moored by the wharfside leapt for their lives. With a deafening roar the mass of stonework crashed over the wharf and into the river, almost burying three lighters in its fall.

From the river the scene resembled an enormous fireworks display, and it lit up the faces of the crowds on the riverside and the occupants of the boats in which enterprising watermen rowed out the many curious spectators who sought a better view from the river.

Workmen's Escape

The fire apparently originated in a rubber store on the top floor. Fortunately only a few workmen were in that part of the building at the time, and they were able to get safely away.

An adjoining warehouse held thousands of chests of tea. Spirits are stored in large quantity in the basement.

Great sheets of flame could be seen shooting in all directions from the huge building and an immense cloud of smoke rolled away for miles.

It was revealed at Bridgeport, Connecticut, yesterday that the Navy Department has ordered all private and naval shipyards engaged on naval construction to speed up work. The Department undertakes to pay any additional cost entailed by the taking on of extra hands and the working of overtime, etc.

walls, whilst the daring fire-fighters occupied every vantage point and poured upon the furnace thousands of gallons of water a second," he said.

"We approached the building. At first the ground was sticky with molten rubber, and as we advanced the depth of the molten mass became greater until we were wading up to our knees. Part of the building had collapsed into the river and sunk three barges, whilst casks of tea were being washed from the wharf.

"Over a hundred firemen were still at work. And they had literally cut the building apart with the aid of a jet three inches in diameter from a fire-float, the Massey Shaw, named after London's first Fire Chief. The pressure on this jet was so great that masonry weighing half a ton was washed away with it. From a 150-feet crane we looked down upon the 100-feet high flames which were still raging when I left."'

As far away as New Zealand the news-wire service had the story of the Thames-side blaze

'BIG LONDON FIRE.
Colonial Wharf at Wapping. LONDON. September 25.

A spectacular fire, fortunately involving no loss of life, broke out this afternoon at the Colonial Wharf, Wapping, and soon after hundreds of firemen, with 60 engines and three fire-floats, were fighting the blaze.

The Colonial Wharf is the largest in this reach of the river, and the floors where the fire was located house rubber, tea and Oriental products. The traffic was suspended in High Street, Wapping, and the neighbouring dockside streets, and later police measures had to be taken to push back the crowds of spectators, as the enormous crane on top of the building threatened to collapse. Reinforcements from the fire brigades of districts further afield have arrived, but the fire is not yet quelled, Efforts are being made to prevent it spreading to adjacent warehouses.'

The Colonial Wharf and the wharf adjoining it on the east side were almost completely burned out. The next warehouse on the east side had its roof seriously damaged by falling walls. The estimated value of this warehouse and its contents was some £60,000. On the west side of the fire there were four warehouses containing stocks of tea valued at about £250,000. The adjacent warehouses suffered water damage, but the efforts of the Brigade and the Salvage Corps had prevented the fire spreading westwards. Beneath the block of warehouses involved in the fire were vaults, under the charge of His Majesty's Customs, that contained 16,000 casks and 14,000 cases of wines and spirits. These vaults received only slight (water) damage.

Major Morris retired from the London fire Brigade in 1938. In his retirement he wrote to the Board of Trade regarding the need of both the Board and ship owners to take the views of Fire Officers in connection with the drafting and implementation of fire regulations affecting shipping. He pointed out that in his last five years of service the London Brigade had had experience with all sorts and conditions of ship fires in the Capital. There were some one hundred and fifty-seven in total, most involving the fire-floats, some requiring two or of these craft.

Although this has no connection to the LFB's river service, here is just one slight digression regarding the career of Chief Officer Major Morris, one that concerns the Crystal Palace fire in 1936. The Crystal Palace had been relocated from its original central London Hyde Park site to the south-east outskirts of London: to Sydenham, in fact, an area that was covered by the Penge fire brigade and its one fire engine and complement of eight men. No one still knows, even after eighty years, precisely why and how the Crystal Palace was set on fire. But on 30th November, at six in the evening, the manager of the Palace, Mr Henry Buckland, noticed a red glow ablaze in a staff lavatory. He called the local firemen and told his workmen to extinguish the blaze before he went on with his duties. Within five minutes fire had swept across the Crystal Palace which eventually had to be evacuated. The closest London fire engines were West Norwood, Perry Vale and Dulwich. They called for massive reinforcements. Major Morris took charge of the 79 London appliances and his 281 firemen who attended the fire that dominated the London skyline as it burned throughout the night. Stories of arson abounded because of the large amounts of flammable material the gigantic structure contained, but the true cause may have been a terrible accident. The fire attracted thousands of spectators and Major Morris had to give the Duke of York a tour of the fire scene when he came to see the disaster for himself.

Major Cyril Clark Boville Morris, CBE MC MIMechE. (Mary Evans)

The new Lambeth river station opens: 1937

The LCC had sought a suitable site for a new fire brigade head-quarters as early as 1930 to replace the outdated, Victorian, South-wark Bridge Road headquarters. Finally, on the 5th March 1935 the Labour-controlled Council approved Major Morris's propos-als to build a bespoke, and showcase, LFB headquarters complex on the Albert Embankment at a cost estimated at £280,000. Its total cost, when fitted out, actually came to £390,000. With the site cleared, building works commenced in May of 1935. The Brigade headquarters complex was divided into two blocks. It was reported at the time to be *'the most efficient unit of its kind in existence'.*

The new London Fire Brigade Lambeth Headquarters and its river fire-float station, opened in 1937. (Mary Evans)

The design brief was for a main block of ten floors and base-ment, comprised of: a seven-bay appliance room, watchroom, breathing apparatus room, control room, gymnasium and canteen, first floor station accommodation, offices and a new fire-float moorings and pontoon. The upper floors were residential quarters for the Chief Officer and senior (principal) officers. Access from the top of the building to the appliance room for fire calls was via four sliding poles.

A Brigade museum was located with the building and a dedicated memorial to those that lost their lives in the course of their duty was provided in the main entrance lobby. To the rear of the main building were balconies on the first, second and third floors that would accommodate 800 people to watch the weekly brigade drills held in the headquarters drill yard, which was 230 feet long and 110 feet wide. Placed in the easterly corner of the drill yard was the 100 foot tall, nine-storey drill tower with its smoke chamber and internal wet hose hoist. At the west end of the drill yard was the covered bandstand.

The Lambeth headquarters was designed by Mr E. P. Wheeler of the London County Council's Architects Department, and the front of the main building incorporated central stone reliefs by

The London Fire Brigade's Roll of Honour, a memorial to those killed in the line of duty, incorporated into the new headquarters' main entrance hall. (Mary Evans)

Gilbert Baye with gold mosaic backgrounds for the first to the third floors. The interior also possesses highly decorated internal reliefs in a similar style. The purpose-built headquarters' steel-framed structure was faced in brown brick laid in English Bond with the ground and first floors and the top of central tower faced in Portland Stone.

Incorporated into the design brief was the erection of a new fireboat pontoon and prow located directly opposite the head-quarters station on Lambeth Reach.

April 1937 saw the partial occupation of the new Lambeth fire station and the closure of Vauxhall fire station – also located on the Albert Embankment – Waterloo fire station in Waterloo Road, and the Battersea river station. May saw the formal transfer of the Brigade Headquarters from Southwark to Lambeth with the new fireboat station opened shortly afterwards. The 'Gamma II' was relocated to Lambeth.

The formal opening of the Lambeth Headquarters by King George VI and Queen Elizabeth. (Mary Evans)

On the 21st July 1937 the London Fire Brigade headquarters was officially opened by King George VI together with Her Majesty the Queen Elizabeth. It was one of the social highlights of that summer with a display of fire drills and rescue work together with an inspection of the men and their appliances. It was also the last occasion that such a parade would see the brass helmet worn *en masse* as it was being replaced by the new style cork helmet. On the Thames the brigade's fleet of fire-floats gathered for the Royal opening along Lambeth Reach.

In March 1938 recruiting in London for the Auxiliary Fire Service started. War was considered imminent. Major Morris, London's Chief Fire Officer, who had overseen the building of the Brigade's new headquarters complex, retired in June 1938. He was succeeded by the Deputy Chief, Commander Aylmer Firebrace RN, whose name would later be given to one of the Brigade's boats (by then renamed fireboats) when it was commissioned in 1961. With storm clouds gathering across Europe the brigade took into service its latest fire-float, the fast-moving 'James Braidwood' which replaced the ageing 'Gamma II' at the Lambeth river station.

The 'Gamma II' was the first fire-float stationed at the Lambeth river station. (Mary Evans)

The 'Gamma II' at the new Lambeth river station in 1937. (Mary Evans)

The fourth of London's fire-floats, the 'Delta II', undergoing her sea trials in 1913. (Mary Evans)

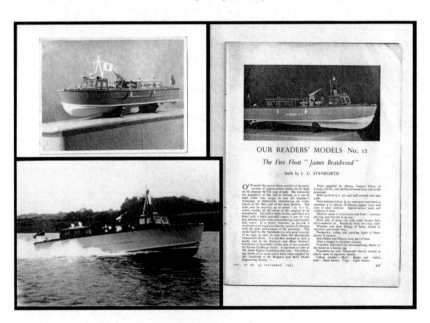

Rare images of the high-speed fire-float the 'James Braidwood'. (Permission of the Massey Shaw Education Trust)

*River firemen from the Cherry Garden river station, in Bermondsey, with
their first aid hand cart that enabled them to deal with calls from the
public made direct to the fire station, near where the 'Beta III' fire-float
was moored. (Mary Evans)*

The 'Massey Shaw' fire-float at her Blackfriars station and displaying her water fire-power, 1935.

CHAPTER 6

The War Years and the River Thames Formation

THE ARRIVAL OF THE 'Massey Shaw' fire-float in 1935, followed by the high speed fire-float, the 'James Braidwood', in 1939 brought the Brigade's river fleet up to four fire-floats. It was, at the time, a force worthy of the London County Council's London Fire Brigade, a fire brigade that was considered to be the finest in the world. However, these were not normal times; storm clouds were rapidly gathering over Europe.

Three of London's four fire-floats ('Beta III', 'Gamma II' and 'Massey Shaw') line up abreast of the new Lambeth Brigade Headquarters on the occasion of its formal opening in 1937. (Malc Burden)

The likelihood of a Second World War was being planned for in early 1931 by the British government, although it did not widely publicise the fact. The then Coalition Government, under the premiership of Ramsey MacDonald, were considering what arrangements would be necessary to cope with concerted enemy aerial attacks on its strategic population centres. London was of particular concern to the Government. However, this was just but one of many major problems facing the MacDonald administration. Not least of their worries were the vast economic troubles the whole country faced in the wake of the Wall Street crash of 1929 and the subsequent widespread depression it caused.

Despite this monetary background, the Home Office, which had responsibility for the Fire Service, held a series of seminars and secret planning meetings to deliver a strategy in the event of war and subsequent fire attacks on the British mainland from the air. London was deemed particularly vulnerable from enemy bombing action. Not least because it was the nation's seat of government and the City of London was crucial to the country's financial and business interests. Both the London County Council and the Chief Officer of the London Fire Brigade, Major Morris, played a key

part in the planning meetings. The reason was simple: London was the hub of the UK's trade and industrial money-making.

The London of the 1930s took on a vastly different look to the London of today. The River Thames provided easy access for shipping to the vast network of extensive docks and associated warehouses. The dockland warehouses, from Southwark on the south bank and Blackfriars on the north bank, ran eastward to the Essex and Kent boarders.

It was recognised by the powers that be at an early stage that it would require a massive expansion of London's and the surrounding counties' fire brigades to deal with fires involving London's central maze of narrow streets, warehouses filled with combustible products such as oils and grains and dockyards with acres of stacked imported timber. Failure to respond to such a challenge could leave London little more than a smoking ruin. With the foresight of the then London Chief Officer and his deputy, Commander Aylmer Firebrace, the creation of auxiliary firemen was approved and the provision of centrally funded emergency firefighting equipment agreed.

The Carron Wharf fire, Upper Thames Street in 1939. Fire crews working on the foreshore and supplied with river water from the fire-floats.
(Mary Evans)

The steady rise of Nazi Germany, and its expansion into surrounding countries, brought about the inevitable conflict that saw Great Britain declare war on Germany in 1939. However, before that day arrived the new Auxiliary Fire Service (AFS) was created and from March 1938 their numbers grew. The work involved in attracting the proposed twenty-eight thousand AFS volunteers, who would supplement the regular London Fire Brigade, was a major logistical exercise. A massive London-wide recruitment drive was launched. Sixty fire brigade vehicles toured London's streets promoting the campaign, recruitment posters were seen everywhere and planes flew over the capital trailing AFS recruitment banners. The River Thames was used to advertise this new fire force too with the Brigade's high speed fire-float, 'James Braidwood', flying similar banners seeking recruits to supplement the London Fire Brigade's expanded river service.

In the shadow of the Tower of London, NFS firemen of the River Thames Formation travel down the river on their way to an incident after receiving a call at the fire station. Signalling from the deck of the boat is Fireman H S Bellingham. Immediately before the alarm sounded, these men were working on the production of paddles for naval assault craft. (IWM)

The area we now call Greater London had, prior to the outbreak of war, at least 66 fire brigades. This included the London Fire Brigade, the largest, which covered the whole of the former London County Council administrative area. Some of these other brigades were one fire engine outfits that only protected a small borough area, while others had four or five stations such as West Ham and Croydon. Buildings and vehicles were seconded into service to house and equip this basically trained corps of AFS firemen and women that had now greatly expanded London's fire service. Meanwhile garages, filling stations and schools, empty since the mass evacuation of children, were taken over and adapted as sub-fire stations.

Whole-time and AFS firemen of the expanded London Fire Brigade at a brigade training exercise at Greenwich, with land crews supported by auxiliary fire-floats personnel. (David Rees)

London had gathered two thousand emergency fire appliances, initially in the form of trailer pumps pulled by London taxis hired for the purpose of being make-shift fire engines. In addition to the regular fireman's fire engines the Home Office later issued 'heavy units', a fire engine looking like a small lorry, either fitted with or carrying a pump capable of supplying eight hundred gallons per minute. The taxis were large enough to carry a crew and the hose was stored in the luggage compartment. The accommodation the 'new' firemen were allocated was frequently poor at best so the new volunteer AFS firemen spent many hours making good their bases and building their own wooden beds. In addition to this they erected brick walls over windows and sand-bagged entrances to protect themselves from blast damage.

The sand bagged frontage of a London AFS sub fire station of a converted shop in Cooks Road, Vauxhall. (Mary Evans)

It was not only the London Fire Brigade that were making extraordinary preparations for the outbreak of war. London Underground had major worries about the likely consequences of enemy bombing of the River Thames itself or its embankment walls, especially at times of a high spring tide. So around the time of that autumn's Munich Crisis, London Underground started preventative measures in case bombing breached the rail tunnels running under the River Thames. This involved nothing more sophisticated than plugging the tunnels with concrete, which obviously meant that they could not be used until the threat of war receded and the obstructions were removed.

On the day Poland was invaded in September 1939, prompting the British declaration of war, more practical plans were initiated. This was the installation of remotely controlled flood barriers at the most vulnerable points on the network, with additional sites being addressed soon afterwards. Although trains running under the Thames were halted during air-raids when the water-tight doors were closed, this allowed normal services at other times. Similar measures were taken at stations in the vicinity of major water mains, e.g. Tooting Broadway, principally to block street access with concrete plugs, although some underground inter-change facilities between different lines were unaffected. Despite appearances, these heavy steel doors were not proof against blast.

It was just before midnight on the 9th September 1940 that some sailors up on deck of the cargo sailing ship, 'Seven Seas', were watching an air raid by German bombers over the Charing Cross railway bridge when an explosion hit the river and a large wave struck the ship. A few moments later, a large fountain erupted out of the River Thames that lasted for about half a minute before dying away. Eyewitnesses by the Hungerford Bridge reported a bomb impact in the area, and the report was confirmed by other people in the area about an hour later.

The bomb had evidently hit something under the Thames, but the Northern Line seemed too far away from the fountain, and anyway, although the anti-flood doors were closed at Embankment and Waterloo Stations, there were no reports from tube staff of any flooding in the tube tunnels. However, the bomb had indeed smashed through the roof of the Northern Line tunnel, or more specifically, a long since abandoned loop of the Northern Line under the Thames that had been in use for just a few years before being sealed shut.

Although not that well known at the time, the London Transport Board were well aware of the existence of the tunnel under the Thames, and surveyors used some access tunnels to get into the area to inspect the bulkhead doors that had been welded into place in the abandoned tunnel.

In 1938 twenty auxiliary fire-floats had been ordered and in 1939 ten more were put into service. These craft supplemented the Brigade's existing four fire-floats: 'Beta III', 'Gamma III', the

'Massey Shaw' and the 'James Braidwood'. The 'Delta II' fire-float, which had been decommissioned, was brought back into operational service. With its greatly increased number of river fire stations London had the largest river-based firefighting force in its history. The additional boats, some of which were open, whilst others were fitted with a small rear crew cabin, all carried two large capacity portable pumps, each with an eight hundred gallons per minute output, and mounted at the front of each fire-float was a monitor. Additionally the Brigade had four Thames barges. Each barge carried four one thousand gallon per minute Dennis fire pumps and had twin holes cut in the stern. Suction hose from the pumps was fed through the holes and placed into the river. The barges could move in all directions, manoeuvred by jets of water from two of the pumps. The other two pumps on the craft were used to concentrate on dock and ship fires.

Supplementary London Fire Brigade fire-floats, equipped with trailer pumps, at Lambeth river station. (Mary Evans)

The basic training was provided by firemen from the London Fire Brigade. Detached from normal firefighting duties, they put the new recruits through sixty hours of practical and theoretical lessons. Whilst some women chose to undertake dispatch rider (motorcycle) duties and others opted for motor driving, most were trained in 'watchroom' duties and necessary procedures for mobilising fire engines and pumping units. Everyone underwent basic firefighter training. They were, of course, civilians. They had volunteered from every trade and profession, from every walk of life. Office workers, labourers, lawyers, tailors, cooks and cleaners had taken up the call to join the Auxiliary Fire Service.

AFS recruits were divided into different categories. This was based on their physical capabilities, their age, gender and skills. Men considered Class B performed general firefighting duties. B1s worked only on ground level, either pump operating or driving. Others recruited from trades on the Thames were classed for River Service work and whilst women could be in the thick of it none performed frontline firefighting duties.

A London Thames barge converted into a floating pump and equipped with trailer pumps at Lambeth river station. (Mary Evans)

With the prospect of war becoming a reality the Air-Raid Precautions Act was passed into law in 1937. Britain was divided into twelve Civil Defence Regions, of which Greater London (and an inner ring of commuter towns close to it) formed one region. Almost a million people were enrolled into the Civil Defence. The vast majority working as volunteers, such as Air Raid Precaution wardens (ARP), ambulance drivers, staffing decontamination units and communication centres. Others were employed in heavy rescue and demolition teams. At the height of the Blitz, moreover, one in six ARP wardens was a woman, and 50,000 women worked full-time for Civil Defence.

Group photograph of some of London River service officers, firemen and firewomen, comprising both AFS and regular London firefighters. (David Rees)

Commander Aylmer Firebrace, who had been the LFB's deputy Chief, became its Chief Officer in 1938. He wrote an open letter to all those Londoners considering enrolment as auxiliary fireman or woman, including the River service, the same year. This was his message:

'Enthusiasm! Courage! Endurance! They are not enough.

To these admirable qualities must be added knowledge and experience, if an efficient firefighter is to be made. Technical knowledge is fundamental if we are to be in a position to conduct a successful fire defence of London, knowledge which will enable us to make the best use of our material. Knowledge of our organisation which will ensure that our appliances and personnel are mobilised just where they are wanted in the shortest possible time.

There is science and an art of firefighting. Most of the science can be learnt at a fire station, but the art can only be learnt at fires. As a seaman is made by going to sea, so a fireman can be made only by attending fires, year after year, as many of them as possible.

The Auxiliary Fire Service is no "paper" force. Its members have enrolled in what must surely be one of the most practical and exciting of ARP jobs, a vitally important branch of the home defence.

Commander A. Firebrace'

A regular London officer instructs AFS river firemen in the use of a rocket line that is being fired from a fire-float. (Mary Evans)

The government had also prepared plans for the evacuation of thousands of children from the threatened area early in 1939. When the evacuation really began in August the plans quickly dissolved into chaos. Many children from the East End were evacuated by boat or train to East Anglia or Kent. On arrival they found the local authorities completely unprepared to accommodate or feed such large numbers. Often, accommodation in the country areas could only be found in the homes of the more affluent – an extremely different environment from the poorer parts of the East End. The result was often a terrible culture clash. Children were sometimes treated extremely badly or abused and they were often miserable. The situation became worse when it was realised that these 'safe' areas might also be subject to air raids. Many children were moved yet again, as far afield as South Wales or the Lake District.

*This **Daily Mirror** cartoon illustrated the change in the public's attitude to the AFS following the fire raids of 1940*

Despite all these frantic preparations for war, London was barely affected between September 1939 – April 1940 and this time became known as the 'Phoney War'. The public and the press frequently gave those who volunteered for duty in the fire service a rough time, labelling them 'war dodgers'. The tide would turn, however, and soon.

The River Service suffered its first fatality during this Phoney War when in January 1940 River Pilot George Sluman, who was employed by LFB died on the 6th January. He was aged fifty-three. He was listed as lost overboard when he fell from the Lambeth pontoon, opposite the Brigade Headquarters, into the Thames. His body was found three weeks later on 18th January at Southwark Bridge.

In May 1940, however, German armies over-ran France and a largely British army, the British Expeditionary Force, was defeated and trapped on the north coast of France at Dunkirk. Responding to a call from the Government an armada of vessels, including many from London and the Brigade's 'Massey Shaw', set off to rescue the besieged troops.

The end of the Phoney War marked an intensification of preparations for the defence of the Port of London. The River service was on high alert. Anti-aircraft guns had been installed around

The Auxiliary Fire Service crew attached to the Massey Shaw fire-float station. Winners of the 1940 Efficiency Cup. (David Rees)

London docks and barrage balloons were located to protect vulnerable areas like lock gates. Many of the port workers volunteered to serve additionally in the Auxiliary Fire Service, especially on the River Service, or alternately in the Port of London's own section of the Home Guard.

On the River Thames, a new River Emergency Service (RES) had been formed to assist damaged ships, help with casualties and clear the river of mines. In addition to its launches, the RES also had fourteen ambulance vessels crewed by a doctor, nurses and boat handlers. The women of the RES were trained in a wide range of skills, from signalling to seamanship.

There were now some eighteen such river fire stations along the length of the Thames, used to accommodate the crews on twenty-four hour standby to man the regular and auxiliary fire-floats. The river-based firefighters had to be ready to confront conflagrations in waterfront warehouses, riverside industries, power stations or gasworks, as well as vessels ablaze on the river. London's thirteen river fire stations were located at:

R1Z Landsdowns House, Richmond
R1Y 31 the Terrace, Barnes
R1X Public draw dock Teddington
R2Z Albert Embankment, Lambeth
R2Y Battersea Bridge
R2X London Rowing Club, Putney
R3Z 9 Carmelite St Blackfriars
R3Y 2a Eastcheap, Billingsgate
R3X Hays Wharf, Tooley Street
R4Z 73 Cherry Garden St, Swark
R4Y South Wharf, Rotherhithe
R4X Curlew Rowing Club, Greenwich
R4W Queen Elizabeth St School, N Woolwich

London and the River Thames waterfront were prime targets for the intensive enemy bombing campaign in the early part of World War II, which became known as the Blitz. Hitler had two objectives: to disrupt trade through the country's largest port; and to break Britain's spirit. However, the Germans were proved to be wrong on both points. The German plan, overseen by Reich Air Marshall Goering, had been to reduce London, and other large populated cities, to rubble and ashes, shattering the infrastructures of everyday life. His aim was to paralyse administration and industry and to leave the population exhausted, terror-struck, and cowering in their shelters. From this onslaught, it was hoped, Britain would sue for peace. Goering's strategic bombing dissolved the clear distinction between the battlefield and homeland. His tactics turned a distant city into an embattled 'home front'. The docks, warehouses, and munitions plants of London were obvious targets; but so were the utilities and transport networks that served them, together with the millions whose labour was the city's lifeblood. This was industrialised war: a *'total war of materiel and attrition'.* The people of London became targets. As such, they faced a choice: they could be mere victims, waiting in the damp and muck of a crowded shelter for the bomb that destroyed them – or they could become combatants in their own right and fight back by simply not giving in to the bombing. Londoners chose the latter.

Deputy Prime Minister Attlee visits Lambeth river fire station and meets the river firefighters on the front line. (Malc Burden)

Throughout the summer of 1940 the Luftwaffe (German Air Force) had targeted the Royal Air Force (RAF), both in the skies over southern England and its bases in the Home Counties, especially across the Southeast. The Germans needed air superiority before they could mount their planned invasion of England. This was the Battle of Britain, and despite heavy losses of men and aircraft, the RAF gradually gained the upper hand, forcing the Germans to change their tactics. The Germans did.

The raids on London began in earnest on 7th September 1940. On 'Black Saturday', a force of 348 bombers, with an even larger fighter escort, arrived over East London and headed up the River Thames. Their targets were industry and infrastructure: Woolwich Arsenal, Beckton gas works and the Royal Docks, then wharves and warehouses all the way from Silvertown to Wapping. Three hours later a second wave arrived. They were guided to their targets by the bright orange glow from hundreds of burning buildings. The 'Massey Shaw', together with all her sister fire-floats, worked throughout that first horrendous night. But this was just the start. On the north of the river warehouses full of sugar, rum,

The morning of the 8th September 1940. Fire-floats at work in St Katharine Dock in the Pool of London. (Mary Evans)

paint and spirits caught fire. Blazing rivers of molten liquid poured out onto the quaysides and onto the water. Preventing a 'firestorm' depended on thousands of firemen, on land and the river, fighting fires while the bombs continued to fall.

The morning of the 8th September 1940. East London's Dock ablaze.
(Mary Evans)

In the weeks that followed London's burning docklands provided a beacon for the German navigators following the Thames upriver. For those on the ground and fighting the dock and warehouse fires, the contents themselves added to hazards they faced nightly. There were pepper fires, loading the surrounding air heavily with stinging particles, so that when firemen took a deep breath, it felt like burning fire itself. There were rum fires, with torrents of blazing liquid pouring from the warehouse doors, and barrels exploding like bombs themselves. There was a paint fire, another cascade of white-hot flame… A rubber fire gave forth black clouds of smoke so asphyxiating that it could only be fought from a distance.

ARP wardens were on active duty during the bombing, enforcing the blackout, guiding people to shelters, watching for incendiaries, attending and reporting 'incidents'. Under such fire and doing this essential work, they were as much combatants as the regular soldiers, manning AA guns, searchlights, and barrage balloons around London. (The ARP suffered 3,808 during the war, 1,355 of them killed.)

An East London dock and shipping ablaze following another night's enemy bombing. (Mary Evans)

Despite the blackout restrictions, the Luftwaffe had a relatively easy way of finding London in the subsequent raids: they simply had to follow the route of the River Thames. Each night the first bombs dropped were the incendiary bombs. These were designed to start fires and provide the following bombers with the most obvious of markers. After the incendiary bombs came the high explosives. Their targets were industry and infrastructure; then, wharves and warehouses all the way from Silvertown to Wapping, Erith to Bermondsey. Three hours later a second wave arrived – guided to target by the bright orange beacon from hundreds of burning buildings.

On that first night of the Blitz, only one in five of London's fire-fighters had had any previous experience, and the dangers faced were numerous and unpredictable. Altogether, during the war, more than eight hundred firefighters were killed and more than seven thousand seriously injured, many of them blinded by heat or sparks. At the end of the ten-week London's onslaught of intensive Blitz, fire-crews were all utterly exhausted by lack of sleep, excessive hours, irregular meals, extremes of temperature, and the constant physical and mental strain.

The firefighters were supported by a first-line defence provided by volunteer Fire Guards, who formed Supplementary Fire Parties, part of Civil Defence. Three people, often women, formed a fire-party, each team equipped with stirrup-pump and sand bucket, each team responsible for thirty houses or one hundred and fifty yards of street. Their job was to locate and extinguish incendiaries and other small fires.

On the river, beside the 'Massey Shaw' and London's other fire-fighting craft, London's air defence precautions included the River Emergency Service. More than a dozen pre-war pleasure steamers were converted to first aid and ambulance boats. They were moored at various points along the river including Silvertown Wharf, Wapping and Cherry Garden Pier, alongside the 'Beta III'.

Fireman Edward Hugo Pike and his river firefighter colleagues battle to contain Blitz riverside infernos, some requiring the attendance of 1,000 pumps. (The family of the late E. H. Pike)

A London auxiliary dedicated fireboat, in her WWII grey livery, getting ready to moor off Blackfriars.

Another example of an auxiliary fire-float, equipped with trailer pumps, passing under Battersea Bridge. (Mary Evans)

To give a taste of what the fire-float crews, and others, endured on the Thames that first night (7th September) it is perhaps best illustrated by a personal account given by Sir Alan (A. P.) Herbert, who was in command of the Thames Auxiliary Patrol's vessel 'Water Gypsy', which was heading downriver:

> 'Half a mile or more of the Surrey shore was burning. The wind was westerly and the accumulated smoke and sparks of all the fires swept in a high wall across the river.'

He pressed on into the clouds of smoke:

> 'The scene was like a lake in Hell. Burning barges were drifting everywhere. We could hear the hiss and roar of the conflagrations, a formidable noise but we could not see it so dense was the smoke. Nor could we see the eastern shore.'

On 3 November 1938, the English humourist, novelist, playwright A. P. Herbert (later Sir Alan), enrolled himself and his boat, the 'Water Gypsy', in the River Emergency Service, which was under the control of the Port of London Authority. Over the summer of 1939, he had taken part in exercises involving simulated air raid and casualty retrieval. In early September 1939, the River Emergency Service reported to their war stations.

As dawn broke, the scale of the destruction was revealed: 450 Londoners had been killed and 1,500 badly injured. Three main railway stations were out of action and one thousand fires were still burning, all the way up the river from Deptford to Putney. They included two hundred acres of timber ponds and stores in the Surrey Commercial Docks, destroying one third of London's stocks of timber – which was badly needed for building repairs in the coming months.

Firemen battling a blaze in Southwark Street, SE1. As water mains were destroyed by enemy action river firemen had to supplement water supplies from the River Thames. (Malc Burden)

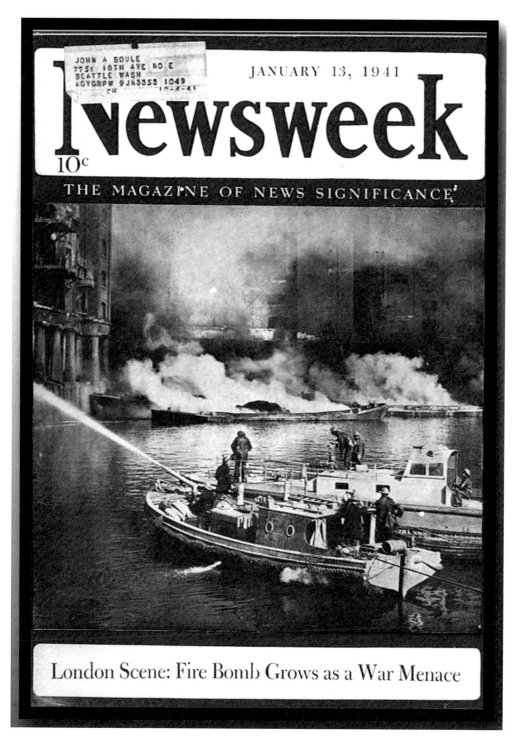

JANUARY 13, 1941

Newsweek

10¢

THE MAGAZINE OF NEWS SIGNIFICANCE

London Scene: Fire Bomb Grows as a War Menace

The cover of **Newsweek** *from the United States showing London's river firemen in action in St Katharine Dock during the first days of the Blitz and which brought the news of the devastation of the Blitz to the North American nation.*

Reports back from the German aircrew and the reconnaissance photographs on this, and the next few air raids, convinced the Luftwaffe high command that they were striking a mortal blow at the nation's industrial and transport base, not least threatening food supplies. They were convinced that if they kept up this onslaught, they would bring Britain to its knees.

The Blitz on London had started. The German bombers struck for fifty-seven consecutive nights and sometimes by day as well, the riverside communities from Woolwich to Lambeth bearing the brunt of the onslaught. Some streets had sturdy, well-constructed public air raid shelters; in others people had to rely on quickly built Anderson shelters made from a couple of sheets of corrugated iron with earth piled on top. The shelters were for the civilians; there was no such safe haven for the emergency services, but especially the firemen, working on the streets and along the river.

The defence of London relied on anti-aircraft guns, searchlights and an early warning system. The Royal Observer Corps (ROC) played a vital role in this as many units were based on the coast and could inform the authorities in London of impending attacks. ROC units based on the East Coast could also give early warning of German bombers coming in from Norway. As the RAF had no night-time fighters then, the German bombers *only* had to cope with AA fire and avoiding the barrage balloons and searchlights.

Meanwhile it was not exactly business as usual for the docks and wharves as traffic was reduced to half its pre-war levels. But more freight was carried by tugs and lighters (barges) since, unlike the roads, the river was never blocked by bomb damage.

The air raid sirens had given the warning as the first wave of German bombers neared the capital. The Surrey Docks and Peek Freans factory in Southwark, which made both biscuits and ration packs for the troops, were among the first to be hit at the start of the Blitz. Minutes later the Tower of London became the target, then Somerset House, Waterloo Station, the Parliament buildings and even Westminster Abbey.

The night-time raids that followed were equally terrible and deadly. Night after night the bombers returned. The Strand, the West End and Piccadilly were attacked. St Thomas's Hospital, St Paul's Cathedral, Buckingham Palace, Lambeth Palace and the

House of Commons were all hit. Between September and November 1940 almost 30,000 bombs were dropped on London. In the first 30 days, almost 6,000 people were killed and twice as many badly injured including London's firefighters.

There were many acts of 'Blitz' outstanding gallantry. One fireman was awarded the George Cross, the Nation's highest civilian gallantry award. Others received the George Medal, tragically some medals and commendations were awarded posthumously. In late 1940 *Acting Sub Officer Richard Henry ASHTON*'s actions saw him awarded the *Medal of the Most Excellent Order of the British Empire (BEM) for Meritorious Service.* (Published in the *London Gazette Supplement* No 35058, 31st January 1941, pp. 611.) About fifty people were cut off by a serious fire and were in danger of being driven into the river by the flames. With great difficulty and while bombing was continuing Sub-Officer Ashton, who was in charge of a fire-float, rescued the stranded people by towing them in a barge, skilfully avoiding other burning barges and disembarked them in safety.

Also awarded the *Medal of the Most Excellent Order of the British Empire (BEM) for Meritorious Service* was *Auxiliary Messenger Samuel STILLWELL.* At a large Docks fire this boy (16) was discovered holding a hose until relieved by firemen. He continued afterwards to deliver messages-and bring drinking-water to officers and men who were unable to leave their positions. Altogether Stillwell was at the fire in the Docks on the first day and night for over 14 hours and on five succeeding nights carried out duties at fires in the same area with great courage. He was quite indifferent to the danger he was in and, although ordered to shelter, he turned up again and again later in the night and the next morning carrying drinking water to the men on the hoses.

At 6.30 p.m. on the 29th December the night attack began in earnest. Baskets and baskets of enemy incendiaries clattered down on the roofs and streets of the City of London. All around St Paul's Cathedral fires sprang up and quickly spread. Some fire bombs fell on the cathedral's roof but all were cast off or extinguished. The water supply in London failed, important mains being shattered by high-explosive bombs. Only by dragging heavy canvas hose across the mud from the fire-floats working in the Thames could water be brought to the bank. In the riverbed firemen toiled, coaxing slimy hose-pipes into a battery of lines for their vital water supply. It was most one of the most notorious raids of the Blitz to date. The enemy's focus was the City of London. An area from Aldersgate to Cannon Street and Cheapside to Moorgate went up in flames. Nineteen churches, including sixteen built by Christopher Wren after the Great Fire of London, were destroyed. Miraculously, however, St Paul's survived. Of the thirty-four Guild Halls, thirty-one were decimated. When Paternoster Row, centre of London's publishing industry, was destroyed, around five-million books were lost.

In the end, around one third of the City of London was laid to waste. However, many of the main business streets, such as Cornhill and Lombard Street, suffered little damage and the Bank of England and the Stock Market were not hit. Two fire officers and fourteen firemen were killed that night. Across London 250 officers and firemen were injured fighting the 1,500 fires that blazed into the early hours of the following day.

The air raids continued sporadically, with major raids on 16 and 19 April 1941. More than one thousand people were killed on each night in various areas across the capital. Finally, on 10 May, bombs fell on Kingsway, Smithfield, and Westminster and across the City, killing almost three thousand and hitting the Law Courts, the Tower of London, and many of London's museums and the House of Commons.

Despite the repeated raids, the docks continued to cope with the flow of imports and exports that kept London and its economy going. After two months of intense attack, in November 1940, damage to the docks was reported to be 'serious, but not crippling'. German expectations that the commercial and industrial life of London could be ruined by air raids proved to be over-optimistic. The docks continued to operate and the yards and factories along the river still manufactured the ships and products that were vital to the British war effort.

By May 1941 43,000 people had been killed across Britain and almost one and an half million had been made homeless. Not only was London attacked but so were many other British cities. Coventry and Plymouth were particularly badly bombed. Few, if any, of Britain's cities escaped enemy bombing. Manchester, Glasgow and Liverpool all suffered major damage, the loss of life and its populations serious injury.

For Londoners, and particularly the East Enders, it had been the winter from hell. Since early September 1940 their homes, and their city, had been pounded almost nightly by the German bombers. In riverside communities from Woolwich and Silvertown, Lambeth and beyond, everyone knew the bomb-damaged streets, the families whose homes had been destroyed or someone who had lost a loved one to the Blitz. But the spring of 1941 brought a respite. Until, that is, the night of 10–11 May, when the bombers returned with an unrivalled fury. It was the night that changed much of central London for ever. One thousand four hundred and thirty-six people were killed and one thousand eight hundred seriously injured in London on that night. The German air force dropped 711 tons of high explosive and an incredible 86,173 incendiary bombs.

In the closing weeks of the Blitz the bravery of London's fire-fighters was never far from the bombing. Fire stations from the outskirts of greater London headed into the fray, many attending the riverside docks and warehouse fires. Sometimes just one or two units had to cope with the most serious of fires. One of the last awards of the Blitz was that of the *British Empire Medal.* (L/G. 35336, 7th November 1941, pp. 6424.) It was awarded to *Section Officer Thomas David YOUNG* (Tottenham fire station, North London). During an air raid Section Officer Young had been on leave but volunteered to form one of the crew of a heavy unit ordered to a fire at a riverside warehouse. After this fire was extinguished, a number of half-submerged barges were seen to be alight. The barges were moored to a ship lying alongside a quay but were lying off from the ship some thirty feet. Young boarded the barges by sliding down the mooring line from the ship's deck and enabled a hose to be got to work on the barges which prevented the fire reaching an adjoining transport ship. Young remained in this precarious position for some hours, even when the barges were in a sinking condition. It was not until a tug was obtained and the barges pushed ashore that help could be given. Young displayed exceptional courage and daring throughout.

The Blitz on Britain was called off in May 1941. Hitler had a far more prized target. In the following month, Operation Barbarossa, the attack on Russia, was launched. The huge military force needed for this attack included many bombers and two-thirds of the German military was to be tied up on the Eastern Front for the duration of the war. Meanwhile it was not exactly business as usual for London's docks and wharves as traffic was reduced to half its pre-war levels. But more freight was carried by tugs and lighters (barges) since the river was always clear of any bomb debris which blocked the capital's roads.

The heavy bombing raids on the provincial cities of the UK had shown that not only were the local fire-fighting resources insufficient at times of greatest need, there was also poor co-ordination of equipment, and their available resources. Even the words of

"In the Service of the Nation"

THE N·F·S GOES INTO ACTION

SCRIPT *by*
"CENTURION"

PICTURED *by*
FIREMAN REGINALD MILLS

PUBLISHED FOR THE
NATIONAL FIRE SERVICE BENEVOLENT FUND
(REGISTERED UNDER THE WAR CHARITIES ACT 1940)

By RAPHAEL TUCK & SONS LT.D

(Firefighters Charity)

command differed from one fire brigade to another which, in turn, frequently led to confusion and misunderstanding. The Government's course of action was to create a National Fire Service (NFS) which came into being on the 18th August. The country was divided into thirty-three, later forty-three, fire areas and grouped together into eleven regions, of which Greater London was one.

Contained in the newly created London Region were five force areas (reduced to four in 1943), plus the newly created River Thames Formation that brought together the fire-float stations of the London Fire Brigade, Kent, Essex and Surrey. Nineteen river fire stations made up the Thames Formation, which now covered an area of the river from Tilbury to Walton-on-Thames. The name of the fire-floats were changed too; they became known as fireboats, which is exactly what they were. Fifteen new river stations had been added and the river firefighter's strength had been increased to 386. They now had a fleet of thirty fire boats and forty adapted barges. Each pontoon was large enough to have two fire-boats and two or three barges moored there.

Created in August 1941, the NFS River Formation and the crest for Fireboat 'Sea Robin'. (Mary Evans)

During 1942 and 1943 twenty-three raids occurred over the London Region. They were however all light in character and the fire service was only called out on five of these occasions. During the long lulls firemen and firewomen took part in the industrial production for the country's war needs. A variety of tasks were undertaken, including assembling, finishing, sorting and testing operations which required little space and only simple tools. Small workshops were set up at fire stations and millions of items were handled including wireless sets, radar equipment, engine parts, aircraft parts and much more. The firemen of the River Formation used their skills in the creation of paddles for assault craft as well as the making and testing of a variety of mine detectors, castings and bomb saddles.

Between the periods of intense and arduous activity there were times when there were few fires or none at all to be extinguished. There was always the need for drills, training, cleaning and maintenance of their equipment and vehicles. Improvements were also made to the firemen's accommodation that had often been provided in unsuitable premises – premises that had

London river firemen undertook work as part of the War Effort during their extended shifts. Here they are making paddles for the Armed Services.
(Mary Evans)

been hurriedly requisitioned to meet the sudden emergencies of war. Garages were built, sheds erected and in one or two cases completely new fire stations built from scratch. At the outbreak of the war there were some twenty-five thousand auxiliaries serving in the London Fire Brigade. By the end of March 1942 there were over forty-two thousand on the whole-time establishment of the London Region of the NFS. At its peak the London Region had some ten thousand fire service vehicles and appliances, including its fleet of fireboats.

Delivery of a new fireboat for the NFS Thames formation. Station No 49. (Mary Evans)

Fireboats came in many guises – here a 'monkey barge' is seconded into service. Seen here with its London firemen crew. (Mary Evans)

A flavour of those times can be gathered from the reminiscences of a London fireman, who in 1942 was allocated to a sub-station in South-East London.

'The Grand Surrey Canal ran through our district to join the Thames at Surrey Docks Basin, and the NFS had commandeered the house behind a shop on Canal Bridge, Old Kent Road, as our Sub-Station. We had a fire-barge moored on the Canal outside with four Trailer-Pumps on board. The barge was the powered one of a pair of "Monkey Boats" that once used to ply the Canals, carrying goods. It had a big Thornycroft Marine-Engine.

I used to do a duty there now and again, and got to know Bob, the Leading-Fireman who was in-charge, quite well. His other job was at Barclays Brewery in nearby Southwark. He allowed me to go there on Sunday mornings when the crew exercised with the barge on the Canal. It was certainly something different from tearing along the road on my fire engine. One day, I reported there for duty, and found that the Navy had requisitioned the engine from the barge. I thought they must have been getting desperate, but with hindsight, I expect it was needed in the preparations for D-Day. Apparently, the orders were that the crew would tow the barge along the tow-path by hand when called out, but Bob, who was ex-Navy, had an idea. He mounted a swivel hose-nozzle on the stern of the barge, and one on the bow, connecting them to one of the pumps in the hold. When the water was turned on at either nozzle, a powerful jet of water was directed behind the barge, driving it forward or backward as necessary, and Bob could steer it by using the swivel. This worked very well, and the crew never had to tow the barge by hand. It must have been the first ever jet-pro-pelled fireboat.

We had plenty to do for a time in the "Little Blitz". The Germans dropped lots of containers loaded with incendiary bombs. These were known as "Molotov Breadbaskets," don't ask me why! Each one held hundreds of incendiaries. They were supposed to open and scatter them while dropping, but they didn't always open properly, so the bombs came down in a small area, many still in the container, and didn't go off. A lot of them that hit the ground properly didn't go off either, as they were sabotaged by Hitler's slave-labourers in the bomb factories at risk of death or worse to themselves if caught. Some of the detonators were wedged in off-centre, or otherwise wrongly assembled.

The little white-metal bombs were filled with magnesium powder, they were cone-shaped at the top to take a push-on fin, and had a heavy steel screw-in cap at the bottom containing the detonator, These magnesium bombs were wicked little things and burned with a very hot flame. I often came across a circular hole in a pavement-stone where one had landed upright, burnt its way right through the stone and fizzled out in the clay underneath.

To make life a bit more hazardous for the Civil Defence workers, "Jerry" had started mixing explosive anti-personnel incendiaries amongst the others. Designed to catch the unwary firefighter who got too close, they could kill or maim. But they were easily recognisable in their un-detonated state, as they were slightly longer and had an extra band painted yellow. One evening, one of these "Molotov breadbaskets" came down in the playground of the Paragon School, off New Kent Road. It had failed to open properly and was half-full of unexploded incendiaries. This school happened to be our sub-fire station, so any small fires roundabout

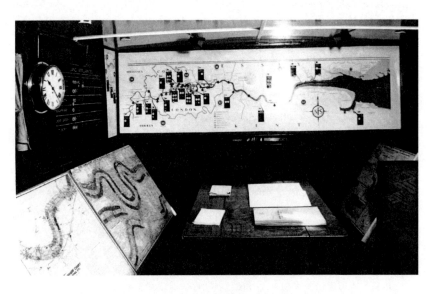

The cabin of a Thames Formation fireboat set up to act as a river 'control'
boat during major fires requiring multiple fireboats.
(Mary Evans)

were quickly dealt with. While we were there, Sid and I were hoping to have a look inside the Container, and perhaps get a souvenir or two, but UXB's were the responsibility of the Police, and they wouldn't let us get too near for fear of explosion, so we didn't get much of a look before the bomb-disposal people came and took it away.

One other macabre, but slightly humorous, incident is worthy of mention.

A large bomb had fallen close to the Borough tube station booking hall when it was busy. There were many casualties. The lifts had crashed to the bottom of the shaft so the Civil Defence "Rescue" men had a nasty job.

On the other side of the road, diagonally opposite the tube station, stood the premises of a large engineering company, famous for making screws, and next to it a large warehouse. The roof and upper floors of this building had collapsed, but the walls were still standing. A WVS mobile canteen was parked nearby, and we were enjoying a cup of tea with the Rescue men, who'd stopped for a break, when a steel-helmeted special PC came hurrying up to the rescue crew's squad-leader. "There's bodies under the rubble in there!" the PC cried, his face aghast, as he pointed to the warehouse. "Hasn't anyone checked it yet?" The Rescue man's face broke into a broad smile. "Keep your hair on mate!" he said. "There's no people in there, they all went home long before the bombs dropped. There's plenty of dead meat though, what you saw in the rubble were sides of bacon, they were all hanging from hooks in the ceiling. It's a bacon warehouse."

The poor old special didn't know where to put his face. Still, he may have been a stranger to the district, and it was dark and dusty in there. The "Little Blitz" petered out in the spring of 1944, and air-raids became sporadic again. With the rumours of Hitler's secret weapons around we all awaited the next and final phase of our London war, which was to begin in June, a week after D-Day landings, with the first of them to reach London and fall on Bethnal Green. The Germans called it the V1. It was a jet-propelled pilotless flying-Bomb armed with 850kg of high-explosive, nicknamed the "Doodle-Bug".

Dated the same year, 1942, a child recalled his experiences of the Thames Formation at Holehaven, Canvey Island, in Essex, part of the London Region of the NFS.

'Aged ten I moved with my parents in 1938 to Canvey Island. We lived there for the whole of the war. There was a wooden barrack, come signal tower that was built the following year just outside the Lobster Smack. Every ship that passed was contacted by Morse and given berthing details for those ships inward bound, and convoy detail and where to anchor off Southend for those outward bound. Also in 1939 the Port of London Authority built a small pier along from the Lobster Smack for the Thames Formation of motor launches manned by firemen and naval personnel.

The line of old Coastguard cottages were empty save for two: one housed a venerable old pipe smoking lady, an ex-Piccadilly flower seller. The only other occupants were the River Thames Formation of the NFS, whose fireboat (an ex rich man's motor yacht with a name like "Serina") was moored just off Hole Haven point. I remember a tanker hitting a mine in the fairway then catching fire which was quickly put out by the firemen on their boat before the Chinese crew were brought ashore wrapped in blankets.

NFS Thames Formation fireboats, B2V, at Holehaven, Canvey Island, Essex.
(Mary Evans)

I also recall boarding half a Liberty ship that was anchored in the Haven having broken her back. (I never knew what happened to the stern half, her forward hold was full of jerry-cans of petrol with planks of American oak separating the layers of cans. The firemen came and could not believe their luck with what they found.'

Prior to the outbreak of the Second World War, throughout the Blitz upon London and during the days of the nationalisation of the Fire Service, the London Fire Brigade/London Region was led, at different times, by three individuals: Commander Aylmer Newton George Firebrace (1938-1939); Major Frank Whitworth Jackson, DSO (1939-1943); and Frederick William Delve (1943-1962). Never in the history of London's fire brigade, some one hundred and thirteen years (1833–1946), had the brigade or its leadership been confronted by such challenges, unparalleled fires or events of such magnitude as to be without precedent. The role and the work of the Brigade was very much in the public's gaze, and particularly during the months of the 'Phoney War', not always favourably. So I provide a brief summary below of the three men that commanded London's land and river firemen/fire-women, a force that at times exceeded forty-three thousand. Two had a nautical background, one was a decorated First World War hero. All three were outstanding characters in their own right and made a positive contribution to the country's war effort as well as making policy that enhanced the Brigade, including its river fire service.

Aylmer Newton George Firebrace was born on the 17th June 1886 in Southsea, Hampshire. His was a naval education, schooled at HMS Britannia. In 1902 he was commissioned into the Royal Navy as a Naval Cadet on board the battleship HMS 'Bulwark', flagship of the Mediterranean Fleet. By July 1905 he was confirmed in the rank of sub-lieutenant, and lieutenant in 1906 serving on the Invincible-class battlecruiser HMS 'Indomitable'. He saw active service during World War I. He subsequently served on HMS 'Centurion', a King George V-class battleship, during the Battle of Jutland in 1916, as a gunnery officer. In 1917, he was promoted to commander and ended the war as the Commander of

213

the Chatham Dockyard gunnery school. In 1918, he was awarded the Bronze Medal by the Royal Humane Society; this medal is awarded to people who have put their own lives at great risk to save or attempt to save someone else.

Commander Sir Aylmer Newton George Firebrace, CBE RN(Retd)

He left the Royal Navy at the end of August 1919. He was 33 years of age. There were limited opportunities in the peacetime Royal Navy so in the same year Commander Firebrace applied to join the London Fire Brigade. He originally applied for the post of Chief Officer but instead was appointed to the lower position of Principal Officer. He was promoted to Assistant Divisional Officer in 1920 and Divisional Officer (North) in 1933. He was promoted to Deputy Chief in 1936, and finally to Chief Officer in June 1938.

In January 1939 he was seconded to the Home Office to oversee the plans, drawn together, to co-ordinate the London Region's sixty-six fire brigades. On the outbreak of World War II, he was appointed as the Regional Fire Officer, London Region. However this posting was purely administrative and prevented him from operationally commanding the region's fire brigades. He was once more seconded to the Home Office in May 1941. The Blitz had forcefully demonstrated that the localised system of fire brigades handicapped an otherwise efficient fire service and needed to be remedied. In August 1941, the National Fire Service was created and replaced the existing one thousand six hundred British fire brigades. Firebrace was appointed to the dual-hatted roles of Chief of the Fire Staff and Inspector-in-Chief of the Fire Services, becoming the first and only person to head all firefighting in Great Britain. At its peak strength, he led approximately 370,000 personnel. This included some 80,000 women, as he was a strong supporter of the employment of women.

In a personal account Firebrace provided a 'professional's' perspective of the area around St Paul's on the evening of the 29th December 1940. It has been taken from the memoirs of this Chief of the Fire Staff and Inspector-in-Chief of the Fire Services. On that particular evening he had been working his way through London to see what needed to be done and what support was required. He started travelling by car from Southwark where serious fires were already developing. Crossing the river he had to abandon the car and walked through the city, taking a route from Cannon Street to the Redcross Street fire station just to the north of St Paul's, where he entered the local control room.

Fire engines line up around St Paul's Cathedral on the night of the 29th December 1940.

'In the control room a conference is being held by senior London Fire Brigade officers. How black, or more realistically, how red is the situation, only those who have recently been in the open realise. One by one the telephone lines fail; the heat from the fires penetrates to the control room and the atmosphere is stifling. Earlier in the evening, after a bomb falls near, the station lights fail, a few shaded electric hand lamps now supply bright pin-point lights in sharp contrast to a few oil lamps and some perspiring candles. The firewomen on duty show no sign of alarm, though they must know, from the messages passing, as well as from the anxious tones of the officers, that the situation is approaching desperate.

A women fire officer arrives; she had been forced to evacuate the sub-station to which she was attached, the heat having caused its asphalt yard to burst into flames. It is quite obvious that it cannot be long before Redcross Street Fire Station, nearly surrounded by fire will have to be abandoned.

The high wind which accompanies conflagrations is now stronger than ever, and the air is filled with a fierce driving rain of red-hot sparks and burning brands. The clouds overhead are a rose-pink from the reflected glow of the fires, and fortunately it is *bright enough to pick our way eastward down Fore Street. Here fires are blazing on both sides of the road; burnt-out and abandoned fire appliances lie smouldering in the roadway, their rubber tyres completely melted.*

The Blitz on the night of the 29th December in the City of London.

The rubble from collapsed buildings lying three and four feet deep makes progress difficult in the extreme. Scrambling and jumping, we use the bigger bits of masonry as stepping stones, and eventually reach the outskirts of the stricken area. A few minutes later LFB officers wisely evacuate Redcross Street Fire Station, and now the only way of escape for the staff and for the few pump crews remaining in the area lies through Whitecross Street.

Message from Mr. Charles Latham

The London County Council has always been proud of its Fire Brigade, but it has never felt more pride than in these last months when regulars and volunteers, merged together in one citizen army, have grappled with the greatest emergency in the history of fire fighting.

The needs of war have now demanded that the London Fire Service should become part of a larger organisation and some of its links with the Council have been temporarily severed. This change will, however, in no way lessen the interest and affection which London feels for its fire fighters, and, on behalf of the Council, I should like to express to all of them our gratitude for their great services, regulars and auxiliaries, men and women, alike.

CHARLES LATHAM,
Leader, London County Council.

The County Hall,
London, S.E.1.
August, 1941.

The scope of the fires that the LFB had to fight and the resources needed were immense. The regional LFB record for the night recorded that:
- *There were 6 conflagrations that needed one hundred pumps each*
- *28 fires each needing over thirty pumps*
- *51 fires needing twenty pumps*

- *101 requiring 10 pumps each*
- *And 1,286 fires which had one pump each.*

Pumps were sourced from the rest of London and surrounding regions to help fight the fires in the heart of the City. Around 2,300 pumps were eventually in use that night. (Just before the war there had been only 1,850 pumps covering the whole of Great Britain. Far more than this were in use in the City alone on that one night.)'

Remaining at the Home Office, Firebrace was knighted at Buckingham Palace by King George VI on the 13th February 1945. He was subsequently appointed Commander of the Order of St Olav by the King of Norway in recognition of his services during the war. He retired on 28 February 1947, after which the National Fire Service had been returned to local authority control. He died, aged eighty-eight, on 8 June 1972.

Frank Whitford Jackson was born in 1887 in Strood, Kent. Little is known of his formative years but the Census records of 1911 shows him living with his father, who was an Assistant Superintendent of Shipbuilding and working for the War Department, in Shooters Hill Road, South London. At 24 the young Jackson was employed by the London County Council as a clerk. Following the start of the First World War in July 1914 he had volunteered to go to the 'front' and on the 7th October was enrolled into the Officers Training Corps of the Royal Army Service Corps. (The Royal Army Service Corps (RASC) was the unit responsible for keeping the British Army supplied with all its provisions barring weaponry, military equipment and ammunition, which were under the remit of the Royal Army Ordnance Corps.) It was the same day as a Cyril Clarke Boville Morris was promoted to Second Lieutenant. Both men would go on to command the London Fire Brigade.

Frank Jackson had a noteworthy war, rising to the rank of Major. He served in France throughout the war and was mentioned in despatches on three occasions for his bravery and outstanding conduct in the field by Field Marshall Douglas Haig, who commanded the British Expeditionary Force from 1915 to the end of the war. He was awarded the Distinguished Service Order

(DSO) in January 1918. (The DSO was established in 1886 for rewarding individual instances of distinguished or meritorious service by officers in war, typically in actual combat.) Jackson remained in the Army until 1919.

In 1920 he applied to join the London Fire Brigade, entering as an officer. His contemporaries were the likes of Major Morris, who had been awarded the Military Cross for his gallantry during active operations against the enemy, and Commander Firebrace RN. By the early 1930s, and with Chief Officer Morris MC now at the helm, Jackson had risen to the rank of Assistant Divisional Officer. Firebrace was the Divisional Officer North, commanding all north of the River Thames. All three moved to the new Lambeth Brigade Headquarters in 1937, when the shadow of war was already discernible on the horizon. Firebrace became Chief Officer in 1938 and Jackson was promoted to become his deputy.

MAJOR F. W. JACKSON, D.S.O.
ASSISTANT DIVISIONAL OFFICER
LONDON FIRE BRIGADE

With Firebrace's departure to the Home Officer the following year Jackson retained the rank of Deputy Chief but was responsible for commanding the London Fire Brigade and its massive influx of auxiliary firefighters and their equipment. Jackson was the Brigade's Chief Officer in all but name.

Major Frank Whitford Jackson, Deputy Chief Officer – London Fire Brigade.

It was under Jackson's leadership that the London Fire Brigade prepared for and then fought the Blitz. Command of the London Fire Brigade has rested with him, and to him was entrusted the responsibility of coping with the many and difficult situations created in the London area by the enemy's attacks. Churchill also added to pressures upon Jackson when he gave him the unenviable responsibility to keep St Paul's intact.

The London Fire Brigade successfully dealt with outbreaks of fire on a scale, and in such numbers, as had never previously been experienced. Particularly noteworthy was the manner in which, in spite of severe handicaps, the public Fire Services operated on the occasion of the enemy's incendiary attacks on the City of London on the night of the 29th December, 1940.

It was to Major Jackson's able and inspiring leadership that the success of the London Fire Brigade was in large measure due. His leadership of the service from 1939 to 1943 was widely considered distinguished. His personal leadership through the Blitz resulted in him being rewarded by King George VI and made a Commander of the Most Excellent Order of the British Empire (CBE). (*London Gazette*, No 35074, 14th Feb 1941, pp. 869.) His citation read: '*He has shown marked personal gallantry on a number of occasions, and in the fullest sense has shared the dangers of his officers and men.*'

Then in January 1943 his was a sudden, and unexpected, departure from what was now the London Region of the National Fire Service, and in what were considered slightly 'acrimonious' circumstances, although what they actually were was never made public. He took on an administration role within the Home Office, directing his energies to fire prevention. In the same year, on the 12th June, his son, also named Frank Whitford, aged twenty and a Flying Officer pilot in the Royal Air Force Volunteer Reserve (196 Squadron) was killed in action over France.

Frank Whitford Jackson CBE DSO died on the 15th June 1955, aged sixty-eight, at his home in Epsom, Surrey.

Frederick William Delve was born on 28 October 1902. He commanded the London Region of the National Fire Service for four years prior to becoming the Chief Officer of the reformed London Fire Brigade in 1948, a position he held for a further fourteen years. He was an outstanding figure in the world of fire. His 93 years spanned the part of a century remarkable for its increase in fire hazards and in developing the essential services for dealing with them.

'Freddy' Delve was the son of a Brighton master tailor. His parents' plans for his education were shattered in 1918 when an over-patriotic 'flapper' on Brighton sea-front mistook the tall, blond teenager for an older man dodging military service, and pinned a white feather to his lapel. To his parents' distress, he went and joined the Royal Navy on his 16th birthday. The war ended two weeks later.

Resigned to Royal Navy life, Delve became a wireless telegraphist. His ship was sent to the Black Sea to evacuate the British Military Missions as the Red Army overran the ports there and for the first time he became aware of the importance of good communications.

By 1922 Delve left the Navy and joined the Brighton Fire Brigade. By 1929 he had passed a series of technical examinations with distinction, been commended for two particularly courageous rescues and promoted at the age of twenty-seven to Second Officer, the youngest in Britain. He moved to the prestigious

Frederick William Delve

Croydon Fire Brigade as its Chief Officer in 1934 and under his leadership they became the first in the country to install radio communications between all appliances and the Croydon HQ.

It was from Croydon that he led his brigade to the legendary Crystal Palace fire in 1936. There, he said, *'for the first time I saw firemen turning their brass helmets back to front to protect their faces from the searing heat.'* It was there too that he developed the skill which was to become vitally important during the Blitz, of relaying hose over long distances and, if necessary, uphill from the water sources to the fires.

Delve was one of a small group of young, dedicated, senior fire officers who had been pressing the Government to take seriously the threat of firebombing in any future war. It was not until after the air attack on civilians in Guernica during the Spanish Civil War that, in 1937, the Home Office set up a committee, on which Delve served, to advise on changes in the fire service in Britain which, at that time, comprised very many different brigades, most with equipment incompatible with neighbouring forces. The ensuing Fire Brigade Act of 1938 established the Auxiliary Fire Service and, for the first time, admitted women to the brigades.

A fireboat of the NFS Thames Formation fitted with radio communications for the first time. (Mary Evans)

In 1941 he became Deputy Inspector-in-Chief of Fire Services, under Firebrace, and when the enemy began their saturation raids on Britain's cities he travelled to their aid with help, advice and, if necessary, support from neighbouring brigades or the armed services. He was awarded the CBE in 1942.

The heroism of the Blitz firefighters could not hide the deficiencies of their equipment and organisation and Delve was, again, among those who persuaded the Government to establish the National Fire Service in 1941. In January 1943 he was appointed Chief Officer of No 5 Region – the whole Greater London area including its seventy craft of the River Thames Formation which he delighted in equipping with radio-communication. It was to prove essential in their work protecting the fleet of support vessels which packed the Thames Estuary, laden with explosives and ammunition, awaiting D-Day.

When the RAF began their intensive campaign against enemy cities, Delve was among the fire chiefs who advised on how to achieve optimum results from fire bombing. Soon he found himself protecting London from the onslaught of V1 and V2 rockets.

After the war, when the NFS was disbanded, Delve remained in London as Chief Officer of the reformed London Fire Brigade. He became the first Chief Officer of the LFB to be knighted whilst still in office. He retired in 1962. He never ceased to grieve for his beloved wife, Ethel who died in 1980 after fifty-six years of happy marriage. 'Freddy' Delve died at the age of ninety-three on the 2nd October 1995.

From 1942 onwards the Thames was involved in the preparations for the eventual liberation of Europe. Hundreds of Thames lighters were converted to carry supplies and equipment for landing on the coast of France on D-Day. Many of these were crewed by Thames watermen, recruited into the Navy for 'Special Combined Operations' for the duration of the war. The NFS Thames Formation had the additional responsibility of keeping the waterway safe from the spread of fire, especially given the large volumes of flammable stores and fuel oil that was being moved by barge and ship on the river.

To ensure that the liberation forces had enough oil and fuel, two flexible pipelines were redesigned, in great secrecy, at the Siemens Brothers factory at Woolwich, south-east London. The pipelines had to be flexible enough to be unwound from a giant floating drum, called a 'Conundrum', and laid on the sea-bed of the English Channel between the UK shore and France. (The pipeline known as PLUTO (Pipeline under the Ocean) supplied a million gallons of oil a day to the Allied forces after D-Day.)

A further contribution made by those who worked on the Thames to the liberation of Europe, including London's firemen and particularly the River Service, was the construction of the sections of the 'Mulberry Harbours'. Used after D-Day the harbours were artificial structures made of concrete sections. These were towed across the Channel and sunk in position to provide shelter for ships and quaysides for unloading supplies for the army. The huge concrete sections were built in drained dock basins at the East India and the Surrey Commercial Docks. Once constructed, they were towed down the Thames and sunk a mile off shore until they were required.

In late 1943, Hitler once again ordered the mass bombing of southern England. As a result, the Luftwaffe gathered some five hundred aircraft to carry out this order. The raids were never of the same scale or intensity as the Blitz, mainly because most of the experienced German bomber crews had been lost over Russia and in other campaigns.

On 21st January 1944, the Luftwaffe bombed London, employing over 440 aircraft in the process. However, due to the lack of experienced crews and the greatly improved British night fighters and other defences, the raid was an utter failure, with only a fraction of the bombs dropped actually landing on London. These raids continued for another three months, by which time the Luftwaffe had been comprehensively defeated, having fewer than ninety serviceable bombers and seventy fighters remaining in Western Europe. Although the 'Baby Blitz' attacks had involved more Luftwaffe aircraft than any other raids on the UK since 1941, the effectiveness of air and ground defences, the relative inexperience of the German bomber crews, and the sheer lack of bomber numbers meant relatively minor damage and few casualties were inflicted.

It was at this time that London's River started to see an upturn in traffic: war supplies poured into the docks as preparations for the D-Day landings, the liberation of Europe was gathering pace. The London Region of the NFS and its River Thames Formation remained on high alert. In this build up to D-Day thousands of troops and masses of equipment were assembled amidst the bomb-sites of Canning Town and Silvertown; and some even camped in West Ham's Upton Park football stadium.

Never in its history had the Thames seen such a fleet – a mix of seagoing tramp steamers, coasters, tugs and barges from the river plus purpose-built landing craft all came together in the estuary. London's contingent for the D-day armada set sail from the Thames estuary for Normandy shortly before midnight on 5 June: a total of three hundred and seven ships carrying fifty thousand servicemen, nearly eighty thousand tons of military supplies and about nine thousand vehicles.

As a slight adjunct to these war time accounts of London's fire-floats, one of the strangest adaptations of fire brigade equipment to be used on an amphibious craft came about in the build up to the D-Day landings. In the Spring of 1944 a Sapper Captain by the name of Holmes visited the famous fire brigade engineering firm of Merryweather in South London's Greenwich. In addition to its two centuries of specialising in building fire brigade appliances and equipment the firm had been making equipment for all manner of tasks in the general war effort.

Captain Holmes had asked the firm if it was possible to adapt one of the one hundred foot turntable ladders to fit into an amphibious assault craft, known as a 'DUKW', and to operate the ladder from the craft. The initial view of Merryweather's was the ladder and its mechanism was much too heavy at some five tons. However, after serious adaptation and changing the rising mechanism they came up with a plan. Some tests were carried out before the idea was adopted by the Admiralty.

It had been impressed on the Greenwich firm that secrecy was absolutely vital, and although some five hundred men and women worked on the project not a hint of their work reached the outside world. Early one morning the completed units, heavily camouflaged headed for the North Devon coast where the Amphibious Wing of the Royal Army Services Corps conducted successful sea trials. The design and installation of these seagoing fire brigade ladders on sea going craft was a remarkable technical feat. The team working on this rush job received a special commendation from the Board of Admiralty. As it turned out the people of Merryweather's had done much more than fulfil an important and arduous contract: they had beaten fate itself. Shortly after their task was completed one of the early 'flying bombs' attacks on London found Merryweather's Greenwich factory. It received a direct hit; the factory lay in ruins.

Taken from the war time accounts of the D-Day invasion these ladder carrying 'DUKWs' were involved in a combined British and American assault on a section of the Normandy coastline. The joint attack involved British crews in motor launches, which could operate in just five feet of water, who were acting as escorts and navigation leaders for the 'DUKWs' carrying men of the American 2nd Ranger Division.

A 'DUKW' carrying a 100 foot turntable ladder at the Greenwich Merryweather's factory in 1944. (Merryweather)

The beach at Pointe-du-Hoc, their landing point, was only ten meters in width as the flotilla approached, and shrinking rapidly as the tide was coming in (at high tide there would be virtually no beach). The beach looked down on Utah Beach to the left and Omaha Beach to the right. There was no sand, only shingle. The allied bombardment from air and sea had brought huge chunks of the clay soil from the point tumbling down, making the rocks slippery but also providing an eight-metre build up at the base of the cliff that gave the US Rangers something of a head start in climbing the one hundred foot cliff.

The Rangers had a number of ingenious devices to help them get to the top of the cliffs. Among them were the one hundred foot modified turntable ladders mounted in the 'DUKWs'. But one 'DUKW' was already sunk, and the other three could not get a footing on the shingle, which was covered with wet clay and thus was rather like greased ball bearings. Only one ladder was managed to be extended. A Sergeant William Stivinson had climbed to the top of the ladder to fire his machine gun. He was swaying back and forth like a metronome, German tracers whipping about him. A Ranger Lieutenant, Elmer 'Dutch' Vermeer, described the scene thus: *'The ladder was swaying at about a forty-five-degree angle -- both ways. Stivinson would fire short bursts as he passed over the cliff at the top of the arch, but the DUKW floundered so badly that they had to bring the fire ladder back down again.'*

On 12th June 1944, shortly after the Allied invasion on the beaches of Normandy, the first German V-1 flying bomb fell on Bethnal Green. In the months that followed, over nine thousand were launched from their ramps in France and Holland and of those fired, two thousand five hundred and fifteen reached London, the rest being shot down by either Anti-Aircraft guns or RAF fighter crews, with some also brought down by the barrage balloons. Despite this impressive defence, another 6,184 Londoners were killed, with nearly eighteen thousand more injured.

The first V-2 rocket fell on Chiswick on 8th September 1944. These frightening weapons were launched from mobile sites in Holland and there was absolutely no warning of them or defence against them. Over one thousand one hundred of these rockets were fired at Britain and they killed 2,754 in London alone. (The last V-2 rocket landed on a house in Orpington on 27th March 1945.)

V-2 rocket attack on Smithfield Market. 1944. (Mary Evans)

That many London firemen and firewomen displayed conspicuous bravery is indicated by the number of national gallantry awards made. In addition to the *George Cross* being awarded twice, one woman and seven men won the *George Medal.* Additionally there were three awards of the *Most Excellent Order of the British Empire (OBE)* and thirteen awards of the *Member of the Most Excellent Order of the British Empire (MBE).* One hundred and eighteen *British Empire Medals (BEM),* plus eleven *King's Police and Fire Service Gallantry Medals (KPFSM).*

During the war 327 men and women of the London regional Fire Service were killed in action (see Appendix III, page 487) and 3,087 were injured as a result of enemy action.

The last gallantry medals to be awarded to members of the NFS River Thames Formation followed an incident in the closing months of the War. It followed a river accident when the MV 'Erinna' and SS 'Mount Othrys' collided and caught fire on the River Thames at Holehaven, in Essex, on 7th January 1945.

Awarded the British Empire Medal (BEM). (*London Gazette Supp* No. 37181, 17th July 1948, pp. 3678.) *Section Leader Robert James WYNNE* of the River Thames Formation, National Fire Service.

Two vessels, one of which was a fuel tanker, collided. Petrol gushed out and was showered over the two ships and on to the water. At the same time the tearing metal sparked sufficiently to cause the petrol to ignite and instantly the two ships were

230

enveloped by flames. Section Leader Wynne who was in charge of the Fireboat 'Laureate' brought his ship alongside the tanker and, undeterred by the fact that all the crew of the tanker except two had abandoned ship, led his crew on board and resolutely tackled the fire with foam. The men worked their way across the ship, across a burning hot deck, using the break of the foc'sle as a screen, to the burst and burning tank on the port side. Gradually the flames were smothered and, out of a cargo of eight thousand tons of petrol, only about three hundred and fifty tons were lost. Section Leader Wynne, by his prompt and resolute actions, saved the ship and prevented what might have been a disastrous fire.

Members of the crew of the 'Laureate' were awarded the *Kings' Commendations for Brave Conduct* in respect of their actions at same incident:

Leading Fireman Frederick Edmund BONNER.
Fireman Reginald John COX.
Section Leader Walter William DIPLOCK.
Leading Fireman Philip Percy DIWER,
Fireman Alfred Charles HUGGINS.
Fireman William George SCRAGG.
Fireman Thomas Henry SETCHELL.
Fireman Frank TYTE.
Norman Harry WILLIAMSON.

On the 8th January, in a letter to Mr Herbert Morrison, the Home Secretary, Winston Churchill said of the Nation Fire Service, *'They are a grand lot, and their work must never be forgotten.'*

From 1945 until March 1948 the National Fire Service was occupied in creating a peacetime service. On the 1st April 1948 the London Fire Brigade returned to local authority control, the London Country Council.

CHAPTER 7

The 'Massey Shaw' Fire-Float

T HE 'MASSEY SHAW' REMAINS one of the, if not *the*, most iconic fireboat ever to have graced the UK's fire service. In 1934 the Fire Brigade's Committee of the London County Council had approved the purchase of a new fire-float for the London Fire Brigade. (They were called fire-floats before WWII and were only reclassified fireboats in late 1941.) This new craft was to take the name of the first Chief Officer of the former Metropolitan Fire Brigade, Captain Eyre Massey Shaw, who was later knighted by Queen Victoria on his retirement. The name of the fireboat was shortened: it was to be simply called 'Massey Shaw'.

The Brigade's specification required a vessel with a shallow draught which could operate on London's stretch of the Thames, its tributaries, canals and enclosed docks. It was to be fitted with a three-inch monitor to direct large quantities of water onto riverside fires together with two discharge boxes each having four-three and half inch hose connections. This would facilitate pumping water ashore and for salvage pumping.

The 'Massey Shaw' was constructed at the shipyard of J. Samuel White & Co. in Cowes on the Isle of Wight, the whole of the pumping equipment being provided by Merryweather & Sons Ltd. The boat cost just over £17,000 and was launched on 25th February 1935 by the wife of the then Chief Officer of London, Major C. C. B. Morris. At 78 feet (24 metres) in length and 50

The 'Massey Shaw' fire-float on the River Thames in 1935. (Mary Evans)

tons in weight the boat was powered by twin 8-cylinder Gleniffer 165hp diesel engines giving it a top speed of 12 knots. Its twin 4-stage centrifugal pumps and firefighting equipment supplied by Merryweather gave the monitor a maximum output of 3,000gpm (135,000 litres). Its monitor was also a formidable piece of equipment, capable of rotating three-hundred and sixty degrees and being able to elevate through an angle of ninety degrees. Her draft was just three feet nine inches which enabled the fireboat to navigate the Thames at most states of the tide.

The 'Massey Shaw', being launched by Mrs Morris, wife of London's Chief Fire Officer. (Massey Shaw Educational Trust)

Within weeks the 'Massey Shaw' was attending one of London's largest riverside fires for a decade. The new fire-float was one of the first on the scene to tackle a fire that had broken out in Colonial Wharf, Wapping High Street, E1 on the 25th September 1935. It was typical of big Thameside fires, the sort which the London fire Brigade, and its former Metropolitan Fire Brigade, had tackled for almost seventy years.

The young Captain Massey Shaw when he came to London as the new Superintendent of the London Fire Engine Establishment. He went on to become the first appointed Chief Officer of London's Metropolitan Fire Brigade in 1866. (Mary Evans)

On completion she was sailed around the Channel into the Thames and was fitted out by Merryweather at their Greenwich dock yard. The 'Massey Shaw' was based at Blackfriars Bridge River Station from July 1935 where she replaced the ageing fire-float 'Delta II'. It was from Blackfriars that she attended a number of major riverside warehouse fires, including Colonial Wharf, Wapping where her monitor was put to good use in restricting the spread of fire to adjoining warehouses.

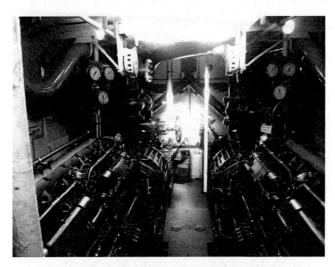

*The engine room of the 'Massey Shaw' fireboat.
(Massey Shaw Education Trust)*

The 'Massey Shaw' and her crew in action at the fire that required sixty pumps to tackle it. The Colonial Wharf, Wapping. (Mary Evans)

The nine-storey warehouse was full of crude rubber and other highly combustible products. It burned for four days. During that time a number of explosions occurred. Sixty pumps, twenty special appliances and the Brigade's fleet of three fire-floats together with some 600 London firefighters fought this huge blaze. Such was the intensity of the fire the walls gradually collapsed and a stream of escaping liquid rubber flowed into the surrounding Wapping streets. The river floats pressed home their attack into the burning building whilst firemen, perched precariously on cranes on adjacent wharfs, directed their jets of water into the flames. Fire engines from every part of London, and its suburbs, brought in men to relieve those who had been on continuous duty for many long hours, a few of whom suffered minor injuries and burns. The district was covered with soot, and the local schools and tenements were uninhabitable at the height of the blaze. For the firemen crewing the fire-floats there was no respite from fighting the flames. However, the 'Massey Shaw', and her sister fire-floats,

The partial collapse of the Colonial Wharf after a series of explosions, with the 'Massey Shaw's' monitor continuing to tackle the fire whilst her pumps also supply the firemen's hose on the adjacent barges. (Mary Evans)

played a significant part in the firefighting. It was reported that the water discharged from the 'Shaw's' massive monitor helped to successfully prevented fire spreading to the surrounding warehouses.

Until 1937 the London Fire Brigade headquarters had been located in Southwark Bridge Road. In July of that year His Majesty King George VI, accompanied by Queen Elizabeth, opened the new headquarters on Albert Embankment, near Lambeth Bridge. The headquarters complex had been designed and built under the direction of the London County Council. It was state of the art for the time. The headquarters included both a land and river fire station, the Brigade's vehicle and equipment workshops, the new recruit training school, and residential accommodation for both the Brigade's senior and principal officers.

The Brigade was then organised into six districts: A to F. It had had three 'Floating stations': station 58 at Cherry Gardens, Rotherhithe, station 65 at Blackfriars, Victoria Embankment, and station 96 Battersea, at Battersea Bridge. Its three fire-floats, 'Gamma II' (1911), 'Beta III' (1926), and the 'Massey Shaw' (1935), formed the River Service and were overseen by Superintendent H. J. W. King. ('Delta II', replaced by the 'Massey Shaw', was held as a reserve fire-float.) The opening of the new headquarters brought about a limited reorganisation of the Brigade. The land stations of Vauxhall and Waterloo were closed down and the Battersea river station transferred to the new Lambeth river station, adjacent to the headquarters complex. The Charing Cross river repair depot was also shut down, fire-float repairs and maintenance being undertaken by the marine engineers now working at the new Lambeth HQ workshops.

With the new river station operational, 'Gamma II' was transferred from Battersea to Lambeth. The 'Massey Shaw' remained at Blackfriars and the 'Beta III' at Cherry Gardens. The River Service had 68 officers and firemen, plus its river pilots (employed by the Brigade but not as firemen) at the three river stations. With the arrival of the new high-speed fire-float, the 'James Braidwood', in 1939 it was stationed at the Lambeth river station. The 'Gamma II' joined the 'Delta II' in reserve. However, both these fire-floats

Smoke billowing from the burning Colonial Wharf in Wapping, and the brass helmeted firemen on the barges dwarfed by the sheer size of this major London blaze. (Mary Evans)

would soon be returned to full operational river service with the increasing likelihood of war being declared on Germany.

The 'Massey Shaw' as she arrives in the upper Thames, having been fitted out by Merryweather's in Greenwich. May 1935.
(Massey Shaw Education Trust)

By the outbreak of the Second World War in September 1939 the London Fire Brigade's regular strength had been increased with some 23,000 auxiliaries. Within that total a considerable number of the auxiliary firemen had been recruited and specially trained for river duties. It was from this number that eight were later selected, together with five regular London river firemen to form a volunteer crew for a very special duty.

Dunkirk

In May 1940 the 'Massey Shaw' was requested by the Admiralty. It was despatched to Dunkirk, via Ramsgate, on 31st May with its volunteer crew of regulars and auxiliaries, plus an attached naval officer in command.

The 'Massey Shaw' adjacent to her Blackfriars moorings in London.
(Mary Evans)

Dunkirk, and the evacuation associated with the troops trapped at Dunkirk, was called a 'miracle' by Winston Churchill. As the German *Wehrmacht* swept through Belgium and France in the spring of 1940, using Blitzkrieg, the French and British armies could not stop the onslaught. The advancing German Army trapped the British and French armies on the beaches around Dunkirk. Some 340,000 military personal were surrounded, and they were a sitting target for the Germans.

Lord John Gort had led the British Expeditionary Forces (BEF). It was he who first raised the possibility of an evacuation from Calais, Boulogne and Dunkirk on 19 May. The Admiralty appointed Vice-Admiral Sir Bertram Ramsey to take command of the planning for this possible evacuation, under the codename 'Dynamo'.

Vice-Admiral Ramsay spearheaded the evacuation of Dunkirk. (Bertram Ramsay was born in 1883. He had gone to sea at the age of 16 as a midshipman. For two years he served on the 'Dread-nought' – a ship that was to change warship designs in the future. Ramsey qualified as a signals officer and then attended the newly set-up Naval War College.) It was from his base at Dover that he formulated Operation Dynamo. It was his plan to get off the beaches as many soldiers as was humanly possible. The trapped British troops included both professional and territorial soldiers, soldiers that Britain could not afford to lose.

The beaches of Dunkirk have a shallow slope, therefore no large boats could get close enough to the actual beaches where the men were waiting. Smaller boats were required to take the men from the beaches and then transfer them to larger ships waiting further off shore. In total 800 of these legendary 'little ships' made the crossing to the French coast. The 'Massey Shaw' was among their number. It is thought that the smallest craft to make the crossing was the 18-foot fishing boat 'Tamzine'. (This fishing boat remains on display in the Imperial War Museum in London.)

Operation Dynamo lasted from the 27th May until the 4th June 1940. It is one of the most celebrated military events in British history despite being as a result of one of the most crushing defeats suffered by the British army. For over six months previously the two opposing armies had faced each other across the Franco-German border. But on the 10th May the German offensive began. After just ten days German tanks reached the Channel at Abbeville, splitting the Allied armies in two. All the Germans had to do to trap the BEF, cutting off any hope of escape, was to immediately attack Dunkirk. Instead the BEF was able to fight its way to Dunkirk, where between 27 May and 4 June a total of 338,226 allied troops were rescued from the Dunkirk and surrounding beaches. It was this escape of British and Allied forces that enabled Churchill to convince his cabinet colleagues to fight on, regardless of the fate of France.

Ramsey had had a number of serious problems to overcome. At the start of the evacuation Ramsey had a fleet of destroyers, passenger ferry steamers and Dutch coasters. What he lacked however were enough small boats to get men from the beaches to the ships waiting offshore. Dunkirk itself had been under heavy bombardment for some days, and the inner harbour was out of use.

The evacuation got underway on the afternoon of Sunday 26 May, when a number of personnel ships were sent into Dunkirk harbour (these were mostly fast passenger ships that had been used on the cross-channel routes before the war, and were manned by Merchant Navy Crews). This type of ship would eventually evacuate 87,810 men from Dunkirk and the beaches, second only to the destroyers. Operation Dynamo itself did not start until 6.57 p.m. on 26 May, when the Admiralty ordered Vice-Admiral Ramsey to start the full evacuation.

Over the first two days of the evacuation 7,699 men disembarked in England, virtually all of them from the harbour.

On 28th May the evacuation from the beaches began to pick up speed, and one third of the 17,804 rescued during the day were taken from the beaches.

On the 30th May more men were evacuated from the beaches than from the harbour. That day also saw the little ships at work, ferrying men from the beaches to the larger ships offshore.

British and Allied losses at Dunkirk were very heavy. The BEF lost 68,111 killed, wounded and prisoner, 2,472 guns, 63,879 vehicles, 20,548 motorcycles and 500,000 tons of stores and ammunition during the evacuation. The RAF lost 106 aircraft during the fighting to protect the British and Allied forces on the beaches. At least 243 ships were sunk, including six Royal Navy destroyers, with another 19 suffering damage.

Hundreds of small, privately owned boats took part in the evacuation from Dunkirk, making their main contribution from 30 May onwards. Anything that could float and could cross the channel made its way to Dunkirk in unknown numbers. Close to 200 of the little ships were lost during the evacuation. Their critically important role was to ferry soldiers from the shallow inshore waters to the larger vessels waiting off the beaches. For around 100,000 men the journey home from Dunkirk began with a short trip on one of the small ships. One such 'small boat' was the 'Massey Shaw'. Other than her maiden voyage the 'Massey Shaw' had never been back to sea. The furthest she had venture downstream was to Ridham in the Thames Estuary. However, her two massive diesel engines had more than enough power to propel her up and down the Thames at 12 knots.

Her first port of call was Ramsgate where they were directed to pick up a Royal Naval officer and provisions. Whilst heading down the Thames her volunteer crew were kept busy painting the shiny brass and metal-work with navy-grey paint.

The original assumption was that 'Massey Shaw' would assist with firefighting operations in Dunkirk port but, on arrival, this proved impractical under the desperate circumstances. Instead, she was instrumental in rescuing some 600 troops – ferrying over 500 troops off the beach at Bray Dunes to larger vessels offshore, where her shallow draught proved advantageous, and bringing over 100 others back directly to Ramsgate over three trips.

It had been over the 29th and 30th May that the 'Massey Shaw's' regular crew had seen tugs coming down the river towing strings of small boats, yachts, lifeboats and even dinghies. Then they heard that they were to follow and that their destination was Dunkirk. Her volunteer crew of thirteen were chosen and with a formal send-off they departed from the Brigade Headquarters river station on the Albert Embankment in Lambeth. Their river and estuary pilot on the first leg of the journey was also a volunteer, a Mr Pinch.

Thirteen was more than her normal crew complement because they had expected to spend several days fighting fires off the French coast without relief. A river pilot took them to Greenwich and then another onto Ramsgate. At Ramsgate a young Royal Naval Sub-Lieutenant came aboard to take command of the 'Massey Shaw'. He carried nothing more than his steel helmet and a chart to show him how to navigate through the minefields across the channel from North Goodwin Lightship to Bray Dunes, the beach where they were to pick up Allied troops.

The 'Massey Shaw' did not even possess a ship's compass, but the firemen had bought one hastily from a chandler's in Blackfriars. There was no time to swing and correct it, which made it rather unreliable since the large steel hull of the fireboat caused a massive deviation. As a result, despite the excellent landmark of smoke from Dunkirk's burning oil tanks, they were well outside the swept channel when they got to the French coast. But their shallow draft enabled them to cross the hazardous sandbanks without grounding.

(Mary Evans)

The scene on the beaches at Dunkirk is best described using the words of Walter Lord from his book *The Miracle of Dunkirk*, published by Allen Lane.

> 'At first glance it looked like any bank holiday weekend with swarms of people moving around or sitting in little knots on the sand. But there was a big difference; instead of bright colours of summer everybody was dressed in khaki. And what appeared to be "breakwaters" running down to the surf turned out to be columns of men. Also dressed in khaki. [...]
>
> The Massey Shaw sent in a rowboat towards one column. It was shortly swamped and sunk as the troops piled in. Then a stranded RAF speedboat was salvaged in the hope that it might be used but fifty men trying to crowd aboard put that out of action as well. Later another boat was found and a line was strung between the Massey Shaw and the beach, and the new boat was pulled back

and forth along the line rather like a sea going trolley car. The boat only carried six men at a time, back and forth it went, ferrying load after load. Finally the Massey Shaw could hold no more. There were now thirty men packed into a cabin which had seemed crowded with six the night before. Dozens more were sprawled on the deck and there was not a square foot of empty space. [...]

It was dark when the Massey Shaw finally set off to Ramsgate. So far she had led a charmed life. The Luftwaffe was constantly overhead. But no plane had attacked. Now, as she got under way, her screws kicked up phosphorescent wake that caught the attention of some sharp-eyed enemy pilot. He swooped down and dropped a single bomb. It was close, but a miss. The Massey Shaw continued on her way bringing home another sixty-five men.'

The crew on her second crossing to Dunkirk comprised mixed fire service and RN personnel transporting a naval beach party. The fires ashore were what the 'Massey Shaw's' firemen crew were used to, but the bursts of high-explosive shells, bombs and anti-aircraft fire were a new experience. Once again, as they steamed parallel to the beach, they saw columns of men wading out in the shallows, waiting to be picked up by a host of small boats. Late that afternoon, they anchored off Bray Dunes.

Using a light skiff, picked up at Ramsgate Harbour, they went ashore and collected the first of the men. Most of the soldiers were non-swimmers and at first, too many of them tried to get aboard. There were many other small boats operating from the beach, but each of them already had its own ship to fill. A line was again made fast, this time to a derelict lorry, and a small boat was used to ferry altogether forty of a company of Royal Engineers aboard the 'Massey Shaw'. The young naval officer, having spent most of the day in the water between the fireboat and the beach, then safely navigated her back to Ramsgate where they arrived next morning. The crew of the 'Massey Shaw' refuelled hastily, got some food and left for another trip. Some of the exhausted firemen were replaced by naval ratings; they brought a Lewis gun on board as a defence against air attack, but this was never used. Another Royal Naval Volunteer Reserve Lieutenant came aboard to command the ship and they brought two stokers to take care of the engines and a beach party commanded by a second young naval officer to handle the embarkation on the other side. They also took a 30 foot ship's lifeboat in tow as a tender.

By eleven o'clock that night they had arrived and anchored off Bray Dunes in ten feet of water with their prow facing the shore. The fires of Dunkirk gave them enough light to work by and the thick blanket of smoke provided some cover from air attack. But the shelling from German guns was relentless. The two naval officers set a splendid example of calm and the beach party rowed ashore, fixing a line to maintain contact with the fireboat. After four or five journeys, the 'Massey Shaw' was full once more with troops pressed together in the cabin and standing shoulder-to-shoulder on deck. Her load of nearly a hundred men was transferred to a troopship at anchor in the channel and she returned to be reloaded.

This was only possible after some engine trouble that the naval stokers, who were unused to the 'Massey Shaw's' machinery, eventually managed to overcome. Stretcher cases now began to arrive and these were hard to handle and transfer to the troopship. They made about five journeys from the beach to a paddle steamer and it was estimated that they embarked 500 men in this way. As dawn broke, the troopship was full and left for England. 'Massey Shaw' returned to the beach and started loading again. At this point, on a falling tide, they began to bump on the sands and were in danger of damaging their propellers but, with their engines throbbing at full power, they just managed to get back into deep water. At 3.30 a.m. they were the last boat to leave that part of the beach. Halfway across the channel, the naval skipper began to have doubts about the compass, but then, to his relief, came across a drifter towing two small boats packed with troops. They followed them into Ramsgate where they arrived at 8 a.m. on Sunday 2nd June, landing 30 or 40 more soldiers.

The 'Massey Shaw' returned to Dunkirk again the next evening with a London Fire Brigade crew. This time they went to the jetty of Dunkirk harbour. It was difficult for soldiers to board her from the towering jetty and she came away empty. After returning to Ramsgate, she was ordered back to London. Off Margate, the 'Emile Deschamps', a French ship which had sailed to England from Dunkirk laden with troops the previous night, was passing her at a distance of 200 yards when it struck a mine and sank almost immediately. The 'Massey Shaw' picked up 39 men, all severely injured, and took them back to Ramsgate. Early on Wednesday, she finally returned to London and as she came up the River Thames she was cheered as she passed each fire station. Finally, the wives and families of all those on board were waiting at the Lambeth Headquarters when the boat docked at the Lambeth river station to great jubilation. The crew were given a splendid reception at the Headquarters station. A total of seventeen London Fire Brigade/London Auxiliary Fire Service personnel took part over the three trips, the most senior being Station Officers H. Youngman and G. A. Briancourt.

Fireman Dick Heyler was a member of the 'Massey Shaw's' Dunkirk crew. He recalled later:

'We knew that things were not good in France. Sub Officer May had called a group of us together and said, "We're in trouble. The British Army is stranded on the beach not far from Dunkirk. Will you volunteer to go over there?" We agreed readily and scampered around getting the things we needed. There was a bit of a delay while we got a certified river pilot because they wouldn't let the Massey Shaw out of the Thames without one, but we eventually got one and shoved off about four o'clock At Ramsgate we tried to get some metal sheeting for the engine covers and some Lewis guns, but as I recall we weren't successful. From this point we had a naval officer in charge of us and flew the white ensign. Our crew comprised Jack Gillman, Beaumont Hinge, "Speaky" Lowe, Mr Youngman and Sub Officer May, who was a really courageous bloke.

There were dozens of boats of all shapes and sizes moving out to cross the Channel. Spitfires and some twin-engine Blenheim's cruised around overhead. Left to my thoughts in the engine room I wondered what I had let myself in for. Many of the crew had been in the First World War, but I was the youngest member of the crew at twenty-two. We had a look out of the hatch occasionally and when Dunkirk appeared on the horizon there was a thick pall of smoke coming from across the seafront. We steamed in towards Dunkirk and then turned along the coast towards De Panne. There were bombers overhead, but I was down below and could only hear things rather than see them which was as much as I wanted at the time. When I did poke my head out of the hatch I could see a French destroyer, completely burnt out.

It was a dead calm sea and there were wrecks everywhere. You could see masts sticking up out of the water from boats that had received direct hits from enemy bombers. In our engine room you could feel the shock waves from the explosions. We were unable to get right into the beach because of our propellers, but smaller boats were picking up soldiers. There was a lot of machine-gunning and bombing going on. Eventually we got soldiers on board from one of the other boats and after a while we could hardly move down there.

Coming up on deck for fresh air I could see the troops still on the beaches. The sky was thick with aircraft while out to sea there were four or five destroyers lobbing some stuff inland. At one stage we wanted to get a line to a launch with our rocket line system but it fell short. I put on a lifejacket, pulled on the rocket line and swam ashore with it. The bombs and shells were coming down all the time and it really was very frightening. Anyway, I swam to this RAF launch which was crowded with soldiers. They said they were stuck until the tide came in, but somebody gave me a hand and we tied a bowline from the Massey to the towing bollard on the launch. A naval officer said we'll never pull them off with all the soldiers on board, he was right, it was useless. Someone on the launch unhooked the line and threw it off. I had to swim back to the Massey.

We had nearly seventy soldiers on board and nearly all of them were drying off in the engine room. A few sat on the upper deck where they could find room. We were on the go all the time. Putting the engines into ahead, stop, astern, stop, ahead, you get the picture.

Eventually we got away at about three o'clock in the morning, one of the last to go. There was a red glow all over Dunkirk and the fuel oil tanks at the entrance to the harbour were well alight. We got back to Ramsgate without being machine-gunned. We had a cuppa tea and digestive biscuit but I remember we were still very hungry and absolutely exhausted. After we had gone off the

Massey they put a Navy crew on board and after they came back from Dunkirk they sent another crew down from London for a third trip.

When we moved out again we were warned about mines which was particularly worrying for us as we had no protection against magnetic mines. We were nearly opposite Margate and I was in the engine room when I heard a tremendous crash. I nipped up the hatch to look and saw a plume of smoke not very far away. It was the Emile Deschamps, a French auxiliary vessel. She had struck a mine. She sank within two minutes. She had something like 350 people on board and nearly all were lost. We picked up 39 survivors, all of them badly injured. The first survivor we picked up saw the monitor of the Massey, thought we were the enemy and tried to swim away rather than be rescued.

[*Topical Press*]

The fireboat *Massey Shaw* returns from Dunkirk, 4th June, 1940.

It was a real mess and we felt so sorry for those poor devils. One man was split like a kipper, from his hip to his heel. We put them everywhere, all of them seriously injured, and covered in blood and with broken arms and legs. To make matters worse just as we were

250

about to move off we got a line round one of our screws and had to put one of the engines off the run.

We signalled to HMS Albury, a minesweeper loaded with French troops, to ask if they could take the injured, but she replied that she had no doctor on board. We were about to head back to Ramsgate when the Albury signalled again to say they'd found some French doctors on board so we went alongside and transferred the injured before making our way back to Ramsgate.

The official homecoming of the 'Massey Shaw' fire-float to the London Fire Brigade's Headquarters river station at Lambeth. (Mary Evans)

As we came off the Massey Shaw we were told that somebody was needed to make a broadcast to Canada, There were no volunteers so, being the youngest, I was chosen. I came home by car and recorded the broadcast about Dunkirk at Broadcasting House. Whether or not it was ever broadcast I don't know because, believe me, I was so tired that all I wanted to do was to sleep.'

Years later and in a subsequent interview regarding the Dunkirk exploits Dick Heyler, who was now a Station Officer in the London Fire Brigade had a strange experience of *déjà vu*. He was to be reunited with one of the very soldiers that he had helped save fifty years earlier. It turned out to be an emotional reunion, one that took place in April 1990 when a John Overy, a former Sergeant with 2nd Royal Horse Artillery, knelt on the now retired, but restored, decks of the 'Massey Shaw' and, like the Pope, kissed the wooden deck. His friends stood there laughing and somewhat bemused.

John Overy told them: *'This boat saved my life.'* He saw the 'Massey Shaw' again in Dunkirk for the 50th anniversary celebrations and was interviewed about his connection to the boat, which brought memories flooding back of that time. His regiment had been in France since the outbreak of war in September 1939. Pushed back by the German onslaught they found themselves, together with hundreds of thousands of other British, French and Belgian troops on the Dunkirk beaches. Operation Dynamo was underway. John's first rescue attempt had ended in failure when the Dutch boat he was on took a bomb down its funnel and sank.

'I was lucky,' he told the reporter. 'I went over the side and swam back to the beach. There were so many dead lying around.' John waited a further two days before his eventual rescue by the 'Massey Shaw'. His story recounted his rescue by the 'Massey Shaw' and its crew.

> 'Enemy bombers constantly flew low over the beaches every ten or twenty minutes. With the onset of darkness, at about 6 p.m., a man [Dick Heyler] had swam to shore from the Massey Shaw bringing a line with him as a guide back to the boat for those awaiting rescue.'

By this stage two smaller craft had already been overwhelmed and sunk in their attempts to ferry troops to larger waiting boats. John had grabbed the line Dick Heyler had secured to the shore line and hauled himself to the safety of the 'Massey Shaw's' deck. He found himself in the crowded company of other servicemen, many injured, and all of them drenched. It took two or three hours to reach the relative safety of Ramsgate and with no first aid equipment the injured were looked after with torn shirts used as bandages.

> 'At first we didn't realise we were on a fire tender. When we realised that these were not seamen but firemen, we all said a silent prayer to them. We were all so glad we had been saved.'

That was not the only meeting on those beaches that would have a fire brigade connection in the years to come. Robert (Bob) McInnerny was a soldier waiting to be evacuated. Charlie Winister was serving in the Royal Navy, one of many sailors sent to the Dunkirk beaches to aid the evacuation and bring the much needed troops back home to safety. The young McInnerny was hauled aboard a ship by Charlie Winister. After the war they both joined the London Fire Brigade and being South London lads found themselves serving in the same division. Charlie was stationed at New

Cross and Bob had come to stand by at the station in the late 1950s. Over a yarn the two men discovered that Charlie, who was serving on HMS 'Gallant', had rescued Bob McInnerny and some of his comrades at Dunkirk. Bob McInnerny was a larger than life character, in the literal sense. As the Station Officer at Southwark fire station he was a formidable fire officer; he also had a wide girth. In fact it was so wide that he was issued with a special body belt to wear when using his Proto BA. Charlie rose to senior rank. Charlie and Bob were also both members of the Dunkirk Veterans Association and were featured on a TV programme in the 1980s called *What's my Secret?* They returned together to Dunkirk, on the 'Massey Shaw' fireboat, to commemorate the 25th anniversary of the evacuation.

The 'Massey Shaw' and her crew returned to her moorings at Lambeth and much to the relief of the waiting families gathered at the Brigade Headquarters for a formal welcome home. The 'Massey Shaw' had come back upriver on Wednesday 5th June and had powered under Tower Bridge. The crew found that they had a hero's welcome from Londoners lining the embankment walls and bridges. Major Frank Jackson, London's Chief Officer, had also arranged for the crew of the first Dunkirk trip to be taken out to the 'Massey Shaw' for the arrival at the Lambeth headquarters. It was something of a surreal sight for Londoners waiting on the Albert Embankment to see the crew muster and then march up the gangway to the pontoon with each man carrying a rifle over his shoulder. Not the normal equipment the public expects a fireman to carry. There were no casualties from the crew but there was recorded from the repairers report what was described as *'various instances of collision damage'.*

In all this the 'Massey Shaw' was to receive two singular honours: she was the only small ship, civilian manned, to be mentioned by Vice-Admiral Ramsey in his despatches to the Lords Commissioners of the Navy. Following their actions three members of the 'Massey Shaw's' crew were awarded gallantry honours. They were published in the *London Gazette* on the 16th August 1940. (Supplement 34925):

Mentioned in Despatches were Auxiliary Firemen Henry Albert William RAY and Edmund Gordon WRIGHT for meritorious services when the Massey Shaw deployed to the beaches of Dunkirk in May/June 1940. (L/G 34925, p 5073.)

It was a rare honour for a civilian, Sub Officer May, to be awarded a Naval gallantry medal, which had hitherto been reserved for Warrant Officers, Petty Officers and Seamen of the Royal Navy and the equivalent grades in the Royal Marines.

It seems highly likely that Aubrey May remains the most decorated operational fireboat officer in the United Kingdom. Following the creation of the National Fire Service in 1941 Sub Officer May was promoted to a Company Officer (Station Officer) and was seconded to the Port of Alexandria. He was awarded the British Empire Medal for gallantry five years later, together with Divisional Officer William. A Ramsey. Their awards, earned at the same incident, were published in the *London Gazette* on the 1st February 1946. The citation read:

Awarded the Naval Distinguished Service Medal: Sub Officer Aubrey John May. (Author)

'*Awarded the British Empire Medal for Gallantry.*
William Alexander RAMSAY, *Divisional Officer, National Fire Service (Port Fire Officer, Alexandria).*
Aubrey John MAY, DSM, *Company Officer, National Fire Service (Deputy Port Fire Officer, Alexandria).*

During the operation of discharging a cargo of octane petrol from a tanker in Alexandria Harbour, Divisional Officer Ramsay was put in charge of special fire precautions. After three days on board the ship a sudden and unexpected underwater escape of petrol occurred. This was very shortly followed by a serious petrol fire in the harbour. Immediately he detected the smell of escaping petrol, the Divisional Officer sent a signal requesting the tanker be taken to sea.

Shortly afterwards the petrol flashed on the water 'about 800 yards away from the ship and fire rapidly began to spread back to the vessel along the stream of petrol. Ramsay, immediately proceeded in a small open motor boat to the fire and drove his boat backwards and forwards through the stream of petrol and strong concentration of high "octane" gases in close proximity to the fire and was successful in breaking up the stream of petrol to the fire, and thus stopping the fire spreading back to the vessel.

In doing this in intense heat he knew that the petrol vapour might have flashed at any moment, which could only have had fatal results to himself. He then supervised the initial fighting of the fire from the fire-boat before returning to the tanker to make arrangements for that ship to be got to sea at once. His very gallant actions undoubtedly saved the vessel which still had about 9,000 tons of spirit on board, arid prevented a major disaster.

Company Officer May was ashore at the time of the outbreak. Immediately he observed the fire he obtained a boat and in about ten minutes had taken charge of the fire-fighting from the fire-boat. In very close proximity to this blazing fire he worked with complete disregard of his personal safety, and after about twenty minutes the fire was under control and finally extinguished. His courage and grasp of the situation very materially helped to prevent a serious conflagration.'

Sub Officer Aubrey May after his award of the DSM (right) and River Pilot Mr Pinch, pictured at the 'Massey Shaw's' Blackfriars moorings. (Massey Shaw Education Trust)

Thereafter the 'Massey Shaw' undertook fire-float duties on the Thames during the 1940/41 Blitz on London. On resuming her normal duties, she was the first fire appliance to be fitted with radio communication. She played a major role during the Blitz, pumping water ashore for the land appliances hampered by huge demands on the water supply, or when bombing had destroyed the water mains. She was especially credited with supplying water ashore which enabled land crews to prevent fire spreading to St Paul's Cathedral on the night of 29th December 1940.

The Luftwaffe had timed their attack on the City of London on 29th December with deliberate precision. There was an exceptional low tide that evening, making it much harder to pump water up to the fire engines. Soon, there were 1,500 fires blazing in London – all but 28 of them inside the symbolic Square Mile. As the fires raged in the narrow medieval streets, the 'Massey Shaw' started pumping up 3,000 gallons of water per minute from her berth next to the Blackfriars Bridge, and would continue to do so throughout the night. Very soon all the local fire stations were empty of their appliances and the fires were spreading around St Paul's. *'That's why we relied so much on the fireboats,'* were the words of one Blitz fireman.

The night of the 7th September 1940: the Surrey Docks are ablaze and the 'Massey Shaw' is in the thick of it, supplying water to land-based crews. (Mary Evans)

To get their hoses to the shore, the fireboat crews had to go over the side onto the bed of the Thames, into thick mud, drag the hose onto the banks and start pumping the water up to where it was required. The 'Massey Shaw's' pumping output was the equivalent of about 20 good firefighting jets, so her role was absolutely vital. That night, 160 civilians and 14 firemen were killed and 19 churches were destroyed.

The Blitz on London initially lasted for 57 consecutive nights from the 7th September until the end of November. Sporadic, but intensive and devastating attacks then lasting until the end of May 1941. In the August of that year, and with the creation of the National Fire Service, the term fire-float was changed to *fireboat*, a term that remains in use today. For the remainder of the war fireboat the 'Massey Shaw' operated under the River Thames Formation of the National Fire Service. In 1947 her open canvas dodger and screen, which gave scant weather protection to the helmsman, was replaced by a fully-enclosed wheelhouse.

London fire-floats supply much needed water to the land crews after enemy bombing destroys the water mains.
(The family of the late E. H. Pike)

An unusual river trip took place around this time when Herbert Morrison MP, Leader of the House of Commons, and Aneurin Bevan MP, the then Minister of Health, came on board the 'Massey

Shaw' and were taken down to the Thames Estuary, during which time a conference took place on board which led to the creation of the National Health Service.

Until its closure in September 2016 a unique remnant of 'Massey Shaw's' Dunkirk history was preserved for posterity at the London Fire Brigade's museum at Southwark. It is the blood-stained flag flown by the fire-float during her role in the evacuations from the beaches. It had been taken as a memento by one of the soldiers rescued and was only discovered some forty-four years later when the man had died and his son had found it among his possessions. It was presented to the museum for safe keeping in 1984. It is hoped that the flag will again be displayed when the Brigade's museum relocates to the former Lambeth headquarters building as part of a redevelopment project in the near future.

The mid-1950s: the 'Massey Shaw' passes Westminster Pier, now the berth of her former sister fireboat the Beta III, which had started a new life as a Thames passenger launch. (Malc Burden)

After the War

From 1945 until March 1948 the 'Massey Shaw' was an integral part of the River Thames Formation, part of the National Fire Service. Her base remained at Blackfriars until 1948 when the river station there was closed and she was transferred to the Lambeth river station. The three river stations were: R80 Lambeth, R81 South Wharf (Rotherhithe) and R82 Woolwich. Following the practice introduced during the National Fire Service, the re-introduction of the post of 'river pilot' on the fireboats was not considered necessary by the Brigade. Firemen-trained boats' coxswains now undertook that role.

The monitor of the 'Massey Shaw' being used at a drill session.
(Massey Shaw Education Trust)

The Fire Services Act of 1947 returned the responsibility of maintaining efficient fire brigades back to the local authorities: in the case of London, to the London County Council. That became effective as of the 1st April 1948. The 'Massey Shaw' was once again a London Fire Brigade (LFB) fireboat, although in truth her crews had never seen her as anything else but LFB. Operating from her river station the 'Massey Shaw' was often called upon as riverside fires occurred on a regular basis. The fireboat also assisted neighbouring fire brigades of West Ham and Essex, which covered the dock system to the East of London and the Kent riverside risks from Erith and Gravesend. But in the post war years the brigade's river service was contracting. By 1953 only two permanent river fire stations remained: R80-Lambeth and R82-Woolwich. South Wharf having been shut down in 1953, first as a temporary measure, then permanently in 1956.

In 1961 a new fireboat arrived. The fireboat 'Firebrace' entered service with the brigade. It was berthed at the headquarters and was moored at the Lambeth river station. The older 'Massey Shaw' was transferred downstream to Woolwich and the leased moorings at the Royal Arsenal. The crew bedded down at night at nearby Woolwich fire station in Sunbury Street. The 'Massey Shaw' was transferred to Greenwich Pier in 1963 and the crew operating out of Greenwich fire station.

The 'Massey Shaw' at her Woolwich moorings in South East London.
(Malc Burden)

In 1965 the London County Council was replaced by the newly created Greater London Council (GLC) and the 'Massey Shaw' suddenly found herself covering far more of the downstream area of the Thames than ever before. On the north bank the West Ham fire brigade area was totally absorbed into the GLC, including the mighty Royal Docks with the Victoria and Albert docks. The formerly Essex and Kent riversides were now absorbed up to the extended greater easterly London boundary.

1966 was the centenary year of the London Fire Brigade. On the 11th November Her Majesty the Queen, accompanied by HRH the Duke of Edinburgh attended the Brigade Headquarters on a rather grey afternoon to conduct a Royal Review of the London Fire Brigade. There was little, that day, the river firemen could do to get in on the act with this land-based display and demonstration of firefighting skills. However, this had not been the case just two months earlier when the Brigade's fireboats were the stars of the show for the GLC's River Pageant; this had taken place on the 9th September.

The display of floodlight massed jets from the brigade's fireboats at the Southbank's Festival Pier provided a never to be forgotten

The 'Massey Shaw' fireboat. (Mary Evans)

spectacle. It was cheers all the way from Tower Pier to Chelsea Reach and back for the 'Massey Shaw' and the brigade's period tableaux barges. The evening was the culmination to a great deal of planning and preparation. Weeks before the event took place four barges were being turned into: a fiery dragon some eighty feet long; a mock-up of the London skyline; a replica Metropolitan fire-float; but the most impressive of all was the barge carrying the brigade's historical appliances. Hidden generators ensured the most effective lighting for each of the individual barges. Junior firemen were pressed into service as the Insurance Company firemen, operating the manual pumps. The 'Massey Shaw' was dressed overall with coloured lights.

One of those to witness the Thames celebrations was the son of Harry Ray, whose father had served on the 'Massey Shaw' and had gone to Dunkirk. His father, who had since died, had been stationed at the Blackfriars river station and he recalled the emotional return to Lambeth when he and his sister, together with his mum, went to greet the crew on their arrival back from Dunkirk.

Having not followed in his father's footsteps and joined the fire brigade, Harry Ray had expected the 'Massey Shaw' to have been scrapped but was delighted to see his father's old fireboat still on the Thames. *'My father took such pride in her engine room, polishing the brass and you could have eaten your dinner off the deck. It was always such great fun for my sister and me to go aboard her when we were young.'*

In 1968 'Massey Shaw' went to the movies, or rather appeared in one. It was a small cameo role for a part she was well suited for and had actually undertaken in real life. The film was the *Battle of Britain*. (This is a 1969 British film directed by Guy Hamilton, and produced by Harry Saltzman, which endeavoured to be an accurate account of the Battle of Britain, when in the summer and autumn of 1940 the British RAF inflicted a strategic defeat on the Luftwaffe and so ensured the cancellation of Operation Sea Lion – Adolf Hitler's plan to invade Britain.) Some of the location filming took place in London and was carried out mainly in the St Katharine Docks area in Wapping.

The older houses were also being demolished for housing estates. The partly demolished buildings represented bombed houses and the disused warehouses which were made to represent an amazingly dramatic effect by the film men would appeared to have set the docks on fire. The presence of the 'Massey Shaw' and her modern day crew added a very authentic touch to the Blitz scene. St Katharine Docks was one of the few areas of London's East End to have survived the Blitz. Many of the film extras were survivors of the Blitz. Almost all the period equipment from the London Fire Brigade Museum was utilised by the film makers in the production of the film.

It was a year or so later that a fireboat, this time the 'Firebrace', was back at the docks for real. The warehouses, built originally by Napoleonic prisoners of war, caught fire and twenty-five pumps and the fireboat were required to battle the blaze.

Because of their very restricted capacity and inability to cope with large modern ships, the St Katharine Docks were among the first to be closed in the late 1960s and were sold to the Greater London Council. Most of the original warehouses, around the western basin, were due for demolition and would later be replaced by modern commercial buildings.

'Massey Shaw's' days as an operational fireboat were rapidly drawing to a close. She was considered uneconomical to maintain and the GLC were drawing up plans to decommission the fireboat. But operationally she was still fighting fires. Her last major ship fire was the 'Paraguay Star' which was berthed in the Royal Victoria Docks, Silvertown East London.

The initial call in the small hours of the morning on the 12th August 1969 had the crews of Silvertown, Plaistow and East Ham fire stations rushing to their engines and heading off to the docks. The crew of 'Massey Shaw' were also rushing to their transport, only it was not the 'Massey Shaw'. The fireboat, berthed at Greenwich pier was locked up and secured each night between calls. The crew's sleeping accommodation, however, was located at Greenwich fire station, just under a mile away from the pier, only five minutes' drive away in the Brigade's personnel carrier, complete with its blue flashing lights, which transported them to the pier and the waiting fireboat.

By the time they arrived at the 'Massey Shaw' and got her main engines started, then cast off the mooring lines, they already knew they had a 'working job' on their hands. The officer in charge at the docks had sent a 'priority' message as soon as he saw the thick smoke pouring from the engine room skylights and the ventilators aft of the funnel of the 'Paraguay Star'.

The 'Paraguay Star' was one of four vessels built after WWII to replace tonnage lost to enemy action. Of six hatch tween-deck construction, they were refrigerated ships, cooled by CO_2 compressors. Chilled beef, carried from Buenos Aires to the European market, was its normal cargo. The No 4 hatch, behind the forward windbreak, contained a swimming pool when on passage.

With accommodation for 68 passengers she operated a regular service to South America, calling at Lisbon, Las Palmas, Rio de Janeiro, Santos, Montevideo and terminating at Buenos Aires, on a seven week turnaround. Her accommodation was described as comfortable rather than luxurious by today's cruising standards. The officer and crew accommodation was somewhat more austere. Powered by her two Babcock & Wilcox steam turbines she caught fire due to an electrical failure in one of her generators.

As the crow flies the distance between Greenwich Pier and the Royal Victoria Docks is relatively short, however the vast curve of the Thames, as it goes around the Greenwich Peninsula trebles the distance. Before the 'Massey' entered the docks the local Divisional Commander had arrived and urgently requested fifteen pumps, all with breathing apparatus to attack the blaze. This was followed by a 'make pumps twenty –fireboats two' message. The first time that both the fireboats had been ordered to the same incident in over a decade.

With the 'Massey' drawing ever closer to the 'Paraguay Star', land crews were making determined endeavours to enter the ships engine room. Moving in from the B Deck, in extremely punishing conditions, they came across two acetylene and three oxygen cylinders, already too hot to handle. Cooling them, the cylinders were put in improvised dams whilst a renewed attack was made on the engine room by other crews in punishing and arduous conditions. It was so hot that the crews had to be relieved frequently and their progress was painfully slow.

The 'Paraguay Star'

As a refrigerated ship, the insulation that normally kept the heat out of the refrigerated spaces now just as effectively kept the heat in. It made the conditions in the ship particularly taxing and exhausting for the firemen groping their way around in almost pitch black below deck. The 'Massey' was secured to the side of the 'Star'. Her pumps were engaged and she was supplying water to the crews on the ship. She also had jets of water playing on the ships side as the conducted heat scorched and burnt the ships paintwork, marking out the intensity of the fire on board.

High derricks were located fore and aft of the seven storey high ship. Thick black smoke occasionally enveloped the 'Massey Shaw' as it escaped from the tall single funnel. (This had the ship owner's big red star painted on its white background). Smoke was also being forced out of the central passenger's accommodation and various vents on the upper decks. Lines of hose fed up the side of the ship from the 'Massey', looking like the thick hawsers that were securing the 'Star' to the quay. The second fireboat, the 'Firebrace', would take at least forty minutes to make the journey down river against the tide.

One thing was certain: the 'Massey Shaw' was not going to run out of water. However, too much water in the ship brings with it its own problems. Problems of stability and in extreme case, the capsizing of a ship when water is trapped inside the vessel causing it to list to one side or the other. The greater the weight of the water, the greater the list the ship could take on. Too much water and you do eventually put the fire out, but with the undesirable effect of sinking the ship in the process.

With the night watch crews being exchanged over with the start of a new day watch at 9 a.m. and whilst minimising any disruption to the continuing attack on the fire, the 'Massey Shaw' and 'Firebrace' fireboat crews remained in situ, their replacement crews transported to the scene by personnel carriers later in the day. By the afternoon the fire had been confined to the engine room. The 'Massey Shaw' remained with the ship for twenty four hours before she was finally released to return to her Greenwich base. Even then the conditions in some areas of the ship were so hot that BA crews were only able to work for short spells as they hacked away amongst the maze of pipes, valves and levers to ferret out and remove every vestige of the smouldering insulation.

An ignominious farewell.

In her last year of operational service the 'Massey Shaw' is credited with attending two major London fires: fires in which she is said to have played an active part. One was the serious fire at the Tate and Lyle's sugar refinery in East London. That she definitely attended and supplied water which helped quell the blaze is a matter of record. However the other fire remains something of a mystery! It was said to be a ship fire on the SS 'Jumna', berthed at the Royal Albert Docks. There was such a ship, but if fire did ever occur it was of little consequence and certainly not one that warranted any news coverage. (The SS 'Jumna' had been a cargo ship of 9,890 tons and was originally owned by the Hain-Norse shipping line. It was later sold to P&O and renamed the Strathnaver in 1975. Two years later it was renamed again, this time called Singapore Progress by Singapore Shipping. The ship was ultimately scrapped.)

The 'Massey Shaw' remained in active service until 1970, when she was decommissioned. There was no suggestion that the former fireboat would be scrapped. She initially passed into the hands of the Greater London Council's Housing Department with the proposal in mind that the 'Massey Shaw' would be the centrepiece of a floating museum on the developing Thamesmead Estate in the

The late Station Officer Peter Capon, of Lambeth river station, looks on at the moored 'Massey Shaw' after she was withdrawn from operational service. (Massey Shaw Education Trust)

early 1970s. For whatever reason it never materialised. For some time she lay tethered near the riverside steps where a century earlier many a Londoner bade farewell as they moved in their chains from the Milbank Prison onto the transports that would ultimately deliver them to Botany Bay. 'Massey' was then relocated to the Woolwich pier, then St Katharine Dock, she was moored and forgotten. Left to her own devices and the Thames tides, for over a decade she laid moored up, slowly deteriorating.

In 1981 a senior control officer from the Brigade's Control Room training centre thought enough was enough and the 'rot' had to stop, literally. Phil Wray was a Brigade control officer working at Lambeth. He launched a project to restore the 'Massey Shaw' to working order. He formed the Massey Shaw Fireboat Trust (originally named the Massey Shaw and Marine Vessel Preservation Society) with the hope of securing charitable status. His endeavours paid off and he had prepared his ground well, having already secured professional appraisals of what work was required to bring back the 'Massey Shaw' to her former glory. The cost of the work was estimated to be £12,750.

With a great amount of hard work, commitment and a dash of good luck the 'Massey Shaw' was brought back from the brink over the next few years. Such was their success that the 'Massey Shaw' was not only able to 'sail' once more on the Thames but she was starting to appear, as a guest artist, in a number of River Thames special events, including the GLC Thamesday celebrations, the Lord Mayor of London Show and most notably an appearance before the Queen and the Duke of Edinburgh at the grand opening of the Thames Barrier.

On the 8th May 1984, the Queen had set off from Festival Pier on the Southbank in her barge, the 'Royal Nore'. 'Massey' joined the procession down river they passed under bridges bedecked with bunting. At Just after 3.30 p.m. the Royal party had arrived at Woolwich Reach. There they took in *the glittering new structure, resembling a row of drowned Sydney Opera Houses'* (The Times). After a short speech, the Queen pressed the button, and the 'flood' gates swung slowly into action. The crew of the 'Massey Shaw' took it all in as they stood proudly to attention on the deck of the fireboat.

Construction of the barrier started in 1974; 18,000 tonnes of steel, and £1.6bn later, the barrier was complete. It had gone operational in 1983 and first used in 'anger' the following year. Covering the opening *The Times* newspaper wrote rather grumpily: *'Its spectacular overruns on price and delivery date, as majestic in their way as the statistics of its novel and unparalleled technology, could stand as an emblem of the industrial history of the seventies and eighties.'* It remains, however, an impressive achievement. Stretching for 520 metres across the river, with the barrier's falling radial gates, as well as rising sector gates that allow for the natural flow of water, and for boats to pass, when laid flat on the riverbed. But when raised into position, an operation that takes an hour and a half, the gates stand 20 metres tall. Weighing 3,300 tonnes, each gate can hold back over 9,000 tonnes of water. Since it was completed in 1982, the Thames Barrier has been raised 150 times in order to prevent flooding in central London. During the wet winter of 2014 the barrier was closed 28 times, accounting for 18.7 per cent of the total closures in its thirty-three year history.

The BBC's first war correspondent, Richard Dimbleby, interviewing the crew of the 'Massey Shaw' on her return to Dunkirk. Standing next to Richard Dimbleby is Station Officer Dick Heyler.
(The family of the late Dick Heyler BEM)

Dunkirk Anniversaries

In May 1965, to mark the 25th anniversary of 'Operation Dynamo', Raymond Baxter, the well-known radio and TV presenter, organised and assembled a fleet of 43 of the original 'Little Ships' of Dunkirk to return there to commemorate the epic maritime event of the evacuation of the British Expeditionary Force in 1940, in which they played such a significant role. It had been decided that such a unique assembly should not just be allowed to disperse into obscurity. The Association of Dunkirk Little Ships was subsequently formed in 1966. The object of the Association is to keep alive the spirit of Dunkirk by perpetuating for posterity the identity of those Little Ships that went to the aid of the British Expeditionary Force during the evacuation of Dunkirk in 1940. In 2008 the Association was privileged to have HRH Prince Michael of Kent GCVO accept the invitation to become the Association's Honorary Admiral which he retains.

The Association have organised a Commemorative Return every five years since 1970. The average age of the Little Ships is now close to 80 years. The task of getting this many elderly, traditional, vessels across one of the world busiest shipping lanes is by no means insignificant. In fact the event remains one of the unique Anglo/French maritime events. With the exception of a small number of vessels that are operated by 'Trusts', such as the 'Massey Shaw', all Little Ships are privately owned and receive no financial or other assistance from any public body.

That first anniversary crossing was notable for many reasons, not least was the fact that the 'Massey Shaw' was still an operational fireboat of the London Fire Brigade. Making up the volunteer crew was one of the original Dunkirk crew who made the crossing in 1940, Dick Heyler. He had since been promoted to Station Officer rank. The event received considerable coverage, especially by the BBC. The crew were interviewed by the late Richard Dimbleby. Dimbleby had originally worked as a news reporter on the *Southern Evening Echo* in Southampton, before joining the BBC as a radio news reporter in 1936. He was their first 'war' correspondent. He had accompanied the British Expeditionary Force into France and covered the retreat too. He later made broadcasts from the battle of El Alamein and the Normandy beaches during the D-Day landings.

The next time the 'Massey Shaw' crossed the Channel was in 1985. Much had been done to make her ready for the trip. A crew of six was to make the return trip on the fireboat with others taking the Cross Channel ferry so they could attend the commemorations in Dunkirk over that late May weekend. Ramsgate-bound, the crew were given a salute of massed jets by the 'London Phoenix' fireboat as she departed down river. At Gravesend safety lines were rigged fore, aft and amidships in preparation of any heavy swells. The original plan was to have pulled in at Sheerness, but with things going so well the fireboat sailed on into Ramsgate harbour and settled down for the night.

The following day, Friday 24th May, thing were not looking so good. The weather had changed for the worse. The convoy of Small Ships, of which the 'Massey Shaw' was now a part, could not cross the Channel. Saturday was better and the Commodore, in charge of the convoy, gave the news that they would be sailing. Upon reaching the Dunkirk Light, the Commodore signalled the 'Massey' and gave her the honour of leading the convoy into Dunkirk.

Sunday was the day of commemoration and memorial services. The 'Massey' got under way and together with the convoy headed back out to sea. The convoy had formed a large circle and an RAF helicopter flew over the centre, dropping a wreath to honour all those lost at Dunkirk. After the official wreath-laying and speeches the only other wreaths laid were from the London Fire Brigade and the 'Massey Shaw' crew jointly with the Royal British Legion. Then it was over. Monday saw the 'Massey' return to London, a round trip of some one hundred and thirty miles with an average speed of almost ten knots, and at times reaching thirteen knots: not a bad achievement for a fifty year old!

It was whilst the 'Massey Shaw' was chugging her way back across the Channel some of her support team were heading in the same direction but on a cross-channel ferry. This was how the 'Massey Shaw' became involved with yet another anniversary. An anniversary that had its origins one hundred years before and by the man whose name the fireboat now carried: Sir Eyre Massey

Shaw. In 1887, the Chief Officer of the Metropolitan Fire Brigade, Captain Shaw, together with Princess Christian, had inspected one thousand volunteer firemen from eight-four brigades at Oxford as part of the Jubilee celebrations of Queen Victoria.

As the support team were sitting in the lounge bar of the ferry, enjoying a pint or two, their conversation was overhead by a member of the Oxford University Press fire brigade. He told them about the about the forthcoming historic anniversary and invited them to attend. By the time they landed at Dover they had agreed the 'Massey Shaw' would be going to Oxford.

It was another first for the 'Massey Shaw'. The fireboat had never been that far up the River Thames. However, before that happened there was the unselfish hard work of the members who made up the crew; plus the hard-graft and endurance given by the other

Only the roof of the 'Massey Shaw' wheelhouse is visible as the boat lays on the riverbed of the Thames. (Massey Shaw Education Trust)

Trust members gritting down and getting the fireboat shipshape. Then there was the small worry about the 'Massey's' gearbox: could it be fitted in time? The gearbox had been taken to an engineering company who had the task of grinding a new one from the casts they had taken. The other small worry was: could the Massey actually make the trip? It was designed for the lower reaches of the Thames, not navigating the thirty-two locks it had to pass through to reach Oxford. Those that knew the 'Massey Shaw' would give testament to the fact that she had very good engines. That said, her navigation qualities were considered much to be desired. Pointing the 'Massey' in the right direction and keeping her on course frequently tested the skills of her helmsmen.

With the new gearbox finally fitted, some other mechanical glitches sorted the 'Massey' set off up river. The first miles passed trouble-free, although there were the concerns of where the crew of eleven would actually sleep. This was resolved by putting sleeping bags down in the wheelhouse, fore-peak, engine room and cabin. Two drew the short straw and slept on the open deck, and were found under a tarpaulin after an unexpected night-time rain shower!

Wednesday 1st July found the 'Massey' and her crew navigating the most hazardous part of her journey westward. It was hazardous because besides being the narrowest part of the river and shallowest with tight bends the 'Massey' found herself in the middle of the first day of the Henley Regatta. Passing through this stretch of water was any navigator's nightmare and the ageing fireboat was not renowned for stopping quickly or suddenly. Some of those supping champers, munching canapés and attending the boating version of a Sloane Ranger's convention... were less than joyous at having fifty tons of fireboat passing through this popular and crowded area at this time, especially as the crew had forgotten to pack their blazers, flannels and old school ties. But many on the banks did give a friendly wave and by the next morning they arrived at the head of the river, Oxford.

The 3rd July was the open day. The crew had given the 'old girl' a good spit and polish. There were some nerves as this was their first real contact with the public. Would anyone come and want to see the 'Massey Shaw'? Well they did, and in force too. The crew were genuinely surprised both by the number of visitors and the interest they showed. A number of Dunkirk veterans were delighted to see one of the 'small ships' on their doorstep and to be able to walk around one of those famous craft in far happier circumstances. That evening the crew were the guests of the Lord Mayor of Oxford at a civic reception at the Town Hall. The following day saw even more visitors and some surprising news about 'Massey Shaw's' history. The crew welcomed on board three ladies, one of whom informed them that her father had been a Station Officer on the Thames fireboats from 1939 to 1945. In fact she had actually been christened upon the 'Massey Shaw'.

The next week saw the fireboat explore places that it had never seen before – Mapleduram and Caversham – before heading back down to London via Henley. Visitor numbers grew as did the press and television interest in the exploits of the 'Massey Shaw' and her anniversary tour. Her arrival at Henley coincided with the tenth Traditional Boat Rally, and she joined other Dunkirk Little Ships in a special presentation procession. That evening the crew joined the thronging crowds as they listened to the London Symphony Orchestra followed by a spectacular fireworks display. The 'Massey' even walked away with a couple of prizes. She had demonstrated how to propel the fireboat through the water using only the propulsion from her monitor and had won the competition for the most unusual means of propulsion. The crew also won the other prize for their London firemen's traditional dress, complete with brass helmets.

Then disaster struck. On August Bank Holiday Monday in 1987 the 'Massey Shaw' *sank*. The fireboat was moored by a barge just off Millbank, on the north side of the Thames and within sight of the Lambeth fire brigade headquarters. A valve had been accidentally left open and river water slowly filled the boat. The first thoughts were that the 'Massey' had been stolen as the duty fireboat crew looked across the river from their pontoon at Lambeth, but the ebbing tide told a different story as the top of the 'Massey's' wheelhouse started to be exposed by the receding River Thames. The Trustees were greeted by the harrowing sight of seeing all their hard work laying on the Thames riverbed.

Massey Shaw 75th Anniversary images. (Massey Shaw Educational Trust)

It was a worrying forty-eight hours as the 'Massey Shaw' lay submerged whilst arrangements were put in place to raise the fireboat back to the surface. The changing tides forced ever more mud and silt into the beleaguered craft. It seemed that there was a never-ending supply of mud to be removed from bilges, engines, electrics and the 'Massey's' nooks and crannies once the salvage operation got into full swing. Plus there was the additional burden of repairing her upper works caused by the lifting operation. However, her fortunes were to smile again on those determined to see her salvaged. Retrieved from the muddy, unexpected, resting place, the Preservation Society members resumed their arduous task of restoring this most resilient of river craft. By the summer of 1988 the 'Massey' was back in business and had joined some of her wartime counterparts in their annual rally.

Returning to Dunkirk became a regular feature in the 'Massey Shaw's' calendar. The fiftieth anniversary was one the crew did not wish to miss. On 21st May 1990 the 'Massey' left the safety of her home in London's West India Dock, with a tank full of free fuel supplied by Total Oil. A day that started in bright sunshine and with only a gentle breeze gave no warning of the weather to come. The 'London Phoenix' fireboat provided a spectacular water salute as it escorted and then bade her adieu.

By Tilbury an ominous change had come over the weather. The wind had increased from the North East and the sky was now overcast and menacing. The river too had become restless and an unpleasant chop made the sailing uncomfortable for the crew. The 'Massey Shaw' had started an uncharacteristic pitch and roll. For the next three hours angry green water hurled over the fireboat's foredeck, bursting right over the wheelhouse. The helmsman had his work cut out holding a course whilst the skipper and the navigator plotted the course from buoy to buoy. Several times she rolled quite badly. At times it seemed that 'Massey' might not reassert herself, but she powered on.

Their arrival at Ramsgate was heralded by the lifeboat's two maroons shooting skyward with a whoosh, followed by their alerting loud 'bangs'. Another of the Little Ships, the 'White Marlin', was in trouble off the Margate Sands. The crews watched with unguarded admiration as the Waveney Class lifeboat, the 'Ralph and Joy Swann', sped out to sea with the waves breaking over the whole of the boat.

The following morning the run down to Dover was a pleasure cruise. His Royal Highness the Duke of Edinburgh arrived in the early afternoon to inspect the convoy. Prior to his arrival Navy divers inspected every vessel for explosive devices whilst the security forces checked all above the water line. For the crossing the weather once again turned foul. It was a fourteen hour crossing that the crew could have done without. Whilst Dover Harbour was like a mill pond, when the 'Massey' was only a mile out to sea she hit a wave and her prow went under, the crew thought someone had given the order: 'Dive, Dive, Dive'. However, whilst the 'Massey Shaw' held her own, the skipper of the 'Papillion' had to be air lifted to safety, and the RNLI had to go to the aid of other craft with engine problems.

Nearing Calais a lone Spitfire flew over the convoy several times finally doing a victory roll directly over the 'Massey Shaw' that enthralled the crew. Sadly it was a short-lived distraction as the weather continued to deteriorate; in fact it became vile, as the little ship neared Dunkirk. It was pitch dark when the vessels finally made port for the night. Thankfully by Sunday, and the offshore ceremony, the weather brought calmer seas. With the service conducted aboard HMS 'Alacrity', the 'Massey' held her station, marking her position with the vast plume of water from her monitor, and clear of the helicopter that had dropped a wreath and which the large flotilla had circled. The return to the West India Dock seemed almost an anti-climax after the excitement of the outward trip, but there would be others.

They followed in 2000 and in 2015, the 75th anniversary. Both were successful journeys, but it was not lost on the organisers that many of the boats attending the 75th anniversary were octogenarians themselves, some many years older. But it was British veterans, now in their 90s, who had gathered in Dunkirk for the anniversary of the historic rescue of hundreds of thousands of Allied troops trapped in the French port by advancing Nazi armies, that the little ships continue to honour. The next big landmark commemoration, the 80th anniversary, is in 2020. It seems that the

'Massey Shaw' has many years ahead of her yet and will continue to play an important part in that played by the little ships.

Mixed blessings

In 2002 a television series on Channel 4 called *Salvage Squad* had the 'Massey' in its sights. The TV team took on the challenge of repairing the fireboat. The programmers had been alerted to the need to carry out repairs to the 'Massey Shaw' after they had requested suitable projects for the forthcoming series. The 'Massey Shaw' proved to be a winner with the viewing public. With some of the work completed in 2002, the 'Massey Shaw' was voted the most popular project for the team to return to in 2003. By the time the Salvage Team had finished upgrading work had been completed in the starboard engine, the fire pumps, fire values and the exterior of the boat.

The 'Massey Shaw' refurbishment programme, 2011.
(Massey Shaw Education Trust)

Then on 1st November 2004 the London Fire Brigade came rushing to the aid of its once proud fireboat. Vandals had attacked the boat at its Greenwich moorings. Fire engines from Poplar, Greenwich, Deptford and Lewisham fire stations battled against rising Thames water to stop the 'Massey Shaw' sinking again. Although about three-quarters of the boat had been submerged on the rising tide, the crews prevented the 'Massey' from going totally under. Finally the Red Watch from Poplar managed to get the boat re-floated and the water was pumped out.

Once again she had been badly damaged by water and escaping oil. The boat was moved to a more secure mooring site. The difficult task of funding the necessary repairs was taxing the resources of the Massey Shaw and Marine Vessels Preservation Society who had taken ownership of the fireboat in 2002.

By this time it was felt by the trustees that a major refit was necessary if the boat was to remain active. They made an application to the Heritage Lottery Fund (HLF) which, after detailed and lengthy negotiations, awarded a sizeable grant to enable some extensive work to be carried out.

In 2009, with the Lottery bid successful, restoration work was started in London. Once that work commenced it became clear that further funding would be required as the work was far more extensive than first envisaged. A second bid was made to HLF for additional funding. This too was successful, which brought the grant to a total of £1.2 million. However, it also resulted in a re-tendering process for the restoration work. The successful bidders were T Nielsen's Boatyard, based in Gloucester Dock, and so the vessel was moved 140 miles for this company to complete the work.

The subsequent engine refurbishment contract was won by Gardner of Canterbury. With the 'Massey Shaw' transported to Gloucester overnight by low-loader in April 2011, she was heading for a major facelift and overhaul. Originally it had been hoped to have the work completed in time to participate in the Olympic celebrations of 2012 as the 'Massey Shaw' had staged river displays for the 1948 Olympics when Great Britain had hosted the games. Unfortunately, due to various complications to the rebuild programme it had to be extended. In the intervening time training was undertaken for the boat crew and shore support volunteers so as to be ready for when Massey Shaw returned to London.

The 'Massey Shaw' fireboat returned to the Thames in December 2013 after a four-year restoration programme. In January 2014 the 'Massey Shaw' was a major attraction at the London Boat Show. The return of the unique craft to the London scene provided an opportunity for members of the public to see the fireboat in action. They do so to this day, and following her renovations, will continue to do so for many more years to come.

Fire boat Massey Shaw

Artist: Peter Kent May. (Massey Shaw Education Trust)

Massey Shaw

(Massey Shaw Education Trust)

(Massey Shaw Education Trust)

No other London fire brigade appliance, or sole piece of equipment, has been responsible for the rescue, or bringing to safety, of so many individuals. Some 710 soldiers were either ferried to troop ships or landed safely on English soil. The 'Massey Shaw' resumed her operational (wartime) duties in London and was one of some twenty other fireboats and floats swept up in the creation of the National Fire Services (London Region) and formed part of the River Thames Formation.

The 'Massey Shaw' at the Lambeth river fireboat station. (Neil Saunders)

CHAPTER 8

The Post-War Period, 1948-2000

T HE END OF THE war in 1945 may have brought the hostilities to an end but the National Fire Service (NFS) remained in place until April 1948.

London County Council/London Fire Brigade, 1948–1965

The new Fire Service Act was passed into law the year before. The Act placed the responsibility for maintaining efficient fire brigades into the hands of local authorities. The London Fire Brigade had its name restored and returned to the oversight of the London County Council (LCC). The Brigade area covered the whole of the LCC's administrative area and the length of the Thames within its boundary. Other fire brigades such as Croydon, East Ham and West Ham that had formed part of the NFS (London Region), were returned to their County Borough Councils. The County Councils of Kent, Surrey, Essex and Middlesex became fire authorities in their own right for the first time. London remained the country's largest brigade with some 2,500 officers and men. The London Fire Brigade resumed its pre-war status on the 1st April 1948. It retained Frederick William Delve as the Chief Officer of the re-formed Brigade.

London County Council/London Fire Brigade cap badge. (Author)

Along the route of the Thames London's heavily populated industrial and dockland areas had been targeted during the enemy bombing raids. The first bombs had fallen during late 1940 and continued until May 1941. The Port of London, Surrey and the Royal Docks were left in a terrible state. Many thousands of high explosive, as well as literally thousands of incendiary, bombs had fallen on the Port of London Authority (PLA) property.

In the intervening post-war years, up until the early 1950s, much of the war damage and reconstruction of the Thames, and the industry it served, had been completed. In fact by the early 1960s dock and river trade had not only recovered, it topped a record-breaking sixty-one million tons. However, in that same decade, and certainly by the late 1960s, London's dock use was in serious decline due to the introduction of containerisation. This had a dramatic effect on the docks and those Londoners dependent on its continuing trade. These 'new' containers, which could hold huge amounts of cargo, along with the greater use of the 'roll on/roll off' method of shipping, led to many dock workers being laid off. In fact they were becoming obsolete. The very nature of the Thames and its industries were changing. The changes would bring about a reappraisal of London's fireboat fleet.

1949: high tides cause flooding at Lambeth; the river station pontoon can be seen in the background. (Mary Evans)

With the return to local authority control the NFS Thames River Formation, which had been enlarged, was disbanded in April of 1948. Kent and Essex fire brigades initially retained the fireboats that covered the lower Thames and the Estuary. Three of London's four pre-war fireboats, the 'Massey Shaw', 'Beta III', and 'Gamma II' were again in the operational control of the LFB. They also took charge of a number of the fire-boats commissioned for the AFS, and later, the NFS.

The 'Delta II' fireboat, unlike her sister craft, was of an awkward design. Had not the war intervened it is most likely that this fire-boat would have been disposed of before the war had started. However, it served throughout the war, supplementing the Brigade's expanded fireboat fleet, despite her coxswains frequently reporting she was tricky to manoeuvre in the strong Thames tideway. The 'Delta' was put up for auction and sold. She ended her days as a houseboat in the upper reaches of the Thames.

The London County Council considered the Brigade had too many fireboats for its operational needs. With the 'Massey Shaw', the 'Beta' and the 'Gamma' resuming their river duties the remainder were placed into cold storage. They were moored at different locations along the Thames, which during the early 1950s, remained one of the busiest waterways in the world. The Thames was also becoming increasingly smelly and polluted. Despite the ingenuity of the Victorian engineers who had increased the flow of the river by building the Victoria, Albert and the Chelsea embankments, in their efforts to rid the river of the putrid mud, it had slowly deteriorated. By the 1950s the Thames was again little more than an open sewer containing virtually no oxygen. The production of hydrogen sulphide in decomposing matter in the river gave off the smell of rotten eggs. The problems were further aggravated by the Thames' fluctuating tides. It could take up to eighty days for river water to be flushed out to the sea in periods of low rainfall.

For those working on the Thames there were the inevitable hazards. It resulted in those engaged on the various ships and vessels plying their trade on the river occasionally falling in, including London's river fireman. Notwithstanding the obvious danger of drowning, a fall into the unsanitary and contaminated water inevitably required a trip to the nearest hospital to have their stomach pumped out and injections provided to prevent infection from waterborne diseases.

Cargo ships, barges and tugs still filled the river right up to London Bridge, the road traffic along Tower Bridge Road being brought to a regular halt as Tower Bridge was raised to allow large ships to pass beneath it. Further up river numerous Thames cruise boat carried passengers from the various piers as the river tours took in London's riverfront tourist sites. Warehouse and quayside cranes lined the river front of Southwark and the City of London, lifting and lowering various bales, sacks and pallets of a multitude of products and cargos either from or onto the barges that lined the river bank or worked alongside moored ships.

It's a digression from the role of London's river firemen but so as to provide a flavour of these post-war years here is a personal insight into that era. Born in 1949, I was a child of the '50s. My childhood was spent in the former Borough of Deptford, with its historic links to both the Thames and the Surrey Docks. We lived near the top of Waller Road, a hill in south London, its steep incline running up from New Cross fire station that fronted Queens Road.

Despite the difficulties my parents had in day-to-day living, most people retained a great pride in, and loyalty to, their country. They seemed to share a common purpose in life. Families stayed together, ours certainly did, through the hard times and everybody knew their neighbours and had a sense of belonging. I seemed to have 'uncles' and 'aunties' up and down the street, few of whom were actually related to me! They would routinely leave their street door 'on the latch' or hang the door key on a piece of string behind the letterbox so that if they were out their children could come and go as they pleased.

From our rear, top floor, rooms we had a clear view of the lines of lattice riverside cranes working either in the Surrey Docks or along the Deptford stretch of the Thames. Occasionally the sound of the ship's fog horns could be heard as the fogs and smog that enveloped London made movement on the roads or the Thames a hazardous journey. London frequently suffered from this dense, yellowish, blanketing smog, known as pea-soupers. They were caused by fog combining with coal fire emissions. In 1952 a particularly thick smog shrouded London and caused the deaths of an estimated twelve thousand people.

Waking up on Christmas morning in 1952 we still experienced the rationing of food and clothes that the older children had endured all of their young lives. It was quite normal to go without sweets, biscuits, crisps and fizzy drinks that would be taken for granted by future generations. Sweet rationing ended in February 1953, and then the most prized thing in our Christmas stocking would be a small, two-ounce bar of Cadbury's chocolate.

Many of us who grew up then have memories of houses that were draughty in winter with curtains hanging behind the street door to reduce the flow of cold air and the frost that formed over-night on the inside of bedroom windows. Warming your vest and underpants up in the bed before you put them on on a cold winter's morning.

However, life was certainly not all doom and gloom. We grew up in a much safer environment than we can ever imagine for children these days. We were able to enjoy the freedom of outdoor life. We played lots of rough-and-tumble games, got dirty, fell out of trees and played on the bomb-sites. The purple stains of iodine were always evident on the grazed knees of boys in short trousers. There was no such thing as health and safety or children's rights. We were taught discipline at home and at school with corporal punishment being freely administered for bad behaviour. There was no mugging of old ladies and people felt safe to walk the streets. There was very little vandalism and no graffiti. Telephone boxes were fully glazed and each contained a full set of local telephone directories and a pay-box full of pennies.

Youngsters respected people in authority, such as policemen and teachers, even the local park-keepers in their brown LCC issued uniforms, knowing that they would get a clip around the ear if caught misbehaving. Home life was much different from today. Everyone seemed to have a gramophone, an upright piano and a valve radio in their front room and there were ticking clocks all around the house. The kitchen was filled with products such as OMO washing powder and Robin starch and a whistle kettle was a permanent fixture on the kitchen stove.

My Dad, like most adults, smoked. There were ashtrays in every room, even in the bedrooms. Many homes didn't have a bathroom so people would either wash in a tin bath by the fireside or take a weekly trip to the local municipal baths where they could pay to have a hot bath in a little more comfort. Toilets were usually outside. My Nan, whose house we lived in, also had lodgers. She had had installed a 'geyser' (a gas water boiler) over the bath, plus she had an inside toilet that always reeked of tobacco smoke!

We always managed to eat lots of wholesome food, which was always freshly cooked. My Mum and Nan always seemed to be baking and because we didn't have a fridge went shopping for groceries almost every day. Perishable foods were bought in small amounts, just enough to last a day. It was quite usual to buy a single item of fruit or a quarter of butter (pound that is). Both the milk and the bread were delivered by horse and cart, with eager neighbours scurrying out with a bucket and a shovel to collect the horse droppings off the road for their gardens,

On Sundays everyone had a roast dinner and cold leftovers for Monday and anything left over was made into stews and pies later in the week. In 1950s half of all young children drank tea with their meals. Bread and beef dripping was standard fare but we cringed at the sight of a curled-up Spam sandwich which was even worse than the daily spoonful of cod liver oil many of us had to consume.

Boys and girls played street games together, such as run outs, hopscotch and British bulldog. In the playground schoolgirls practised handstands and cartwheels with their skirts tucked up under the elastic of their navy blue knickers, while the boys played conkers. We travelled in third-class compartments on train journeys to the seaside. In 1956 they were renamed second class; the change didn't move you any higher up the social ladder but it made you feel there was a bit less of a social gap. At the seaside you wore a knitted bathing costume on the beach.

Saturday mornings saw us heading to the pictures up the Old Kent Road. Pathé News, cartoons and a feature film. The manager would regularly stop the film and threaten to send you all home if you didn't behave and the solitary usherette was often forced to run for cover. It was controlled mayhem with the stalls and circle filled with children cheering for the goodies and booing the baddies. It introduced us to The Lone Ranger and Zorro and the slapstick comedy of Mr Pastry. When the film ended everyone stood for the National Anthem and stayed until it finished playing.

Dusty, old-fashioned sweetshops had high wooden counters jam-packed with boxes of ha'penny chews and other sweet delights. I remember Lucky Bags and frozen Jubblys plus getting a sore tongue from sucking on gobstoppers, aniseed balls and Spangles. Then there were those old Smith's potato crisps. The salt was in a twist of blue paper and you always had to rummage around for it at the bottom of the bag. All your one-shilling-a-week pocket money would go on sweets and comics (£sd back then).

There was something cosy about growing up in the '50s in which most children retained their childish innocence to the age of 12 or 13 and enjoyed a carefree life full of fun and games. The stresses of adolescence and then adult life could wait. We children were lucky.

Many historians consider the 1950s as a prosperous decade. Record quantities of imports and exports passed through London's docks. The reconstruction effort remained in full swing. Skilled labour was now being actively recruited from Commonwealth countries and was helping to build and staff London's new hospitals, houses and schools. The population was in excess of three and quarter million, and growing. Manufacturing firms flourished during this decade, particularly those making consumer goods such as televisions, washing machines and radios. 'White collar' jobs were on the increase as an office boom brought over fifty thousand new jobs to London and service took a bigger share of London's overall economy.

All this activity resulted in a busy operational workload for the London Fire Brigade, including its three working fireboats. Whilst it was nothing on the scale of the worst days of the Blitz, it was enough to place serious demands on the Brigade and the role of the fireboats on the river. Tragically, occasionally some incidents would bring some of its operational procedures under serious scrutiny – none more so than in the wearing and use of breathing apparatus, which was now also carried on two of the fireboats. Change was hard fought and slow. Following a series of major London blazes between late 1949 and 1958 where firemen, wearing breathing apparatus, lost their lives, changes to procedures were finally enacted.

The first of these fires occurred in the basement of Covert Garden Market. It started during the morning of the 20th December with the last fire engine leaving at 1.40 p.m. on the 22nd December. Station Officer Charles Fisher, from Clerkenwell fire station, died during the very difficult and arduous firefighting operations. In his subsequent report, given on the 24th January 1950 to the Fire Brigade Committee of the LCC, Chief Officer Delve surprisingly reported that in his opinion the brigade's organisation had been satisfactory despite the death of one of his

officers and an internal inquiry which found the following proce-
dural deficiencies:

- There was no method of recording the names or time personnel entered or exited the building.

- There was no minimum charging pressure for the Proto
breathing apparatus oxygen cylinder. Some cylinders were
only two-thirds full.

- Proto oxygen breathing apparatus sets had no warning
devices to alert the wearer they were reaching low cylinder
capacity and should therefore begin to withdraw.

- Firemen were allowed to work alone in breathing apparatus
so they had no immediate help if they encountered difficulties.

- There was no radio communications between firemen inside
to those outside and vice versa. Line signals, when and if
employed, had to be used. Worse still, there was none between
individual firemen wearing breathing apparatus, or other
firefighting crews. (When seeking urgent outside assistance in
the rescue efforts for Station Officer Fisher the firemen barely
made it back to street level. Valuable time was lost, with the
final tragic consequences.)

- Breathing apparatus was donned outside in fresh air but the
mouthpiece wasn't inserted in many cases until the crews
were inside the building. Communications problems between
crew members were overcome by removing their mouthpiece
so they could talk, or shout, to one another. The delayed use
of, or the total removal of, the set's mouthpiece meant there
was no protection from firemen inhaling the surrounding
toxic atmosphere with its immediate and long term effects.
This gave rise to London, and other whole-time, firemen
being known as 'smoke-eaters'.

- No 'guidelines' were in operation. For a fireman to search
for people reported trapped in a building or to locate the
seat of a fire it was practice to use a hose line to guide subsequent crews into the building. At Covent Garden crews had
to follow a working hose line, in this case hose that was
submerged by up to four feet of water.

It took a long time to service the sets on the fire ground so there was a slow crew 'turn around' time for them to be prepared to re-enter the 'job'.

The procedures above were later, and in some cases many years later, implemented for both LFB land and river firefighting crews. However, as a direct result of this tragic fire the Brigade did introduced a nominal roll board which was placed in all fire station watchrooms, including the three river stations. The names of crews were appended at the start of each watch and adjusted throughout the day as necessary. Firemen wearing BA had the letters BA added after their names. These boards were not carried on appliances responding to incidents, though. Other than the nominal roll board, the general procedures for the use of BA did not change between this fire and the next fatal fire that occurred in 1954.

This second fire, which cost the lives of Station Officer Frederick Hawkins and Firemen Arthur Batt-Rawden and Charles Gadd, all serving at Clerkenwell fire station, also happened in the Covent Garden Market area. It started in a five storey warehouse at 3 p.m. on the 11th May 1954 and spread with rapid ferocity. It continued until approximately 11.30 p.m. on the same day. (It was soon obvious that the lessons to be learnt were some of the same as experienced at the 1949 basement fire.) An internal investigation again found that no recording, or supervising, of firemen entering and leaving the fire wearing breathing apparatus had taken place. In fact one fireman was only accounted for when a roll call was taken back at the fire station. Other shortfalls found there was still no means for a fireman to summon assistance in an emergency. It had taken fire crews nearly an hour to locate a trapped colleague after the building collapse, and there were no evacuation signals to warn firemen to withdraw if signs of a building collapse became evident.

It was not until the following year, 1955, that the Home Office issued a general Fire Service Technical Bulletin (No 2/1955). This set out, and stressed, the importance of two fundamental points of good BA procedure. These were:– that BA should be donned and started up in fresh air before the wearer entered an incident; also if the wearer's nose clip or face mask become dislodged for any appreciable amount of time he should return to fresh air to avoid the inherent danger associated with the exposure to noxious atmospheres. But there was nothing from a national level to provide a more detailed guidance on procedures for the operational use of BA in Brigades.

It would take the deaths of two further firemen, Station Officer Jack Fourt-Wells and Fireman Richard Stocking, once again from the ill-fated Clerkenwell fire station, before a radical review of BA operational procedures was finally enacted. This major fire started the early hours of January 1958. A fire had broken out in the basement of Smithfield Market.

(Pathé)

This fire proved to be one of the most notable in that it included a local procedure established by the London Brigade in 1956 following the second Covent Garden Fire. This was the provision of a Control Point set up to record the entry of firemen into the BA incident. The Control Point consisted of an ordinary blackboard and, written up with white chalk, it recorded individuals' names, their station and time of entry and their time due out. This

Scores of London fire engine attending the Smithfield meat market fire, January 1958.
(Mary Evans)

procedure proved to be invaluable and was able to indicate later in the incident that two men were overdue and missing.

Immediately following the disastrous fire at Smithfield with its tragic loss of life, and the previous fatal fires at Covent Garden, there were calls for a more comprehensive schedule of BA procedures to be formulated. These calls came from Delve himself, Leslie Leete, his Deputy Chief, plus Mr Horner who was the General Secretary of the Fire Brigades Union (FBU). In addition the FBU circulated its twenty thousand membership a questionnaire on possible procedures and invited suggestions with a £100 prize for the best ideas.

By February, and due to the outcry over the recent deaths of firemen, the Home Office set up a Committee of Inquiry into the operational use of BA. It appeared from its first meeting that some efforts had previously been made by the Home Office to establish a procedure for the use of BA but nothing had been circulated to brigades on the progress made. By June that year twelve UK brigades were circulated with a trial procedure. In August observations and recommendations had been received by the Committee of Inquiry which prepared an interim report. In that October FIRE SERVICE CIRCULAR 37/1958 was issued. It detailed the findings of the Committee of Inquiry and recommended the following:

- A tally for every individual BA set that recorded the wearer's name, the cylinder pressure and time they entered an incident.

- A Stage I and Stage II control procedure for recording & supervising BA wearers.

- The duties of a BA control operator.

- The duties and procedure to be followed by BA crews

- A main control procedure at incidents where there was extensive use of BA.

All British fire brigades were requested to report their observations and recommendations, in the light of experience, by the end of November 1959. There was no immediate specifications for the design and use of guide or personnel BA lines, but recommendations were, however, made in respect of a specification for both a low cylinder pressure warning device and a distress signal device.

It became clear that the use of BA required more firemen to be thoroughly trained in its use and tested on its procedures. Guidance on the selection of firemen as BA wearers were later provided in another Fire Service Circular (32/1960) and issued in July 1960. It recommended:-

- 18 months operational service before any BA training.
- A possible age limit for wearers. (50 years of age.)
- Standards of fitness required.
- Two BA wearers per appliance equipped with BA.

The slow improvements to BA procedures took over a decade to reach the point outlined above. However, back at the start of the 1950s the London Fire Brigade, and under Delve's command, other major changes happened which included a review of its fireboat fleet, which was by then in a marked decline. The London fire-float 'Beta III', the forerunner of the 'Massey Shaw', was the first to go. Then the 'jewel' class 'Amethyst', 'Diamond' and 'Sapphire', the WWII fireboats, were all sold off. These had arrived in London in 1943, joining the NFS River Formation. Each craft was fitted with four heavy emergency pumps capable of an output of three thousand six hundred gallons per minute. After the war replacements and spares for these three timber-built craft had become difficult to obtain.

However, the demise of the 'Diamond' fireboat caused some embarrassed faces in London Fire Brigade circles when in the early hours of the 12th December the fireboat actually caught fire! Then moored at the headquarters Lambeth river station, the crew of the 'Diamond' found themselves fighting a fire in the fireboat's pump room. The outbreak was quickly attacked using foam, first from three foam extinguishers, then a foam making branch. Supported by the land crews of Lambeth fire station the blaze was brought under control in a relatively short time.

The fire was discovered to have been caused by petrol vapour igniting when the boat's engines back-fired. Considerable damage was caused to the 'Diamond', affecting the superstructure of the pump room, the wheelhouse and after-cabin, and with a fifth of the pump room itself and its contents burned. The fire boat was considered beyond economic repair and was not returned to operational service. It was disposed of by the London County Council in 1954. It was followed by 'Amethyst' and 'Sapphire' in 1957, together with Brigade's own high speed fireboat, the 'James Braidwood'.

By 1953 the brigade's river fire stations had been reduced to three. Two were active stations, Lambeth and Woolwich, and one a non-operational reserve station, located at the South Wharf pier, near to the Pageants Wharf fire station in Rotherhithe Street, South London. This had been built in preparations for the oncoming war. South Wharf was temporarily closed in 1953 and permanently closed in 1956. It was later demolished.

The London Fire Brigade Headquarters underground control room, showing the station distribution board and R80, Lambeth river station. (Malc Burden)

The 'James Braidwood' remained stationed at Lambeth river station whilst the 'Massey Shaw' operated from the Royal Arsenal's Woolwich pier. With a greatly reduced peacetime river fleet the numbers of river firemen, which had stood at well over three hundred during the war, had shrunk to under fifty. In addition to the operational fireboats there were also two motorised fire-boat tenders. These were normally towed behind each of the fireboats and then used for getting hose ashore when the fireboat was working at a blaze from mid-stream. The two tenders were named 'Peony' and the 'Ravensbourne'.

There was one other additional operational fireboat in London, the 'Crocus'. It belonged to the Auxiliary Fire Service (AFS). The AFS had been reformed in 1948 and was part of the much larger Civil Defence Corps. This was a civilian volunteer organisation which had been established in Great Britain and was to be mobi-lised, and take local control of the affected areas, in the aftermath of a major national emergency, principally a Cold War nuclear attack by the then Soviet Union (USSR). Initially the AFS had been issued with old National Fire Service equipment. The role of the AFS was to provide mobile firefighting columns that could be deployed to those areas that had suffered a nuclear attack. (It was assumed by the Government planners that the local firefight-ing capability would most probably have been destroyed.) The old NFS equipment was quickly found unsuitable for the task, and so in the 1950s the AFS was totally re-equipped. This included one thousand Green Goddess (Bedford RLHZ self-propelled pumps) fire engines, Land Rovers, motorcycles and support vehi-cles such as pipe carriers, mobile kitchens, and foam and water carriers. London also had an AFS auxiliary fireboat. This AFS craft was originally designed for services as a re-fuelling launch by the British Overseas Airways Corporation (BOAC) for use in Southampton Water in conjunction with its boats. It had been subsequently converted and modified to incorporate fire-fight-ing equipment and placed into service with London's AFS force. (The AFS would be later abolished in 1968 by the Prime Minister Harold Wilson as part of a programme of Government cutbacks.)

One of Delve's most serious concerns was the state of the brigade's accommodation needs. Most of its stations were old ones, more suited to the horse drawn fire engines of the past. The London County Council had previously agreed a comprehen-sive programme of rebuilding and re-siting fire stations as early as 1949. However, the financial difficulties prevailing at the time made any rapid modernisation programme unrealistic, if not impossible. Government grants would only be given if the Home Office (which was responsible for the Fire Service) approved them. The Home Office was most reluctant to do so, and in any event there were far more pressing demands for new housing, schools and other important infrastructure projects. Hardly any new fire stations were built in London before 1956.

There were some notable changes, however. The London County Council had decided to abolish the street fire alarms in 1949. These alarms had been a source of increasing false and malicious calls, although the very last street alarm did not disappear from the streets until 1958. But most notable were the improvements in the area of the Capital's fire prevention arrangements. Many thousands of inspections were made by the Brigade each year, plans were examined, fire prevention requirements prescribed and certificates of suitability issued. Officers specialising in fire prevention now attended all large fires to gather information, watch the effects of particular hazards, and give advice as to means of checking the spread of fire and undertaking investigations into the cause of the fire and breaches of fire safety regulations.

The 'Beta III' in her new guise as a Thames launch at the Festival pier
in 1954. (Helen Symonds – betaiiifireboat.com)

The London Fire Brigade's post-war regeneration presented Chief Officer Delve with a number of problems, and his reduced river service was not high on the list of his priorities. By the mid-1950s two of the Brigade's former fireboats were disposed of by the LCC, although they did not say goodbye to the River Thames entirely. The 'Beta III' went in 1954 and was purchased by a Thames river cruise company which converted her into a Thames passenger cruiser, working from Westminster and Charing Cross piers. The 'James Braidwood', which was never really suited to the rigours of a working fireboat on the River Thames, was eventually sold off and later purchased by the Scout Association for use by the Sea Scout troop based at Battersea.

'Beta III' berthed at Westminster Pier, London taking on passengers for River Thames pleasure cruises. (Helen Symonds – betaiiifireboat.com)

In 1961 Frederick Delve made London Fire Brigade history. He became its first Chief Officer to be knighted whilst in office. It was the same year that the London Fire Brigade took delivery of its first new, custom made, fireboat since the end of the war. Named 'Fire-brace', she had been built in Anglesey. This impressive and sturdy craft had made her way around the Welsh and English coastline entirely under her own power – which is more than could be said for some of the crew, including the Brigade's workshop engineers who had accompanied the craft, as they succumbed to sea sickness on the less than friendly seas. The 'Firebrace', on the other hand, had no problems coping with the varied sea conditions. She cut a striking figure as she travelled up the River Thames on her maiden voyage and stopped off at the London County Council's headquarters, next to the Festival Hall, for a photo call.

The 'Firebrace' replaced the ageing 'Gamma' (which was also converted into a Thames river cruise craft). The 'Firebrace' took her place at the Brigade headquarters river station at Lambeth, the 'Massey Shaw' fireboat covering the downstream reaches of the Thames. The new fireboat was named after Commander Aylmer Firebrace, a former Royal Naval Officer who had been London's Chief Officer for only twelve months prior to the outbreak of the Second World War. Gifted with a brilliant mind and exceptional organisational skills, Commander Firebrace was seconded to the Home Office and was the principal architect of the Fire Service's war time organisation and, later, he oversaw the establishment of the National Fire Service from 1941 to 1948. He never returned to the London Fire Brigade. As the Chief Inspector of Fire Services, he worked from his offices in the Home Office. Knighted prior to his retirement in 1948, he died in June 1972.

The 'Firebrace' fireboat at the Lambeth river station, 1961. (Mary Evans)

The 'Firebrace' was a purpose-built craft. An all-welded steel vessel she was sixty-nine feet long, she had a beam of thirteen feet nine inches and a maximum draft of four feet eight inches. Her hull was divided into four watertight compartments, which comprised the chain locker, hose locker, engine room, crew accommodation and galley and stern stowage. Her two powerful Dorman diesel engines provided the boat with a maximum speed of nearly twelve knots. Two similar engines provided the drive for her Merryweather fire pumps. All the engine room controls were operated from the forward wheelhouse which had a connecting door leading to the crew's accommodation and a small galley. Access to this area was also possible from the stern of the boat. The 'Firebrace' was fitted with two sets of pumps, each capable of pumping two thousand gallons of water per minute at one hundred pound per square inch (nine thousand litres at seven bar). Fitted with an auxiliary generator it delivered AC electricity at 240 volts. Her deck fittings include a hydraulic-powered winch on the forward deck and a hydraulic powered capstan on the after deck.

Mounted on her deck, immediately behind the wheelhouse, was the boat's sole monitor, its maximum four inch nozzle capable of throwing a solid stream of water hundreds of feet into the air and discharging three thousand gallons per minute (thirteen thousand five hundred litres). More importantly, it could reach the tops of any riverside wharf or warehouse standing on the banks of the Thames, delivering tons of water per minute in the process. She was equipped with two sets of radio apparatus: one maintained contact with Brigade Control, though the other was for use with walkie-talkie equipment to provide communication between ship and shore. Twin rudders were fitted to the craft to give manoeuvrability.

With its distinctive livery of red and black bodywork, and white painted pump outlets and fittings, she soon became a regular, and commanding, sight as she patrolled the upper reaches of the Thames from Wapping to Teddington weir. If one fireboat was unavailable, the other would cover the whole length of the Thames. The normal minimum crew for the 'Firebrace' was seven; this included the officer in charge, coxswain, engineer (who remained on board), and four to crew the tender. In fact the work of the firemen afloat was, and remains, very different from that of their namesakes on land. Naturally, basic fire-fighting training is the same, and when working side by side at an incident they work to the same rules of engagement and procedures. However, the firemen afloat must command an elementary knowledge of both seamanship and navigation. A great amount of time, and training, is given to the problems which hardly arises on land, that of how to get to a fire, and when there, how and where to position and secure the craft. Knowledge of the state of the tides and tidal flows is vital if safe mooring is to take place and which allows a fireboat to safely rise and fall with the tide. It is not only the skills on a fireboat that have to be perfected; the river fireman must be fully conversant with small boat handling too. Skiffs were in constant use as tenders to fireboats, taking hose ashore, dropping an anchor midstream to position a fireboat when the monitor was at work, or even rescuing someone fallen in the river: all required water-borne skills and coordination.

London's latest fireboat, the 'Firebrace', in a 'photo call' by the Houses of Parliament. (Mary Evans)

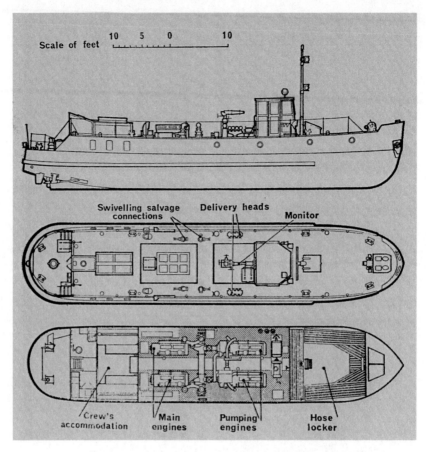

Diagram of the 'Firebrace'. (Source: HMSO-MoF)

Greater London Council/London Fire Brigade, 1965–1986

Great London Council/London Fire Brigade cap badge. (Author)

London welcomed another new fireboat in 1966 – athough this time it was more of a 'hand-me-down' vessel. The fireboat 'Fire-flair' had originally been built for the War Office in 1955. At sixty-five feet long and steel-hulled, she had been placed into service with the Royal Army Service Corps. Then on the 10th June 1961 she was jointly commissioned by Kent and Essex Fire Brigades to provide fire cover on the River Thames between Barking Creek and the Thames Estuary, and berthed at Denton Wharf, Graves-end, Kent. With a top speed of ten knots she had four monitors mounted two for'ard and two aft of the craft and was capable of pumping 1,500 gallons of water per minute. When the Kent and Essex fire brigades contracted a fire-fighting tug company to provide fire cover, the 'Fireflair' was sold to London and became the Auxiliary fire services' fireboat. With the AFS disbanded in 1968 the 'Fireflair' was transferred into the LFB and placed into service as the reserve fireboat and saw active service at both river stations when either the 'Firebrace' or the 'Massey Shaw' was unavailable either due to maintenance or repairs. The 'Fireflair' was disposed of by the Greater London Council in 1975.

The former Kent Fire Brigade fireboat, 'Fireflair'. (Kent County Council)

Footnote:
'Fireflair' was subsequently converted to a houseboat, and it retains that current use. The old fireboat underwent an extensive tasteful conversion. The upstairs accommodation was divided into two. A beautifully deco-rated lounge was installed complete with classic wooden panelled walls and a built in fireplace. The new owners created windows allowing plenty of light into the boat, new glass doors lead into a fitted kitchen/dining area. A panelled stairway from there lead to the downstairs accommo-dation which consists of a large double bedroom and a further bedroom or an office/study. The retained original opening portholes on both sides provide light and airflow, a reminder of the boats character and its history. Additional accommodation on the former Fireflair consists of two large storage areas, a family bathroom and utility room. The boat was also fitted with full centrally heating, using kerosene. The refit incorpo-rated a comfortable deck space at both ends of the boat.

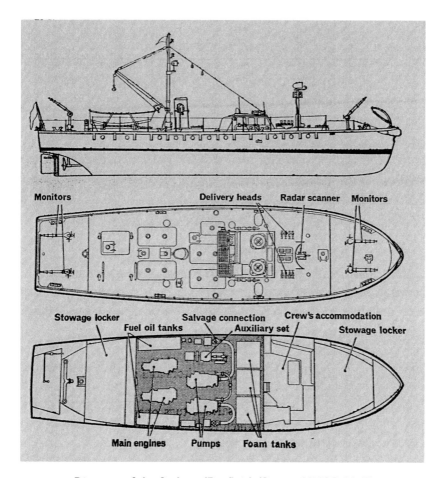

Diagram of the fireboat 'Fireflair'. (Source HMSO MoF)

In the modern post-war history of the London Fire Brigade there have only been two fifty pump fires. On both occasions fire-boats not only attended but made a significant contribution to the successful extinction of those fires. Given her wartime (Blitz) experience the 'Massey Shaw' fireboat was no stranger to major conflagrations. Here, together with many 'older' WWII serving firemen who had fought such fires during London's Blitz, they were reunited fighting this North London inferno.

On the 22 September 1966 the 'Massey Shaw' fireboat attended her second largest peacetime fire of her long career (the first being in 1935). In fact, it was the biggest blaze that the recently enlarged London Fire Brigade had encountered. Almost three hundred firemen, fifty pumps and many other specialist fire engines were brought into action at Bambergers Ltd, an enormous timber yard in Tottenham, N17. The national press and television news described it as the largest fire London had seen since the Blitz. The incident was also remarkable in that a malicious false alarm to the very same site had been made only two hours before the genuine fire calls were received.

In a comprehensive report of the outbreak, the then Chief Officer Leslie Leete stated that the site, belonging to the timber importing firm of Bambergers Ltd, covered an area of 475 x 420 feet. It was bounded on the west by a road, to the north by a recreation ground and bounded by the River Lee, with the rear gardens of private houses to the south.

The vast timber stock, which comprised mainly teak and plywood and veneers, was brought by barge up the River Lee and off-loaded by means of electric cranes on overhead gantries under a continuous roof. At the time of the fire, there were eighteen lorries and articulated trailers parked in the south-west corner of the yard. A number of other lorries and trailers, laden with timber, were parked in the gangways between storage sheds in the north end of the building. Lying off the towpath alongside the River Lee were twelve 'dumb' barges, several of which were fully loaded with timber and covered with tarpaulins.

At 9.28 p.m. on that September night a call was received by exchange telephone at the Brigade's Northern control room located at Wembley fire station. The caller was evasive in giving an accurate address but was heard to say: 'Fire – Bamberger, High Road, Tottenham, near the school.' Three fire engines were ordered in response to that call, two from Tottenham fire station and one from Stoke Newington fire station. The engines from Tottenham station, with Station Officer Hogg in charge, proceeded through to the entrance gates of Bambergers, having observed no sign of any fire en route. The machine from Stoke Newington entered from the opposite direction but also noted no sign of any fire. When the first crews from Tottenham arrived at Bambergers, two women standing by the entrance approached Station Officer Hogg and said that there could not possibly be a fire there as they had just left the premises.

Station Officer Hogg summoned the night-watchman and proceeded with his crews to carry out a systematic, thorough search. The whole area was covered and no trace of any fire was found. The local telephone exchange were asked to verify the telephone call and they stated that it was made from a public call box at the Manor House tube station, some considerable distance from the Bambergers site. After satisfying himself that there wasn't any fire anywhere in the immediate vicinity, Station Officer Hogg sent a radio message back to the Wembley control room saying the call was a 'False Alarm'.

The night-watchman at the premises had accompanied Station Officer Hogg and his crews during their search. He too was convinced that there was no fire anywhere on the site. His duties included patrolling the premises at 90-minute intervals requiring him to clocking-in at various check points. At about 11.30 p.m. he was summoned to the entrance gate by the enquiry bell where somebody told him that smoke was coming from one of the sheds near the southern towpath end. He went to investigate and seeing flames called the fire brigade.

At 11.44 p.m. the first of three calls were received by exchange telephone at the Wembley control room to a fire at Bambergers. The same two fire stations were dispatched, with Station Officer Hogg again in charge. This time an additional fire engine from Stoke Newington was sent. As Station Officer Hogg approached the address he observed a huge slow-moving column of black smoke over Bambergers' timber yard set against the night sky.

Upon his arrival Tottenham's pump-escape was driven into the yard. Two lines of hose were immediately laid out, water being supplied from a nearby hydrant and an attack on the fire was made. Station Officer Hogg sent a 'priority' assistance message by radio at 11.50 p.m. making pumps five. When he looked into the building he saw that the fire appeared to be spreading swiftly along the south wall in a westerly direction. One minute later he made pumps eight. With the arrival of the appliances from Stoke Newington its crews started to provide a further line of hose into the building. As they did so a flashover occurred and it appeared run along the wall on the south side of the premises from east to west. The crews from Tottenham were ordered back from the seat

The 'Massey Shaw' fireboat at the 50 pump Bambergers fire in Tottenham after navigating the River Lea. (Look at Life)

of the fire by their Sub Officer. However, they had great difficulty in getting clear of the rapidly spreading fire and had to run for it. Three of the five firemen in Tottenham's' crew sustained burns to their backs. The flashover spread at such a rate that it reached their point of entry to the timber storage area before they were clear of it.

At 11.54 p.m. Station Officer Hogg made pumps ten, and he ordered his pump-escape to pull back out of the timber yard. The fire spread with extreme rapidity from south to north; along the back of the premises and adjacent to the River Lee. Just five minutes after he arrived Station Officer Hogg had made pumps twenty. The crews who had pulled back at the time of the flashover were ordered to break the couplings of the hose abandoned in the timber stacks. Fresh lines of hose were brought to bear on the fire which some of the crews managed regardless of the burns inflicted on them. A police constable was instructed to have the nearby houses evacuated. As more reinforcing fire engines arrived the attack on the fire was directed from both the north and west flanks. With the arrival of Assistant Divisional Officer Spring from the local Divisional Headquarters, he took command. He was only in command for eight minutes before a more senior officer arrived and immediately assumed command of the still rapidly growing fire.

With a Divisional Office in charge ADO Spring took responsibility for fire-fighting at the rear of the adjoining houses to the timber yard. As he entered a house next to the fire he saw that the 24 foot high corrugated iron wall at the south side of Bambergers was white-hot for the whole of its length. Four lines of hose were brought through the houses and firemen got jets to work to cool the corrugated iron wall and protect the houses from fire spread.

In the meantime, the Divisional Officer had established a control point at a nearby road junction. The wind was moderate but the fire was still spreading. Fires of this intensity create their own wind currents. Two pumps crews were ordered to gain access to the River Lee, to supply hose lines from the river. The occupants of private houses opposite Bambergers were warned to be ready for immediate evacuation as the fire continued to spread. At fifteen minutes after midnight pumps were made thirty, with six radial branches required. The 'Massey Shaw' fireboat was also dispatched to the incident.

The 'Massey Shaw' left her moorings at Woolwich shortly after midnight. She proceeded up the Thames to the River Lee's entrance on the north bank. Passing Silvertown she entered Bow Creek before following the route of the Lee. After the vast widths of the lower reaches of the Thames the River Lee seemed to close in on the fireboat as it navigated it way north to the Tottenham fire. By Homerton the 'Massey's' crew had no doubts where they were heading as the glow in the far distance was acting like a homing beacon.

With the fire now involving the whole site, involving six single-storey buildings covering an area of 300 x 200 feet, hose-laying lorries were increased to three. The fire was being attacked on all sides. Holes were made through the fences to the River Lee using pickaxes and hand axes and lengths of suction hose were passed through and additional hose lines got to work. At the same time more lines of hose were laid out across the recreation ground, to augment the supplies to pumps, and further fire engines were sent into the recreation ground to assist in providing water from the river where firemen got jets. These were also got to work along the towpath and positioned on the dumb barges to protect the timber stacks with which several barges were laden. A deputy Assistant Chief Officer took command just before 12.30 a.m. He made a swift assessment of the deteriorating fire situation, with its vast area and continuing rapid spread, and sent a message: 'Make pumps fifty.'

With the subsequent build-up of appliances and crews more were allocated to each side of the fire. There were soon 15 jets on the south side preventing the spread to the private houses. There was danger from flying brands setting fire to houses in the surrounding streets and patrols were instituted to deal with any outbreaks of fire.

Deputy Chief Officer Mummery was the former Chief Officer of the Middlesex Fire Brigade prior to the creation of the Greater London Council in 1965. This was his old patch. He took command and directed the attack which was steadily increased so as to cover the 3,000 gallon overhead diesel oil storage tank, the three-storey office building and the vulnerable 2,600 gallon petrol storage.

At 1.06 a.m. the Deputy Chief was able to send a message stating that progress was being made in containing the fire. Shortly after this the Chief Fire Officer arrived and assumed control of the fire-fighting operations. At 1.36 a.m. he was able to send a message saying the fire was surrounded. The fire was brought under control at 2.45 a.m. By this time the fire had involved nearly the whole of the 13 timber storage sheds, covering an area of 420 x 300 feet, and eight lorries and trailers in the timber yard. It had also damaged the office building and the other single-storey buildings and structures in the yard. Strenuous efforts by the brigade, and the crew of the 'Massey Shaw', had prevented the fire involving the petrol and diesel storage tanks or any of the nearby houses, although several had suffered minor damage. Forty-four jets, four radial branches and the 'Massey Shaw's' massive monitor were used to extinguish the blaze – the biggest in London since World War II.

The supposed cause was recorded as 'doubtful'.

The London Fire Brigade celebrated its centenary in 1966. One hundred years prior the Metropolitan Fire Brigade, under Captain Massey Shaw, was created: 1866. The name changed to the London Fire Brigade in 1904. 1966 was also the Tercentenary of the Great Fire of London. Both these notable events were celebrated that year in style. Her Majesty Queen Elizabeth, accompanied by His Royal Highness Prince Philip, attended the Brigades Centenary Review at the Lambeth Headquarters in the November. Prior to that the Greater London Council (GLC), in conjunction with the Brigade and the former newspaper, the London Evening News, marked the three hundred anniversary of the Great Fire of London in sensational fashion and on the River Thames.

It was not very often that Londoners got the opportunity to see all of the Brigade's fireboats at work, at the same time, and on the same stretch of the Thames. The GLC had only been in power for fifteen months when it decided to stage the largest River Thames extravaganza in London's local government history. It was almost three hundred years to the day that the Great Fire had swept through the central parts of London. It blazed from Sunday 2nd

Montage of the Thames River Pageant. (London Evening News)

September until Wednesday 5th September 1666. The fire completely gutted the medieval City of London, inside the old Roman city walls. It threatened, but did not reach, the aristocratic district of Westminster and King Charles the Second's Palace of Whitehall. It consumed over thirteen thousand houses, eighty-seven parish churches, St Paul's Cathedral and most of the buildings belonging to the City authorities. It is estimated to have made seventy-thousand of the City's eighty-thousand inhabitants homeless.

Massed jets display on barges and London's fireboats.
(London Evening News)

The true death toll remains unknown but it is traditionally thought to have been small, as only six verified deaths were recorded. Although this reasoning has since been challenged on the grounds that the deaths of the poor and middle-class people were not accurately recorded, if at all, since the all-consuming heat of the inferno would have cremated many victims, thus leaving no recognisable remains.

319

As already discussed (page 25), the 'Great' fire had started at the bakery of a Thomas Farriner (or Farynor) in Pudding Lane, shortly after midnight on the 2nd; it spread rapidly west across the City of London. The use of the major firefighting technique of the time, the creation of firebreaks by means of demolition, was critically delayed owing to the indecisiveness of the Lord Mayor of London, Sir Thomas Bloodworth. By the time large-scale demolitions were ordered that Sunday night, the wind had already fanned the fire into a firestorm which defeated any such measures. The fire continued north on Monday into the heart of the City. By Tuesday, the fire had spread over most of the City, destroying St Paul's Cathedral and leaping the River Fleet to threaten Charles' Royal court at Whitehall. The battle to quench the fire is considered to have been finally won by two factors: the strong east winds died down, and the Tower of London garrison used gunpowder to create effective firebreaks to halt further spread eastward. The social and economic problems resulting from the disaster were overwhelming. Despite numerous radical proposals, London was reconstructed on essentially the same street plan used before the fire.

To commemorate the three hundred year anniversary an enormous flotilla had gathered to recall that catastrophic fire. It was the largest spectacle of fireworks, light-show and pageantry London had even seen staged on the River Thames. The London Fire Brigade fireboats were to take centre stage. On the evening of the 9th September the pageant unfolded. It had brought together the 'Massey Shaw', the 'Firebrace' and the 'Fireflair', in addition to scores of volunteer off-duty firemen and firewomen plus squads of London's junior fireman, all dressed in period costumes. Before hundreds of thousands of spectators, who had lined the embankments and watched from vantage points along the Southbank and the northern Westminster shoreline, the various tableaux were staged on barges, ships and craft of all descriptions. Massed jets shot into the night sky, cleverly illuminated by the co-ordinated firework display.

There was one other event, but that was not one open to the public. A massive combined exercise involving five thousand firemen and firewomen of the AFS took place in the London's

Royal Docks. On Saturday the 3rd of September one thousand vehicles and fire engines moved on London from every Civil Defence Region in England and Wales. Representatives came from one hundred and eighteen separate fire brigades.

Overnight accommodation has been secured at Army and RAF camps surrounding London. Feeding and refuelling of the vehicles and other miscellaneous arrangements fell to the London Fire Brigade and its AFS detachment. The aim of the exercise was designed to test the arrangements for assembling such vast numbers of mobile and light columns and to engage them in an incident that stretched some two and half miles in length. There had not been such a deployment of fire service resources since the height of the Second World War's Blitz and the other enemy attacks on mainland Britain.

At 9 a.m. on the 4th September the command was given, 'Go Go Go', and the exercise began. Massed crews converged on Victoria East and West Dock and the Albert Dock complex. Quayside pumps, pumps in AFS rubber rafts and over one hundred light portable pumps provided water to four hundred jets in a mock attack following a simulated 'Cold War' attack on London. The weather that day was atrocious; it rained heavily right throughout the whole exercise. If the spray from the massed jets did not soak most to the skin, the weather did. With some five thousand gallons of tea consumed one of the lessons learned was that there were insufficient lavatories in the dock area to cope with demand! By 3.15 p.m. everything had been cleared away and the various contingents began their long homeward journeys.

My own contact with the river service came at either end of my long career in the LFB. I had been posted to Lambeth fire station in 1967. A former junior fireman, Lambeth fire station was my first operational posting after leaving training school at Southwark. Lambeth comprised both a land station and a separate river station. A mere teenager, I loved riding the fire engines and had little interest in the fireboat on the other side of the Albert Embankment. But serving at Lambeth fire station meant doing out-duties to the fireboat if they were short of personnel. But before you could do that you had to undergo a RST course. Whilst

I did everything in my power to avoid this, one day I ran out of options. I was detailed to get over to the float and do my River Service Training (RST) course. I was not a happy man! That said, the memories of the course provide a first-hand account of some of the duties and the operational roll of the river fireman. The training lasted for two complete tours of duty, four day shifts and four night duties. I was not considered a crew member during that time but just the 'boy' under instruction This is a flavour of those two weeks spent on the Thames and the events that occurred on my last night duty.

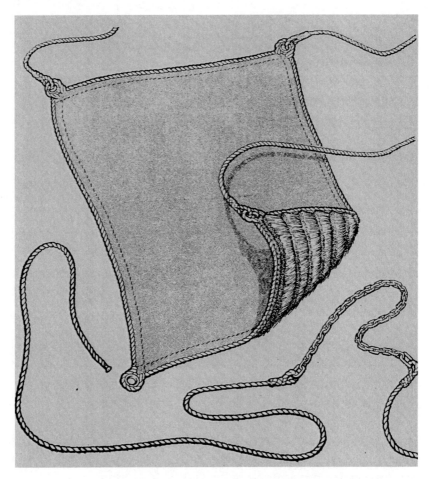

Fireboat collision mat. (Source: HMSO MoF)

Despite my reluctance to spend time on the fireboat I found myself soon eating humble pie. It was far more interesting and informative than I had ever thought possible. Being taken out training on the river was an eye-opening experience. I discovered what a wide range of equipment the fireboat carried, from its pristine breathing apparatus sets to its hot (oxy-acetylene) cutting gear. From coir lines – grass-lines are special ropes that float on water – to collision mats that just might stop a boat disappearing under the water... I learnt of the drills and manoeuvres required of the 'Firebrace' and its fireboat crew. The boat required a qualified coxswain and an engineer at all times, plus, if he was not the coxswain, an officer in charge. Station Officer Ken 'Dodger' Long was the Red Watch's fireboat's governor. He loved the river and was a fount of knowledge regarding all things riparian. His knowledge was encyclopaedic. He was also an excellent trainer and made my course interesting and varied. The days were filled by performing man overboard drills, rowing the skiff whilst pulling hose ashore, pumping vast quantities of water out of the river and putting it back in again. If only the fireboats attended more working jobs it would easily be much more interesting, but as this happened only rather infrequently you can see why I did not relish this particular RST qualification and spending more time than was necessary on the fireboat.

The time passed very quickly. There was so much to absorb, from fenders to anchors; what knot had to be applied to different moorings, like a round turn and two half hitches on a pile, or a rolling hitch on a chain, whilst a waterman's hitch had to secure the skiff to the fireboat. I began to understand the difference between 'steering' and 'sheering' and the importance of 'steerage way'.

New words were added to my fire brigade vocabulary: words like 'abeam', 'athwart', 'bulwark', to the likes of 'gimbals' and 'thwarts'. My time was not wasted and the fireboat crew, who were all former experienced land firemen, clearly took a great pride in what they did and went about their work in a quiet, unassuming, yet totally professional way. I was seeing these old 'floaties' in a completely new light. Then on the last night duty of my short training course I was to see just how hard the fireboat's crew worked when called upon to do so. Although a couple of calls, or 'shouts', had the 'Firebrace' mobilised during those two weeks we never once actually arrived anywhere. We were always returned to base, unwanted and unloved. Late into the evening on my final night duty Lambeth's station bells sang their tune and the dutyman in the station watchroom illuminated a white light. It was a shout for the fireboat.

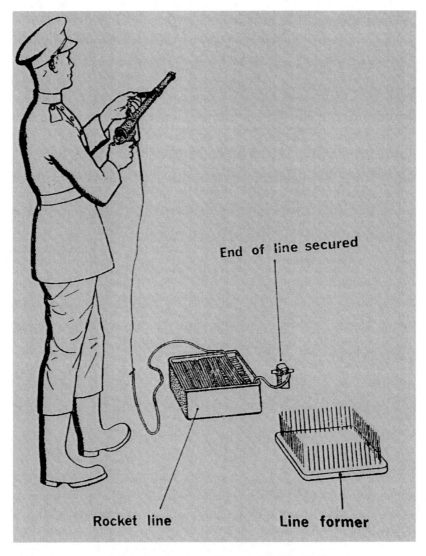

Fireboat rocket line. (Source: HMSO MoF)

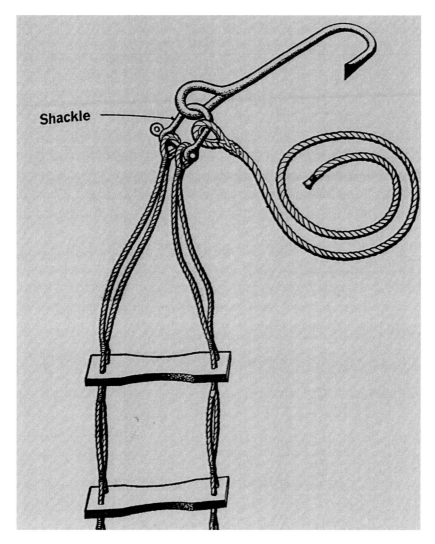

Shackle

Fireboat boarding ladder. (Source: HMSO MoF)

Leaving the land station and crossing Albert Embankment that night, I ran down the gangway onto the pontoon. Whilst the experienced hands cast off the 'Firebrace's' mooring lines I went to the wheelhouse and waited for an opportunity to ask where we were heading. I knew we were going downstream on an ebbing tide, so not all the two weeks' training had been totally wasted. Station Officer Long told the crew that we were ordered to 'Fire in a warehouse, Battle Bridge Lane, Tooley Street, SE1.' The warehouse was upstream and adjacent to Tower Bridge on the south side of the river. The call was on Dockhead's ground. Even with the tide behind us the fireboat was not renowned for its rapid speed and swift arrival at an incident. As we approached Charing Cross railway bridge we heard over the fireboat radio the message transmitted from 'Bravo two-four-two' (Dockhead's pump). It was a priority message making pumps *ten*. Calmly, Station Officer Long announced, 'We've got a job lads', which I thought amusing given that the youngest crew member was at least twenty years senior to me. There were still four bridges to clear, Waterloo, Blackfriars, Southwark and London before we saw Tower Bridge and the blazing warehouse on its southern approach. The tide had now run its course. By the time we reached Southwark Bridge the Thames was at its low water mark. One of the older 'floaties' who was busy making a brew in the galley below called out, 'It means bloody hose ashore by skiff.' It was the first and only time I've had a cup of tea going to a shout!

Wheelhouse of the 'Firebrace'. (Source: HMSO MoF)

Clearing the next bridge, another priority message came over the radio, this time from 'Bravo One Zero' (the B Division BA control van) making pumps fifteen and requesting the ETA of the fireboat. This fire would eventually become a thirty pump fire. 'Blimey, we're wanted,' mused the coxswain whilst trying to get the maximum revs out of his engines. From the wheelhouse we could see the glow illuminating London's night sky and casting strange flickering shadows over Tower Bridge. Navigation charts were pulled from the wheelhouse drawers as the Station Officer and the coxswain conferred and looked for anchorages and low water lines. A message was dispatched to Brigade Control by Station Officer Long giving our ETA as five minutes and requesting instructions from the fireground as to what was required.

As we cleared London Bridge the Hays Wharf head office was on our starboard (right) side, its white clean stonework making it a distinctive feature of the riverside façade alongside the old and dirty buildings that surrounded it. Three large sculptured reliefs, symbolising Capital, Labour and Commerce, fill the centre of the building's river frontage. It was this company's warehouses that totally dominated the vast warehouse and wharfages that run between London and Tower Bridges; these included Chamberlains, Cotton, and Wilson's wharves. Many were now lying idle or empty, their former days of hectic trading and unloading goods from all over the globe now consigned to the history books from when London had been the Port of the Empire. Gaps in the riverscape told the story of those already lost to the ravages of fire; others would follow before developers would once again bring life and wealth back into the area, not least with the creation of London Bridge City and the conversion of warehouses to prestigious inner city apartments and flats.

The fireboat was detailed to lay offshore and supply water to the quayside, to feed the pumps that would redirect the water to crews fighting the fire. The large, ugly brick warehouse was well alight by the time the fireboat stood by at its station laying about fifty yards from the exposed shoreline. The quayside stood thirty feet above the shoreline; here the river frontage, that included Mark Brown's wharf, had enormous baulks of timber sunk into the riverbed. This timber had been used to construct a wooden jetty where once-famous ships, like the 'Baltic Trader', would have moored to discharge their valuable cargoes of goods and commodities. Now it was just rotting and derelict, providing yet another obstacle to getting the hose and much needed water ashore.

The fireboat crew had been busy getting long lengths of flaked three and a half inch hose ready, coiling lengths of grass line that would be used to pull the heavy lengths of canvas hose ashore. The Station Officer had already decided it was too dangerous to use the rocket line from the boat but his crew could use it from the shore to fire over the boat. It would trail a thin line that would be connected ultimately to a grass line that would haul the hose through the water onto the shore. I was seeing at first hand the methodical workings of the boat's crew. On land firemen were frequently like sprinters, going for the quick, all-out physical assault required for a snatch rescue, or the speedy attack on a blaze. But here they were like marathon runners, maintaining a steady powerful rhythm, preparing for the long haul.

The skiff, which had been towed, was now pulled to the side of the fireboat; two hundred feet of flaked hose line was placed aft, the rocket line box placed forward, and wearing lifejackets for the first time four of the crew prepared to row ashore. With the end of the hose line connected to the fireboat's pump outlet they rowed and trailed the hose line out behind them. Crews who were waiting on top of the jetty had lines thrown down to pull up the hose to deliver the desperately needed water. I was watching all this activity, detailed to remain on the fireboat. As the skiff crew reached the shore the first man jumped clear, immediately sinking into slimy ooze that came up to his knees. It took the combined efforts of all four men to haul the single line of hose though the mud to the jetty wall where it was hauled aloft and connected to the first pump. Giving the 'water on' signal the hose was charged with water. It took on the image of a giant python. The hose steadily engorged with water as it snaked a path through the mud-filled foreshore, then rose up and slithered up the jetty wall.

Two of the firemen from the skiff moved onto their next task. Still wading through the oozing mud, they found a vertical, rusted, iron ladder and climbed to the quayside carrying the rocket line in its special carrying box. Positioning themselves opposite the 'Firebrace' they opened the box and removed the hand-held rocket launcher, which looked like a large flare gun. In the box, made up on a special 'former', was a thin nylon line that was secured at one end to the rocket. Taking the former out of the box the line formed a criss-crossed neat pile. With one end tied to the rocket and the other secured on the jetty the fireman holding the rocket gun took aim over the fireboat and pulled the trigger. With a whoosh the rocket passed over the 'Firebrace's' wheelhouse before landing in the river, the line now lying across the fireboat. Pulling in the end attached to the rocket, it was quickly secured to a long line, in turn that line was tied to a 'grass line'. With the coupling of a length of three and half inch hose secured it was pulled back to the fore-shore by the crew on the jetty. With the line of hose connected to a pump the fireboat crew retrieved the grass line and repeated the process again and then again. It had taken almost forty minutes to connect the final length to the second pump, but now an endless supply of water was available to the firegound that the fireboat could, if required, supply at four thousand gallons a minute.

Their initial duties done the skiff crew row back to the fireboat. They were almost unrecognisable, caked from head to toe in stinking river mud and slime and they stank to high heaven. A smiling Station Officer Long told the hard working crew, 'Don't even think about going below until that lot is washed off,' before he returned to the warmth of the wheelhouse to monitor the pump controls.

We pumped water all night. There was little hope of saving the warehouse which had been engulfed in flames. But the firemen successfully prevented its spread to the adjacent warehouses. As dawn broke the early shards of light showed the full extent to which its collapsing empty floors had left high exterior walls dangerously exposed and unsupported. Crews had been withdrawn during the night and reluctantly fought the fire from the outside – not the London way. With the roof finally gone the building was just a shell as the first of the morning commuters were heading into London for the start of another working day.

Fire crews would continue their work and extinguish the last remnants of flame and hot spots make the remains of the building safe for the demolition crews to move in. (The site would, for now, become yet another temporary car park, once the remains of the warehouse were demolished and the land cleared.) With the day shift fireboat crew delivered by personnel carrier and crews exchanged we made our way back, somewhat wearily, to Lambeth. The 'Firebrace' remained at the scene of the firefighting operations for the whole of that day, initially tied up at the jetty and as the tide ebbed she moved back mid-stream on the Thames. My two weeks' familiarisation had ended in style. I had learnt something about the Brigade's fireboats, but more importantly I had learnt about the people that crewed them. I came away with both a greater appreciation of the role of the fireboat and an even greater admiration for the crews who had been, in the main, long-serving land-based firemen who had transferred their skills of firemanship to the fireboat. As river firemen they brought a new dimension to the role of a firefighter, ones that they might not use every day but when they did won my respect and admiration every time.

The Brigade's Lambeth workshop marine engineer checking the 'Firebrace's' engine room. (Source: HMSO-MoF)

Dudgeons Wharf

The morning of the 17th July 1969 was a very warm and sunny day. At 11.22 a.m. Millwall's pump escape and pump, Brunswick Roads pump, the foam tender from East Ham and the fireboat 'Massey Shaw' were dispatched to Dudgeons Wharf on the Isle of Dogs in East London. It would be a nine-nine-nine call and its aftermath that would be forever remembered in the history of London's Fire Brigade.

A fire had broken out in one of the huge oil storage tanks at Dudgeons Wharf, on the Thames waterfront. This wharf was situated on East London's Isle of Dogs and located between the riverfront and Manchester Road. The tank, which was empty but not purged, had a capacity of twenty thousand gallons. The demolition workers believed they had actually put the fire out. The land fire crews, which totalled twelve in number, arrived to make sure it was. At this time the 'Massey Shaw' fireboat was still en route to the scene.

Over one hundred tanks, of various shapes and sizes, had stood on the Dudgeons Wharf site. The demolition contract had been approved and issued, and the contractors had started their work in earnest on the 30th June. Previously, on the 4th of July, a serious fire had occurred at the site, a fire that resulted in eight fire engines and a fireboat attending before it was brought under control and extinguished. The site, on the fateful day, was now in varying stages of demolition.

However, a miscalculation would lead to a horrifying explosion that sent six men – five members of the Brigade and a demolition contractor – to their deaths. They believed that the sixty feet high 'No 97' storage tank in question to be empty and were inspecting the tank when efforts to remove a securing nut from a manhole cover at the base of the tank proved fruitless. A demolition worker started to remove/loosen the nut of the inspection cover using an oxy-propane cutting torch. When the flame of the torch was applied to one of the securing nuts the roof of the tank, on which the firemen and contractor were standing, blew off almost instantaneously, the explosion hurling the six men high into the air.

Ariel view of the Dudgeons Wharf tank farm during demolition.
(Dudgeons Wharf Inquiry Report)

Other fire crews, police and nearby dockers raced to the scene to search for the men. The injured were ferried in a fleet of ambulances to Poplar Hospital. A neighbour, living close by in Manchester Road, reported: *'The explosion rocked our flats, it was just like the Blitz all over again.'* Local mothers ran to the nearby Cubitt Town Primary school, fearful of their children's safety. Wreckage from the blast landed one hundred and fifty feet away from the site of the blast. A demolition worker, who helped find the bodies, was metal-cutter Roy Measom, whose friend Richard Adams, known as Reg, was the demolition worker on the top of the tank and who was killed. He later told news reporters attending the scene, *'When I looked up the firemen were flying around like paper dolls. The air was full of helmets and debris. There was no need to cut into the tank,'* Roy added. *'The fire was out. We should have left it to cool, not take the inspection plate off.'*

In the immediate aftermath of the fatal explosion Station Officer Harold Snelling, who was in charge of Brunswick Road's pump and fireman Ian Richards, who was the driver of East Ham's foam tender, went to the aid of their fallen colleagues. The force of the exploding oil tank had thrown both men off a pathway, down an embankment into a deep pool of oil and water. Station Officer Snelling was completely submerged. Both suffering from shock, they were helped back on their feet by the workmen and the oil was already affecting their eyes. They were told a fireman had fallen into the exploded tank; they climbed a 35 feet high wall into the tank, using tank side ladders, to commence the search. Making their way through thick sludge, many feet deep in places, they reached the half-submerged body of a fireman whom they knew to be dead. Disentangling the body from the wreckage they carried him a dry spot where he could be lifted by line. On being ordered out of the tank they became so ill they had to be removed to hospital for the treatment of shock and the oil in their eyes. For their actions Harold Snelling and Ian Richards were both awarded a Chief Officer's Commendation for their attempted rescue of a fireman at the disaster. Both men were subsequently awarded the British Empire Medal for Gallantry.

The East End went into mourning for its tragic loss. Hundreds of firemen from all over Britain arrived the following week for the funeral of their comrades from Millwall (Sub Officer Michael Gamble and Firemen Alfred Smee), Brunswick Road (Firemen John Appleby and Terence Breen) and from Cannon Street fire station (Fireman Trevor Carvosso – who was standing by at Millwall). They formed a guard of honour four deep as the coffins, draped in Union Jacks, were carried into All Saints Church at Stratford. Crowds lined the East London streets to see the five turntable ladders bearing the coffins arrive, with brass-helmeted trumpeters sounding *The Last Post*. The London Fire Brigade Missionary, Jack Woodgate, spoke of the six men, including civilian Richard Adams, as 'comrades in death'. After the church service, traffic came to a halt and passengers got off buses to pay their respect as the firemen's cortege made its way slowly to the City of London Cemetery. It was the greatest loss of life in the London Fire Brigade from a single incident since the Second World War, three decades before.

Footnote:

In 2009 the London Fire Brigade's Commissioner Ron Dobson formally unveiled a memorial plaque commemorating the site of the Dudgeons Wharf disaster and 'the lives of the six men who on the 17th July 1969 sadly became comrades in death.'

ParaquayStar fire.
1969.
Royal Victoria Docks.

THE DAILY MAIL, TUESDAY, A

T MEAT SHIP

Royal Victoria Docks.

(Pathé)

In 1969 the combined efforts of both the Brigade's fireboats were required at two quite different incidents. The first was a major fire that occurred on the SS 'Paraguay Star' on the 2nd August. (See also page 265.) This ten thousand ton refrigerated cargo and passenger ship, laden with frozen meat and general cargo was berthed in the Royal Victoria Dock when it caught fire. Shortly after 5 a.m. the fire was discovered and three fire engines, a turn-table ladder and emergency tender, plus the 'Massey Shaw' fire-boat from Greenwich were immediately ordered. As soon as the Divisional Commander arrived and saw the seriousness of the fire he made 'pumps fifteen'. Together with the reinforcing fire engines the fireboat 'Firebrace', from Lambeth, was also sent on.

The fire was immensely difficult to tackle. Hazards and dangers were encountered by the firemen at every turn. Oxygen and acety-lene cylinder were soon discovered adjacent to the engine room. Already too hot to handle they had to be made safe and cooled by spray jets.

The severe heat made working conditions for the firemen wearing their one-hour duration oxygen breathing apparatus extremely difficult and exhausting. Both heat stress and heat stoke were a constant danger for those working in the very high temper-atures and humidity in the bowels of the ship. Both the 'Massey Shaw' and the 'Firebrace' were engaged in boundary cooling as the fire scorched and buckled the ship's deck plates and bulkheads. Shortly a message 'make pumps twenty' was sent. BA crews had to contend with not only the severe heat but also with the dense oily smoke that meant visibility was almost non-existent. After fight-ing the fire for some six hours, under the severest of conditions, the strenuous efforts of the firemen had contained the fire to the engine room and machinery space.

In addition to the active firefighting both fireboats' crews assisted with salvage work using their ejector pumps to discharge excess water from the ship, whilst they and the land based emer-gency tenders also supplied auxiliary lighting into the ship. Two foam tenders were also brought into use and numerous relief pumps, each carrying breathing apparatus, attended to relieve the exhausted crews who had in many instances entered the ship twice after changing their oxygen cylinders for a fresh one. It was two days later that the fire was finally extinguished.

Then in November a near-disastrous Thames collision brought the two fireboats back into action together again on a stretch of the Thames, at the very edge of greater London boundary and which separated the counties of Essex and Kent. On a fog-shrouded river the two ships collided. It was twenty-eight minutes past midnight when the motorised barge 'Beefeater', laden with one hundred and twenty thousand gallons of petrol, collided with a Japanese cargo ship, the 'Yamaguchi Maru' being escorted by the tug 'Sun 21'. The impact was so severe it threw the crew of the 'Beefeater' into the winter chilled river.

Calls were received by both Essex and Kent fire brigade controls some seven minutes later. Essex responded to the north shore and Kent went to the Tilbury landing where a Port of London (PLA) fire tug 'Gunfleet' was ordered to take the fire crews out to the collision. Meanwhile the 'Yamaguchi Maru' and the 'Sun 21' had been searching for survivors and had managed to locate and rescue three men from the river. When the 'Gunfleet' arrived on scene it was established that two members of the 'Beefeaters' crew were still missing. At 1 a.m. Kent fire brigade requested the assistance of the LFB. Their call was received by the Brigade control at Lambeth who sent two fire engines from Erith fire station and ordered both the 'Massey Shaw' and the 'Firebrace' fireboats to the scene. Two minutes later Essex fire brigade contacted the LFB's Eastern Command control room at Stratford, seeking assistance. They sent fire engines from Wennington and Hornchurch to the rendezvous point, together with the major control unit and the foam tender from East Ham was moved to Wennington, to be close at hand if required.

The first London officer on the scene sent a message detailing what had occurred, confirmed two men were still missing and requested an ambulance at the scene. At 1.25 a.m. the PLA confirmed that the 'Beefeater' had capsized and was spilling its flammable cargo into the river. With a flood tide carrying the petrol upstream engineers at Littlebrook, Belvedere and Barking power stations and the Ford Motor Company works at Dagenham were warned of the possible dangers. Three Metropolitan police launches patrolled the area warning shipping and people on nearby wharves of the imminent hazards.

With the two fireboats standing by, the capsized 'Beefeater' was successfully beached on the north shore, at about 2.30 a.m. opposite Cunis Wharf. Fire engines on the south side of the river were returned to their stations. However, petrol was still leaking from the barge. By 1040 a.m. a message from the PLA warned that petroleum spirit had moved up river as far as the Royal Docks and the Woolwich Ferry pier. Jets from the two fireboats were used initially to break up the petrol spill on the surface of the water. At 12.30 p.m. the PLA made the decision to tow the damaged barge downstream, where salvage vessels would attempt to right it. PLA divers were brought in and they plugged the vents to prevent any further spillage whilst the barge was relocated. Jets from the fire-boats were again used to prevent any danger of the petrol being ignited whilst this difficult work was being undertaken.

As the salvage work continued the two fireboats remained at the wharf to provide fire-cover for the operations. The incident was finally closed down at 8.01 p.m. the following day. The bodies of the two missing crew members were recovered some days later.

In London's borough of Southwark, the large Surrey Docks finally closed to river traffic in 1970. London's docks were in their death-throes. The age of the riverside industries was almost over. With the changes in delivery systems, the old industries of North Southwark began to close down or relocate. It is estimated that half of the manufacturing jobs in Southwark alone were lost in the period from 1971 to 1986. Other London riverside boroughs quoted similar statistics. By the mid-1980s all the local major manufacturing factories were vanishing, leaving large areas of industrial wasteland. Along the riverbank, the empty wharves ran from Blackfriars Bridge to the middle of the Rotherhithe Penin-sula, from Wapping to Silvertown. In those affected boroughs, warehouses and factories, which had once dominated the local life of the area, stood empty and derelict. Alongside this ran the closure of local shops and social clubs, cinemas and recreational centres, leaving housing estates often isolated in the middle of nowhere, especially in those areas once dominated by London's formerly thriving docks.

The 'Firebrace' attending a major fire at St Johns Wharf adjacent to the Metropolitan river police station, Wapping in the 1970s. (L. Bradbury)

(Source: London Evening News)

Reviewing London's fire cover was not new; both the London County Council and later the Greater London Council (GLC) had required the Brigade to undertake such studies. In the review of 1969/70 the GLC considered that there were cases where the Brigade afforded cover higher than the national guidelines. These reviews were, in part, driven by pressure from the government for fire authorities to find ways of reducing or revising cover to the minimum levels. The government's intention was simple, to save money. Yet despite this pressure, and the reduction on some of London's land-based fire cover, the GLC decided to retain its two fireboats, the 'Firebrace' and the 'Fireflair' (the former London Auxiliary fire service fireboat). The 'Massey Shaw' had by then reached the end of its economic life and had been withdrawn from service.

The 'Firebrace' became involved in London's largest fire of the decade when on a hot August afternoon it was in the initial attendance to a fire in Wilson's Wharf, Battle Bridge Lane, Tooley Street. It proved to be one of the fiercest and most difficult fires that the post-war London Fire Brigade ever had to face. It would last nearly thirty hours, involving all three watches It was ironic that this should be the same location that cost the life of the Brigade's very first Chief Officer, James Braidwood, when in 1861 he was buried under a collapsed wall in a warehouse blaze that took several days to bring under control. (The Brigade was then called the London Fire Engine Establishment.)

Wilson's Wharf was built on the site of that first devastating fire, part of the Hays Wharf Company's great rebuilding scheme, and had opened in 1868. Starting life as a coffee and cocoa wharf it later became the company's first wine and spirit bottling department. Just over a century later it now lay unoccupied, having previously undergone conversion to a refrigerated warehouse and major cold store.

For the day (White) watch that afternoon station routines had been underway for nearly an hour; some stations performing drills, others considerably extending their lunchtime game of volleyball. Some stations pumps were unavailable for calls, either because they were engaged in outside inspections or 'off the run' (not available) waiting repair of a mechanical defect at the station or to be repaired at Lambeth workshops. When the 'bells went down' at Dockhead, Southwark and Cannon Street fire stations only their pump escapes were available to attend the call that would eventually summon another one hundred fire engine crews to the scene.

Those three machines responded at 2.48 p.m. and were joined by a turntable ladder from Barbican fire station. But already the blaze was drawing considerable attention as it rapidly gained a hold in the warehouse's interior. With the second of many subsequent calls received, Brigade control sent on Whitechapel's pump and Lambeth's fireboat 'Firebrace'.

The six-storey warehouse had an irregular shape and sat tightly wedged between other wharfs. On the riverside was a wide vehicular jetty where previously goods and products had been delivered to its one hundred and fifty foot wide riverside access. It was also one hundred and fifty feet from this side of the building to the far side, which faced Tooley Street. Various raised open and covered iron bridges were connected to surrounding wharves. Unable to stem the rapidly developing fire with an extinguisher, contractors beat a hasty retreat from the building, leaving their oxy-acetylene cutting plant in situ. It was sparks from their hot cutting that had ignited combustible tape on the pipe-work insulation. It had spread to the building's insulation material itself, four-inch thick, very flammable expanded rubber. Even as the contractors were running out of Wilson's Wharf and as fire crews drew closer, the hot and smoky atmosphere was being trapped inside this now disused cold store. The windows and loopholes had been bricked up, making the building a veritable fortress, turning large parts of the complex into a vast brick oven, superheating the interior.

Five minutes after the first call was made the officer in charge made 'pumps four, BA required.' With crews unable to make an easy entry into the building and with the smoke thickening by the minute, pumps were made eight, two minutes after 3 p.m. (The new-style BA guidelines were about to get their baptism by fire, if the crews could actually penetrate into the warehouse, that is.) These modified guide lines had pieces of string bound into the line. Placed at regular intervals were two sets of tags, set six inches apart: two long tags and two knotted tags. Getting 'knotted' was the rule of thumb to finding your way out.

With the fireboat arrived and awaiting instructions, concerted efforts were being made to enter the building despite the heavy smoke pouring from all the available openings on the third and fourth floors. After thirty minutes of fruitless searching by BA teams, probing in the hot but accessible areas of the warehouse there was still no sign of fire, just the constant build-up of intense heat. As more appliances arrived, sweating men laid out more lines of hose to increase the number of jets available. The fireboat now moored against the jetty of Wilson's Wharf was already supplying its maximum discharge from its two massive pumps. Firemen were using the interconnecting bridges to direct jets into the conflagration, they themselves being protected by water spray from other jets from the turntable ladder and from pumps.

In the space of forty-five minutes pumps went from fifteen, to twenty, and then thirty. Command of the fire changed hands so quickly that no single plan of action could be properly implemented until the Chief Officer, Joe Milner, finally took command at 4.16 p.m. He faced daunting problems, taxing even his considerable know-how of commanding major incidents from his time in charge of the Hong Kong Fire Brigade. He had all his Headquarters' principal officers at his disposal, including the Deputy Chief. It would take their combined experience and expertise to direct operations at this incident, which was now extremely serious, due to the complex layout of the building, the thickness of the walls and lack of access points. The heat build-up, deep inside the structure, was likened to a potter's kiln operating at its maximum temperature.

Despite the tenacity and doggedness of the firemen, the tremendous heat and smoke posed major problems for any of the crews fighting to establish a bridgehead to counter the blaze. Contractors working alongside firemen tried to break open some of the bricked-up windows at third floor level with elementary breaking-in gear, club hammers and cold chisels, but little or no progress was made. Meanwhile those BA crews that had made exploratory forays into the building were slowly being forced back out by conditions so severe that their exposed skin blistered.

Two workmen came forward with pneumatic drills in an attempt to break through the bricked-up windows. They assisted firemen and worked in the most difficult conditions for nearly thirty minutes before they had to be withdrawn for their own safety as precarious and unstable cracks appeared in the walls above them.

The smell of the fire was ever-present anywhere in the vicinity of London Bridge. For those starting to come into their fire stations, ready for the Blue Watch night shift, the teleprinter messages in the station watchroom conveyed the story of the afternoon's events in stiff fire brigade speak. What the messages could not convey was the true extent of the gruelling and arduous conditions that the crews and officers were having to struggle against. In truth they were fighting a battle that would be near impossible to win.

The fire had brought both Headquarters' day related officers and Lambeth's night shift firemen alike to the viewing gallery of the Brigade control, in the basement of Lambeth HQ. All were keen to connect with this breaking news story that was only two station grounds away. The activity within the control was composed yet the control staff appeared tense, not because they were being watched, but because they knew the fireground messages conveyed far more meaning and drama than the simple wording that the informative messages portrayed. The whole control room hushed as the priority message from the Brigade control unit was received by the control room radio operator. All eyes turned to him as he told the control unit to go ahead with its priority message. 'From the Chief Officer at Wilson's Wharf, Battle Bridge Lane, make pumps fifty.' The radio operator repeated the message back and timed the message at 5.12 p.m. Gasps of surprise filled the viewing gallery.

The Brigade's Senior Control Officer of the watch organised the mobilisation of the next twenty pumps, then set about the task of arranging standby appliances to cover empty stations. The special cover stations retained their pump escapes but there were lots of empty stations all over central London. Restricted mobilising (where reduced attendances were sent to all calls) had been in operation since the make pumps thirty but another large incident up could see the fire cover in London reach desperate, possibly dangerous, levels. This is something that the Chief was well aware of, as he had at one stage considered making pumps 'eighty', which would have been unprecedented in peacetime fire-fighting in London.

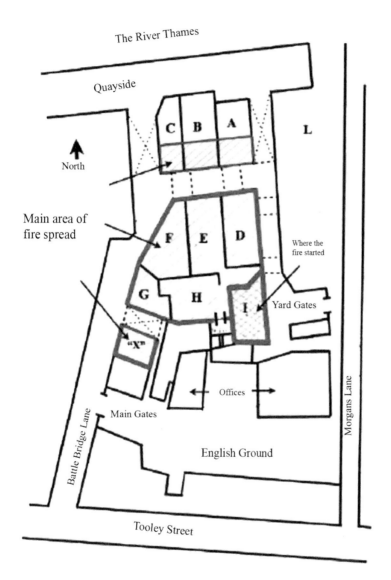

Plan of the Tooley Street fire. (Stephen Jacob)

That evening at many London fire stations there was no fire engine to ride. All station routines had been cancelled and early suppers ordered in anticipation of reliefs being ordered to the fire. Special arrangements were made to get the Blue Watch night

343

shift fireboat crew to the 'Firebrace' and bring the day shift crew back to Lambeth. As the 6 p.m. roll call was being taken a violent flashover occurred in the warehouse; whether it was the acetylene cylinders exploding or the massive build-up of flammable gases from the insulation igniting was never determined. Nonetheless three BA firemen working from a covered bridge-way connecting two warehouses were injured. One was rushed to hospital suffering serious burns to his hands and face.

The fire was now so severe that crews were concentrated on confining the spread of the fire to an area bounded by Battle Bridge Lane, English Lane and the river. Several floors of the building had collapsed and fire was finally breaking through the building's face at ground, first and second floor levels. After the change of watch the organisation of getting the day shift crews returned to their stations and exchanging them with the night shift personnel added to the pressures on the control unit staff. Maintaining the attack on the fire was vital; any weakness in the containment now being put in place would allow it to quickly spread to surrounding property.

By 7 p.m. large cracks had opened up in the eastern and southern walls of the warehouse. Whilst belching flame and smoke, the release of pent-up heat enabled crews to make better progress with the assault on the fire in the surrounding sections of the complex. These were the scenes that greeted us when the pump, which I was riding prearranged overtime, then Lambeth's Emergency Tender, returned to the scene. Parked fire engines filled Tooley Street. Others were arriving, some preparing to return weary crews to their station, to exchange crews and immediately return. Some crews, tired, wet, grimy and smoke-stained, were cradling cups of tea in their hands. Others, clearly exhausted, sat in the street, some dunking biscuits in mugs of tea, whilst many were having a well-earned drag on a cigarette or pulling their trusty pipe from an inside tunic pocket. Senior officers, looking equally weary, mixed freely with the firemen and chatted, unified in battling a common foe.

Some of the relief pump crews arrived around the same time, 7 p.m. They carried their BA sets over their shoulders as they negotiated their way over a multitude of hose lines that filled the narrow access lanes. It was a tribute to the accuracy of the hand drawn fireground plan displayed on the Brigade's control unit that they found the crews they were relieving in the general area indicated. As one crew neared its position and passed under a connecting bridge, two white-helmeted figures emerged from the swirling thick smoke above. The Deputy Chief, accompanied by his staff officer (wearing a walkie-talkie radio on his back), crawled out from the smoky second floor, leaned over the iron bridge, retched violently, before both turned around and crawled back in again.

So intense was the fire at this stage that complaints of smoke drifts were received as far away as Bethnal Green in East London and there were reports of smoke drifting into some underground stations in the City. The mixed cacophony of sound was even punishing the firemen's hearing. The loud cracking of timbers, the crashing of internal walls, the humming of pumps working at high pressure, combined with the thud of the jets hitting brick walls. The echo of these sounds reverberated in the confined spaces they were working in. It seemed to be trying to drown out the frightening noise of the fire but failing, which rose above the sound of everything else. This fire had become a whole body experience, affecting every one of the firefighter's five senses: sound, sight, touch, smell and taste.

Suddenly the attention of those on the ground was drawn to movement on the overhead connecting bridges as firemen ran away from the fire then, dropping one level, ran back into the building. It transpired that a Sub Officer, who had been moving in the smoke across the sagging floor, had suddenly stumbled, overbalanced and fallen through the already weakened floor on to the debris laying on the floor below. What those below saw was the prompt actions of his crew, retracing their steps and gaining access to the first floor. They crawled their way through the debris to comfort him as he was placed on an improvised stretcher and carried, in considerable pain, to safety and the first aid area.

Just before 9 p.m. the situation seemed to have improved and Joe Milner sent the 'fire surrounded' message. Crews were re-deployed at this stage to prevent the fire from 'jumping' across the narrow Battle Bridge Lane to adjoining premises.

Now radial branches, looking like military mortars, were throwing vast quantities of water on to the burning building, many fed by the fireboat still on station mid-stream. As the flames reduced so, like skirmishing troops, the crews moved forward consolidating the bridgeheads gained earlier. The building, once red with anger, was now obscured by dense rolling smoke as the cooling water overcame the flames, the choking smoke blinding the weary firemen as they moved closer at every opportunity, going for the final kill.

By the time the next phase of reliefs came the fire in the complex had been subdued. It was now confined to the top three floors of a warehouse in the corner of the site. Crews continued to be exchanged throughout the 11th and 12th August, extinguishing pockets of fire. Relief crews continued the work until only the smouldering ruins, tall, gaunt and with dangerously cracked walls, belched out nothing but steam. The last pumps left the scene at 5 p.m. on the 12th August.

The damage to the complex consisted of three-quarters of all the floors being severely damaged by fire, heat, smoke and water; half the roof was destroyed. Twenty jets, eight radial branches and two hundred Proto BA sets had been used to quell the blaze. National newspaper reports, covering the fire, said that *'three hundred firemen had fought the blaze of the century on the banks of the Thames and that three firemen were injured.'* There was little or no follow up news. The incident was not considered sufficiently newsworthy, despite the fact that the effort of containing the conflagration took three days and only the actions of London's firemen prevented it being a blaze of catastrophic proportions.

Despite the lack of recognition from the nation's press, such was the nature of this incident, with its organisational affects, that the Chief Officer sent a general teleprinter message to reflect his appreciation of the hard work from all those involved in what proved to be a most testing period for the capital's fire brigade.

'TO ALL STATIONS, DIVISIONS, COMMANDS, BRIGADE TRAINING CENTRE.
GENERAL MESSAGE.
FROM THE CHIEF OFFICER.

I SEND MY SINCERE COMPLIMENTS AND APPRECIA-TION TO ALL MEMBERS OF THE BRIGADE ON THE DILI-GENCE WITH WHICH THEY HAVE MET THE ABNOR-MALLY ARDUOUS DEMANDS OF THE LAST 36 HOURS. THE DETERMINATION AND FORTITUDE OF PERSON-NEL AT THE TOOLEY STREET FIRE AND THE TIRELESS DEDICATION WITH WHICH ALL OTHER OPERATIONAL PERSONNEL AND CONTROL ROOM STAFF HAVE MET THE ADDITIONAL DEMANDS ON THEIR RESOURCES AND STAMINA ARE A PLEASING COMMENTARY ON OUR 'ESPRIT DE CORPS' AND ARE IN KEEPING WITH THE HIGHEST TRADITIONS OF THE BRIGADE.

I WILL TAKE THE EARLIEST OPPORTUNITY OF REPRE-SENTING MY APPRECIATION OF YOUR VERY FINE WORK TO THE GREATER LONDON COUNCIL. MEANWHILE THE CHAIRMAN OF THE FIRE BRIGADES COMMITTEE HAS ASKED ME TO CONVEY TO YOU ALL HIS PERSONAL ADMIRATION OF YOUR EFFORTS AND DEVOTION TO DUTY.

J MILNER. CHIEF OFFICER.'

During 1971/72 the then Ministry of Technology engaged in a feasibility study on the use of a Hovercraft firefighting capability in the London Fire Brigade, either to replace or supplement its existing fireboat cover. The study decided that if a Hovercraft were to be brought into service it could be based at the new fire station being proposed for the City of London, one that was to replace the Cannon Street station in Queen Victoria Street which had been earmarked for closure. Named Dowgate, the new fire station was incorporated into the Mondial House development that was built to accommodate Europe's largest telecommunications and switching centre. Mondial House was designed to withstand attacks from the IRA and was, at the time, considered one of central London's most famous eyesores. It was once described by Prince Charles as resembling a 'Typewriter'. Dowgate fire station remains located in Upper Thames Street, on the Thames riverbank. The Hovercraft, despite extensive trials, never saw the light of day. The general prevailing financial climate was the principal factor for the Greater London Council (GLC) not progressing the Hovercraft option at that time. They never did.

THE HOVERING FIREFIGHTER

(Source: London Evening News*)*

In 1971, after thirty-six years, the 'Massey Shaw' was withdrawn from service. The 'Fireflair' was the replacement boat at the

Greenwich river station. In the same year the Chief Officer, Joe Milner, undertook a combined study of waterborne provision and helicopter support. The GLC was considering the use of helicopters in the discharge of its various statutory authority responsibilities, e.g. highways surveys. The helicopter was considered to provide support which would including assisting firefighting and rescue tactics including river incidents. The helicopter options, whilst considered an effective provision, fell victim of cost-saving considerations and was not formally pursued by the GLC.

Footnote:

The London Fire Brigade did eventually bring helicopters into use in a trial operational role. The reviews were mixed with the final consideration being its cost effectiveness compared to its operational role. Cost outweighed its use so the idea was scrapped. In the current financial climate there are no plans by London's Fire Authority to revive the scheme.

Of significance at this time was the Brigade's evaluation of 'Sea Trucks'. This was a fast landing craft, constructed in glass reinforced polyester which afforded a high degree of reserve buoyancy. It had a speed of thirty-five knots and carried two light portable pumps with a combined capacity of 2720 litres (600 gallons) per minute. The craft was extensively trialled during 1972 and found great favour with the Lambeth-based crews. The report presented to the GLC's Fire Brigade Committee sought a positive recommendation for its introduction to the Brigade. The considerable advantages of this vessel were stated as being;

- Its comparatively shallow draft;
- Its considerable speed with minimal wash and freedom from PLA restrictions in its use on the Thames;
- Its flexibility and versatility in getting hose ashore;
- The 35 feet model provided an enhanced load capacity with minimal reduction in speed efficiency.

When tested by the Greenwich fireboat crews the Sea Truck experienced extensive hull damage during the trials. This, it was alleged, was due to inappropriate handling and grounding on the Thames shorelines. However, the outboards were two six cylinder Mercury's engines and they ran them without any water cooling and literally melted the cylinder head of one. Following this substantial damage marine engineers, brought in to investigate, found 'the *Sea Truck had been driven to destruction'*. They stated that despite its military application, they had never seen one in such condition. A senior LFB officer is reported to have told the marine engineers that it was often stated that you could give a fireman two indestructible steel ball-bearings, put him in an empty enclosed room, and he would lose one and break the other! The marine engineers did not argue with the officer. No GLC funding was forthcoming for the necessary repairs and all future trials were discontinued. No charges were brought on those alleged to have allowed the damage to occur.

In 1975 the 'Fireflair' was sold off and one year later the 'Firebrace' followed a similar path. After much debate two craft of an identical design were purchased as replacement fireboats; they were the 'Fire Hawk' and 'Fire Swift'. The first to arrive was the 'Fire Swift' that went to Greenwich, the 'Fire Hawk' taking up her station at Lambeth in 1976. These sister craft were just forty-five feet in length, with mono hulls made from glass-reinforced plastic; both had a maximum pumping capacity of one thousand two hundred gallons per minute. They were built by Watercraft Ltd, in Shoreham, West Sussex. The 'Swift' had cost the GLC forty-five thousand pounds; a year later the cost had risen to sixty thousand pounds for the 'Hawk'.

Footnote:
In an issue of the magazine Motor Boat and Yachting, *a south Devonshire couple saw an advertisement that the GLC had placed for the purchase, by tender, of the former London fireboat 'Firebrace'. The boat's specification exceeded their wildest dreams of securing a suitable craft to use as a workshop, living space and office accommodation, part of their project to make a small harbour for yachts at Torpoint on the River Tamar in Plymouth. Five thousand pounds had been their ceiling for a suitable craft, but after adding a couple hundred more they sent off their sealed bid to the GLC. A telephone call told them that their bid had been*

accepted and that they were now the new owners of this 'Firebrace'. All they had to do now was to get her back to south Devon. At three thousand pounds for the road transport costs that was quickly ruled out of the question. They simply could not afford it.

Collecting the 'Firebrace' from her Lambeth moorings the new Devonshire owners were overwhelmed by the kindness and hospitality afforded them by the Lambeth river firemen, who were clearly delighted, and relieved, that their former fireboat was not to be broken up; but was, with some minor additions, to be used as she was. It was an emotional farewell for some of the river firemen who watched their beloved fireboat cast off and steer downstream towards new permanent home. In fact some river firemen even helped the new owners on the first leg of their journey. Most notable was Tom Bell, a Sub Officer on the river, who had taken the trouble to get the new owners familiar with the 'Firebrace'. At Woolwich the 'Fire Swift' joined the 'Firebrace' and escorted the former London fireboat to the Greater London river boundary.

The boat made good progress down the Thames, having refuelled en route. It was now getting dark and at Canvey Island the real navigation started, going from buoy to buoy. They had to use the 'Firebrace's' searchlight to find the buoys and more than once found themselves stuck on a mudflat. But the 'Firebrace's' powerful engines managed to pull them for backwards. The following morning, at 1.00 a.m. and having continued throughout the night they found themselves near the Goodwin Sands off Folkestone, and with an engine bleeding oil at an alarming rate. Buckets and washing up bowls were placed strategically around the engine and the oil put back into the fuel tank.

London Fire Brigade fireboat 'Fire Hawk' on her sea trials. (Malc Burden)

That morning, with calm seas and warm sunshine they continued past the south of the Isle of Wight before the next problem struck. The fuel pump packed up. It was only with a great deal of 'Heath Robinson' engineering skills that a solution was found and the boat continued its onward journey. The mid-day weather forecast did not bode well as a deep low pressure system was heading their way from the Azores. By evening time it had arrived and the boat was off Portland Bill and the bad weather arrived. By now the forward monition of the boat was driving her bows down into the oncoming sea. As the seas rose the waves washed right over the boat. Waterfalls of water swept into the accommodation windows. This was not the normal River Thames environment for the old fireboat. The heavy seas were giving her a decidedly uncomfortable motion that some aboard found difficult to contend with.

With both the wind and sea becoming more 'lumpy' over the next two hour they contacted the Brixham Coastguard. The Coastguard informed the crew that a Force Nine was heading their way, and it would be imprudent for the 'Firebrace' to stay out in the open water. Slowly heading for the relative safety of Brixham the Firebrace's crew nevertheless had to endure two and half hours of the most uncomfortable rolling as they made for calmer waters. Finally, sheltering in the lee of large fishing vessel, they were able to turn in for a couple of hours of much needed sleep.

As the final morning dawned bright and sunny they made for their destination, Ballast Pond at Torpoint. However, the weather and the sea conditions were not going to let them off lightly. Rounding Start Point the swell came sickeningly on to the beam of the boat, something they endured for the next seven hours. With their safe arrive at the boatyard there was a feeling of pride and achievement in bring the 'Firebrace' to her new home. A home where she still remains today.

In July 1979 the Conservative-controlled GLC published a public consultation paper on the 'Future Development of the London Fire Brigade'. The service had moved to a two-shift, four-watch, forty-two hour week, from the previous two-shift, three-watch, and forty-eight hour week. Increased staffing costs to cover the forth watch was met, in part, by a drastic reduction in the number of London's fire engines and its specialist appliances.

Once again the reduction, and changes in the nature of the risks on and alongside the River Thames led the GLC's Fire Brigade

Committee to believe that the river service required change. Reviewing its fireboat provision, and in response to the government's continuing fiscal pressures, it drew up policies to take account of the significant changes to the nature of London's riparian and river risks. Subsequently the downriver station, which had been moved from Woolwich to Greenwich Pier in 1963, was closed. The Brigade's only remaining fireboat station was at Lambeth, despite serious concerns as to the site's suitability covering the operational effectiveness of the downstream fire cover provision. This reduction in the number and changes to the nature of the fire risks led the GLC to the conclusion it was sensible for the LFB to enter into contractual arrangements for the provision of a firefighting vessel/fire tug for its downstream fire cover. Kent and Essex fire brigades had at the time similar arrangements. Whilst many of the service cuts did take place, the removal of dedicated fireboats in London was not one of them.

'Fire Swift', sister craft of the 'Fire Hawk'. **(London Fireman *Magazine*)**

Footnote:
After their disposal both the boats were converted to commercial use. The 'Fire Hawk' currently resides in Falmouth, whilst the 'Fire Swift' was last reported residing in Gibraltar.

The start of the New Year in 1980 brought with it tragic consequences for one member of the London Fire Brigade. In its history the London Fire Brigade only ever had one fireman perish in a ship fire. His name was Stephen Maynard. He was a Leading Fireman serving on the Red Watch Poplar fire station, in East London. He died aged twenty-six years of age.

The motor vessel 'Rudi M' was an eight hundred ton Panamanian registered liquid gas tanker, and in the winter of 1979/80 she had come into Regents Canal Dock, off the River Thames in East London, to undergo a re-fit.

On the 17th January, the crews from Poplar Fire Station (F22) received a call to a ship fire in Regents Canal Dock. The dock was located on Poplar's fire station ground. The fire was caused by workers using hot cutting equipment within the ship. It was quickly tackled by the crews and extinguished. Work on the boat continued throughout the following week until the fateful morning of the 25th January.

The Red Watch at Poplar had reported for duty at their normal time, 6 p.m. on Thursday, 24 January. Station Officer Tony

The fatal fire on board the Rudi M in Limehouse Basin.
(London Fire Brigade)

354

Westbrook was the officer in charge; his junior officers that night were Sub Officer Dennis Hurley, his deputy, and Leading Firemen John Bailey and Stephen (Steve) Maynard the junior officers. It was a typically busy night for Poplar, with a number of calls in and around the station's ground and the pump, with the Station Officer in charge, spending a large part of the night fighting a twenty-five pump fire at the Chelsea Flour Mills in West London.

That Friday morning saw what looked like a clear day ahead and around 8.30 a.m. a number of the oncoming Green Watch started to appear for their day shift that commenced at 9 a.m. Having had a long, busy, night duty a few of the Red Watch had been relieved early by members of the Green Watch now riding for Red Watch personnel.

At 8.55 a. m. a call was received at the Stratford Fire Control from workers on the 'Rudi M'. There was a fire in the ship's hold. Once again the contractors had accidentally set alight to insulating material in the ship's tank.

The bells went down at Poplar fire station ordering its pump escape and pump, together with the pump from Shadwell fire station to the fire. Upon their arrival the fire was evident in the hold of the ship. A four man breathing apparatus crew consisting of Leading Fireman Maynard and a fireman from Poplar's Red Watch with Poplar's Green Watch Sub Officer and one of his firemen. The crew entered the ship, taking with them a firefighting jet.

Conditions within the hold were exceptionally hot, very smoky and visibility at zero. One of the firemen withdrew to the jetty to get a pair of gloves but was ordered by Station Officer Westbrook to go back down into the ship and get the breathing apparatus crew to withdraw. The fireman returned to the hold and passed on the Station Officer's order. The two Green watch members exited first, followed by the Red Watch fireman with Leading Fireman Maynard bringing up the rear. Upon reaching the top of the ship's ladder the fireman noticed that Steve Maynard was not behind him. He immediately went back down the ladder into the ship.

All of a sudden the hold of the ship erupted into flame and dense smoke. The fireman was badly burned. Leading Fireman Maynard did not manage to escape; he tragically lost his life.

Footnote:
In 2010 members of Steve's family, retired members who attended the fire, local senior and principal LFB officers lined up the side of the dock as a new plaque to commemorate the anniversary of Steve's death was unveiled. The Limehouse Basin, the scene of the Rudi M fire, had changed totally from the time of the fire but the memories for that tragic incident hadn't.

Within three months London's firefighters fought their second major ship fire, although thankfully not fatal this time. On the 27th April 1980 a fire started on the 'Old Caledonia', a former paddle-steamship, moored on the Victoria Embankment and converted into a floating restaurant. The fire rapidly engulfed the vessel, spreading throughout the length if the ship. Crews tackled the blaze from both land and river, but the ship could not be saved. Ironically the ship that was to replace the 'Old Caledonia' suffered a similar fate. Whilst in Bute dry-dock in Cardiff the turbine steamer, 'King George V', built in 1921, caught fire and was destroyed.

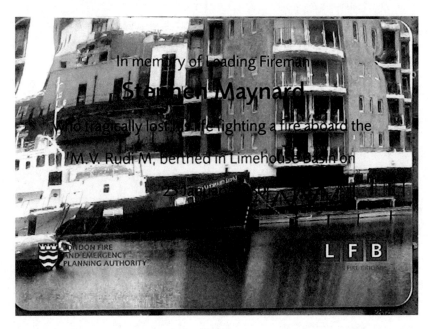

(Author)

The 'Caledonia' 'restaurant' ship fire on the Victoria Embankment.
(Gerald Paul)

Up until the 1980s London's fireboat crews took great pride in knowing their ground, or in the river firefighter's case, knowing their waterways. They knew the various nooks and crannies that made up the River Thames; where they could navigate and where they couldn't. In addition to the various skills that made them effective firefighters they were also required to know the state of the river, its ebb and flood tides and the Thames's powerful tidal flows and eddies.

One such nook still remains: St Saviour's Dock. It is a small dock located on the south bank of the River Thames, some 420 metres east of Tower Bridge. It was where the Neckinger River enters the Thames. Today it forms the eastern end of the picturesque and historic Bermondsey embankment which starts at Tower Bridge known as Shad Thames. On the other side of the Dock is Jacob's Island.

The area was once notoriously squalid. It was often described as 'the very capital of cholera' and 'the Venice of drains'. In the mid-1800s it was covered with a scum almost like a cobweb, and prismatic with grease. Charles Dickens famously set portions of his novel *Oliver Twist* in the area of Shad Thames, at a time when it was an area of notorious poverty known as Jacob's Island. Dickens gave a vivid description of what this unsavoury place must have looked like at the time of the novel in 1837:

> *'[...] crazy wooden galleries common to the backs of half a dozen houses, with holes from which to look upon the slime beneath; windows, broken and patched, with poles thrust out, on which to dry the linen that is never there; rooms so small, so filthy, so confined, that the air would seem to be too tainted even for the dirt and squalor which they shelter; wooden chambers thrusting themselves out above the mud and threatening to fall into it – as some have done; dirt-besmeared walls and decaying foundations, every repulsive lineament of poverty, every loathsome indication of filth, rot, and garbage: all these ornament the banks of Jacob's Island.'*

The dock would have been familiar to generations of London's river firemen, especially those from the former 'Beta III' river station at Cherry Gardens Pier. The Dock had previously been the setting of many a major riverside warehouse fire, most notably the Concordia Wharf fire.

Whilst the Dock area was in the process of considerable regeneration the previous history of the area was the last thing on the mind of Sub Officer Ian Pettit as he reported for duty on the evening of Monday 16th July 1984. He had been detailed to ride in charge of the 'Fire Hawk' fireboat at Lambeth's river station together with its White Watch crew. He was unaware of it then, but he and his crew were going to be the last to have a working role at a major fire in the 'Fire Hawk' which, together with her sister craft the 'Fire Swift', were about to be replaced by a new generation fireboat – the 'London Phoenix'.

The role of a London river firefighter had been greatly devalued by the Brigade's management policies by the 1980s. Lambeth was the only river station, the mooring for both the 'Fire Hawk' and her sister craft the 'Fire Swift'. It was more a berth than a separate fire station. The fireboat no longer warranted its own dedicated crew. The personnel at Lambeth fire station might be riding a land fire engine one day and the fireboat the next. Its crews did get some training; the firefighters got a whole two days! The boat's coxswains did undertake an intensive four-weeks assessed course in boat-handling skills and river-based knowledge. But the rot was about to stop. The new fireboat was nearing its completion and would soon start her sea trials. The policy of alternate crewing would, before long, be reversed and Londoners would, once again, benefit from dedicated river firefighters.

1984 proved to be a pivotal year in the history of the Brigade. Later that year would come the fatal King Cross fire and the tragic loss of so many lives including that of Station Officer Colin J Townsley, from Soho fire station, who was posthumously awarded the George Medal. That fire would bring about radical changes both to London Underground but also the London firefighters' uniform. The brigade's hook ladders were removed from its fire engines and consigned to the history books, as were the London Salvage Corps (LSC). Created in the same year as the Metropolitan Fire Brigade in 1866 (under Captain Massey Shaw), the LSC were disbanded by their owners, the insurance companies.

The Fireboat 'Fire Hawk' at her Lambeth moorings. (Craig Bert Weeden)

The 999 telephone call to a fire in Java Wharf in Shad Thames, Bermondsey was received by the control room staff in the fire brigade control, located at Croydon, in the very early hours of Tuesday morning. The Croydon control staff were responsible for receiving all emergency calls and mobilising fire engines south of the River Thames. Details of the Shad Thames call were entered onto the control officers mobilising screen; a call which was on Dockhead's fire stations' ground. With the necessary details verified by the mobilising officer the required station call bells were actuated from the control room, whilst simultaneously the selected fire station teleprinters started to print out the ordering slips to the incident. One such station where the bells had awakened slumbering firefighters was Lambeth. Its fireboat formed part of the predetermined attendance for all fire calls to Shad Thames.

Dockhead fire station is located in Wolseley Street, a stone's throw from St Saviour's Dock, albeit on the eastern side of it. As Dockhead's crews sped up to Tooley Street, turned right, and then right again into Shad Thames and Java Wharf, the 'Fire Hawk' had cast off her mooring lines and Firefighter Chris Savage, the fireboat's coxswain, had cleared Lambeth Bridge and was heading down river on the remains of that night's flood tide – a tide that would attempt to impede the 'Fire Hawk's' progress. The other fire engines that made up the initial attendance were hastening through the deserted Bermondsey and Rotherhithe streets towards Java Wharf.

With some distance still to cover the crew of the 'Fire Hawk' were monitoring the boats radio and they knew that they now had a working job on their hands. The priority message had just told them so. The first officer in command had discovered a serious fire situation at Java Wharf and immediately summoned reinforcing fire engine crews. Other such messages would follow as the crews struggled to contain the intense fire devouring the wharf.

As Chris Savage coaxed extra revs out the 'Fire Hawk's' engines, Sub Officer Pettit conferred with him over the navigation maps checking water depths, which on a flood tide they both knew would be favourable, at least for now.

By London Bridge the fireboat crew could see the glow of the blaze in the night sky. What they could not see, but knew was happening, were the strenuous efforts being made by the firefighters at the scene to secure a bridgehead in their attack on this all-consuming fire. Whilst the building had lain vacant and empty for some time there was every reason to suspect the fire could, and would, spread to the five- and six-storey adjoining terrace warehouses unless the fire was contained, and swiftly too. However, despite their determination and tireless persistence the firefighters were hampered in their efforts. The access they had to Java Wharf was only from the street frontage in Shad Thames. Java Wharf had been built right on the side of St Saviour's Dock. There was no pathway, no landing area at the rear. It was also flanked by other equally tall wharves standing right on the edge of the Dock. The land firefighters had no viable access to the rear, especially as the Dock was now full of water.

With almost one hundred firefighters and fire officers on one side of the blaze the 'Fire Hawk', and its crew of six, pulled into the Dock. Chris Savage navigated its restricted opening and Sub Officer Pettit made an assessment of the predicament that he had found himself in. He issued crisp instructions and from the opposite dock wall, and tied up, the 'Fire Hawk' crew commenced their attack on the fire. It was the only attack being made from the Thames. Pettit had ordered the fireboat monitor to get to work and its two portable fire pumps were soon discharging their maximum output. With some satisfaction the crew noticed that they were making a useful addition to the overall firefighting. However, it had not escaped their attention just how bloody hot the fire was. They could feel the radiated heat from the opposite side of the narrow, short cul de sac St Saviour's Dock.

Sub Officer Pettit was no novice fire officer. An experienced firefighter, he had seen large warehouse fires before and knew of their unpredictability, especially when burning with the intensity of this one. He was aware that cracks appearing in the brickwork of a building were likely to be followed by an imminent collapse. So in addition to directing his crew he set himself the task of monitoring the upper floors very carefully. After about an hour he noticed the tell-tale signs of cracks starting to appear at a high level. He immediately ordered the fireboat to be moved.

As the 'Fire Hawk' was unsecured and Chris Savage repositioned the fireboat in the Dock, part of the upper floor finally collapsed. Its brickwork, weighting probably over a ton, fell into the water exactly where the 'Fire Hawk' had been moored. A plume of muddy river water shot skyward and the resultant waves bounced off the surrounding Dock walls. It is highly likely that without Pettit's vigilance the brickwork hitting the fireboat would have sunk it, plus the real possibility of death or serious injury to its crew members.

Now the 'Fire Hawk' was not like the fireboats of old: fireboats like the 'Massey Shaw' and the 'Firebrace' with their massive monitors that could throw a column of water hundreds of feet into the air. However, its monitor was no pipsqueak either. As the coxswain worked to keep the 'Fire Hawk' on its new position, lines from the bow were secured to two separate points on the Dock walls to counter the jet reaction of the monitor, something which could push the fireboat further and further away from the fire. The river firefighters were having to combine all their firefighting skills with their river craft.

At about 5 a.m. it became very apparent that the tide was going out and that the 'Fire Hawk' was going to be left high and dry in St Saviour's Dock. Sub Officer Pettit ordered a halt to their fire-fighting and for Chris Savage to make full speed for the main river: something they managed to achieve, but only just, for at low tide they observed two furrows in the Dock's mud-filled floor, made by the fireboat's prop shafts.

Due to the ebbing tides, and after five hours of continuous work, the fireboat had to retreat to the middle of the Thames. Here Sub Officer Pettit received a message from the incident commander, Deputy Assistant Chief Officer Brian Butler, to report to the Control Unit. Brian Butler was one of the Brigade's most respected principal operational officers. He was a force to be reckoned with. His leadership and innovative tactics in dealing with the Brixton riots in 1981 resulted in him being awarded the MBE. He was in command of this major blaze and he wanted to hear from the young officer whose radio messages had interspersed his own on the Brigade's main radio scheme from this incident.

However, for Sub Officer Pettit getting to report to this formi-dable officer was easier said than done. With the 'Fire Hawk' in the middle of the Thames the draught of the fireboat would not allow it to get close to land. So Ian Pettit flagged down a passing Police launch and hitched a lift. They took him and his crew shore and returned them again later. As for Brian Butler, he was clearly impressed by the actions of the fireboat crew and told them so. What Sub Officer Pettit did not tell Brian Butler was that in the 18 months he had occasionally ridden the fireboat this was the first fire both for himself and most of his crew. Brian Butler also happened to be the B Divisional Commander; this was his patch, and very little got past this astute officer.

Sadly, not all the B Division senior officers were so judicious. Returning to the river station around 6.30 a.m. the fireboat crew caught the early morning radio news which talked of the biggest blaze in years that had just occurred on the banks of the River Thames. Then, prior to 7 a.m. a Divisional Officer made a surprise visit to the river station on his way to the Divisional HQ at Clapham. He had hoped to catch the river firefighters still in bed! All that he could find fault with were the crews' life-jacket coats still in the station office, which he said should not be left hanging around. Sub Officer Pettit suggested that this officer's time might be better spent listening to the radio news; then he would know that they had been fire-fighting throughout the night rather than making his nit-picking comments.

A couple of months later Sub Officer Pettit and the White Watch fireboat crew received Letters of Commendation from their Divisional Commander, Brian Butler MBE, for their noteworthy actions on that memorable night.

St Saviour's Dock, showing the refurbished Java Wharf, now residental accommodation. (Ian Pettitt)

Footnote:
Java Wharf lived to survive another day, only as another of the up-market and expensive riverside residential properties. Today it boasts daytime porterage, lift access and secure parking space in St Saviour's Dock with its attractive and historic waterfront.

The Rise of the 'Phoenix'

In April 1985 'London Phoenix' was placed into operational service. The 'Phoenix' was built as a catamaran. For some inexplicable reason the river firefighter's called her 'Nellie', a name she was always affectionately known by, to those that served on her.

At 60 feet (18.9 metres) long and 23 feet (7.3 metres) wide it was originally thought the boat would provide a stable platform for a seventy-foot articulated Simon Snorkel hydraulic platform arm. Her twin Perkins diesel marine engines developed six hundred and twenty horse power pounding through her three-bladed twin propellers. A water salvo could be discharged from her four deck monitors mounted fore and aft fed by her two fire pumps that were capable of pumping two thousand gallons (nine thousand litres). There was also a foam monitor mounted ahead of the boats wheel house. Sadly the snorkel never made it through her sea trials, and it was touch and go whether the engineer operating the snorkel would either. Working in the Solent, near Southampton, the engineer was in the snorkel's operating cage, at the end of the hydraulic arm, and had swung out to a ninety degree angle to the

Artist's drawing of the new 'London Phoenix' fire and rescue boat.
(From the original painting by Divisional Officer Lawrenson, LFB)

boat. The 'Phoenix' caught the rise on the wash from the Red Funnel Steamer ferry, making her crossing to the Isle of Wight. The stresses caused by the wave proved too much for the arm and it snapped at the end of the main extension, throwing the engineer into the water. Fortunately, with only his pride injured, he was rescued and taken back on board. The manufacturer did not try another arm, instead they shortened the original and added an extra monitor to the end of it. As for the remainder of the sea trials, they proved successful and 'Phoenix' sailed up the Thames to her fire brigade moorings at Lambeth.

Special accredited training courses had to been undertaken by all those selected to serve on the 'Phoenix', plus those chosen as the reserve crew members. Despite the frequent calls, especially to riverside calls to automatic fire alarms actuating, the boat was rarely got work. There was the odd occasion where the 'Phoenix' came into her own, like the riverside warehouse blaze at Wapping, filled with newsprint, and the 'Phoenix' delivered water through four lines of hose taken ashore hour after hour without interruption. It was, after all, what a fireboat was designed to be, a floating pump that would never run out of water. However, as a subsequent review discovered, there were downsides to the 'Phoenix' too – none of which were brought to the attention the Fire Brigade Committee, not that the Committee bothered to enquire about them anyway. So when the Chief Officer presented his report seeking approval for the purchase of the 'Phoenix' and asking them to spend one million pounds on the new fireboat it was approved.

Taking up her station at the modernised Lambeth river station pontoon, because of her vivid colours she stood out amongst the myriad of Thames craft plying their trade upon this waterway. Although the Thames remained a highway through the heart of London, its dominant use is perhaps more recreational use than that of the past. With a top speed of twelve knots and an economical speed of seven knots London's new fireboat patrolled the entire length of the greater London Thames, removing the need of assistance of firefighting tugs for the lower reaches of the river.

'London Phoenix' on patrol on the Thames. (Paul Wood)

The present, apparently, peaceful river is rife with menace for the unwary river-man or river-woman. In the depths lies debris large enough to pierce the slender shell of the boat and lay bare her innards for the hungry river. It is the fireboat crews' job to spot and log these potential instruments of destruction.

On the bridge, a broad platform encased in aluminium alloy and glass overlooking the two forward water monitors and a powerful foam making jet-master monitor, the Station Officer maintains his command position. Close at hand he has river firefighters (trained to obey him). Charts and gauges inform both him and the coxswain of the depths and hazards when approaching the shoreline and landing stages.

His deputy, the Sub Officer, stands by the marine radio and radar to relay to the bridge the movements of shipping and any London Port Authority instructions. The coxswain is constantly manoeuvring the boat to keep clear of obstructions and other vessels whilst reading the constant intricate eddies, the currents and the prevailing wind and keeping the vessel on its course. The boat's controls which the coxswain's experienced hand finely tunes to control the speed of the hefty engines. Batteries of lights, alarms and dials easily confound the uninformed eye of untrained observers. Visitors sadly soon became all too frequent guests on board the latest acquisition to the London Fire Brigade's armoury. An armoury with which it aims to defend Londoners from danger and disaster on the river.

The monitor firepower of the 'London Phoenix' demonstrated at training and at a London riverside warehouse blaze. (London Fire Brigade)

The 'London Phoenix' at the modernised Lambeth river station pontoon.
(Mary Evans)

London Fire and Civil Defence Authority: London Fire Brigade, 1986–2000

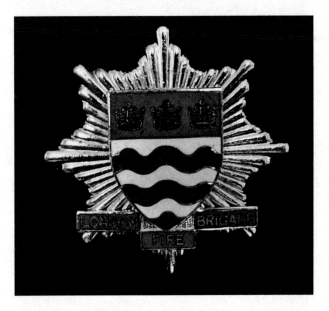

THE GOVERNMENT OF MARGARET Thatcher had been pushing for the abolition of the GLC, and the other six Metropolitan authorities, for a few years. When the Local Government Act (1985) was finally published, the Bill faced considerable and concerted opposition and it was only narrowly passed into law. In the autumn of 1985 it received Royal Assent and the final nail was hammered into the coffin of over one hundred years of London-wide local government. The GLC and the 'Mets' ceased to exist from the 1st April 1986.

However, prior to its abolition the GLC's Public Service and Fire Brigade Committee approved the purchase of the 'London Phoenix' and the 'Fire Hawk' now became the brigade's reserve fireboat.

The London Fire Brigade had been seeking approval to commission a new fireboat (at a cost of one million pounds) during the early 1980s. However, when the Chief Officer submitted a report seeking approval to purchase the craft his report extolled the virtues of the proposed replacement boat whilst skilfully omitting to highlight its possible shortcomings. With less scrutiny than might normally have been applied to such an expensive purchase, the outgoing Fire Brigade Committee (the GLC Fire Authority) sanctioned the purchase.

The home of the London County Council and the Greater London Council, County Hall on London's South Bank ceased to be the home of London's local government. The building was subsequently converted into a hotel and the home of the London Aquarium. (Mary Evans)

The 'London Phoenix's' rapid rescue craft. (Alan Dearing)

The 'Marchioness' disaster was a fatal collision between two vessels on the Thames in the vicinity of Kings Reach, located between Southwark and Cannon Street bridges at 1.55 a.m., Sunday 20th August 1989. Fifty-one people drowned. The pleasure boat 'Marchioness' sank after being pushed under water by the dredger MV 'Bowbelle'. The later formal inquiry blamed poor lookouts on both vessels, and inadequate instruction of both crews.

The prelude to the disaster started at 1.15 a.m. when the 'Marchioness' cast off from Charing Cross pier on a calm moonlit night. The party atmosphere on the boat was reported to be happy and carefree on the boat with its invited passengers enjoying themselves on both the upper and lower decks. At the same time, the 80 metre long dredger 'Bowbelle' had departed from Nine Elms in Battersea to the Shipwash dredging grounds on the Thames. The dredger was approaching Cannon Street Railway Bridge when it struck the 'Marchioness', first from behind, and then on the side, rolling her over.

Immediately the young people on board, now terrorised, tried to get off the boat. The 'Bowbelle's' anchor, rigid in its fixed and high position sliced through the upper deck of the 'Marchioness', shearing off the roof section. As the 'Marchioness' rolled over and took in water, the 'Bowbelle' continued to push the passenger boat. The smaller craft capsized. In seconds guests were thrown into the fast flowing flood waters of the Thames. It was like a bicycle being run over by a lorry.

The 'Marchioness' was plunged into darkness and turned over. Furniture was thrown around, trapping and injuring many of those on board. As the ship sank, the waters rose around them and many were swept out into the Thames. For the fortunate, the return to the surface meant they had fought only half the battle. Of those who escaped from the vessel a quarter would die in the water. Many of those rescued had to survive in the Thames for at least 15 minutes.

Some lucky passengers clung to debris floating nearby, others to structures in the water in their attempts to not be swept away. Eighty-nine people were rescued within ten minutes but another fifty-one people, including the skipper of the 'Marchioness', died, many trapped helplessly below deck. Of the deceased, 24 were recovered from the sunken hull. The majority of the survivors had been on the upper decks at the time of the collision. It had taken little more than 30 seconds to sink the 'Marchioness' with 131 passengers including crew and catering staff on board.

'London Phoenix' fireboat and the rapid rescue boat on its stern.
(Paul Wood)

Station Officer Peter Humphreys had been the officer in charge of the Brigade's fireboat that night, the 'London Phoenix'. They could have been one of the first emergency service vessels on the scene given the relatively short distance from their moorings at Lambeth to Southwark Bridge. However they were ordered at 1.55 a.m. to a call reporting a boat sinking with 20 people on board in the water off Chelsea Embankment. They, and their rapid response craft, the 'Dory', headed in the opposite direction to the disaster scene. The duty captain at Woolwich marine radio service had misheard and thought the location was Battersea Bridge. He had given the misheard location to the police, who unknowingly sent the fire brigade in the wrong direction. At the subsequent inquiry the Captain said, *'I can't explain why I heard Battersea Road Bridge rather than Cannon Street Rail Bridge.'*

At the time of the collision a strong flood tide was running and the night sky was clear. Some eleven minutes later the 'Phoenix' was instructed by the mobilising control to turn about and head downstream to Kings Reach. The Dory had gone on ahead of the Phoenix and at 2.13 a.m. the Dory crew reported lots of flotsam in the vicinity of Blackfriars Bridge. Twenty minutes after the collision the fire brigade was given the real location. When they arrived at Blackfriars Bridge they could find no survivors.

Passengers on the vessel 'Hurlingham' rescued more than twenty survivors. A police launch managed to drag twenty-two people on to their boat, a boat which was designed for three crew and two passengers. Another police launch managed between 15 and 20. In all, 80 people survived.

Although the search continued for most of the night, no one was found alive after the first 30 minutes. The 'Phoenix' had taken a position upstream where the strong incoming tide might take survivors or carry bodies. At 3 a.m. the 'Phoenix' crew recovered the body of a young female almost opposite the fireboat's moorings at Lambeth. With one body on board they continued their search upstream reaching Hammersmith Brigade around 4.45 a.m. before returning to the Police pier at Wapping to hand over the body. The 'Phoenix' was later ordered to Putney Pier to collect the remaining bodies that had been swept up river on the tide and recovered, though this instruction was later cancelled. No other bodies were recovered until the following day when the wreck was raised east of Southwark Bridge. Here 24 bodies were found in different sections of the boat. Over the next few days the remaining 26 bodies were gradually recovered along the river.

Footnote:

The 'Marchioness' had been one of the little ships involved in the evacuation of the Dunkirk beaches in 1940. Adjacent to the site of the disaster a memorial to the victims was erected in the nave of Southwark Cathedral. Every year a service of remembrance is held for the fifty-one who lost their lives on that tragic night.

In the mid-nineties the Brigade's Fire Cover Review, conducted during 1995, highlighted that the river service was *'inefficient and expensive owing to the very nature of the vessel involved.'* The 'London Phoenix', which had been hailed as a state of the art craft when its procurement was recommended to the former GLC Fire Brigade Committee, was found to be wanting. The review discovered, or rather confirmed, what was already known: that the fireboat frequently took too long to attend calls, that the call had already been dealt with by land crews so the fireboat was returned before even reaching the incident.

That same year I was one of two senior officers tasked with *'reviewing the current role and provision of fireboat cover on the river'* – where else would it be? – *'and its efficiency in relation to its cost effectiveness'.* It was a major undertaking. Its findings would question the need for a fireboat at all in London. However, London's Fire Authority made a determination that in discharging its statutory responsibilities it would maintain a fireboat as an integral part of its operational strategy. I would not see the new millennium serving in the London Fire Brigade – my medical retirement had seen to that. London would, however, see a new style fireboat introduced into the Brigade.

Postscript:

Two of the London Fire Brigade's former fireboats found themselves both relocated to the South-West of England. The 'Fire Hawk' undertakes fishing charters whilst the 'Firebrace' is awaiting a restoration project to return her to her former glory.

The former fireboat 'Firebrace'. (John Price)

The 'Fire Hawk'. (John Price)

CHAPTER 9

Firefighters Rowing Boats on the Thames

EVEN FROM ITS EARLIEST days London's fire brigades have had its firemen rowing boats on the River Thames. In fact the very first firemen, in James Braidwood's time, were recruited from sailors and Thames lightermen and watermen into the London Fire Engine Establishment. Besides the qualities that these men brought to his fire brigade Braidwood realised that virtually nearly every building on or near the River Thames was associated with ships and the various cargoes these craft brought into, or carried from, London and its many docks. In fact the Pool of London was given the title of 'the larder of London'.

London's first fire-floats were powered by oars, so who better to man them than firemen who knew the ways of the river? For many years the fire brigade remained the predominant occupation of former sailors, as it was only these men who were accepted as recruits into Massey Shaw's Metropolitan Fire Brigade – although this requirement was later dropped by the London County Council, and after the name of the brigade had been changed to the London Fire Brigade at the beginning of the twentieth century. However, firemen rowing boats, or skiffs, did not change for many years, although it was not seen in such a sporting sense back then. Their function were mainly fire service related, such as firemen rowing hose ashore at a riverside blaze by skiff from the fire-float. This was required either because of the state of the tide or the lack of sufficient draught, which prevented the fire-float(s) getting anywhere near the river's bank.

It is not certain exactly when the first Thames rowing competition involving firemen took place. However, in 1906 the first river race was recorded. It started when the firemen of the 'Alpha' fire-float, moored at Blackfriars, challenged the Royal Naval ratings of HMS 'President', moored a short distance away on the Victoria Embankment, to a 'whaler race' on the Thames. With the exception of the war years the Whaler Race was held every year after that. By 1911 a crew from the Metropolitan Police River Police joined in the annual race. By 1923 a team from the Royal Naval Reserve brought the competing crews to four.

Prior to the start of the First World War in 1914, London's firemen had held a regatta on the River Thames. Competition between station crews had been popular in the London fire brigade for years. Pathé newsreels recorded various forms of competitions taking place at the turn of the century at the London Fire Brigade's headquarters in Southwark Bridge Road. These competitions, against the clock, included both pump competitions and wheeled escape competitions. By 1918 Pathé had even recorded footage of the London firemen's Thames regatta.

Tragically, 1918 was the same year in which Fireman Edward T. Woolf, who was stationed at the Cannon Street fire station, drowned whilst practising for a regatta off Chelsea Reach, near Pimlico in Westminster. His boat capsized and its crew of four fell into the Thames. Whilst three of the crew struggled to the nearby foreshore Edward Woolf never surfaced. His body was later recovered from the murky waters of the Thames.

From 1904 until the Second World War the London Fire Brigade was divided into six districts, A to F. Firemen rowed representing for their respective districts. These districts later were reorganised into just four Divisions (A-D) after the War, and when the fire service returned to Local Authority control in 1947. The format of the Whaler Races essentially remained unchanged for the next seventy years or so, with Divisional competitions, followed by the Brigade inter-divisional completion and the winners representing the Brigade in the Fishmongers Cup race. Teams of five, together with a coxswain, rowed the one and half ton, clinker-built naval whalers.

With the opening of the new London Fire Brigade head-quarters at Lambeth, located on the Albert Embankment, and with the combined opening of a new river fire station a regular Whaler Race course was established in 1937. The starting point was mid-stream and directly opposite Lambeth river station. The crews rowed the one mile six hundred yard course downstream to HMS 'President', the finish line. In the wake of the whalers a flotilla of spectators' craft followed the crews, cheering, yells of encour-agement echoing across the river. The London County Council had funded the impressive Royal George Trophy, to commemo-rate King George VI opening the new headquarters the same year. The winner's name was inscribed on the trophy, which was kept on public display in the main entrance lobby and Memorial Hall glass-fronted cabinets; these were filled with a striking collec-tion of silverware that had been presented to Brigade and Brigade competition cups and shields. The annual Brigade Whaler Race

Montage of the first River Thames firemen's regatta.
(Source-Pathé News)

winners each received a pint tankard whilst the runners up took home a half-pint tankard.

The races traditionally took place on a Saturday afternoon, but training for the event on that stretch of water took place at any time the individuals could get together on the Thames. The winning Divisional crews were frequently granted special leave, when on duty, to get extra training in, especially if their Divisional Officer thought his team had a good chance of winning that year. The Brigade winners were certainly given some leeway to increase their performance, after all the Brigade's reputation was at stake.

It was not unknown for furtive figures to be seen skulking along the riverside trying to see how the opposition were performing in training, especially the Metropolitan Police river service with whom the Brigade battled for supremacy.

Brigade crews battle it out in the final of the Brigade's Annual Whaler Race opposite HMS 'President' which was moored on the Thames Embankment. (The family of the late Vic Rawson BEM)

Just prior to the outbreak of the Second World War the Worshipful Company of Fishmongers, one of the twelve great Livery Companies of the City of London, donated a magnificent challenge cup for the annual inter-service Whaler Race, hence the name by which the race is currently known: the Fishmongers' Cup. The Fishmongers' Cup become a popular highlight in friendly inter-service rivalry. After 1947 the London Fire Brigade had established itself in a dominant role, and their crews became the first to achieve more than three consecutive victories.

Throughout the 1950s and 1960s the LFB won the Fishmongers' Cup more times than it lost it. By the 1970s the Brigade's winning crew were engaged in wider rowing competitions too. They held a commendable record in the Ports Jubilee Regatta Whaler Races.

Not satisfied with just whaler racing in the early 1970s, the Brigade established the marathon skiff race. The skiff were slightly shorter and lighter than the whalers and made of fibre-glass, not timber. This was a thirty-one mile slog from the Lambeth head-quarters to Eel Pie Island, Twickenham. And back. A good winning time was in the region of five and a half hours' non-stop rowing, a time that eroded as the race progressed over the years. Eight to ten teams entered the annual event, some Divisions being less than enthusiastic about rowing on the Thames than others. However, for those that did they could all guarantee one thing: blisters on their hands and backsides, and very aching limbs by the end of the marathon pull. Competition was keen amongst the teams. It is a testament to the endurance, strength and stamina of the compet-itors that in a particular race that decade only sixteen minutes separated the winning crew, in a record time, and the tenth crew that brought up the rear.

The Shrimpers Regatta

The winners of the Fishmongers' Cup in 1972, a team from the LFB's B Division, with a crew from Brixton, Clapham and Lambeth fire stations, were invited to row against the profession-als, the Thames Watermen and Lightermen, in that year's Shrimp-ers Regatta. These people row, and race, Thames barges for fun! This new event to the Thames calendar, a marathon race, had been running for four years, and had been started by the Worshipful Company of Watermen and Lightermen.

(Even at over five hundred years old the Watermen and Lightermen's Livery Company is still not one the City Of London's twelve great Livery Companies. However, from ancient times the Thames was a recognised main highway for moving people and goods from the Estuary to London and beyond. The use of ferries was the only link across the Thames before the Romans built the first London Bridge. The importance of the trade that the river provided was highlighted by a survey conducted in 1598. It found that some forty thousand men earned a living on or about the River

The winning London Fire Brigade whaler crew from the inter-services annual Thames race in the early 1950s. (Mary Evans)

Thames. The Act of 1514, passed by Parliament of Henry VIII, regulated the fares charged on the Thames. However the Watermen, who carried passengers, continued to act independently, so an Act of 1555 appointed Rulers of all Watermen and Wherrymen working between Gravesend and Windsor; thus the Company was born. The Act of 1555 also introduced apprenticeships for a term of one year for all boys wishing to learn the watermen's trade and this was extended to seven years by a further Act in 1603. Since 1827 the Worshipful Company has been governed by a Court of Assistants, which includes an annually elected Master together with four Wardens. Their present Livery Hall dates from 1780 and remains the only original Georgian Hall in the City of London. The Doggett's Coat and Badge is the oldest continuously run single sculling race in the world and is run in conjunction with the Worshipful Company of Fishmongers.)

The marathon course is thirty four and half miles, stretching from Gravesend to the 'Mid-Swatch' buoy off Sheppey and back. Ideally, the crews row down on the ebbing tide and row back on the flood. There is about one and half hours' slack water with no tidal assistance to the halfway mark.

The London Fire Brigade got their whaler shipshape, the crew somewhat apprehensive competing against these River professionals and on their own 'turf', in waters that the river men knew intimately. The starter, in his Doggetts Coat and Badge, finally gave the crews the off. Various launches carrying first aid, umpires, press and officials kept bobbing up from nowhere and asking if each of the crews were all right, before trying their hardest to make sure they weren't by belting off creating a lot of turbulence in the water. By a sustained effort the LFB crew had managed to pull themselves into fifth place, a feat that rather surprised the officials and amazed the crew. Aboard their boats the crews each carried supplies, flasks of soup, tinned fruit juice, chicken legs and slabs of cheese. The teams were expending a lot of calories each and every hour, especially as most were rowing at 25 strokes per minute throughout the six hours' duration of the race.

When they reached the halfway point, the LFB team were now in third place, from starting in last place. The Committee boat following the race radioed the positions back to the crowd assembled around the blackboard at the starting point. Every one wondered what the LFB were going to do; some officials wondered if it had been a mistake even inviting the Fishmongers' Cup winners, a team that were not given very good odds, in fact were considered as rank outsiders.

Unfortunately the LFB crew had expended too much in the first half of the race and had insufficient momentum to maintain their performance on the return leg. Each of the crew needed a breather, and the coxswain took turns to allow each of the rowers time for a quick snack. The crew in fourth place saw the movement in the boat and the apparent loss of pace and they quickly pulled themselves into third place. With three crews ahead the of the LFB crew, still in sight but well clear, and no sight of any the crews still behind then the team settled down for the long pull home. This is the time when the metal of any oarsman is tested, it is both a mental and physical assault on their reserves. Muscles ache, fatigue sets in. Yet with the finish in sight the LFB crew gave a spirited sprint finish to good applause, and hoisted their oars in naval fashion in salute to the crowd.

They waited to cheer the following crews home, clapping in the next two but never seeing the final crew, who still had seven miles to row to the finish line. The Master of the Worshipful Company of Watermen and Lightermen had lost his worried frown by the time he awarded each LFB crew member with his certificate and publicly praised the London Fire Brigade team in its first attempt and the crew's endurance, skill and determination at this premier of Thames marathon races.

Firemen in rowing boats did have a far more serious side, no more so than at Lambeth's River Fire Station where its crew were occasionally required to pull for all that they were worth for a much different reason: someone's life depended on their combined skill and the speed in reaching them in time in the fireboat's skiff. The skiff was normally attached to the fireboat, and was towed behind it whenever proceeding to a fire or special service call on the river. However, the practice with anyone reported to have jumped into the Thames in the vicinity of the river station was for some of the fireboat's crew to jump immediately into the skiff and row to the person in the water, whilst the fireboat started up her engines, cast off and backed up the skiff crew. It was a system that worked and lives were saved because of it.

My own award of a Chief Officer's Commendation, for rescuing a woman from the River Thames opposite the Brigade Headquarters, and *'carrying out mouth to mouth resuscitation in difficult and dangerous conditions on the 5th March 1968'* had such a crew rushing to our aid. I was assisted by my Station Officer, Donald Brown, who received a Chief Officer's Letter of Congratulations for his actions. The fireboat's skiff crew returned the unfortunate woman to the pontoon, before her removal to hospital by ambulance. Thankfully she eventually made a full recovery. I was subsequently awarded the Queen's Commendation for Brave Conduct partly because I was only nineteen years of age at the time of the rescue and still a probationer fireman.

B22 river firemen Les Porter, Ron Edwards and Jim Fullicks rowed to the rescue recently when a man fell into the Thames from Lambeth Bridge. Les, Ron and Jim (pictured above) rowed to where the man had drifted, pulled him out of the water and returned to the riverboat pontoon. Shivering, but otherwise unhurt, the 40-year-old man was taken to hospital where he made a quick recovery.

(Source: London Fireman *Magazine*)

Located between Vauxhall and Lambeth Bridges, the river fire station was better placed to have a chance of rescuing those 'jumpers' who wished to end their days with a watery grave. The skiff's crew were not always successful. The powerful pull of the Thames' eddies or the state of the tide could easily sweep a person away. Occasionally there was never a chance of rescue as some jumped in the Thames after weighing themselves down with heavy objects placed in their pockets.

Leading Fireman Ron Parke leaving St Thomas' Hospital after his check-up following his Thames rescue ordeal. (London Evening News)

Ron Parke was a Leading Fireman. He worked at Mitcham fire station in South West London. On this particular day in June 1971 he was not even on duty. Whilst crossing Vauxhall Bridge Ron Parke saw a young woman jump into the River Thames from Vauxhall Bridge. Throwing off his jacket and shoes he immediately dived into the Thames to save the woman, who could not swim. The ebbing tide was flowing swiftly and carried them both downstream. His efforts to reach the southern foreshore, by Albert Embankment, were hindered by the strength of the tide so he supported the woman's head above the water whilst keeping himself and the woman afloat. A member of the public, who saw what was happening, ran to the fireboat river station to summon assistance. The fireboat crew manned the skiff and raced to the assistance of the pair, who were now about 100 yards upstream from the fireboat pontoon. Ron Parke was now feeling the extreme strain of supporting the woman and keeping her alive. Both were lifted from the water by the skiff's crew and after a check-up in hospital both were released to go home. Leading Fireman Parke was commended by the Chief Officer for a remarkable rescue from the River Thames. He was subsequently awarded the British Empire Medal for Gallantry.

Fireman Malcolm Roe had been a former Royal Navy sailor and in 1975 was a fireman on the Lambeth River Station. Members of the public had raised the alarm that a person was seen in the river near Lambeth's river pontoon. Fireman Roe immediately ran to a skiff and prepared to row to where a person's head was seen bobbing, some ten feet from the embankment wall. However, knowing that time was of the essence he dived, fully clothed, into the water and swam to the person's aid. Grabbing and supporting the person he started his return towards the pontoon and the skiff that was being rowed towards by other river firemen. The person then put up the most violent and desperate struggle. In trying to maintain his hold on the person Fireman Roe was pulled under the water and held there. He had to let go of the person so as to return to the surface and get air. He then lost contact with the drowning person. Fireman Roe was now suffering from the effects of taking in and being in the water and was pulled into the skiff. He was returned to the pontoon and taken to St Thomas' Hospital but not detained. The fireboat, assisted by police launches, continued the search but no person or their body was recovered. Fireman Roe was presented with the Royal Humane Society *Testimonial on Vellum* for his attempted rescue of the suicidal person.

In 1991 Firefighter Jeffery John Simpson, from Shadwell fire station, was awarded a *Chief Officer's Commendation* for his gallant action in rescuing a young boy who had fallen through ice on the River Thames at Shadwell Basin on the 10th February. He was also subsequently awarded the St John Bronze Life Saving Medal.

On the 21st December 1998 Poplar firefighters were called to a special service incident at Limehouse Basin, near the Commercial Road, E14. The call was to a child in the water. Two firefighters were told not to rig in their fire gear en route to incident by Sub Officer Cunningham. On their arrival a child was confirmed to be under the water. A crowd of hysterical onlookers pointed to an area of water where two police officers were already in a boat probing the water with their oars trying to locate the missing child. The two firefighters, secured to lines and held by Sub Officer Cunningham and another firefighter, entered the freezing water and swam towards the boat.

Mud and pollution reduced visability to almost nil in the three metre deep water. The two had to dive and search for the child by touch. On his third dive Firefighter Cotton located the lifeless boy and with Firefighter White's assistance hauled him into the boat where they immediately started resuscitation and chest compressions. Sub Officer Cunningham, meanwhile, pulled the boat back to the quayside using the lines tied to the firefighters. The still lifeless boy was passed to the Sub Officer who continued with the resuscitation. A passing doctor came to assist and detected a slight pulse. Mouth to mouth was continued by Firefighter White. The boy was removed to hospital by air ambulance, where he made a full recovery. (The doctors estimated that the child had been under water for about 10 minutes.) Firefighters Mark Cotton and Craig White were awarded the Chief Officer's Letter of Congratulation; and the Royal Human Society Resuscitation Certificate and Sub Officer Terry Cunningham was awarded the Royal Human Society Resuscitation Certificate and an Assistant Chief Officer's Letter of Commendation.

In December 2007 Firefighter Graham Hainsworth, then aged 54 and serving at the Lambeth River Station, took his work home with him and used his training and river experience to good effect. Although off duty, and in the company of his family, he saved a member of the public and a crew member of a river-boat from drowning in the Thames.

Graham was an experienced crew member of the Brigade's Thames fireboat. He and his wife Pauline, plus daughter Laura, were members of a party that had enjoyed a 'Take That' concert at the O2 Arena in Greenwich on the evening of the 8th December. Following the concert and just after midnight they boarded a Thames Clipper passenger boat from the return journey to central London. As their boat neared Canary Wharf Graham heard a woman scream out that a man had fallen overboard at the back of the boat. There was little light; in fact it was almost pitch black. Then Graham spotted a man's head bobbing in the water. The man was struggling to stay afloat. The Clipper crew reversed the engines and assembled a rescue ladder and hung it over the guard rail. Graham recalled later that: *He was a big chap wearing a heavy coat. He was too cold to grab it.*

Graham grabbed a life ring and threw it to the man. With the boat now alongside the man the Clipper's young crew members did not seem to know what to do next. So without any hesitation Graham climbed down the recovery ladder. Graham saw the man was *'in and out of it by that time.'* He knew, given the time of year that it only takes a few minutes before hypothermia starts to set in. Graham had managed to grab the distressed man by the collar, holding his head above the water. In the meantime another young man had come down the ladder holding an inflatable life jacket. The next thing Graham saw was that this man had fallen in the river too and was in danger of being carried away by the tide. Graham immediately locked his legs onto the ladder and made a desperate grab for the second man. He was now holding both men as he watched the blue flashing lights of a police launch drawing closer.

Police officers and crew member then managed to haul both men up onto the craft where they were removed to hospital. Not wishing any fuss Graham and his family slipped away when the boat docked at the London Eye. Here he picked up his car and drove home. That was the last Graham thought about it. However, the police made inquiries about the modest man who had gone to the rescue of first one man, and then another. Unbeknown to Graham, reports were made out and forwarded to the Brigade. They came to the attention of the Assistant Commissioner who considered if Graham's actions were worthy of formal recognition. The news story also got the ears of a newspaper who contacted the river station for a comment. That is best left to the fireboat officer-in-charge, Bob Anderson; he told the press that: *'Graham was now being recommended for a top Brigade commendation. I feel that Firefighter Hainsworth demonstrated extreme courage and professionalism and as a direct result of his actions the first casualty's life was undoubtedly saved and possibly that of the crew member too. This incident shows that by using his vast experience and with little regard for his own safety Firefighter Hainsworth was a credit to the London Fire Brigade and I feel this should be recognised by the brigade. He saved two young men from almost certain death.'* The Brigade's Assistant Commissioner agreed. Graham was issued with a Certificate of Commendation.

Then in March 2011 the crew of Fulham fire station rushed to Wandsworth Bridge, SW6, where a person was threatening to jump into the Thames. Their crew manager Christopher Batchelor took decisive action to prevent the person jumping to their probable death and for his actions was awarded an Assistant Commissioner's Commendation.

Paris to London Row

Firemen rowing on or along the River Thames had occasionally more to do with just racing each other. It actively involved raising money for charity. Very occasionally it involved more than just the River Thames. Three teams of south London firemen, mainly from Brixton fire station undertook the challenge in August 1981.They were to row a naval whaler from Paris to London in relays, and hopefully in the process row themselves into the record books in addition to raising thousands of pounds for two national charities.

Their efforts had to be independently adjudicated and two sea-faring men come forward to take on the task. One was a

Master Mariner from the International Marine Organisation and the other was Lieutenant Commander Mike Bedwell of the Royal Naval Reserve, from HMS President (then still based in the heritage ship moored alongside the Victoria Embankment) who happened to be the owners of the naval whaler used for the exploit.

Mike Bedwell published a report of his first contact with London Firemen in both his own in-house magazine and the award-winning magazine of the London Fire Brigade. This is an abridged version of his original story.

"'Your sleeping space is a bit primitive but it's all been swept out." I had to take Station Officer Dave Pike's word for the swept bit, for the primitiveness of the penthouse area of Brixton fire station extended to the wiring which makes a gallant, but vain, attempt to bring amps to dark places.

However it was only to be for one short night since at the crack of dawn we had to be on the 6.30 a.m. SEALINK Dover to Calais ferry. All this in preparation for the London Fire Brigade's self-inflicted challenge of rowing one of the Royal Naval Reserve's whalers back from Paris into the heart of London. I got in on the act as both an interpreter and, more importantly, as an adjudicator for The Guinness Book of Records, *whose pages the firemen hoped to grace.*

The following day started at 3.00 a.m. An hour only made possible by my first taste of firemen's coffee and their style of banter, which I was to become all too familiar with in the succeeding days. I meet David Bruce, my fellow adjudicator who owned up to being a Master Mariner and was therefore a natural for taking charge of the Calais-Dover-London legs. I was also introduced to the delightful Henrietta, employed as a second interpreter and luscious leavener of this otherwise all male loaf.

The journey to Paris went like clockwork, thanks largely to the generosity of Sealink, the main sponsor [and] the co-operation of the French police and firemen. We benefitted from the French firemen's hospitality when we stayed, as their guests, in the biggest "sapeur pompiers'" barracks in Paris. That evening we were treated to a meal that was light years away from my previous evening's foray to a Brixton chippy.

Memories of the rest of the week became increasingly blurred as the marathon row progressed. Raw details were of course recorded in the official log, maintained by David Bruce and myself: times under way, in and out of locks, changes of crew, (a maximum of fifteen rowers formed the three crews, rowing in relays).

The French waterways was usually interesting, never stupendous and sometimes monotonous. Most of the locks were large commercial affairs, only on the Canal de Calais did we encounter a do-it-yourself English style lock. Elsewhere the locks were somewhat inhuman monuments of hydraulic architecture watched over from Heathrovian control towers with whose countless steps we interpreters became all too familiar. Often we were required to sweet-talk the lock keeper into allowing us priority over other commercial craft, a task which was made easier with the French tolerance of "crazy English" and by the thoroughness with which Dave Pike had done his homework on letter-writing and jacking up presentation plagues.

It was the people rather than the place that made the event so special. There can be no occupation that transcends nationality more than that of the fireman and the camaraderie that was so evident between the Londoners and their French opposite numbers was enough to melt the most chauvinistic heart. More than once I was in one of the escorting vans when we found ourselves outside a fire station. In fact by the end of the week I was beginning to believe it was no coincidence. Within minutes we would have our feet under the table with people we had never meet before. Helmets would be exchanged, equipment would be demonstrated, corks would be drawn and perhaps most welcome of all to a reluctant camper like myself, hot showers could be taken.

For those lucky enough to be in the whaler at the time, Messrs Dolezal, Bryant, Pryke, Pike and Rance plus yours truly, the most treasured memory must be our arrival at a small village near Noyon. It was towards evening and we were behind schedule but the local part-time "pompiers" had turned out in their best bib and tucker to line the approach to the next lock. It would have been churlish to have refused the Champagne that, after the obligatory mayoral words, awaited us.

But my final words must be for the rowers themselves and here there is no need to exaggerate. Their unconventional technique and style might raise an eyebrow on the least anchor-like of naval faces, but for sheer guts, stamina and determination no praise is too high. One day they were struggling through the very disturbed waters of the Canal du Nord under an unkind sun, the next toiling through the Canal de Calais, whose neglected, weed infested water had the consistency of undercooked packet minestrone. Finally, of course, came the biggest challenge of the Channel and the River Thames, which was accomplished under tug escort in something under 34 hours of non-stop relay rowing, a third of them plugging adverse currents which for one frustrating hour allowed less than half a mile to be covered.

All this was done not under the cloistered steak-for-breakfast regime with which Oxford crews prepare for their annual paddle but in expedition conditions where sleep was often short and the food, for all the valiant efforts of the chef, Bob Irwin, was notable more for its carbohydrate than its protein. Minor tensions were inevitable but these were released in an unremitting earthy and stoical humour that was designed to sting but never to injure. It was both an honour and a privilege to see at close quarters the type of individuals that make London's fire brigade.'

The whaler crew reaching the Port of Calais and before their non-stop marathon row back to London and home. (Author)

393

All three crews are on the Thames for the final leg from Greenwich to Tower Bridge in their Paris to London marathon row. (Author)

The jubilant whaler rowers from the London Fire Brigade celebrate their successfully completed trip on board HMS 'President' in London. (Author)

It was in the last year of the 1970s that two teams of London firemen got a real bee in their collective bonnets about a rowing adventure on the River Thames. One that not only involved rowing, but rowing the whole one hundred and eighty-six miles of its navigable length, from Lechlade in Gloucestershire to Southend Pier in Essex, and in the fastest possible non-stop time. One team

394

came from the East End of London, namely Poplar fire station, whilst the other came from a South London fire station – Brixton.

It was a marathon event that hadn't been undertaken before, although a team of doctors from Guys Hospital had been entered in *The Guinness Book of Records* for their achievement in rowing an 'eight' from Oxford's Folly Bridge to Westminster, a distance of one hundred and twelve miles. Brixton was the first to throw down the gauntlet and hoped to complete the gruelling endeavour in about forty hours. These various attempts over the preceding years, in addition to expending the surplus energy of various firemen undertaking this feat of endurance, also raised many thousands of pounds for various charities, including the Firemen's own National Benevolent Fund (now called the Firefighters Charity).

The Brixton five-man crew made their attempt in a skiff, four rowing and a coxswain. They set off in the evening twilight and before long were rowing in the dark with just a small light mounted at the front of their boat for illumination. Thirty minutes before a new day started they had passed through the first eight locks of the total of forty-five. Three hours later they were rowing in the most atrocious weather; pouring rain made rowing very uncomfortable. By that afternoon the crew were behind their self-imposed schedule and feeling tired. After thirty five hours of rowing they passed through the forty-fifth lock. Another three and a half hours sees them at the Lambeth River station: they have a flat battery for the light and ten hours of rowing ahead of them.

After Lambeth the gods are against them. The tide starts to flood and high winds create rough water and one or two passing pleasure craft try their hardest to swamp the skiff with their wake. The crew of the Greenwich fireboat come to give moral support, and more importantly hand out mugs of steaming Bovril.

The fireboat crew also passed on the news that the HM Coastguard would stop the crew rowing in the lower reaches of the Thames as insufficient attention had been given to the provision of lifejackets. The crew never had any! The row was aborted after one hundred and fifty miles and forty-six hours' rowing. It was not all bad news as with the sponsorship money raised a valuable piece of equipment, which detected eye disease, was purchased for the International Glaucoma Association.

In 1981 the East London firemen did row themselves into *The Guinness Book of Records*. They had learnt a lot from the abandoned Brixton experience, not least how not to upset HM Coastguard. They too used a fibre-glass skiff and the five-man crew completed their row in the impressive time of fifty-three hours and two minutes.

But in 1981 the Brixton firemen happened to be on different rowing 'jolly'. (See Paris to London above.) However, with the bit now firmly between their teeth, plus the disappointment of not getting the Paris to London marathon row in the record books, in May 1983 they set off from under the stone built bridge that crossed the Thames at Lechlade, and the point from where they started their record-breaking attempt. It was a different crew and a very different boat. Instead of the lighter skiff they had chosen to row the much heavier naval whaler. It had a crew of five, plus the coxswain and a highly motivated support crew. Everyone that had to be contacted was contacted and even the HM Coastguard was happy with our preparations this time.

The first strokes of the whaler's long oars hit the Thames water in the wee, wee hours of the 5th May. The sky showed the signs of a new dawn, a glimmer of light breaking on the eastern horizon and marking the direction that we were heading for: Southend and its mile long pier. An adjudicator had to monitor our progress throughout the record attempt, so we had taken two in order to cater for their comfort stops and rest breaks. The pair sat huddled together in the chill morning air on the small support boat that accompanied the whaler in the upper reaches of the Thames. Getting through the forty-five locks was achieved with clockwork precision.

However, it was not all plain sailing, as whilst the locks remain open twenty four hours a day, at night when the lock keepers are snuggled up warm in bed, the locks are unlit and the area is incredibly dark. Torches held by the support crew guided us towards the opened lock gates, with our own measly little light on the prow of the whaler warning them of our approach. Operating the locks in the dark was an arduous task for the support team and they were crucial to the success of the row.

With twenty-four hours' rowing under our belt we had Oxford-shire on one bank and Buckinghamshire on the other. The first shards of light that day saw the support boats crew looking a little glum as the fresh night air had chilled them to the bone. The row was planned to get the maximum benefit from the natural flow of the river and to minimise the effects of the incoming spring tides. We had plenty of experience rowing against a Thames tide and it was never easy. Twice a day the Thames tides rise and fall. The velocity of the flowing water varies considerably in different parts of the river. The rates at London Bridge can be between one to three knots but can be as high as seven. We had hit the adverse tide and someone had put a brake on the whaler's progress. It would be another five hours before the next slack water and an ebbing tide.

The second night brought back the blackness of the night, and it was incredibly dark. It was like rowing blindfolded. Only the radar and the marine radio of our now seagoing escort tug gave any warning to others of our position. With the darkness came another change of tide that made every endeavour to carry us back to the point we had spent the last few hours rowing from. It was also bitterly cold.

It was the creeping light of a new dawn that showed the distant Essex coastline, on the coxswain's left, shrouded in an opaque film of morning mist. The whaler was made to be rowed at sea. It was on home ground but the conditions were not conducive to our record attempt. Not only were the adverse currents stronger than we have encountered previously, the prevailing breeze was not helping much either.

At 6.10 a.m. that final morning the tug moved off from our stern and positioned itself off Southend Pier, the finish line. The last sixteen minutes were agonisingly slow as we drew nearer and nearer the pier but never seemed to arrive. Then at 6.26 a.m. our one and half ton whaler passed the marker with us still pulling strongly: a new 'world' record for rowing the length of River Thames in a time of forty-seven hours and fifty-six minutes. *The Guinness Book of Records* had no hesitation in accepting our record-breaking time that had knocked five hours off the previous best time.

Footnotes:

1. There were other record attempts, but never in a naval whaler. The Brixton record still stands.

2. In 2004 a crew, which featured an Olympic medallist, completed the course, known as the Giant Meander, at 10:57 BST on Saturday, in a time given on their website as 30 hours, 57 minutes and 20 seconds. The existing record, set by a five-man crew from Lower Thames Rowing Club in 1993, had stood at 38 hours and 43 minutes. The crew were using a traditional Thames skiff rowing boat. Their distance from Lechlade Bridge to Gravesend Pier was one hundred and sixty-five miles.

3. 2007. A single oarsman completed the same 165-mile route (Lechlade Bridge to Gravesend Pier) in 43 hours, 40 minutes and 56 seconds between April 7 and 9. The same 51-year-old rower also holds the record for rowing the English Channel single-handedly in less than three hours.

4. By the new millennium the rowing traditions between the emergency services were in serious, and terminal, decline. It was a combination of service cut-backs and the decline of the whaler rowing boats themselves. The London Fire Brigade no longer boasts any 'heavy' boat section and the Fishmongers' Cup has not been competed for in over a decade or more. The last Fishmongers races were competed for using Thames Cutters as no one could find four matched Whalers. The last of the emergency services to maintain a whaler were the Metropolitan Police's heavy boat club. Even that finished when their key people retired.

Firefighters rowing on the Thames in whalers is now nothing but a distant memory. It is yet another example of a fine Brigade tradition that has become little more than a hazy reminiscence in the minds of retired river firefighters. Sadly, it also something that probably won't feature very highly in the Brigade's own recalling of its history.

CUP
— ANNUAL ROWING RACE —
8th. SEPTEMBER 1990

Hosted by THE LONDON FIRE BRIGADE

CHAPTER 10

A New Millennium

The changing face of the London Fire Brigade and its river fire service

The Lambeth headquarters of the London Fire Brigade which faces the river fire station on the Albert Embankment, SE1. (Author)

THIS IS THE LAST chapter. 1996 had been the closing chapter of my own long London Fire Brigade career. The London Fire Brigade was changing and I had been caught up in those changes. Mine had been an extraordinary journey from a young lad of 16, joining the Brigade as a junior fireman, then rising from fireman into senior rank. I had never actually served on a fireboat, my brief encounter with one only lasting two weeks many moons before and in the late 1960s. By the early 1990s the Brigade's sole river fire station at Lambeth had been one of my twenty-three fire stations – fire stations that I had day-to-day 'operational' oversight of as the head of operations covering South West London.

The decision of the Brigade's Medical Examiner, the year before, had meant I was to be pensioned off as a result of a due to service accident early on in my career. (An injury that was, ironically, caused by a steel first aid box that had launched itself at me unexpectedly, and at a rate of knots, when the fire engine I was riding stopped suddenly.)

My final months in the LFB were spent performing 'light duties'. I was out of the operational loop. A senior officer without portfolio. Then, together with a close senior colleague (in a similar state of flux), we were tasked to conduct an in-depth review of the Brigade's river fire service. It was part of a wider Fire Cover review of the London Fire Brigade. We both relished our task. We did not pull any punches. Our report was published in the November of 1995. It highlighted surprising facts, some of which caused consternation among our principals. Its recommendations lay gathering dust for a while, before finally they saw the light of day in October 1997, and after we had both retired. It would bring about a change in the Brigade's fireboat provision.

The Brigade's fireboat the 'London Phoenix' had been acquired in 1983. The 'London Phoenix' had been provided, and maintained, by contractors. She was increasingly proving to be unsatisfactory. The Brigade's top management considered that, in the light of the proposed dockland developments and anticipated growth in riverside redevelopments, a Brigade-owned firefighting vessel was now required. Our report had shown that London's land-based firefighting crews were capable of dealing with fires and incidents in riverside properties. Only on relatively rare occasions were they assisted substantially by the 'London Phoenix' fireboat, or the 'Fire Hawk' in its reserve fireboat role. It was considered that only mid-stream fires were the main role for the fireboat.

Based on the findings of our original review London's Fire Authority had authorised the Brigade to draw up a new fireboat specification. The Director of Technical and Property Services was to invite tenders for the purchase of two new fireboats. The specification, in brief, required the vessel to be capable of rapid response (thirty knots) from the Lambeth river station with a boat crew of four to meet, at predetermined pick-up points along the river, and transport up to five land-based firefighters with their equipment to an incident in the middle of the river. Once the fire-fighting crew were aboard, the vessel could reduce speed because the number of rendezvous points available should ensure that the journey to the incident would be relatively short.

The fireboat design required a bow ramp to be fitted which would enable the firefighters to embark and disembark from the boat on to slipways or jetties which are located at strategic points on the river. The aim was to reach the pick-up point safely within a maximum of thirty minutes from mobilisation.

An independent diesel-driven fire pump and monitor were to be provided to fight fires either directly from the vessel by way of the monitor, or by hose to a branch which could be taken onto another vessel or the shore. It was envisaged that the vessel would be in the order of thirteen metres in length and approximately 3.5 metres in beam. The vessel would be driven by twin diesel engines and jet drives to eliminate the risk of the propellers being fouled by debris in the river. (A frequent occurrence with the 'Phoenix' that required the services of a diver, or the propeller damaged when operating in shallow water.)

Eight companies had initially registered an interest, each providing financial and technical details. Brigade officers made visits to seven of the eight companies to examine their facilities and discuss with their designers the outline design specification. The eighth company was discounted as they were not boat build-ers. All the seven companies visited were considered suitable to be included in the tender process. Of the seven companies invited to tender, one subsequently declined, two did not bother to respond. Four companies completed the tendering process.

These four companies proposed three basic types of craft. One, a landing craft design; the second, a conventional boat with below deck stowage and a hinged ramp arrangement on the bow, the third, a landing craft vessel where the wheelhouse was mounted near the bow. All three types met the basic design specification.

There were both advantages and disadvantages in the three designs of craft offered to the Brigade. Both types of landing craft had a low-hinged bow door which was ideal for beach landing compared with a high-hinged ramp. However, the disadvantage of this design is that the closeness of the working deck to the water line lessens stability. The lower-hinged ramp is easier to use when recovering people or items from the water but has the disadvantage that water could flood the craft.

Both the landing craft design had the aft deck (high level) segregated from the fore deck (low level) by cabins which means that any equipment which is loaded on the stern, say from a jetty, had to be carried through the wheelhouse and down a ladder to the lower deck to allow it be off loaded from the bow ramp. In a more conventional boat the equipment and crew can embark over the side and move the equipment around the deck without having to enter a cabin and negotiate several steps.

The tender submitted by Alnmaritec Ltd was the preferred tender and provided for a more conventional type of vessel built from a marine grade aluminium alloy, with a flat deck allowing easy access from the stern to stem with one step down but no entry required into the cabin. The overall length was 14.2 metres with a 4 metre beam. Alnmaritec's proposal was for the 240-volt generator and fire pump to be mounted in one of the voids and remotely controlled from the boat's wheelhouse. The fireboat's insulation meant that the environmental noise for the crew would be low. There was only one cabin in their design to accommodate both the crew of four and the five 'land' firefighters, which also enabled the fireboat's officer in charge to be in full control of all personnel. All the crew and passenger seats were fitted with lap and diagonal seat belts, with the fireboat crew of four having suspension seats since they will travel at high speed to the rendezvous points. To overcome any visibility problems the foreword ramp was fitted with mesh panels.

In 1999 the Brigade took delivery of its two new generation fireboats, the 'Fire Dart' and the 'Fire Flash', the LFB's current fireboats. These craft had been designed to attend a wide range of emergencies along the river and riverside properties. As well as their statutory firefighting duties they were also capable of responding to other lifesaving tasks on the river and would work alongside the Royal National Lifeboat Institution's Thames's rapid rescue service. With one of the fireboats on immediate standby, the second is held in reserve and used for training. Each fireboat is powered by two water jets and the boats fitted with a bow ramp that can be lowered when beaching on the foreshore. On board are pumps, mud mats and cradles as well as a monitor that can deliver water from the Thames at 1,850 litres (400 gallons) per minute at ten bars (150 pounds per square inch).

**The 'Fire Dart' and 'Fire Flash' at the Lambeth River fire station.
(Paul Wood)**

Footnote:
Both the 'London Phoenix' and 'Fire Hawk' were sold off, both finding a new role as private commercial boats. At one point there was deliberation that the river station should be considered for other possible uses under the Brigade's accommodation strategy. As it was discovered that there was little prospect of income from its sale or lease the station remained, and still remains, in use.

The 'New Millennium' was a term widely used in the late 1990s to describe the coming of the 21st century. For most the 3rd millennium began on January 1, 2000 (although in truth it actually began on January 1, 2001!). As the new century came about, so changes were heading the way of the LFB and to its river service, not all of which were welcome. On the evening of those Millennium New Year celebrations tens of thousands headed in to London to see the new century in, many of them on and around the banks of the River Thames. The celebrations passed without any significantly high demands on the Brigade's resources, including that of its fireboat. The fireboat did, however, attend five calls to various persons fallen into the river between 6 p.m. on the evening of the 31st December until 9 a.m. on the morning of the 1st January. The fireboat crew also assisted in release of a trapped casualty from Westminster pier whilst additionally attending a fire call during that same night.

The start of the New Year in 2000 was not only the start of a new millennium. London had a new regulatory authority, and its first elected Mayor. The Greater London Authority (GLA) had been born. It was created as the top-tier administrative body for Greater London. It consisted of a directly elected executive Mayor of London, the first being Ken Livingstone (the former Leader of the Labour-led Greater London Council) together with an elected twenty-five member London Assembly. The authority, established following a local referendum, was given most of its powers by the Greater London Authority Act that was passed into law in 1999. (This was later added to by the Greater London Authority Act of 2007.)

It still remains London's strategic regional authority today. It has powers over transport, policing, economic development, and fire and emergency planning including policy on London's fireboats. It oversees three functional bodies: Transport for London, the Mayor's Office for Policing and Crime, and London Fire and Emergency Planning Authority. The planning policies of the Mayor of London are detailed in a statutory London Plan that is regularly updated and published. The GLA is mostly funded by direct government grant and it is also a precepting authority, with some money collected with local Council Tax. The GLA is unique in the British local government system, in terms of structure, elections and selection of powers. The authority was established to replace a range of joint boards and quangos, including the quango that had previously overseen the London Fire Brigade since the abolition of the GLC in 1986.

The London Fire and Emergency Planning Authority (LFEPA) is the body that runs the London Fire Brigade and it works with the London Borough Councils and the Common Council of the City of London in planning for civil peacetime emergencies. The Authority's statutory obligations were originally set out in the Fire Services Act 1947, which was later repealed in 2004 by the new Fire Services Act. (This was introduced, in part, in the wake of the 11th September 2001 terrorist bombings involving New York's Twin Towers and the subsequent 'Bain's Review' of the UK Fire Service.) The LFEPA's stated principal aim is: *'Making London a safer city by minimising the risks and social and economic costs of fire and other hazards'.* It sets policy, strategy and the budget of the London Fire Brigade, whilst remaining accountable to the people who live, work and visit London and to the London council taxpayers, whose money helps to fund their fire service.

Within just a few weeks of New Year's Day, and in the wake of the 'Marchioness' disaster (20th August 1989) ten years earlier, Lord Justice Clarke had been required by the Deputy Prime Minister, John Prescott (who held the duel posts of the Secretary of State for the Environment, under whose umbrella the fire services sat), to undertake an Inquiry into safety on the River Thames. The 'London Phoenix' had assisted in those dramatic rescue operations in 1989. Lord Justice Clarke had held his first public meeting in September 1999. At the very start of his Inquiry he acknowledged that many safety changes had already taken place, whilst others were in the active process of being implanted.

Lord Clarke's completed report ran to three volumes. His findings took full account the earlier 'Marchioness' 'Hayes' report (conducted by John Hayes, Secretary of the Law Society) and the Coroner's resumed inquest. As a result of that inquest, held in April 1995, the coroner's verdict had included twelve river safety recommendations.

Following the fatal 'Marchioness' disaster in 1989, which had killed fifty-one people, there had been a continuing series of river accidents on the London section of the Thames, not all of which involved the London Fire Brigade or its fireboat. The worst accident was a fatal speedboat incident at Richmond weir. There had been an additional collision between a passenger-carrying vessel and a commercial craft. The damage in that case was superficial and no injuries resulted from that accident. There had been a number of fires on board passenger vessels post 'Marchioness', one so serious that it spread from the engine room to the superstructure. In his report Lord Justice Clarke stated: *'It has been suggested to me, in truth, it is now the risk of fire rather than collision that poses the most significant safety risk to passenger vessels.'*

When considering the issue of the avoidance of casualties Lord Justice Clarke held the view that the regulation of safety on the Thames (post 1989) had improved almost beyond recognition, and he cited the numerous individual advances. When considering the resources available to deal with incidents in the Inquiry area (London's River Thames) he expressed the view that: *'Two new [London] fireboats have been purchased and were in use. Although provided for firefighting purposes, that are available and equipped for rescue work. The two new craft are rapid response vessels.'*

Lord Justice Clarke made comment about the Brigade's new generation fireboats, the 'Fire Dart' and 'Fire Flash'. *'There is no doubt that those two vessels are a most valuable addition to the SAR [Search and Rescue] resources on the Thames. They are capable of 30 or 32 knots and one of them will be available for immediate deployment, fully crewed, at any time of the day or night. Unless that vessel happens to be responding to a fire at any particular time, it will therefore be able to immediately answer a call for SAR assistance. [...]*

They are capable of taking many more people on board than many of the other vessels which are likely to respond to an emergency on the river. I understand that they could, if necessary, even take as many as 50, although not without difficulty. I observed one of the two new fireboats in action during a live river exercise on the 27 October 1999. It was pointed out to me during this exercise that the fireboats have the advantage of a ramp at the bow which can be lowered into the water to facilitate access to the fireboat from the water.'

In its submission to the 'Clarke' Inquiry the London Fire Brigade explained that the river firefighters have special training packages that include coxswain training, crew commander training and fireboat crew operator training. This training was delivered through a mixture of internal and external courses provided and overseen by the National Sea School at Gravesend, in Kent.

In his Inquiry conclusion Lord Justice Clarke drew attention to the well-developed emergency plans (including those of the London Fire Brigade) put in place post 'Marchioness', but he remained concerned that they may not be adequate to meet all foreseeable types of emergency.

The horrific, sickening and catastrophic events that took place in New York City on the 11th September 2001 may seem a world away from anything to do with London's fireboats; but the tragic consequences of that suicidal terrorist attack left in its wake far more than the two thousand, six hundred and six fatalities – fatalities that included three hundred and forty three of New York City's firefighters. The repercussions of that day went global. No single event since the Second World War has made such a profound impact on world events. Its consequences are still being felt right to this present day. History has already shown that the American-led coalition of Western powers (by launching armed aggression, first against Afghanistan and then against Iraq) led to a tide of anti-Americanism and surge of support for fanatical Islamism across the Muslim world and beyond. Those wars have cost tens of thousands of lives and caused mass destruction. The billions of dollars expended on them was financed largely from borrowing, which in turn lead to destabilising the world economy. The threat caused by acts of terrorism is now a core strategic concern of Government, and in London the London Fire and Emergency Planning Authority.

London's population density, the concentration of critical infrastructure and its national (and global) profile as a centre for business and tourism mean a high proportion of UK government domestic security and resilience resources are required in terms of both expenditure and dedicated trained personnel. The London Fire Brigade is an integral part of the capital's 'first responders'. The current London Resilience arrangement, which includes the

Brigade's fireboats, arose from the findings of the post 9/11 review that was led by senior civil servants and members of the emergency services. They reported that, while the capital was generally well prepared for major incidents and catastrophes, a 'new strategic emergency planning regime' was necessary to meet larger scale challenges. London's fireboats play a role in those emergency plans for the capital.

In January 2001 a new search and rescue service for the River Thames was announced. The Government asked the Royal National Lifeboat Institution (RNLI) to provide lifeboat cover. This was the first time the RNLI was specifically covering a river rather than estuarial and coastal waters. The request came as a direct result of the findings of the Thames Safety Inquiries into the collision between the pleasure cruiser 'The 'Marchioness' and the dredger 'Bowbelle'. By 2002 a RNLI lifeboat station was established on the north shore at Tower Pier. A 40-knot E-Class lifeboat was put into service on the 2nd January. The London Fire Brigade and the Metropolitan Police were on longer the only kids on the block when it came to search and rescue arrangements for the tidal reaches of the River Thames.

The RNLI lifeboat. (Royal National Lifeboat Institution)

As with the Brigade's and the Met Police's boat stations, the RNLI station was crewed continuously and provided an immediate response. It was co-ordinated by the Maritime and Coastguard Agency (MCA) from the PLA control room at the Thames Barrier. Two of the three-person crew at each station were full-time, the third crew member a volunteer. Target times for the RNLI rapid response boats were 15 minutes, from their two London stations and the additional stations at Teddington and Gravesend. The Tower RNLI lifeboat station, which is approximately mid-point between the Lambeth fireboat station and the Mets' Wapping Police boat station, covers approximately a fifteen-mile stretch of the Thames from Barking Creek up to Battersea. However, these limits are only a guide. If either the Gravesend or Chiswick lifeboats are involved in incidents at the easterly and westerly limits of their areas respectively, then other craft, including the Brigade's fireboats, are called to incidents as and when required.

Joint training between the RNLI and the Brigade's fireboat crews became a regular feature in addition to their close co-operation during search and rescue operations on the River Thames.

Footnotes:

In 2004 a framed RNLI gallantry certificate, signed by Surgeon Rear Admiral F. Golden and the RNLI Chief Executive, was awarded to Helmsman Mike Sinacola, Mechanic Michael Neild and Crew Member Will Lawrie for their exceptional devotion to duty in carrying out first aid on a seriously injured woman in difficult circumstances, their combined actions instrumental in saving the woman's life.

The new RNLI facilities on the Waterloo Pier lifeboat station were started in 2005 and completed in 2006. The Waterloo RNLI station was the busiest RNLI station in the UK in 2015.

Up to, and including, the spring of 2015 London's RNLI lifeboat crews have saved 420 lives since they began their operations on the River Thames.

In 2002 there were occasions where the River Thames had no London Fire Brigade fireboat cover. The UK firefighters nationally, including London firefighters and its fireboat crews, had taken on the government in the biggest industrial clash for more than a decade. The rumblings had begun back in that spring. The Fire Brigades Union had launched its campaign for a rise in the basic salary from £21,531 to £30,000. The government was very determined not to fund, what it saw as, an inflationary pay claim nor lose out in a trial of strength with the 'unions'. This clash resulted in a very flammable mixture of industrial unrest. The local authorities (the fire service national employers) originally offered a four percent rise, with anything additional only coming from an independent review, set up by the government, under Sir George Bains.

However, the firefighters refused to have anything to do with the Bains Review. Instead they voted by almost nine to one for strike action. The deputy Prime Minister, John Prescott, took personal charge of the peace-making. Yet despite what was described as robust 'industrial language' after several meetings between him and the FBU, the FBU's leader, Andy Gilchrist, thought he was finally making progress. But when Bains published an interim review report that recommended an eleven percent rise over two years, but conditional on sweeping, and drastic, changes in fire service working practices, the firefighter's Union finally decided it was time to walk and not talk. It was the first national fire strike in 25 years. The result was that the armed forces had to take over, providing 'emergency' fire cover across the whole country. Equipped with ageing 'Cold-War' Green Goddess fire-engines the troops responded to fire and rescue emergency calls, with some hesitancy at first, then with growing confidence. Temporary emergency arrangements were even made to secure fire-fighting tugs for any fire incidents on the River Thames.

After the first 48-hour strike came another frenzied round of talks took place between the Union and the Employers. An all-night session appeared to produce agreement giving a two-year, 16 percent pay deal. Their agreement never saw the light of day as John Prescott intervened. He publicly attacked both the FBU and the national employers for signing what he described as a 'bouncing cheque' – something they expected the central government to fund. The Union then took its membership out on a ten-day total strike, the FBU believing that firefighters now occupied the moral high ground. But the government fought back vigorously. It used the apparent success of the troops in replacing the firefighters as a weapon against the FBU. One Government Minister after another lined up to say the troops had coped well with their limited resources. (Which was true to a degree.) The FBU, in turn, insisted that not all emergency calls had been answered and the military had failed to tackle fires as effectively as firefighters. As the eight-day strike ended, both sides started upon a long, bruising battle. Some of the scars of that battle continue to linger until today, especially as the nature and culture of the fire service changed. During that heated dispute London's fireboats remained moored at Lambeth whilst the river firefighters picketed the entrance to their river station pontoon.

Even without the FBU strike, the first couple of years of the 'noughties' were charged with the usual moans from London's firefighters, and of rising dissatisfaction in the LFB. Yet deep down the majority knew it was a job that was to be treasured. That was certainly the case with the river firefighters who had an affinity with the River Thames, its culture and its people, as strong as their kinship to the Brigade.

London's fire brigade does not operate in a vacuum. It is influenced by outside factors and has to respond to them. Whilst some of those serving considered that the whole ethos of the 'old' discipline regime in the Brigade was changing, and not necessarily for the better, the LFB remains an organisation employing almost seven thousand people; an organisation where its 'people' policies are required to reflect the modernisation of employment law and current employment practices. The amended Fire Service Act of 1947 was already over fifty years old. Its related Discipline Regulations had not been amended either in a decade and most considered them to have passed their sell-by date. Many believed the changes made by top management, the ones that removed the perceived 'military' aspect of the firefighter's job, was taking a too soft approach. Regardless of those concerns, a cultural change was taking place across the LFB. Its new firefighter recruits, arriving at the Brigade's training school, enjoyed a different set of values with their rebranded 'Trainers' over what twenty-year service firefighters had experienced with their recruit training under the former 'Instructors'. There appeared a misperception of new entrants openly questioning former values, of marching and saluting whilst at Training School as having no place in the fire service of the twenty-first century. Some 'old school' members of the Brigade believed it all a step too far and a few even voiced those concerns. A few paying the penalty of putting their heads above the parapet as management appeared willing to invoke disciplinary sanctions, even if they were wrapped in the new style 'employment' practices now so in vogue. However, the fear that changes in the Brigade were misdirected and going too far has yet to be realised. The feeling expressed around the fire station mess table that the 'job' would all too soon go the way society was heading – one in which it was no longer considered acceptable for parents to be allowed to discipline their own children, a nanny state – was not in evidence on the incident ground. Theirs remains a job where disciple really does matter, both on the land and on the river. The very nature of fire has not changed. The manner in which it is tackled and fought by the Brigade, in recent times, has. Only an independent external audit will determine just how effective and successful the changes have been. This have yet to be established.

The biggest change to hit the Fire Service since its de-nationalisation after the Second World War occurred in 2004. A new Fire and Rescue Services Act was passed into law that year. It changed many former working practices. It had been brought in to replace the Fire Services Act of 1947. The 2004 Act also repealed several other existing acts, many going back five decades.

That 2004 Act saw the formal introduction of something called the Integrated Personal Development System (IPDS): a system that the London Fire Brigade had played a major part in, both in its development and extended trialling. All future fire service training and development would be based on identified needs and risk-assessed by addressing the 'risk critical' development requirement of operational personnel. A series of National Occupational Standards had been devised and published which set out to describe the skills, knowledge and understanding needed to undertake a particular task or job to a nationally recognised level of fire service competence. In respect of the river firefighters, as with their land-based counterparts, these standards included the various roles undertaken and required of London's fireboat crews. The river firefighter development programmes were an expanded package of learning that gave opportunities to build on their knowledge, skills and understanding to meet the identified training needs of a firefighter and their specialist river role. Their training include specialist external courses as well as learning in the workplace, i.e. the river.

The 2004 Act had also removed the previous fire service single level entry system for operational staff. It now facilitated multi-level entry. This change meant suitable external staff could be recruited directly into roles other than firefighter and enabled in-service staff with potential to progress more quickly. London's firefighters saw graduate entry introduced. The graduates started at the Brigades training school at Southwark. (The Brigade later outsourced all its training, including recruit firefighters training, to a private company, currently Babcock's plc. For the first time in the history of the London Fire Brigade it did not provide the majority of its training in-house.) The graduates then undertake a few placements at fire stations before going to the Fire Service College at Moreton in Marsh (Gloucestershire) before coming out as a Watch Manager (previously a Station Officer). They then attain Station Manager Status within a year. Each of the four watches at Lambeth river station includes a Watch Manager who is overseen by a Station Manager.

Lambeth's river fire station has a unique feature amongst the 112 fire stations that comprised the London Fire Brigade in the early 2000s. In fact London river fire stations always had it; none have ever had an actual fire station ground. The fireboats cover the length of London's River Thames. It is all the fire stations that line the north and south banks of the Thames that have their respective stations ground extend to the mid-point of the river. The fireboat simply maintains its primary function of being a floating pump and acting in support of the land based crews and, when required, acting as a rescue craft, a function that was diminishing as the new century took hold and the River Thames landscapes continued to change, changes that continued to see a reduction in riverside fires and travel distances for the fireboat that meant land crews, in the main, dealt with the incidents as they occurred and without the aid of the fireboat.

The Thames changing river-scape: a former warehouse converted into
plush riverside apartments and 'lofts'. (Author)

In the continuing efforts to enhance river safety on the Thames the fireboat was involved various training exercises. In 2006 a series of special joint exercises were conducted by the Marine and Coastguard Agency (MCA). They involved London's River Thames 'first responders'. The first such exercise took place in

July. It involved the emergency evacuation of a Thames passenger vessel which was involved in an accident/collision where it was not possible to undertake normal disembarkation to either dry land, attending vessels or other lifesaving rivercraft. Most UK registered passenger vessels operating on domestic voyages, including Thames river trips, are required to carry one or more life rafts. However, the viability of these life rafts, and in particular 'open reversible inflatable life-rafts (ORILs), as an evacuation platform had previously been questioned. The main concerns related to the evacuation procedures and the feasibility of towing an ORIL and its occupants to safety, especially in a Thames current or its tidal stream. These exercises were planned to ascertain, among other things, the feasibility and effectiveness of an ORIL as an evacuation platform, as well as assessing the evacuation of a passenger vessel utilising attending rescue craft, namely the brigades' fireboat and the RNLI lifeboat.

The second exercise, also held in July, was again conducted by the MCA in partnership with the RNLI, the Metropolitan Police Marine Support Unit, the London Fire Brigade and Seaweather Marine Services Limited. Its aim was assess the dynamic and lateral stability and general behaviour of an ORIL while under tow in a tidal current. The raft was also observed when drifting freely in the vicinity of obstructions that a deployed ORIL would likely encounter in a Thames environment. It was found in both exercises that the rescue vessel crew's boats need to have sufficient power and manoeuvrability to control and, where appropriate, tow the life-rafts and be aware of the effect of the wash of the rescue vessel when approaching the ORIL.

The third exercise, held in October, involved a domestic passenger ship evacuation on the River Thames. The exercise formed a part of a larger training day for the Passenger Boat Association members. In this exercise eighty volunteers on board a twin-decked passenger vessel were successfully evacuated after supposed damage resulting from a mid-stream collision. The chosen methods of exit were recorded, although the majority of the evacuees utilised the life-rafts provided. Further trials were later conducted, after the main evacuation exercise had been completed, using people with reduced mobility (again volunteers) to assess the effectiveness of the arrangements (both equipment and operational) for evacuating such passengers.

The last of the 2006 exercises, named 'Palm Tree', was held on the on the Thames during November. Its aim was primarily intended to test the co-ordination and communication between London's emergency services in the event of a major maritime incident on the River Thames. The exercise involved the evacuation of many passengers from a passenger vessel moored mid-stream and the search for, and rescue of, persons who had abandoned the vessel directly into the water (represented by mannequins) The fireboat played a major part in this exercise as did the RNLI, the Metropolitan Police Marine Support Unit, and the London Ambulance Service. Additional involvement came from the Royal Air Force, the Department for Transport, the London Boroughs of Hammersmith and Fulham and Wandsworth, and the Port of London Authority. Both the fire service and the RNLI was commended for their parts in the exercise programme.

**The London Fire Brigade's fireboat powering down the Thames.
(Colin Court)**

'Special services' are emergency calls made to the fire service that don't involve fire. They happen on the river as well as on land.

Not all involve people but come under the heading of 'rendering humanitarian services'. Sadly not all of them have a happy ending.

On Friday 20 January 2006 a juvenile female Northern bottle-nose whale was discovered swimming in the River Thames in central London. According to the BBC, she was five metres (16 feet) long and weighed about seven tonnes (24,400 lb). The whale appeared to have been lost, as her normal habitat would have been around the coasts of the far north of Scotland and Northern Ireland, and in the seas around the Arctic Ocean. It was the first time the species had been seen in the Thames since records began in 1913.

Strenuous efforts are made to save the whale, sadly all too late.
(Colin Court)

The day before reports from the Thames Barrier control team were made to the British Divers Marine Life Rescue (BDMLR) that one, or possibly two, pilot whales had come through the barrier. This turned out to be the bottlenose whale. The BDMLR started to monitor the whale's reported movements. The following morning a Mr David Dopin was on a train when he phoned the authorities to say that he believed he had been hallucinating, as he thought he had just spotted a whale swimming in the River Thames. Throughout that morning more and more whale sightings were reported. The whale was finally projected into the wider public eye when the bottlenose whale was captured by television cameras and became the top London news story of the day.

The whale beached several times during that day as the tide went out. Members of the public went onto the foreshore to encourage the whale back into deeper water. Concern grew to grow for the mammal's wellbeing. Bottlenose whales are used to swimming in seas up to 700 metres (2300 feet) deep, but the Thames has a depth of only five metres (16 feet) at most. The whale was also injured as blood was now visible.

As night approached there were signs that the whale may have swam out with the current, from London towards the sea. An unconfirmed sighting by a BBC cameraman placed the whale in Greenwich Reach area around 9 p.m. The area was subsequently searched but nothing was found. There were no further sightings until 1.10 a.m. the following morning at Battersea, after the tide had changed. The whale's position was monitored until 3.30 a.m. when a Marine Mammal Medic called the monitoring off as the whale would not get stranded on a high tide.

On the 21st January the assistance of the Brigade's fireboat and crew was requested. At The Port Authority officials had started observing the whale again at 7.30 a.m. It was decided that the BDMLR would have to assist the whale as she was not strong enough to swim out of the Thames unaided and she had been losing ground against the tide. There was fear later that day that the whale might have perished as she had not been seen for some time. She was spotted again by a Port Authority boat at 9.26 a.m. near the Albert Bridge. The BDMLR had decided it was time to act. With significant help from the Brigade, Port of London Authority and the Metropolitan Police, BDMLR medics had decided to deliberately beach the whale at low tide on a sandbank, and then move her out of the Thames. By midday they captured the whale. They covered her eyes to prevent her from panicking, and made a medical examination.

After two hours, the whale had been slowly, and gently, lifted onto a barge by crane near the Albert Bridge. By this stage there were thousands of people watching the situation develop from the banks of the river. Images were seen across the world. The excitement of the previous day had disappeared. It had been replaced by serious concern that the whale would be unable to survive much longer. As the barge rushed along the Thames towards the sea, news channels provided non-stop coverage of the journey. It reached the Thames Barrier at approximately 5 p.m. Later, despite the darkness, it was reported that crowds were lining the Queen Elizabeth II Bridge to catch a glimpse of the barge.

As each hour passed concern grew for the whale's health. The medics considered she was taking a turn for the worse due to being out of the water, as well as slowly being crushed by her own body weight. At 7.08 p.m. and heading to the sea the on-board vet confirmed the whale had sadly died after suffering from convulsions.

From 2007 the London Fire Brigade was led by its new Commissioner Ron Dobson. (Other UK fire brigades still used the term 'Chief Fire Officer'.) He had a turbulent few years and faced many challenges. Then in 2011 he retired – well, not quite! After quitting his £200,000 a year post, and allegedly receiving an estimated £700,000 retirement package, he walked straight back into his former job, his re-employment being agreed behind closed doors at the London Fire Authority council meeting. A meeting from which the public were excluded.

His tenure as Commissioner found him frequently at the centre of controversy, as he strove to steer the Brigade forward through a significant period of modernisation against a background of increasing financial pressure and budgets cuts because of reductions in Government funding and its grants to local authorities. Inheriting the former Commissioner's 2nd London Safety Plan, Dobson carried forwarded the plans aims to improve the impact the Brigade had in making London safer. His plan was to create a modern fire and rescue service which works hard to stop emergencies happening in the first place and when they do to always respond quickly and effectively when called to a fire or other emergency. At its core was the philosophy that prevention is better than cure. By reducing the actual number of fires breaking out reduces the hurt, distress, property damage and economic loss which they cause.

The 2nd London Fire Safety Plan included a review of fire boat service based on a pontoon at Lambeth. The review concluded that the Brigade should maintain a fireboat service, but rather than the two boats they had at that time (one permanently crewed and one available for use as required, staffed by crew from Lambeth Fire Station), there should be just a single, permanently crewed fire boat. The second vessel to be used as a reserve or for training. The review also recommended that the river station should be treated as a fire station in its own right, rather than as part of Lambeth Fire Station with its own station commander. The current fireboat engines will also be upgraded to provide a faster response, be more fuel efficient and produce fewer exhaust emissions.

Since it had been opened in 1937 the London Fire Brigade Headquarters building had housed both Lambeth fire station and Lambeth river station personnel. In 2007 the HQ complex was put up for sale. The fire station and river station remained (for now), but the powers that be, the Commissioner's policy board, were out to make a quick buck. It was the time of the London property boom and this prime riverside real estate was considered a 'golden egg', its sale boosting the LFB coffers and paying for the building of other much needed fire stations. It never happened. Despite the Headquarters staff decamping to the former, now converted, Royal Mail sorting Office in Southwark's Union Street, and in the shadow of the Brigade's Southwark Training Centre at considerable cost, and moving from a freehold building into a leased building, the Lambeth redevelopment never got of the drawing board. It still remains unsold.

Then in September 2008, to add to the financial woes of the LFB – and, in fact, the global economy – the collapse of Lehman Brothers happened. This sprawling world-wide bank almost brought down the world's financial system. In the UK it took huge taxpayer-financed bail-outs to shore up the banking industry. The ensuing 'credit crunch' turned what was already a nasty downturn into the worst recession in 80 years. Massive monetary and fiscal stimulus prevented wholesale depression and the age of austerity started. The ripples of the financial crisis were felt everywhere; local government and the London Fire Brigade were not spared. Failures in finance were at the heart of the crash.

In August 2008, the then Labour Chancellor, Alistair Darling, in an interview with the *Guardian* newspaper, said the current downturn would be more 'profound and long-lasting' than most had feared. He was right, it was. Hard and difficult decisions had to be taken in the London Fire Brigade to balance its allocated funding to meet its needs. Staffing reductions, station closures, withdrawn fire appliances reduced London's fire cover from its pre-2008 levels. Yet despite the reduction in fire calls and workload on the Thames the fireboat escaped unscathed. Even when fourteen fire stations were listed for closure in 2014, and ten were actually shut down, the river fire station never featured on any hit-list. Its strategic importance remain intact. This seems set to continue.

Rescuing people from the Thames can sometimes involve the fireboat crews in extracting individuals trapped in the Thames mud. (Colin Court)

The fireboat crew responding to people threating to jump into the river from London bridges is nothing new. Sadly, sometimes they arrive too late; their duty then rests with a search and hopefully recovery of a body. On the 7th April 2008, however, there was a much happier outcome. Both the fireboat and land crews had been summoned by a 999 call to a man threatening to leap to his death from the Millennium Bridge.

(Jonathan Buckmaster/Express Newspapers/N&A Syndication)

With the fireboat 'Fire Dart' positioned in the river below, Firefighter Khalid Obadele, from Euston fire station's fire rescue tender, had climbed onto the bridge, helped by a colleague, and had edged himself out over the river towards the man who was in a precarious position and agitated state on the other side of the safety railings. As the agitated man waved him back, Ff Obadele, wearing a safety harness, wrapped his legs round the man and strapped him to his own body before he rolled him off the bridge edge, lowering himself and the man to the waiting fireboat.

Firefighter Obadele was subsequently awarded a Letter of Congratulations for his gallantry. The 47-year-old was also named as England's bravest firefighter in 'The Spirit of Fire Awards' run by the Fire Services National Benevolent Fund charity. Khalid later said: *'It hasn't made any difference to my life. It's my job. But my mum has got all these newspaper clippings on the wall. It's kind of embarrassing going into her house.'* He had been with the fire rescue team at Euston fire station for eighteen years. He said of the incident: *'The man was about 70 feet up and was saying he was going to jump. We were determined to save his life. He wasn't going to jump, not with us there.'*

The 'Fire Flash' on a training exercise on the Thames. (Paul Wood)

London's new breed of fireboat continued to play an active role in the safety of those working and travelling on the River Thames working side by side with the other waterborne emergency services. On the 18th August 2011 the 'Fire Dart', together with other major players in Thames River safety, responded to the sinking of the 'Chieftain' tug boat when it capsized and sank with the loss of one life by Conveys Wharf off Deptford Reach. The PLA. Metropolitan Police river service, the RNLI and the Brigade all attended the scene but it took a three-day search to finally locate and recover a body. The tug was later raised to the surface by a river crane mounted on a barge.

The 'Fire Dart' attending a six pump fire on the Woolwich ferry, South East London. (Mary Evans)

The sinking was later attributed to the floating crane rig the 'Chieftain' was towing jack-knifing onto the tug. It was the second Thames fatality that week, the first being a nineteen year old who was crewing the Woolwich Ferry and was dragged overboard by a mooring rope while releasing lines securing the ferry to a mooring buoy. The nineteen year-old had had suffered head injuries and did not regain consciousness after he was rescued from the water following the accident on the South-East London based ferry.

In 2012 the Government published its framework for the fire services in England. In his Ministerial foreword, Bob Neil, the then Minister of Fire and Rescue Services wrote: *'We are rightly proud of our fire and rescue authorities. The professionalism, courage, and commitment of our firefighters in ensuring that our communities are safer places, less exposed to the destruction and devastation caused by fire exemplifies all that we rightly value in a public service.'*

The framework required all English Fire and Rescue authorities to make provision to respond to incidents such as fires, road traffic accidents and emergencies within their area and in other areas in line with their mutual aid agreements and reflect this in their integrated risk management plans. In London the fireboat remained part of the London Fire Brigade plans to achieve this.

The 'Fire Flash' taking part in the 2012 Thames Pageant to celebrate Her Majesty Queen Elizabeth's Diamond Jubilee. (Mary Evans)

On the 3rd June 2012 the 'Fire Flash' fireboat was shining like a new pin. It had somewhere special to be and was one of six hundred and seventy boats taking part in the Thames Diamond Jubilee Pageant. It was part of the celebrations of the Diamond Jubilee of Elizabeth II. The Queen, Prince Philip and other members of the Royal Family were aboard vessels that took part in the parade. The parade had been organised by the Thames Diamond Jubilee Foundation, and funded by private donations and sponsorship.

The vessels taking part that day included military, commercial, and pleasure craft. According to the Guinness World Records, it was the largest ever parade of boats, surpassing the previous record of 327 vessels set in Bremerhaven, Germany, in 2011. Sailing vessels and others too tall to pass under the bridges were moored as an 'Avenue of Sail' downstream of London Bridge with smaller craft in St Katharine Docks. Whilst the LFB's 'Fire Dart' maintained operational fireboat cover of the Thames and, in part, provided fire cover to the numerous craft taking part, the 'Fire Flash' was crewed by volunteer river firefighters. It was estimated that one million spectators watched from the banks of the Thames by British media companies. The pageant was broadcast live by the both the BBC and Sky News and was subsequently broadcast around the world on other networks. More than 10 million tuned into to watch the BBC's four and a half hour coverage that attracted an audience average of 10.3 million viewers.

The 999 summons for assistance had the 'Fire Dart' speeding up river to Twickenham at 5.29 a.m. on the morning of the 26th November in that year. A fire had started on a barge used as a houseboat, which quickly gained a hold and grew in intensity. So much so that the fire spread to a second boat, also used as a houseboat. The boats were moored off Ash Island near Hampton Court Road in East Mosley.

Despite its thirty-five knots speed (40 miles per hour) the 'Fire Dart' had a considerable distance to cover, almost to the boundary between Greater London and Surrey. From its river station on the Albert Embankment to Ash Island is, as the crow flies, thirteen miles' (20 kilometres') travel distance. However, the snaking River Thames increases that distance to over twenty miles for the fireboat as its wake spreads across the width of the narrow Thames, disturbing those asleep in the house boats, a regular problem for the fireboat who have to arrive as swiftly as possible while occurring the wrath of other River users!

The 'Fire Dart's' travel time meant that the crews from Kingston and Twickenham fire stations, plus a fire engine from Surrey Fire Brigade, didn't only beat them to the incident by a wide margin but almost extinguished the blaze before the fireboat finally arrived. Not that the land firefighters had an easy task, as they first had to navigate their way across a weir in almost pitch darkness to reach Ash Island; they had to transport their light portable pump and the hose to the far end of the Island before they could start to tackle the blaze. Working their way through the mud and with minimal lighting, it was a most challenging incident and they worked strenuously to battle the flames.

The crews had the fire under control by the time the 'Fire Dart' arrived but were grateful of its pumps as the fireboat lifted water from the river to finish dousing the flames on the two burning barges. One of which was so damaged by the fire it sunk. The Watch Manager, Guy Pendilham, one of the twenty-five firefighters on the scene, later gave a press interview regarding the incident. *'A man was asleep on one of the boats and was alerted to the fire by his smoke alarm going off. This may well have saved his life and demonstrates just how vital these smoke alarms are. We gave out free smoke alarms to the other boat owners in the area. Crews are going back again today to offer fire safety advice and smoke alarms to anyone else who may need it.'* With its task done the 'Fire Dart' made its way back to Lambeth at a more sedate pace.

When the 'London Phoenix' fireboat patrolled the Thames emblazoned on the side of the fireboat the words 'FIRE AND RESCUE'. With its departure and the arrival of the RNLI stations on the Thames there was a notable decline in the number of river rescues the new fireboats were called to, although they did still attend such incidents. The RNLI high speed rescue boats had made their presence felt despite the fact that fifteen people still accidentally, and tragically, lost their lives in the River Thames during 2012, according to the Royal National Lifeboat Institution. The charity lifeboat organisation had saved the lives of sixteen people in the River Thames during 2013 and had rescued a further three hundred and forty-four. In the four years since 2009 thirty-four people have accidentally died in the River Thames, with men accounting for 82 percent of fatalities during that time. Slips and falls by the side of the river accounted for 21 percent of deaths. By comparison, swimming and general leisure activities on the water accounted for 18 percent of fatalities over the four years. In 2012 alcohol was recorded a factor in three deaths on the river.

In stark contrast to the Twickenham incident, some river incidents occur on the river fire stations doorstep and they are the first on the scene. Such was the case on the 30th May in 2013 when the prompt actions by the crew of the fireboat saved the life of a man who had entered the Thames near Vauxhall Bridge. In the early hours the fireboat from Lambeth river fire station deployed within 60 seconds of a call from the coastguards and started to search the river. They were joined by a RNLI lifeboat and a boat from the Marine Police. The 'Fire Dart's' cre, using their thermal imaging equipment, spotted the man despite the pitch black conditions and scooped him out of the water with their cradle. They wrapped the semi-conscious casualty in blankets and administered oxygen whilst they returned to the river station where a London Ambulance Service crew were waiting to take the man to hospital. Justin Coo, the river fire station Station Manager, said: *'The fireboat crew had to overcome very challenging conditions with the wind, tide and lack of light and the coastguard said we undoubtedly saved the man's life. The man was suffering from the effects of hypothermia but semi-conscious and breathing. He is not thought to be seriously injured.'* The fireboat crew rescued the man within five minutes of their call.

In that August the fireboat, the RNLI lifeboats and the Marine Police once again combined forces to stop a former Dunkirk 'Little Ship' from sinking on the Thames. The eighty-nine year-old 'Bluebird of Chelsea', which had 13 people on board, sent out a Mayday call at around 8.30 p.m. on a Wednesday evening saying she was holed and rapidly taking on water. The boat was in the Pool of London. The lifeboat from Tower Lifeboat Station was first on the scene and discovered the veteran motor cruiser sinking by the stern some one hundred and fifty metres from the Lifeboat Station. The holed vessel was in imminent danger of rolling over but just made it to the pier where RNLI crew helped to secure her and assisted the passengers and crew to safety.

Four small pumps were used on board 'Bluebird of Chelsea', which prevented the boat sinking entirely and until the fireboat arrived with its larger pumps. The fireboat crew then pumped it out sufficiently to expose the hole. A resourceful firefighter then plugged the hole with a traffic cone until the vessel was rendered safe.

('Bluebird of Chelsea' had been built by Thornycroft at Hampton in 1924 for the then world land speed record holder Sir Malcolm Campbell. During the Dunkirk evacuation in 1940 she was commanded by yachtsman Lt Col Barnard and ferried troops from Dunkirk harbour to larger ships waiting offshore.)

Fires involving strange structures are not uncommon events on land, but on the river they are not an everyday occurrence. But such was the case on a September in 2013 when an amphibious tourist boat, known as a 'DUKW', caught fire just downstream of Lambeth Bridge and near the Palaces of Westminster. Just after midday a total of twenty-eight tourists and two crew members had to be rescued after a fire broke out in the London DUKW Tours craft they were travelling in. A number of those on board, including some children as young as six, jumped into the river fearing that the vessel was about to explode. The 'Fire Dart' was one of the first emergency service vessels on the scene. Its crew quickly gave aid to those in the water and rescued others including the crew members from the DUKW. The incidents attracted large crowds on the river banks and Lambeth and Westminster bridges as smoke billowing from the stricken vessel. News crews were quickly on the scene too and images of the rescues and the aftermath went global.

The 'Fire Dart' extinguishing the burning 'DUKW' prior to towing her away.
(Unknown)

Three people, including a pregnant woman, were treated in hospital for smoke inhalation, while others were treated by paramedics for the effects of cold and shock. An Australian passenger later said: *'We saw smoke, we saw fire and my husband and I said "I think we better jump into the river," and we did. We're Australian, we can swim.'* Elissa Wood, a Londoner who was on the tour with her parents visiting from Australia, said, *'The first we knew of the fire was when they noticed smoke pouring from the front of the craft. We saw the tour guide and the captain look at each other like "this is a real problem" and then they encouraged us to put life jackets on and jump off. It was really hot. The flames were really hot and it was confusing. We weren't sure what was happening so it was scary.'*

The initial call for help from the crew of the DUKW, named 'Cleopatra', went to the Port of London Authority control room at Woolwich, which in turn passed the call onto the London Coastguard (part of the Maritime & Coast guard Agency) and the emergency services. The Coastguard then made the incident known other vessels which were nearby, one such vessel being a Thames Rib – a high speed pleasure craft which was close at hand. A number of passengers were treated at the river bank by paramedics, with no serious injuries. However four passengers were taken to hospital as a precaution for smoke inhalation.

While all of the passengers and crew were quickly accounted for, the emergency services admitted the incident could have easily had tragic consequences. Lambeth's river fire station manager Simon Tuhill said, *'Most of those on board were visitors to the UK, with some coming from Holland, Sweden, Brazil and Australia. They were pretty pragmatic about it all. Obviously it was pretty scary for them. It isn't every day you sink in a boat in the Thames.'* Whilst the fire-ravaged vessel was towed away from the scene by the 'Fire Dart', Port of London Authority, the London Assembly and the Marine Accident Investigation Branch all announced they would be starting separate investigations into the incident.

The London Assembly later conducted a cross party inquiry into the DUKW fire and evacuation on the Thames. The Committee of Inquiry subsequently published its findings and recommendations. They were delighted to hear how effectively the emergency services had responded to the incident and commend the London Fire Brigade, the Maritime and Coastguard Agency, the RNLI, the London Ambulance Service, the Marine Policing Unit and the police helicopter for their respective and co-ordinated roles. Its Chairperson considered that the degree of co-ordination across so many agencies was exemplary and lessons have clearly been learned from previous Thames experiences. The London Assembly had previously highlighted in other similar investigations that communication within and between agencies is the key to successfully managing incidents. They found that in this case, communication clearly had worked well both over telephone and radio channels and between staff at the scene. The search and rescue operation was stood down after 18 minutes when the Coastguard received confirmation from the police that everyone had been accounted for. In light of how busy the Thames is, the complexity of the river and its tidal nature, it is vital that the Mayor and the London Resilience Forum remain satisfied that the co-ordination mechanisms and necessary plans for dealing with a major incident on the River Thames are in place and regularly reviewed. Given the evidence presented to the Inquiry and from their findings they were satisfied that this was the case.

Presenting its evidence the Marine Policing Unit of the Metropolitan Police Service, in a written submission, concluded that the incident *'could not have occurred in a better location from the perspective of its close proximity to Lambeth London Fire Brigade fireboat station. This meant that the casualties could be quickly taken to a safe and warm environment that would have undoubtedly reduced the trauma incurred by them. [...] Had the conditions been different, the consequences of the fire could have been much worse.'*

The findings of the investigation by the Marine Accident Investigation Branch found that unprotected buoyancy foam packed around the engine compartment of a duck boat led to the fire on board the 'DUKW' in September 2013.

Footnotes:
The amphibious 'DUKW' was one of a number of amphibious vessels belonging to a London tours company which offered pleasure cruises along the Thames. These refurbished craft are the same style as those used to ferry troops during the D-Day landings. In earlier months a number of problems had beset the company and these craft. In that July the Marine and Coastguard Agency had grounded seven out of nine of the boats operated by the tour company over safety concerns. The company had been running tourist services on the River Thames since 2002, carrying more than 200,000 passengers.

Two generations of fireboats reunited when the 'Massey Shaw' fireboat,
now a heritage vessel, moors at the Lambeth river fire station and
alongside her modern counterpart, the 'Fire Dart'. (Nigel Saunders).

In 2013 the historic former London Fire Brigade fireboat 'Massey Shaw', which played an important part during the Blitz and at Dunkirk (see Chapter 7, page 232), returned to London after a one million pound restoration programme. The iconic fireboat also starred at the London Boat Show that year. The 'old' fireboat had been transported by road from Avonmouth following restoration work that was carried out at a Gloucester shipyard. She was then relaunched in the West Country prior to her sea trials and inspections.

The 'Massey Shaw' was relaunched at Wood Wharf in the Canary Wharf complex on the Isle of Dogs. The launch marked a remarkable chapter in the fireboat's story and provided a memorable day for the Massey Shaw Preservation Society which has spent several years fund-raising and working on the vessel. Her final restoration was only possible with extra funding awarded from the Heritage Lottery Fund.

We are reaching the end of 2015. This final chapter is drawing to a close. As it does so Station Manager Darren Tulley was the man then in charge of London's only floating fire station. Twice a day the Lambeth fireboat pontoon, located on the Albert Embankment and directly opposite the former Headquarters building, rises and falls with the changing of the Thames tides. Darren has been in his current post for almost two years, his own fire service career starting in Surrey before his transfer into the London Fire Brigade. This may not be his last promotion in the role of a Brigade 'Manager', or his last posting, but for now he is very much a round peg in a round hole. He is in tune with the river, its way of life and many of the people who work on it.

The London Fire Brigade's fireboat at her Lambeth station. (Colin Court)

Darren oversees the four watches that make up London's river fire and rescue service, which has in recent years seen far more emphasis on its 'rescue' role than 'fire'. There has been a steady decline in the number of incidents attended by London's fireboat. In 2008/9 the river service attended some two hundred and seventy eight 'shouts'. In both 2014 and 2015 the fireboat averaged out at one hundred and forty calls per annum, a fall of almost fifty percent. In this last year eighty-five percent of all calls were deemed non-fire calls. Nine rescues were performed by the fireboat crews in this twelve month period, with six of those rescued having sustained injuries. Between June 2014 and May 2015 only twenty fire calls were attended by the fireboat; of these, nineteen were considered a noteworthy fire, the remaining fire being classified as a 'secondary' fire, which may have involved nothing more than burning rubbish. The London Fire Brigade keeps no record of what actions the fireboat undertakes at such incidents – if any action is taken at all.

Each of the four watches currently consists of seven firefighters. This includes the Watch officer, who is also termed a manager. There is also a crew manager, who can deputise, subject to their individual skills set, for the Watch manager in their absence. Some choose not to do so, in which case a reserve river service trained officer is sent to take change of the fireboat.

The current Lambeth fireboat pontoon is a far cry from its predecessor that was opened, together with the new headquarters building, in 1937. Then it comprised two huts on a pontoon where the river firemen would spend their day shifts, returning to the land station to eat their meals and to sleep in the large dormitory on the fire station's first floor. In the intervening years the two huts were replaced by two slightly larger prefabricated single storey buildings. But by the early 1980s both the pontoon and its buildings were in urgent need of replacement. Today's LFB river firefighters have their own self-contained, purpose-built, stand-alone fire station.

London's previous fire authority, the London Fire and Civil Defence Authority, had commissioned the complete replacement of the old Lambeth river fire station and pontoon back in the late 1980s. Work was started in the early 1990s by F. L. Steelcraft Ltd, who were based in West Wales. Their winning design provided for the construction of a floating structure measuring ten metres by forty metres. It contains plant rooms, locker rooms, gymnasium and lecture room all of which are housed within the steel hull. A lightweight, steel-framed, aluminium-clad structure contains the dormitory accommodation, showers, offices and the station's mess room and kitchen. The river fire station, with its long, low, horizontal profile is not considered obtrusive on the Thames riverscape. Its superstructure, which is painted black in order to lose the bulk against the water, and the station buildings are simple in form yet pleasing to the eye with its clean and elegant design. The pontoon provides ample mooring space for the two operational fireboats, with additional mooring facilities for other emergency service river craft if required.

Joint training Thames exercise involving the fireboat crew and a 'line-rescue' firefighter. (Paul Wood)

Each of the four fireboat watches work the same shift pattern as their land-based counterparts. It currently consists of two day duties, two night duties, followed by four leave days. Each day shift starts at 9.30 a.m. and finishes at 8 p.m., nights naturally being from 8 p.m. to 9.30 a.m. the following morning.

In addition to the core skills required of all London firefighters, river firefighters are required to acquire additional river based competences. Each watch must maintain the requisite numbers of coxswains to cover leave and training. Reserve personnel can only work operationally on the fireboats if they are River Service trained. All fireboat training is currently provided by external trainers since the Brigade's policy has seen all its training 'outsourced'.

The watches place strong emphasis on their 'operational readiness'. Every shift begins with a roll call, where updates on both operational matters and appropriate navigational issues on the Thames are noted prior to the daily inventory checks being undertaken. This is followed by the morning or supper time 'cuppa'. Equipment training, boat drills, and practising various procedures feature heavily on all day duties. These are interspersed with visits and combined training activities with other waterborne emergency services, i.e. Metropolitan Police Marine Division and the RNLI. Joint training is also undertaken with the land station crews with a Thameside risk, including Battersea fire station crews who are equipped with specialist waterborne rescue provision.

Another unusual features of the 'floating' river fire station, besides that it has no fire station ground, involve mobilisation. Whereas all land appliances are only mobilised via the LFB's fire and rescue Control Room, the fire boat can be ordered to incidents either by the fire brigade control or the Marine and Coastguard Agency (MCA) via its Thames control centre.

Unless it is defective or undergoing routine maintenance the 'Fire Dart' fireboat is the main operational boat of choice. The 'Fire Flash' acts as the reserve and training fire boat. For ceremonial duties the 'Fire Flash' will normally attend with a trained reservist crew. When required, and if a section of the Thames is required to be closed, both fire boats can be operational; one boat covering upstream of a closure or the restricted movement of vessels and the other covering downstream of the closure.

The new Lambeth river fire station and pontoon on the Albert Embankment, SE1, built at a cost of £1.1 million. F. L. Steelcraft Ltd completed the facility in early 1991. This modern river station has come a long way from the two original small timber huts, with their corrugated metal roofs, that comprised Lambeth's first river station that opened in 1937. (Paul Wood)

It is London Fire Brigade policy that its firefighters do not enter 'moving water' unless they have been subject of specialist training and are suitable equipped and are wearing appropriate waterborne rescue protective clothing. Fire brigades, including London, have in recent years received adverse publicity and hostile comments about the reluctance of some firefighters to take immediate action when members of the public are in danger of drowning or are difficulty in waterways (rivers, lake, ponds or canals). There are ten London fire stations with a waterborne rescue provision (inflatable craft and water safety suits) that are strategically placed across the capital. The personnel at these stations have undertaken specialist training in water rescue techniques within a range of water environments. They are able to interpret the impact of water flow, hazards such as obstacles and mud and use appropriate lines to perform a variety of rescues whilst applying safe working practices. Their skills include casualty assessment and understanding the relationship with the selection of rescue response together with the ability to apply rescue swimming skills in a variety of environments.

It remains a reality that London's firefighters and their officers sometimes have to work in very dangerous and dynamic operational environments. This includes, at times, exposure to dangerous and unpredictable situations when attempting to save life and mitigate other emergencies. On many occasions the River Thames has proved itself to be a challenging place to perform rescues from. There is undoubtedly a legitimate expectation by the London public that its firefighters put themselves at risk to protect others. The London Fire Brigade also has a duty to protect property and the environment. Emergency river incidents can develop at speed and in unexpected ways, so by its very nature, operational activity in the Brigade, but especially of its fireboat crews, represents significant challenges for the application of health and safety law.

On the Thames, and as far as the fireboat crews are concerned, rescues from the water forms part of their basic RST (river service trained) course and is an important element of their continuation training. This effectively covers person-over-board and persons in the river, for which the fireboats carries throwing lines, a 'Jasons' (rescue) cradle and mud paths and its associated equipment. Fireboat training and its operational procedures are vitally important. That said, it is not possible to risk assess and train for every possible scenario that its firefighters or officers might face. In their recent (2013) policy document the Chief Fire Officers Association publicly supported the use of generic risk assessments across the UK fire service. This is something that is supported by *risk awareness and dynamic assessment along with the safe person concept'*. In other words, the right person in the right place at the right time with, of course, the appropriate training, equipment and procedures. However in an important caveat the Association went on to say: *'We recognise that decisions will need to be made in emergency and dynamic situations that with the benefit of a 20/20 hindsight investigation may not bear scrutiny and question. So the idea of London river firefighters standing back and doing nothing when faced with the possibility of their inaction leading to someone, in difficult circumstances, in the*

Thames drowning appears remote in the extreme.' Some of Lambeth's fireboats' firefighters take this life saving duty so seriously that they form, in their off-duty time, voluntary crew positions and ride with the fulltime crews of the RNLI high-speed rescue boats based on the Thames.

As the year 2015 was drawing to a close both boat and line-rescue techniques were combined when on the 18th December a man got himself in a precarious position on the southern side of London's Southwark Bridge. Lambeth's fireboat, together with the fire engine from Lambeth fire station and the Fire Rescue Unit from Battersea fire station, with its specialist line rescue crew, attended the scene. In difficult, and at times, testing conditions the man was first made safe before a line rescue team secured the man and together with a line rescue team member was lowered onto the waiting fireboat below. It was yet another example of the close co-operation and training between land and river based crews that brought an incident to a satisfactory conclusion.

Southwark Bridge rescue, 18th December 2015. (LFB)

London's river has always carried people, both for business and for pleasure. Whilst the nature of its riverside has changed beyond recognition since the latter part of the twentieth and now into the twenty-first century, its popularity as an attraction has not diminished. Boat journeys on the Thames in London in 2013 rose to a record 8.5 million, thanks in large measure to tourists taking advantage of that year's fine summer. This number rose to 9.8 million in 2015. The number of river journeys increased year on year, with commuter trips up by twenty percent. The new Mayor of London, Sadiq Khan, has projected a target of twelve million passengers being transported on the river by 2020.

New piers are planned with a new pier opening in 2016 at Battersea Power Station and two more being built at Convoys Wharf and Enderby Wharf in 2017 plus opening extension works at three central London piers – Bankside, Embankment and Westminster Piers. The Putney to Blackfriars River Bus service has seen a 130 per cent increase in passenger numbers since its re-launch in April 2013. An additional two morning and three evening sailings have been introduced.

Combined land and river crew training plays a vital role in the Brigade's ability to deal with incidents occurring on the River Thames and its environs. (Paul Wood)

The outgoing Mayor of London, Boris Johnson, expressed the view that *'The River Thames plays an integral role as both a key artery for commuters and a wonderful avenue for tourists too.'* But with the growth in projected passenger numbers comes the need for continuing vigilance and readiness by the river emergency services to deal with waterborne accidents and incidents whenever and wherever they may occur.

As I draw this history to a close the political control of the Fire Service nationally has reverted to the Home Officer. The current Conservative Government policy is to abolish London's Fire and Emergency Planning Authority and to transfer its powers directly to the newly elected Mayor in due course. London elected its new Mayor, the former Tooting Labour MP Sadiq Khan, in May 2016.

In the meantime the Brigade's fireboat(s) continue to have an integral part to play in London Fire Brigade's forward thinking fire and emergency safety strategy. Work is in hand on the procurement policies to secure the next generation of London's fireboats. Interesting times await as the new Mayor's vison of London unfolds. These will determine what the future direction of these fireboats may be.

Maybe Londoners will see a multi-agency approach in the every demanding thrust of the present Government to bring about year-on-year budget reductions. Maybe even closer collaborations between the Brigade, the Metropolitan Polices' Marine Division, the RNLI, and the Marine and Coastguard Agency that could deliver 'economies of scale'?

For now it's a matter of watch this space. Today the story of London's fireboats still continues. But whatever the future holds these fire-floats and fireboats have had a fascinating past and the generations of firemen and firefighters that crewed them have, at last, had their story told.

APPENDIX I

A River Fireman's tale – The last 'shout'

Part One

Danny was always considered a bit of a wag. He had been born close to the smell of the river, the River Thames that is. His earliest years were spent in the labyrinthine streets of Wapping, to the East of what would become Tower Bridge. His schooling was basic to say the least, but this bright lad absorbed and understood everything he was taught. It helped him survive the rigours of living an impoverished existence in squalid rooms in the shadow of the East London docks. His was the age that Dickens sought to bring to the wider public's attention, although Danny never got to see any of the benefits of the slow progress of social change.

At sixteen years of age he signed up to join the Royal Navy, having already learnt the benefits of being big for his age and the power of exaggeration by lying that he was almost eighteen. As no one asked for any proof he signed the bit of paper and became a prospective 'Tar'. Danny had joined what was reputed to be the greatest navy in the world at the time. A product of the Victorian age, it was a navy characterised by rapid change and ship building developments. Older seamen bemoaned the change from sail to steam but now serving on the Dreadnought class battle cruise they conceded some of the changes were for the better. However, the social classes were still very clearly defined, exposing the gulf that existed between the Royal Navy's officers and its ratings.

Danny had not been sad to see the back of the tiny ginnels; the alleyways filled with drunken gambling sailors; the criminal lairs; the whorehouses and opium dens that filled Wapping. The Royal Navy turned Danny from a boy into a man. He had 'crossed the line', the thirteenth parallel, twice by the time he really was eighteen years of age. He recalled with a wry smile the ceremonies that tested the ability of new crew members to endure the hardships of life at sea. The ceremonies were frequently rough and sometimes cruel, but Danny had endured his ordeal with a fortitude that belied his age. Very few would now consider taking such liberties or advantages of the lad that had grown into an alert and powerful man.

It was the sudden death of Danny's father, killed in a Wapping street brawl, which brought his life in the Navy to an unexpected end. He was required to assist in the care of his now infirm mother and the Lords of the Admiralty had agreed a compassionate, honourable, discharge. Danny returned to the East End of London and now needed a new job. The Metropolitan Fire Brigade only recruited former sailors, so to Danny it seemed like an ideal choice.

Selection into the Metropolitan Fire Brigade (MFB) was not easy. In fact it was very difficult, with only a small percentage of those applying ever being accepted. Its Chief Officer, Massey Shaw, only recruited sailors into the MFB since he believed that after a seaman's training that they would have learnt the meaning of discipline and would be strong and hardy. Potential recruits were tested for their strength and health. Those few that were accepted then spent the next three months at the headquarters station under instruction before joining a fire station.

The strength test lived up to its name and pushed Danny hard, although not to his limits. Accepted, with a letter of recommendation from his Chief Petty Officer on the Dreadnought, Danny reported to the newly opened MFB headquarters, located south of the Thames in Southwark Bridge Road, in the spring of 1879. The Brigade's Chief Officer, Captain Eyre Massey Shaw, had managed to persuade the Metropolitan Board of Works to build him a new headquarters, as the one in Watling Street, in the City of London, had grown too small for London's expanding fire brigade. Shaw had only been partly successful and the Board, always keen not to spend money, had adapted an existing hat factory and added the rest of the headquarters to it. The site now had a new fire station, workshops, Shaw's six bedroom home and accommodation for the firemen who worked and trained there. Danny was required to live in the single man's lodgings at the Southwark HQ during his training. He also paid 6d a week rent for the privilege of doing so.

His first posting was to the Ratcliff station in Limehouse, East London. At the end of the nineteenth century the whole riverside district of East London was a notorious slum area. Danny knew that all too well. He had grown up in those very streets. Streets of poky terraced houses that were squeezed along canals and railway lines, timber mills and sawmills, lead-works and coal yards, dry docks, ship repair yards, factories and workshops. The area was heavily polluted and had bad sanitation. It remained overcrowded and had one of the highest levels of child mortality anywhere in London. A statistic that Danny was only too aware of as one brother and two sisters had all died before their respective third birthdays.

Life for Danny at the fire station was almost a continuous duty. The manual fire pumps had been replaced by steam driven pumps, that the firemen rode, but were still pulled to the fires by a pair of 'Tilling's' specially trained horses. Tilling's ran a successful London horse-drawn bus company, but leased his horses to the fire brigade. The horses also pulled the stations' escape cart; which carried the fifty foot wheeled escape ladder. Danny had proved himself a reliable and competent sailor, now he was carving himself a similar reputation as a fireman. In his first year he had rescued a woman and her two young children from certain death in a blazing riverside dwelling.

His reputation was further enhanced with the rescue of a fellow fireman from the Shadwell Basin in the closing months of 1902. Their engines had been summoned to a barge fire. It would take a while for the fire-float from Southwark Bridge to arrive on the scene so the Ratcliff firemen got to work. Danny's colleague was about to step on the barge 'Skipper' to assist in extinguishing the fire when he caught his foot on a coil of rope and missed his footing. He fell headlong into the murky dock water, entering the water between the barge and quayside. Danny heard the splash and when he turned round saw that his colleague, Fireman Haggetty, was missing. Danny jumped back onto the quay, looked over the edge and saw Haggetty struggling in the water. Danny yelled, 'Man Overboard,' and laid flat on the quayside before reaching down to grab his friend's hand. Senior Fireman Harris, who was in charge of the steamer ran to Danny's side and laid down beside him grabbing Haggetty's other hand.

Both men tried to pull the fireman from the water, but were unsuccessful. A rope was brought and Harris managed to pass it to Haggetty whilst Danny kept the man afloat. Haggetty grasped the rope with both hands and the pair on the quayside tried to pull the man from the water, still without any success. Haggetty was by now feeling the severe effects of the cold water and he told his colleagues that he could not hold much longer. Danny took the free end of the rope and tied it around himself, telling the other firemen now gathered around to hold the rope. Danny next jumped into the dock landing besides Haggetty. The coldness of the water took Danny's breath away and he also gasped in a lungful of polluted dock water. Grabbing hold of Haggetty he pulled him towards himself before passing a loop of the rope around the exhausted man's chest and securing it with a knot. With Danny pushing and those on the quayside pulling they raised the stout figure of Haggetty back onto dry land. With Danny joining Haggetty both men were now suffering from their ordeal and blankets were brought and wrapped around the shivering pair.

Returning to the fire station Danny was congratulated by his colleagues, especially Haggetty, who considered that Danny had saved his life. The Station Superintendent was far more reserved in his praise for Danny. This powerful and accomplished former East London boxer simply told Danny his actions would be a matter of a formal report together with the loss of his and Haggetty's brass helmets caused by their unauthorised swim.

That report eventually arrived on the desk of Captain Wells, now the Chief Officer of the Brigade. He read carefully the report and the endorsement of the East London District Officer. At the time of the fire there were six barges moored at the spot where Haggetty fell; two lines of three secured end to end and liable to move in the prevailing wind. Haggetty had admitted that if Danny had not entered the water when he did and tied a line to him he would have gone under and most likely have drowned. The water was some feet below the edge of the quay. A strong north-easterly wind had been blowing at the time that could have pushed the barges against the quay which would have crushed both men in the water. Both men were fully dressed in their firemen's uniform at the time; Haggetty's helmet came off when he fell in and Danny's falling into the dock when he threw it down.

Wells put the report down and made an annotation in the margin. It was the following year, 1904, that Danny stepped forward at the fire brigade headquarters to receive his gallantry medal from yet another new Chief Officer. The name of the brigade had also changed. It had taken an Act of Parliament to give it the title that Londoners always referred to it: the London Fire Brigade. Something which Danny considered still the same wine, just a new bottle.

That same year also saw Danny on the move. He had been a first class fireman for some time, now he was promoted to senior fireman and had been transferred to the Brigade's latest fire-float 'Alpha' moored by Blackfriars Bridge.

Whilst Danny had reservations about his transfer his wife certainly didn't. Included in Wells' annotation for the gallantry award was a recommendation that Danny and his wife be afforded better accommodation when it became available. They were moving from their two rooms at Ratcliff to three rooms at the Whitefriars fire station which also served as the fire-floats family accommodation. However, Danny's tenure at Blackfriars was rather short lived as in 1906 another new fire-float was commissioned, the 'Beta II'. It was moored in Rotherhithe at the Cherry Garden Pier. Danny's family, which now included a baby son, relocated to the nearby Cherry Garden fire station accommodation. Although Danny had to move south of the Thames he felt very fortunate, in fact he felt blessed.

The clipper had delivered a cargo of wool from the farthest part of the British Empire, possibly her last? The Captain's daughter had pleaded with her mother to be allowed to see her father's ship moored off Oliver's Wharf in Wapping. The mother acquiesced and they set off from their Greenwich home on the morning of the clipper's arrival in the Pool of London. The clipper was still waiting for a quayside berth so had temporarily moored by some barges, laying side by side back to the quayside, some distance from the northern shoreline. The wife and the young daughter had been transported to the ship by a wherryman from the Cherry Garden pier, almost opposite from where the clipper lay waiting to dock with its valuable cargo. The pilot of the 'Beta' fire-float watched as the powerful arms of the wherryman pulled on his oars, quickly covering the short distance across the Thames to the clipper.

The clipper was a masterpiece, the pinnacle of sailing ship design. Her composite hull of timber and iron was sleek and strong, while her three masts could hold a spread of canvas that propelled the ship at up to 15 knots. As a result, she spent the late 1870s speeding across the high seas, establishing a reputation as one of the fastest clippers afloat. Her speed not only translated into prestige, it also translated into profits for her owners. The clipper helped bring the new tea crop from China, which was incredibly fashionable amongst the tearooms and parlours of Victorian London and Bath. The first batches of the new tea harvest was highly coveted and thus the first tea cargo to arrive fetched only the highest prices. The annual tea race was a Victorian sensation: ships progress were reported by telegraph and would be followed in the newspapers. Even huge bets were laid on the outcome. The clipper was never first to the finish line, but she was still one of the fastest.

When the clipper was first launched it was already the Indian summer of the great sailing ships. The Suez Canal had opened offering steamships a shorter route to the Far East, and slashing approximately two months off their journey time. The winds of the Red Sea and the Mediterranean were not suited to the clippers. Consequently, the increasing speed and cargo capacity of steamships soon rendered sailing ships unprofitable. By the late 1880s, the clippers had been pushed out of the tea trade.

The ship's owner was determined, however, to turn her fortunes around. Therefore, in 1895, he hired the excellent but eccentric present clipper captain: Captain Barrett. Barrett recognised that the clipper's commercial edge now lay in the dangerous wool run to Australia. In this arena the clipper once again excelled, setting speed records between London, New Zealand and Australia. For a decade she established her fame through her lightning voyages, but by now she was approaching the end of her life expectancy and would soon cease to be profitable.

It was the very same fire-float pilot who noticed the smoke rising from the aft hold of the clipper. He immediately raised the alarm and summoned the 'Beta's' crew to action. The pilot's alarm call was relayed by telegraph to the fire stations of Whitechapel, Shadwell and Cannon Street, plus the new self-propelled steam driven 'Fire King' engine at Bishopsgate. The 'Beta' already had her stream-up for a scheduled trip to the fire-float's repair depot at Charing Cross, so she got underway in record time. It was almost unheard of for a fire-float to arrive first at the scene of any fire on or along the Thames. But today was the exception to the rule as the 'Beta' navigated her way across the Thames from the Rotherhithe shoreline to the smoking clipper.

The first land firemen to arrive looked on from the Wapping quayside as the Beta secured herself alongside the clipper. It would be a while before these crews could traverse the barges and start to tackle the evident blaze on the clipper. There was considerable confusion aboard the clipper despite the best efforts of a very anxious looking Captain Barrett to direct the efforts of his crew's attack on the fire. Although contained in the aft hold vast quantities of thick smoke were caught in the fresh westerly breeze and was carried downstream. The choking smoke was clearly affecting the crew and the master appeared to be even more agitated with each passing moment. It was a situation that he would normally have handled given his calm characteristics. He seemed anything but calm and the tears filling his eyes had little to do with the smoke.

'My wife and child are trapped below,' he yelled to no one in particular on the 'Beta'. 'I can't get down below to reach them, help me please,' he pleaded.

The fire-float's main function in life was the supply of water to the land crews via hose taken on shore or directing vast quantities of water at a fire from the monitor mounted on the fire-float's deck. Its crew now had a rescue situation on their hands, something that they rarely, if ever, encountered. But Danny's years of experience kicked in as he skimmed up the clipper's access ladder onto the deck where he stood before the worried master. 'Show me,' demanded Danny above the commotion that was going on around him. Hoses were being passed up to clipper's crew from the fire-float with its firemen leading the crew with gruff instructions full of expletives. Meanwhile the land crews were making painfully slow progress clambering over the barges, whilst dragging their hoses, in their attempts to reach the clipper from the shore.

The aft companionway steps lead down to the stern accommodation and the captain's private quarters, quarters where he had left his wife and daughter when the alarm was raised, thinking it was a safe refuge. He was wrong. Whilst he had run up onto the deck to see what was happening, smoke seeped through the vents from the hold. It quickly filled the corridor, trapping the mother and daughter below.

Although some firemen had access to rudimentary smoke-hoods, a primitive form of breathing apparatus, none were carried on the 'Beta' or any other fire-float. Danny had not become immune to the toxic effects of smoke but was considered to be a regular 'smoke-eater' by his fellow firemen. He seemed to be able to work in that hostile environment for longer than most of his contemporaries. He was well versed in the skills of working in smoke. Nevertheless, as he entered the smoke-filled lower companionway he felt the effects of the escaping heat straight away. Clearly the fire in the hold was growing in intensity. If the land crews did not hasten their progress a very serious fire would soon break out. The clipper would have to be abandoned, leaving the water from the firemen's hoses being directed onto the burning ship from the relative safety of the adjacent barges and from the 'Beta's' monitor.

At the bottom of the wooden steps, steps that Danny descended backwards to protect his face from the heat, he crouched low to the floor. The smoke was already making Danny's progress slower than he had hoped. The acidic taint of the smoke was filling his mouth and nostrils, whilst the smoke irritated his lungs. The corridor ran from left and right, with the captain's cabin laying directly ahead of him and running across the stern of the clipper.

Danny was no stranger to ships. Although the last time he had served on one was twenty-seven years before. He crouched low, very low, his nose almost touching the floor. He tried the door immediately in front of him; it would not open. The captain never indicated that he had locked his family in his cabin; maybe the wife had locked it in her panic, thought Danny. He tried the handle again and put his weight behind the door and pushed. As he did so he struck the form of a woman who had collapsed immediately behind the door. Danny pushed harder and both she and door moved in an arc into the cabin's interior. Danny grabbed at the woman's clothing and pulled her out into the corridor. Without ceremony he hoisted the unconscious woman up onto his shoulder before starting to retrace his path back on to the deck. On the steps Danny was having problems breathing. The smoke was getting thicker by the minute. He struggled up onto the deck, once again passing through the entrance to the ship's officer's accommodation. Willing hands took the captain's wife from Danny as he gasped in lungfuls of the smoke-tainted air.

Danny's thoughts immediately turned to his own children and the anguish that the father of the still missing child must be feeling. There was not a moment's hesitation before Danny turned around and returned below in search of the girl. The smoke had got worse. It was thicker and the conditions hotter. Danny felt his lungs burning, his eyes were stinging and he could not see a hand in front of his face as he descended the steps to the companionway. As soon as his feet touched the floor he fell on all fours, where the conditions were only marginally better. Despite the tears streaming from his eyes he was able to see a couple of feet ahead of him through the fog like gloom. He crawled back into the master's quarters and saw the girl sprawled across the floor. Adrenaline boosted his reserves and he reached out and pulled the child towards him. She was unconscious and making a strange gurgling breathing sound, but was alive. Returning the same way he came in was now impossible: the smoke was much too thick and the heat levels were closer to the floor.

He dragged the child into the nearest port side officer's cabin, the side where the 'Beta' was working from. The room was full of smoke but Danny knew exactly what he was looking for and found it. It was the room's porthole. Opened, it was large enough to pass the child through, but he knew he could never follow her. The open porthole and the escaping smoke attracted the attention of the ever vigilant 'Beta's' pilot. He was not a fireman, but was responsible for guiding the 'Beta' along the Thames. He immediately manoeuvred the ten or so feet to get the 'Beta' closer to the porthole and the girl. Her head hung limply down and her shoulders protruded from the opening. The pilot rushed forward to take the girl's unresponsive arms as, with the last of his remaining strength, Danny pushed her bodily through the opening.

On the deck above hoses had been made ready to bring to bear on the fire in the hold. With the hatch covers removed the order was given as the pilot now held the child safety in his arms. There was no sign of Danny.

The removal of the hatch covers had two immediate results. It allowed the jets of water to be directed at the burning and smouldering bales of wool, but it also allowed a sudden and violent inrush of fresh air into the previously enclosed, oxygen-starved space. The effect of the air reaching the fire was disastrous. The flames spread with an explosive force, a force that the hold alone could not contain. A cloud of superheated gas expanded in the hold. Whilst much of the force vented upwards, into the sky, some of it vented sideways, through vents and gratings into the bowels of the clipper and the officer's quarters where Danny was now desperately trying to save himself. It was too late for Danny. The superheated gases filled the accommodation space: its force was such it completely blew out the master's stern cabin windows. Hot gases seared Danny's throat and burned the lining of his lungs. He collapsed and died at the bottom of the steps, his escape route, only feet away from fresh air and safety. It would take a couple of hours to bring the fire under control and two more before Danny's body could be recovered from where he fell.

Danny was buried with full Brigade honours. The Chief Officer led the funeral cortege from the Southwark headquarters. Just behind Danny's own wife, baby son and daughter were Captain

Barrett, his wife and their daughter. Danny's second gallantry medal lay besides his first, and together with his brass helmet they were placed on his flag-draped coffin as it was carried, in procession, to the Fireman's Corner at Highgate Cemetery in north London. Danny's widow was only afforded a small widow's pension and given time to find new rented accommodation in nearby Deptford. Danny's children never got to understand fully why they had no father. Their mother never got over the grief of their father's loss and she certainly never forgave the fire brigade for his untimely death. When the children did ask about their absentee father they were told he had been a sailor and had died at sea. Their mother did not get re-married and always struggled to make ends meet after the life-changing consequences of Danny's heroic actions.

The London Fire Brigade, and London's public, honouring those that died in the line of duty as the funeral procession leaves the Brigade's Southwark headquarters and marches to the Firemen's Corner in Highgate Cemetery. North London. (Mary Evans)

Part Two

Danny was always considered a bit of a wag. This south London lad had grown up in the shadow of Surrey Docks and his old man was a Docker. He was one of a disappearing breed now. Whilst not a cruel man he didn't spare the rod either where Danny was concerned, not least because of the antics that his only son got up to. Although Danny did, privately, think this may have had something to do with his Dad never having known his own father, who Danny had been named after and who, he had been told, was once a sailor and had died at sea.

The local beat-bobby was a frequent visitor at Danny's house, either bringing him home to face the wrath of his father or to take Danny down the station to help the police with their enquiries. Most of the time it was not even Danny's fault but rather the encouragement of his two younger sisters who could twist Danny around their collective finger to nick the occasional Jamboree bag from the local sweet shop or sneak them into the picture house, via the fire exit door, and getting three cinema viewings for the price of one. Danny was no hardened criminal, he was just a street wise kid.

Then it happened, the fire. Danny's sisters had bunked off from school and had popped home whilst their Dad was working in the docks and their Mum laboured in the nearby biscuit factory. For all his faults Danny loved school, especially PE where he was considered quite a gymnast. What started the fire was never determined, but start it did. Possibly a spark from that morning's fire in the front room meant to dry the washing on the clothes horse, or the remains of the old man's fag when he popped home with a couple of bottles of 'export' gin that had 'fallen off the back of a lorry' that very morning.

The fact that Danny's sisters were at the house was unfortunate to say the least. It was also something that had unintended consequences. Discovering the fire the two teenage girls acted promptly. Grabbing the key that hung from a piece of string, just inside the letter box, they opened the front door. When you don't have a lot what little you have is precious. To them it was their money box in the first floor bedroom, something that contained all the wealth they had in the world. Almost eleven pounds seven shillings and six pence, what with this year's Christmas money from their maternal Granddad and a favourite Aunt. So after running past the blistering front room door, with hot brown smoke forcing its way underneath and melting the lino on the floor, the pair flew up the stairs.

The 'nosy old cow' across the road had, as usual, been peeking from behind her net curtains. She had seen it all. The girls coming home when they shouldn't be; panicking to get into the house; then rushing in; and now the smoke billowing out of the open front door. Sitting in her wheelchair there was little she could do other than dial nine-nine-nine when the smoke appeared to her to have suddenly turned into flames. Her last words to the lady who had said, 'Fire Brigade,' was: 'Please come quick, the two girls are still in the house.'

Danny was taken aback when the policeman came to the school to collect him, not least because he had not nicked anything for the past month. But Danny didn't argue when the copper said, 'Come along with me son.' The last time he had argued the copper gave him such a clip around the ear it had made his ear bleed! However, this copper seemed somehow different, he was concerned. 'There has been a problem, son. Your Mum and Dad are at the hospital.' 'Are they hurt?' asked Danny, trying to work out why both would be at the hospital at the same time. 'Has me Dad been in a fight again?'

'No son, it's your sisters. They were in a fire, your house caught alight. The fire brigade got your sisters out, but they were hurt. Your Mum and Dad are at the hospital with them and they wanted you there too.'

Danny had not seen his Dad cry before, not even when he came home with a broken nose after the hook of the dock crane hit him full in the face. He had seen his Mum cry plenty, especially when his Dad had spent the weekly wage down the pub on a Saturday night. But this was different, his parents just hugged each other and tears rolled down their respective faces. The man in the white coat was talking softly to them as Danny drew nearer. 'Everything will be alright. It will just take time.' Danny's Dad hugged his son.

The first time Danny could recall him doing so. 'They were burnt Dan – but they will be OK.'

Danny had never seen anyone with burns before. He hadn't expected to see so many bandages. All he could see were his young sisters' eyes closed tight. The pair looked like Egyptian mummies. Drips were connected to their arms and the two shared their own small room. It was a long day that turned in to a long week when five days later, and within an hour of each other, both his sisters regained consciousness. The long wait was over. The long path to recovery had started.

Danny and his Dad where given a polite, if not an exactly warm, welcome at the local fire station when the pair had gone to say a heartfelt thank you. Danny had not met firemen before, not close to anyway. He had lobbed some bangers at some when they tried to put out the street November 5th bonfire a couple of years back. Now meeting them they seemed modestly shy talking to him about saving his two sisters. The man with the white shirt, who the firemen called 'Guv', said the fireman that they should really thank was still off sick. He had badly burnt both his hands whilst rescuing the two girls. 'When he comes back, I will tell him you called round.' So with a final thank you Danny and his Dad left the fire station – but for Danny that visit had sparked something much deeper. He wanted to become a fireman. Which is just what he did.

Now sitting on his foot locker at the brigade's only remaining river fire station he found it hard to believe it was almost all over. He was still only a fireman, only these days he was called a fire-fighter. So many changes had taken place over the years. He was still considered a wag and one of the fittest on his watch. 'I am getting bloody soft,' he mused as he thought back to that fire that had left both his sisters with the scars that reminded all three why Danny had chosen to become a London 'firefighter'. Now he was counting down the final days with mixed feelings. He had enjoyed his time. He had made some wonderful mates and meet a couple of real 'plonkers' along the way too. Promotion had not been his bag, despite having all the 'old' promotion exams under his belt he loved what he did and he loved where he did it, on the River Thames.

Before he transferred to the 'river' eight years before he had got himself two 'official' Chief Officer pats on the back from a couple of jobs where he had performed rescues. His record at the Emergency Service's Commonwealth Games pentathlon had remained unbeaten for five years before some young whippersnapper from up north finally took his record from him.

His own two teenage girls were almost finished college and he had been offered a lucrative sports coaching position, post retirement, so things were looking good. He had remained a man of action. Not for him the option of sitting it out in the sticks: he liked the river station and its fireboat too much. He would have served thirty four years, nine months and ten days when he finally walked up the prow of the pontoon at the end of the next shift. But his sisters' involvement in that fire, all those years ago, had been playing on his mind recently. Something he put down to his impending retirement.

He also thought that it was time to go. The Brigade had changed and not necessarily all for the better in his opinion. A young watch officer at the adjacent land station was good on theory, so it was said, but Danny had seen little evidence of it being put into practice, especially given that this station's watch would, if there was a short cut, take it. But those thoughts were quickly dispelled as the house bells started to play their familiar tune and Danny made his way to the fireboat, where he was the coxswain that day, and departed on the umpteenth shout of his long career.

Danny started his penultimate final night duty. Tomorrow would be a special watch dinner and he was coming 'off the run' when both retired and serving land and river colleagues where coming along to say adieu. Danny, a talented musician, had promised to bring along his trusty banjo into work and play a couple tunes of farewell. But not tonight. Tonight he was just riding, not steering, the fireboat and he had young Andy at his side, the pair being at opposite ends of their respective careers.

He liked Andy. In fact Andy was no rookie, he had ten years' service under his belt but he was the latest transfer onto the boat and therefore the 'junior buck'. He was eager to learn about the river and could listen. He was enthusiastic, sometimes a bit headstrong but not afraid of getting his hands dirty. Danny thought that, given time, Andy would make as good a river firefighter as his land experience had already proved him to be. Danny thought he would likely make a good fire officer too given the chance.

The call came in the first moments of the night shift. Danny had an eerie, uncomfortable, feeling as soon as he saw the ordering slip to the ship fire. He had no idea why.

She was a beautiful ship. Now a heritage craft lovingly restored after her early working days as a clipper, first transporting tea from the Far East before transporting wool from Australia and New Zealand in the latter part of the 1800s and early 1900s. After a fire on the ship near Wapping, of which there were scant details, the clipper had been sold to a Portuguese company, who renamed her the 'Dowager'. After repairs the ship spent the next 25 years transporting cargoes between Portugal, Africa and the Americas. In the 1940s, she was purchased by a former clipper captain who remembered the clipper from her glory days. He had brought her to Plymouth where she was part-restored and opened to the public.

By the 1980s the clipper was facing the scrapyard. Saved from obscurity by a sailing ship eccentric, and a healthy grant from the Lottery Fund, she first became a youth training ship before reinventing herself as a cruising sail-ship. The timbers that were once pounded by the storms of Cape Horn now came under a new threat. Years of exposure to the elements had taken their toll and comprehensive conservation of the ship was again required. The clipper's extensive holds, which had carried tea, then wool and even coal, had been painstakingly converted into accommodation for those wealthy enough to book the clipper for private charters and trips on the once-famous tea routes to the Far East.

Now the clipper loomed tall above the rapidly approaching fireboat. She was tethered to her temporary moorings, moorings that completely separated her from the Thames's southern shoreline by almost fifty metres, and was opposite Butler's Wharf. Like many of the wharves this had undergone a remarkable transformation into riverside apartments, and like the clipper herself, its appearance may have looked like the original design purpose but its use now was solely directed to those much higher up the food chain.

The 'Dowager' had returned to London for a refit and a major overhaul of her engine. As a sail ship originally there had been no engine room, but a conversion had taken place in the 1920s and a powerful propulsion system added to prevent the ship becoming becalmed in windless waters when the captain had a schedule of cargoes to collect or deliver. News of her return to London had featured on the news and despite her years the clipper maintained an air of grace and dignity that somehow was missing from the multimillion-pound, custom-built, sleek cruising yachts that only the super-rich could ever afford. Danny had found himself inextricably drawn to the clipper for reasons he could not fully understand. He had put it down to the clipper's individuality, something that set her apart from today's mass-produced vessels.

This was the first occasion that this grand old lady of the sea had made her way back up the Thames estuary in many years. She first encountered what seemed like engine trouble at Gravesend. The engine trouble had obviously gotten worse and what was originally thought to be some localised overheating had started a fire. A pall of oily black smoke now hung lazily over her as she lay at her moorings. It rose high into the London evening skyline, caught in the soft summer breeze, taking on the appearance of some giant's umbrella as the smoke spread outwards with its handle pointing back down to the engine room deck vents. From Tower Bridge the column appeared solid, but as the fireboat drew closer Danny saw it was anything but. It was a violently gushing stream of evil-looking, black inky smoke, defying gravity and spewing its toxic products up towards the clear blue sky above.

The 'London Phoenix' fireboat cut a dashing figure as it powered downstream on the ebbing Thames tide, adding a few extra knots to its not inconsiderable speed. Some had originally thought the fireboat a 'white elephant', others a case of empire-building by the out-going Chief when he convinced the Greater London Council, in its dying days, to buy a new fireboat. But 'Nellie', as the floaties had affectionately name her, soon proved her worth and was a vast improvement over the two so-called fireboats she had replaced – fireboats that most considered better suited for a day's sea fishing. Neither had been equipped with its own integral fire pump, had only a minimal pumping output, and discharged its water through a pipsqueak of a monitor mounted on the front of each of the boats. The 'London Phoenix' was the UK's most state of the art fireboat.

Unlike land-based fire engines, which could race through London's streets at brake neck speed, 'Nellie' travelled at a more sedate pace, even if her twin Perkins diesel engines could provide three-hundred and forty brake horse power. With one eye fixed on the smoking clipper Danny noticed the evening crowds being drawn to the waterfront like iron filings to a magnet. The eastern side of Tower Bridge was crowded with onlookers as the 'Phoenix' passed beneath it. What had initially appeared to be a few hundred spectators were quickly escalating into the thousands – each, it seemed, intent on capturing the unfolding drama on their camera phones or digital cameras, some clearly hoping to capture that image that would go viral. Soon they would have serious competition as the twenty-four hour news crews descended on the scene to capture, and scrutinise, this 'live' breaking news story.

It would be for others to worry about the press intrusion, for Danny had spotted something far more worrying. There were people on the deck of the clipper, none of whom were taking a leisurely stroll either. There seemed every sign of genuine panic. This was going to be a television news editor's lead story. Whatever happened next, good or bad, would be broadcast live as it happened, if it wasn't already.

Danny could not recall the 'London Phoenix' ever being the first to reach an incident. The 'Phoenix's' high-speed rescue craft crew had pulled individuals from the Thames from time to time, but they were only first because nothing else had been sent to the incident. Danny noticed the first of the land crews arriving, crews from the Bermondsey-based Dockhead fire station and the adjacent Southwark fire station. They too, for the moment, could only join the other spectators, who were still increasing in number at every possible riverside vantage point. For some, their vantage point was a private balcony overlooking the river and Danny had a double take as he saw people bringing bottles of wine as they sat down in their comfy patio chairs to gawk at what was happening below. Danny hardly ever swore, but made this an exception as he muttered, 'You sick effing ghouls.'

Station Officer Alan Bradley was an experienced operational officer. He had been on the 'London Phoenix' since the day it was commissioned, even going on her sea-trials in Southampton Water. Alan could easily have risen to senior rank but had a much greater love than just pure career ambition. It was a love of the Thames and working on the river. When he had been selected as one of 'Phoenix's' four watch Station Officers he thought that he had died and gone to heaven. He combined his extensive operational experience of running one of the Brigade's busiest operational stations, Brixton, with an almost encyclopaedic knowledge of the River Thames, its moods and its various risks and hazards. Off duty Alan and Danny were the best of friends; their respective daughters had even attended the same grammar school together. On duty, however, they maintained a professional relationship, one based on mutual trust and respect in each other.

Alan Bradley had been analysing and assessing all he saw as the 'Phoenix' readied to reduce speed and berth on the upwind, riverside, of the clipper. It was not an easy task on a fast flowing ebbing tide. He had already made contact with the clipper's Master using channel 16 on the 'Phoenix's' VHF radio, as well as advising the Port of London Authority (PLA) of his intentions. Those on the clipper's deck had been watching the fireboat's approach and their reactions ranged from restrained panic to controlled desperation as the clipper crew attempted to comfort and control those who were clearly passengers on the clipper. Some were wearing life jackets, others just carried them. They huddled by the rail, looking frightened and all awaiting rescue from the burning ship. The clipper's lifeboat pods, located at the stern, were engulfed in choking smoke and the quick release mechanisms were unreachable.

The 'Phoenix' was the first emergency services boat to arrive on scene. Other boats would soon follow. The Metropolitan Police River Service station at Wapping, was on the north downstream bank, only a short distance away. Its police launches and crews were, however, already patrolling various parts of the Thames and were not close at hand. The Royal National Lifeboat Institution Thames lifeboat was moored at its base at Charing Cross pier; its coxswain, who had been monitoring Channel 16, had raised the alarm and its crew were now en route.

Alan Bradley saw what needed to be done and immediately set about doing it. If the fireboat arriving first at an incident was unusual, its officer in charge sending the first 'priority' assistance message was unheard of in the brigade's recent history. Station Officer Bradley made 'pumps ten' whilst instructing the additional appliances to rendezvous at the Butler's Wharf quayside. He also requested the urgent attendance of the Metropolitan Police, RNLI and the PLA to assist in the evacuation of the clipper and to transport land crews to the 'Phoenix' and the clipper for search and rescue purposes and to fight the fire.

Station Officer Sue Garton was in the first week of her new role as the substantive watch officer at Dockhead fire station. She was also the first land officer to arrive on scene and was for the moment, at least, the Incident Commander, even if she could not get to the fire. She had watched the Phoenix pull aside the clipper and heard Bradley's message request ten 'pumps' at the scene. She felt like an onlooker but did not act like one. She and Bradley had talked on their respective hand-held radios and now she got the Dockhead and Southwark crews ready to transfer to the 'Phoenix' by police launch before boarding the clipper. Breathing apparatus sets, hose, branches and lines were got ready and lifejackets put on. She stood on the quayside impatient that she was still standing there and not climbing aboard the fireboat.

Sue Garton had the physique of an athlete, which in fact she was, albeit an amateur Southern Counties running champion. She also had the looks of a fashion model, which she wasn't. She had been Alan Bradley's junior buck at Brixton when she was first posted to a fire station after completing her recruit's course at Southwark training centre. Garton had been a star recruit. At just 22 years of age she had been a star probationer firefighter too. She combined her intelligence with more than a generous measure of good old fashioned common sense. She had no feminist agenda, displayed by a couple of the early female entrants to the brigade and which had tarnished the reputation of other female firefighters joining the macho world of the London Fire Brigade back in the day. Despite the passage of time, and the increased numbers of female fighters, the legacy those few early activists had left caused some male counterparts to tar all subsequent female firefighters with the same brush. A few were just anti female firefighter regardless of how good and competent they proved themselves.

Garton had been Brixton's first female firefighter. Any misgivings the watch might have had were soon dispelled as she proved herself to be a quick and willing learner. She also gave as good as she got in the cut and thrust of fire station life, its black humour and firefighter's antics. By the time her appointment was confirmed she had become a trusted and much liked member of the watch. Woe betide the foolish, and ill-informed, stand-by male firefighter who made a disparaging remark against firefighter Garton, one that was based on her gender alone. In particular Bunny, the watch mess manager, who had a daughter the same age as Sue, had re-arranged the front teeth of one such sexist culprit. In the years that followed Garton and Bradley had become friends, in fact off duty much more than just good friends. But he was a married man and she had a career ahead of her, so they parted as friends. They still were. She was destined for greater things and higher rank.

The loudspeaker on the 'Phoenix' told the anxious individuals awaiting rescue on the clipper what was happening next. The tannoy also broadcast its message to the microphones of the numerous news crews that had been setting up in ever increasing numbers. His instructions, now broadcast live on the news networks, was meant to reassure those waiting that they would soon be safe. For some they had already waited too long. The wind direction had shifted slightly and was swilling around the upper deck. Those waiting on the deck had watering eyes and their pleas for help were interspersed with fits of coughing. Then suddenly a man jumped into the Thames, followed by two more. The first was in danger of being crushed between the 'Phoenix' and the hull of the clipper. It was only the lightening reflex of the fireboat's coxswain that saved the man from certain death as he put the fireboat into full astern. A line was quickly thrown to the man by the crew of the fireboat and he was hauled from the Thames.

The second man was picked up by the first Metropolitan police launch to arrive. The third man was not so lucky. He had hit the water at an angle. Even though he had only jumped fifteen feet or so from the deck's railings, the surface tension of the water was sufficient to prevent him entering the water cleanly. He was thrown backwards, cracking his head on the steel plating of the ship's hull. He was rendered unconscious and disappeared under the water. The tide carried him downstream and the RNLI boat followed with the crew making an urgent search for the drowning man. By now it was 6.20 p.m. in the UK and 1.20 p.m. on the East coast of the United States. The American television networks were clamouring to get 'live' coverage of the unfolding action in London with its very real human interest angle in the heart of the capital. The BBC's evening six o'clock news brought live images of the scene to the nation.

Alan Bradley was thankfully totally unaware of any of this news frenzy; he had far more pressing issues to contend with. Again he told those waiting, in his calm and authoritative voice, not to jump from the clipper, but to await rescue. However, that didn't stop another two, a man and woman, from jumping from the clipper onto the deck of the 'Phoenix'. Alan heard the man's ankle snap, with a sickening noise, as he landed awkwardly on a delivery hose outlet mounted on the fireboat's deck.

London's emergency service have a combined major incident plan, a plan that includes major incidents on the River Thames. The fire brigade's primary areas of responsibility at a major incident remained life-saving through search and rescue; firefighting; rendering humanitarian services; salvage and damage control; and the safety management within the inner cordon. All this Alan was well aware of and, given what was unfolding and was likely to unfold, he sent his second priority message, declaring this a 'Major Incident'. 'Now the shit will hit the fan,' he mused as he quickly followed this up with an informative message telling his control room, and the duty brigade senior officers, what was occurring at the incident in stilted fire brigade radio speak.

He was trying to recall the mnemonic that had been put together to list his major incident priorities but he gave up, as in essence it was the same as any other major fire he had ever attended. He went through the checklist in his head...

1. Survey the scene as you approach, consider your safety, and try not to get involved in rescue work. That last bit isn't going to happen, he thought!

2. Assess the situation on your arrival, consider the possibility of a major incident, and gather accurate & concise information. 'Done and doing that,' he said out loud to no one in particular and he made a note on his message pad.

3. Estimate the casualties and approximate numbers of dead, including the injured number of survivors. Five so far, one possibly dead and a boat load waiting to get evacuated. He would speak with the police next on channel 16.

4. Access & egress. Well, he thought, once we get aboard we will know more; and he summoned his Sub Officer to organise a reconnaissance BA crew whilst making ready the 'Phoenix' to take on board those needing rescue in concert with the police launches.

5. Consider if evacuation is necessary and safe exit routes. 'After we get them off the clipper I will,' he said to a bemused-looking coxswain, who was beginning to wonder if his Guvnor was cracking up under the strain – but doubted it.

6. Qualify the type of incident and its size, including what is involved. 'Done that'; and he mentally ticked it off his must-do list.

Alan knew that until relieved by a more senior officer he was in charge, even if the land Station Office might have similar aspirations, but this was not a 'pissing contest' and he also knew Sue Garton would be doing the same as him if the roles were reversed. So as the Incident Commander he had his initial plan of action to deal with the developing situation; he had asked for additional resources; and he now set about briefing the police on what to do next.

With rescues to be performed the time for undue caution had long since passed. Both Station Officer Bradley and Danny had joined the London Fire Brigade when its simple tenets were: saving life, fighting fire and rendering humanitarian services. For them nothing had ever changed and this job encompassed all three. The 'Phoenix's' Sub Officer looked at Danny and Andy and said, 'Come on lads, it's BA and topside for us. The Guvnor wants us on that boat.' The BA sets were compressed air sets and weighed around thirty pounds each. Worn like a backpack the air cylinder is carried on the wearer's back and a torch and safety warning device are worn at the front and secured to the BA harness. In theory these sets are meant to last for approximately forty-five minutes, but hard work and exertion greatly reduces the duration of the set. As they checked and donned their BA sets the Sub Officer's set developed a high pressure air leak. He had to change his set. Danny and Andy were in no mind to wait and climbed up aboard the clipper. It was not an easy task given the numbers who were eagerly trying to get off, some assisted, and a couple being carried, either onto the 'Phoenix' or into one of the two police launches now at the side of the clipper. Danny's first words to Andy since they had arrived were, 'You stay close to me Andy'; the next he mumbled under his breath: 'I bloody hate ship fires.'

The firefighting tactics are built around procedures. Firemen's deaths had brought some of them about. People's lives could depend on them being implemented and then monitored properly. In its recent history this was the first mid-stream ship fire with people requiring rescue. Station Officer Bradley had frequently reminded his senior officers, who had only about half his operational experience, that such procedures were the guidance of wise men and the observance of fools. None chose to agree with him. So now in addition to supplying water, a casualty handling station, the forward command location, the 'Phoenix' was also the entry control point for their BA crew, and the subsequent BA crews, entering the ship. Bradley gently touched the wooden surround of the wheelhouse for luck saying, 'Don't you let me down Nellie,' as he went to organise the first arrivals of the land crews who were aboard a police launch, six of which were now at the scene.

The RNLI crew had located the unconscious man about a half of mile downstream of the clipper. When he rose to the surface he was not breathing. Desperate efforts were underway to try and revive him as the rescue boat speed towards the nearest predetermined rendezvous point to transfer their casualty to a waiting ambulance and its paramedic crew, one of fifteen ambulances ordered onto the major incident by the London Ambulance Service – ten of which were standing by in Tooley Street on the south side and five by the Wapping police river station on the north of the Thames.

Some twenty passengers had been assisted from the clipper by both the police and fire service personnel. This did not include the five that had taken their lives into their own hands and jumped ship, one of whom was still fighting for his. Some of the casualties required oxygen, suffering from smoke inhalation, whilst a crew member had severe burns to his face and arms.

Throughout the clipper's Master had remained on the main deck, assisting where he could but increasingly looking uncomfortably anxious and extremely worried. When Danny approached him he suddenly understood why. Four people were still unaccounted for. They included two of the crew and the Master's wife and daughter whom he had collected from Greenwich pier, near the family home in Greenwich Village, on the last leg of the journey. They were last seen heading to the Master's stern cabin, as his young daughter had required the loo. They had not come on deck when the alarm was raised. No one had seen them since.

By 6.24 p.m. land crews were now being ferried out to the Phoenix by police launches. Sue Garton had organised the first two teams and now joined the third with her own Dockhead crew and the first senior officer to arrive at the incident, Station Commander Adrian Butler. He was old school: he still referred to himself as an Assistant Divisional Officer, and he had thirty years' operational experience under his belt. He carried a few extra pounds these days but at fifty years of age, and with a weakness for good red wine, he thought he was entitled to. At 6.25 p.m. the Port of London Authority stopped all river traffic between the east of Tower Bridge and the west of Wapping river police station.

The list of tasks were testing Alan Bradley to the full. He was relieved to see the face of Station Officer Garton heading towards him; he was even pleased to see the face of the senior officer standing by her side. Someone who had the well-earned reputation of being a good fire officer first and a pen-pusher and a management 'Yes' man second.

As the clipper's Master briefed Danny and Andy about his missing wife and daughter and the other two missing crew members they were joined by two more BA crew members. For the second time that evening Danny had a strange, unexplainable, feeling about the clipper but he put the dark thoughts to the back of his mind. He did not have the time to consider them now.

The obvious pain of knowing that his family was missing was etched across the Master's face. A third, four-person, BA crew joined the others, this one armed with a hose line and instructions to make an immediate attack on the fire in the engine room. 'That's settled then,' said Danny. 'You three search for the two crew members and we will search of the Master's wife and daughter,' before he turned to face the Master and told him, 'We *will* find your family and bring them back to you.' Danny wondered if he would return with them still alive, but his face gave no indication as to these secret doubts as he noticed the increase in the smoke levels swilling around the deck.

Danny had the Master's brief wired into his brain. The clipper was designed on three levels. The upper deck, on which they were standing, and two lower decks. The immediate deck below was the revamped staterooms for the passengers, dining rooms and galley, the passenger lounges and the officers' accommodation, plus the Master's stern cabin. The lowest deck was the crew's accommodation, the ships stores, sail room, anchor locker, refrigeration room and the engine room and its adjacent generator room. The Master's brief had explained that there was a fore and aft main entrance to the decks below. In breathing apparatus both were now accessible to the firefighters. There was also an emergency access ladder passing up through the ship on the Port side. It was located in the mid-ships area on the lower deck and exited, via at hatch, onto the main deck.

Assistant Divisional Officer Butler had formally taken charge and sent a message to that effect to control at 6.29 p.m. He was a believer in Alan's Bradley's philosophy of procedures being for the guidance of wise men, and anyway there was no procedure for fighting a fire on a ship moored in the middle of the Thames from a fireboat. So he played it by ear. He had ordered the BA entry control point be set up on the entry to the deck of the clipper. If lives had not been in such danger he might have done things differently, but they were. He may have been many things but when it came to firefighting tactics Butler was no fool.

As the pair handed in their BA tallies to the entry control officer, Danny thought this was a job for the old Proto BA sets, but they had been withdrawn many years before. However, those oxygen rebreather sets had had a longer duration, and if things got really bad, and you got into difficulty, there was a facility were you could make the set last for up to four or five hours. One of the downsides, once the Proto mouthpiece was put in the mouth, it was like a gag, because you were never meant to remove it to talk, although some old hands did just that. Plus, the mouthpiece invariably tasted of strong disinfectant. On the plus side of the sets they were now wearing the full face masks meant you could talk with ease, even if it did sound like you had a mouthful of marbles when you spoke. For just a second Danny recalled the reassuring plip-plop sound of the Proto's mica valves in the breathing tubes, as you breathed in and then exhaled. Sometimes progress sucks, thought Danny.

As Danny and Andy headed towards the aft entrance Danny patted Andy on the shoulder to reassure him. 'You will talk about this BA job around the mess-table for the rest of your career. It is certainly one hell of way of ending mine,' he said. Andy could feel the pounding of his heart as they moved down towards the smoke-filled companion way below.

The Master's wife knew the layout of the ship as well as her husband. But her daughter didn't just need the loo, the unfortunate child could not, in fact, get off of it. A bout of gastritis had hit her suddenly and unexpectedly. The delay, when the fire alarm sounded, meant that when the woman opened the cabin door she was confronted by a wall of acrid smoke that blocked her normal exit route to the upper deck and safety. Covering the child's mouth with her hand and holding her own breath she made a dash of the small service door leading down to the lower deck, which would take the pair to a passageway that ran the length of the clipper and lead them ultimately to alternative exits. The mother helped the child descend the difficult steep raking ladder and the smoke

472

started to follow them down, meeting the trail of thin smoke coming up.

There were no lights on in the ship; if there were, they did not illuminate much, if anything at all. Through the dim beam of their personal torches Danny and Andy saw the vague outline of luxury fittings that looked eerie in the smoke-obscured light that filtered through the occasional porthole opening.

The pair swiftly made their way to the stern cabin and started to search. The following crew were tasked to search for the two missing crew, last reported to be in the galley on the 'tween' deck. As Danny and Andy moved carefully forward any sound they made was drowned out by the shrill screech of the ship's fire alarm. 'I wish some bugger would switch that off,' said Andy, when suddenly it stopped and they heard their fire-boots scraping softly on the ship's timber lower deck. They meticulously, and speedily, searched the Master's cabin and its ante-rooms, finding no one. Which was just as well, as in this smoke, without breathing apparatus, it would be highly unlikely that anyone could survive in that noxious atmosphere for long. They started to retrace their steps, desperation starting to creep into their search pattern as the smoke appeared to getting even thicker, reducing the chances of finding the mother and daughter alive.

Working their way systematically around the companionway wall, it was Danny who discovered the service door slightly ajar. Since the alarm had stopped Danny and Andy found themselves surrounded by a strangely eerie silence that was only broken by the sound of their breathing. Shadows bobbed and danced around the pair with every step they had made. Danny was beginning to feel the clipper was some sort of elaborate optical illusion, for he was sure the ship was much bigger on the inside than it appeared from the outside.

The watertight service door passed through one of the three metal bulkheads fitted to the ship when she had been first built. In sailing ships it was usual to have at least three watertight bulkheads, two being placed at some distance from the extremities and one in the mid-ship part of the vessel. In the 1940s the aft engine room had been encased in an additional bulkhead, with its vents passing upwards through the ship. The collision bulkhead forward was a requirement of Lloyd's. Watertight doors had been fitted in order to afford ready passage between the different compartments. In the passenger areas they were held back in an open position; in all other parts of the ship they were kept closed. Now as Danny and Andy passed through the small bulkhead door, that someone had left open. Danny hoped that it had been the mother trying to lead her child to safety.

Their intention of holding onto each other was scotched at the small watertight door. Staying in close contact was not going to happen, the near-vertical ladder saw to that. It was necessary to go down it backwards, one at a time, in the nautical fashion. Each man was on his own. Yet despite the urgency of their task there appeared little sign of imminent danger. The smoke prevailed but drifted in the air. Andy descended first and within a couple of steps was enveloped in the smoke with only the bobbing of his torch beam marking his progress down. From somewhere below came the sound of a muffled explosion. Neither heard the sound of the bang but Danny felt the force of the blast as he waited his turn to descend. He shouted to Andy but got no reply. The hot air found the exposed skin around the edge of Danny's facemask, not enough to burn him but enough to make him fear for the well-being of his colleague below, who still had not responded to his call.

Danny started his descent not knowing what to expect when he reached the bottom. There was no noise, no sign of fire, nothing was happening, just Andy sitting on the floor looking at something ahead of him. The smoke was thicker here, but the beams from their torches managed to penetrate it somewhat, like car halogen headlamps penetrate fog, with the path of their two beams clearly visible.

Andy was scrabbling about on his knees. Danny assumed he had tried to avoid the blast of heat, but Andy had, in fact, fallen to his knees. What he had seen, or thought he had seen, had made him feel strangely weak, almost faint. When Andy spoke it was a few, excited, garbled words. Not at all like the assured young man that Danny knew. Telling his friend to take his time and to speak slowly Danny heard Andy say in a more controlled tone: 'Someone is down here Danny. It is not the woman and child, but a man. He stood there holding a lantern,' pointing ahead. 'I could not believe my eyes, but I am sure he wants us to follow him.'

Danny thought Andy must have fallen and banged his head, or he was having some sort of hallucination. But he looked to where Andy had pointed, yet all he saw at first was smoke. Then a flicker of light caught his eye and it had nothing to do with their torch beams. The outline of a dim figure stood only feet away, partly shrouded in the veil of smoke. Danny's first reaction was that it must be one of the missing crew members and he called out: 'Don't worry mate, we will get you out.'

There was no reply, the figure just stood there waiting. But there was something decidedly odd about the newcomer's appearance. For the first few seconds it eluded them. Only the bottom two thirds of the figure could be picked out. He, for he clearly had the outline of a large man, and was wearing what looked like a uniform coat. Without saying anything Andy and Danny thought it must be one of the ship's officers, maybe the ship's engineer, then their torch beams reflected light off the two rows of silver buttons on his dark coat. It was then Danny realised it was not an officer's coat at all. It was one of the old-style fire tunics, with its two lines of distinctive chrome buttons down the front. Danny knew exactly what he was looking at because he had worn one of the very same tunics when he first joined the brigade. They had been wearing that style of fire tunic for decades, ever since the days of Metropolitan Fire Brigade in fact. The figure remained silent, but there was little doubt that it expected them to follow him, which is what they did.

The figure stayed ahead of them, the glow from his lantern marking his position in the smoke-filled passageway. Danny was starting to worry, and not just about the stranger's presence. The pair had worked hard and conserving their air had not been easy. Now they were very close to their turn round time, the point that they should start to leave the ship if they were not to run out of air. But neither had they located the Master's wife and child and they seem to have located someone that actually knew his way around the ship. Then Danny remembered, the figure had found them.

The engine room was surrounded by a steel watertight bulkhead. Whilst the metal plates prevented the free movement of water they did nothing to stop the heat from the fire in the engine room being radiated into the surrounding space – space that included the ship's stores, and it was one such store where the heat rose to such levels that it started a secondary fire. Whilst much of the smoke from the engine was filling the evening sky and pouring upwards through the main deck vents, it was the storeroom fire that was filling the lower decks with its lethal smoke.

The figure moved about another half dozen paces and then stopped, his lantern held by a small watertight door on the ship's port side. The pair hesitated, but the figure pointed to the door. It seemed agitated, or maybe the hand signal indicated his frustration, it was hard to tell. Then he was gone, disappeared into the smoke.

Danny and Andy started to follow him but stopped suddenly by the door. Caught on the handle was a small piece of cloth. The type of material that might have come from a child's dress. The figure was forgotten for a moment as they opened the door. At the foot of the narrow vertical shaft, passing up through the ship, lay the woman who was cradling her daughter. Both were unconscious yet miraculously still alive, although the mother's pulse was barely discernible.

Danny looked for their guide, the furtive figure hardly visible as he stood motionless, watching. Still the stranger made no sound, but gave the briefest of smiles before suddenly disappearing. It was then that Danny realised that, whoever he was, he was not wearing any breathing apparatus. There was something else about the figure that hit Danny. He suddenly realised what the connection to the clipper meant for him. But there was not a moment to spare, not if the lives of the woman and child were to be saved.

'Get up that ladder Andy and open that bloody hatch cover double quick.' Andy did and pushed the hatch cover open, allowing the trapped smoke to drift upwards. His sudden appearance, well almost, alerted those standing on the deck. But before words could be exchanged Andy was already on the way back down as the first firefighter moved closer to investigate. 'Don't follow me,' shouted Andy, now nearly a third of the way down, 'we have casualties coming up.'

Whilst Andy had shinned up the metal ladder Danny had removed his facemask, having first taken a deep breath of the life-sustaining air. He opened the additional flow valve, extra air filled the face mask that he now held against the two unconscious faces in turn, giving extra attention to the child. It was difficult to do in the cramped space at the base of the shaft. The smoke and darkness adding its own problems to the extreme nature of his task and trying to resuscitate the two females at the same time. Dim light filtered down from above, as the noise of Andy's rapid descent moved ever nearer and provided a glimmer of hope in this, the most desperate of situations.

Danny had a plan and it was a plan that Andy did not like, not one tiny bit. But there was no Plan B. Danny disconnected the facemask from his BA set and connected it to Andy's additional facemask connection. Now both facemasks were supplied from the air in Andy's cylinder. Andy placed the spare facemask over the child's face, cradling the child across his arms. The smoke was making breathing very difficult for Danny, probably impossible for the woman at his side. Calling on all his reserves Danny took off his BA set completely and removed its cylinder from the holder. He threw the harness out of the doorway, and now as it lay there completely still on the floor the automatic distress signal unit, attached to Danny's set, started it urgent, piercing, alarm call. An alarm call that was meant to summon help.

Andy started his ascent for the second time, the child laying across his arms, the facemask giving her access to air. It was an even more difficult climb than before as he could not hug the ladder and his cylinder was dragging on the shaft wall behind him. Below Danny was making determined, if not frantic, efforts to keep himself and the mother alive. He placed the air cylinder between them and, in turn, gave himself and woman blasts of air. Danny had no intention of recalling a failure on his very last operation shift. 'God it's getting effing hot,' he uttered. The pair were as low a Danny could get them and there was not enough space to close the access door of the shaft and shut out the heat.

The noise of Danny's distress alarm was now audible on the deck but Andy's progress up the ladder prevented anyone getting down it. Fighting the fire in the engine room had been progressing well, even though the conditions in the clipper were now dire. The earlier small explosion had been caused by a pressurised canister going off in the store room. Whilst not causing significant damage it had ruptured cooking oil containers, whose contents had spilled to the floor and spread into the passageway, where considerable quantities of hot thick smoke spilled out from the store into the passageways. The heat was rising to such temperatures it was bringing the oil to its spontaneous ignition temperature and it only need the slightest spark to ignite it. It found one.

Suddenly a firefighter's face appeared at the hatch opening on the main deck. Her eager hands reached in as Andy lifted the girl skyward, disconnecting her facemask from his BA set. The firefighter grabbed her arms and the herculean efforts of both firefighters got the girl safely onto the clipper's deck. Andy was ordered out of the shaft by ADO Butler. An Assistant Chief Officer was now standing on the deck, the incident commander. He had ordered Butler to oversee the rescue operation from the shaft, not that Adrian Butler needed telling what had to be done. Andy still had both feet on the last rung of the vertical ladder when he heard the sound from below.

Later, at the Coroner's Inquest, Andy would describe the sound as a 'Whoosh then a vroom' and believed that his feet were on fire as the thick black smoke and flames blasted out, via the hatch opening, into the evening air. He gave his evidence on crutches; the burns to his legs would heal, eventually. He recalled shouting down for Danny and said that time stood still as all he could hear was the muffled sound of Danny's Automatic Distress Signal Unit giving its warning wail. The Brigade's own report would inform the Coroner that the 'backdraught occurred when the heat from the fire in the engine room built up to such a degree so as to spontaneously ignite spilled flammable liquid in a lower deck storeroom. The fire had raced through the lower part of the clipper with explosive force that was solely directed to the shaft that acted like a chimney flue. That flue effect had saved the lives of the other firefighting teams below, before the fire consumed all the available oxygen and quickly subsided without spreading further below. It was stated that neither of the two firefighters (Danny and Andy) were wearing BA communications equipment.'

Adrenalin, and the love of their comrade, drove the BA search and rescue crew down into the charred bowels of the ship. Despite the hot conditions Station Officer Sue Garton led her crew in the most difficult and distressing of situations. Whilst others doused the fire using jets of water, Garton refused to give up hope as they recovered Danny and the woman. The woman was clearly dead but no one was prepared to make a similar pronouncement on Danny. He was raised by line from the base of the access shaft and rapidly brought back up onto the deck. Others recovered the Master's wife's body. Danny's disassembled BA set told its own story, the empty cylinder had lain between them, Danny holding the outlet to the woman's mouth. Resuscitation on Danny never ceased, and despite the swift transfer from the clipper to police launch, then onto the waiting ambulance and even as it sped through the London streets to the nearby Guys hospital. Danny, and later, the wife were pronounced dead upon arrival. Of the two missing crew members one escaped, in the initial panic, onto a police launch. The other's body was found in the clipper's engine room where, it was assumed, he tried to tackle the fire when it was discovered.

Danny's funeral would have made him proud. He had been to enough in his time. Alan Bradley and Sue Garton led the six pall-bearers in their unenviable duty, three either side of his Union Flag draped coffin. It was an emotional affair, made all the more so by Danny's imminent retirement. His two daughters stood out as they both paid a moving and articulate tribute to a 'wonderful Dad'. After the service the pair showed an inner strength few could have credited as they circulated amongst their Dad's colleagues and friends, many of whom had watched the girls grow up into attractive young ladies. Then an old man approached them, tears filling his eyes. What they each noticed first were his hands. Both were shaped like a claw and had once been badly burned.

'I never actually met your Dad,' said the old man. 'He did come to see me once, to say thank you but I was off sick. I had burned these,' he said raising his scarred extremities. The girls immediately thought of their aunts. 'I never did return to work so I always kept an interest in what your Dad did and the way he did it. When I was pensioned off he made me so proud of what I once was.

Somehow he always made me still feel connected to the Brigade. I just had to come to say thank you and to say goodbye to him.'

They thanked the man as they attempted to comfort him. 'There was something else you should know,' he said. 'It is about that ship and your family history,' he continued. 'The problem is I don't know if this is best time or if you even would want to hear it? Don't worry, it is nothing bad about your Dad,' the man interjected seeing the worried look appear on their faces. 'Honestly it isn't.'

'Maybe another time,' said one of the sisters as their resolve at the day's events was rapidly starting to evaporate.

The London Fire Brigade's Roll of Honour in the Memorial Hall at the Lambeth Headquarters. (Keith Nesbit)

They never saw the old man again. Whatever it was he thought better about sharing it. It was two months later that the immediate family were invited to the London Fire Brigade headquarters at Lambeth to see their father's name, that had been inscribed into the Brigade's Roll of Honour, unveiled during a simple and short memorial service. Bradley, Garton and Butler were all there and a few other faces they knew and many they didn't. After the brief ceremony the two girls wanted to stand by the memorial for a few moments just on their own. The others left, to give them some personal space. All but one man, that is. He was someone that they had not noticed before. He seemed to have come out of the shadows, and yet there was something very familiar about him. He was not terribly old, maybe late fortyish if the girls had to guess. It was how he stood, his stance that struck a powerful chord, reminding them of how their Dad used to stand. They thought that the uniformed chap must be something to do with the Brigade's museum, a guide possibly, as he wore one of the old style fire tunics, dark trousers and black leather fireman's boots. The man moved to Danny's daughters' side, all three now looking at the beautifully sculpted memorial wall and its crafted Roll of Honour scrolls, starting with the first Metropolitan Fire Brigade fireman killed on active duty in the days of Captain Massey Shaw.

'Did you know,' he inquired without looking at them, 'that your Dad's grandfather's name is on that Roll of Honour too?' The girls knew little of their Dad's grandfather, only that he had apparently died at sea. Their uninvited companion pointed to one of the scrolls, the first, which recorded the early names who had perished in the line of duty. The pair looked up in disbelief. There, the eighth entry, they saw their family name: SHAW. They read the citation aloud, neither aware that the other was doing so to too.

1904. Fireman Daniel (Danny) SHAW. Died fighting a fire off St Katharine's Reach, Wapping.

The looked to the very last scroll and the final name entered on it; that of their father.

2003. Firefighter Daniel (Danny) SHAW. Died fighting a fire off St Saviour's Reach, Bermondsey.

The pair turned to speak to the man. He had disappeared. They asked the others waiting outside who the stranger was. The others looked bemused and all said that hadn't seen any such man inside. They told the girls that no one had left the Memorial Hall before they had just exited. It was then the daughters recalled how the man in the old fire tunic had smiled at them. It was exactly the same the way their Dad would smiled at them whenever he left to go on duty.

The Massey Shaw Education Trust

Registered charity: 284970
Company number: 1636306

(Bryan Jones)

The picture above is taken off the French coast in 2015. From the mast is flying the burgee of the Little Ships of Dunkirk, which is the Cross of St George defaced with the badge of Dunkirk. This can be flown by any boat that was participated in the evacuation in

1940. The Association had received an official invitation from the Mayor of Dunkirk to return to Dunkirk in May 2015 to commemorate the 75th Anniversary. Not long after this picture was taken a number of the smaller boats had to turn back as it was too choppy. The 'Massey Shaw' carried on rolling with the waves but never gave cause for concern.

About us

The Massey Shaw and Marine Vessels Preservation Society (the Society) is a charitable trust operating under the authority of the Charity Commissioners for England and Wales and trades as the 'Massey Shaw Education Trust'. The Trust came into being in 1981 and was established by a group of e-firefighters and enthusiasts who had worked on board the 'Massey Shaw'.

Our Mission Statement

The purpose of the society is simple:

> *To advance public education in the history of marine vessels in particular by the preservation and public display of the 'Massey Shaw' fireboat.*

Funding

The Society is an independent organisation which receives no core funding. Its work is financed by grants and through income generated by membership subscriptions, donations, sale of merchandise and public displays.

Board of Directors

The Society is managed by an elected Board of Directors who oversee the running of the Trust. All directors are volunteers who come from a wide range of professional backgrounds (e.g. Fire Officers, Civil Engineers, Boat Builders and Surveyors). They give their time and efforts free to promote the aims of the Society and oversee the Trust.

How you can help?

As an octogenarian the 'Massey Shaw' is a true 'London' vessel. She is believed to be the only remaining example of a working fireboat of her type in Europe. The Society are constantly seeking volunteers. People who can help us maintain the vessel and undertake training as crew members. Additionally, the Society aims to promote our education projects and digitise our fire-float and fireboat archives to allow further access to the public.

We are completely self-funded by donations and grants. This enables us to attend public events and continue to promote the heritage of the vessel and its ties with the London Fire Brigade.

If you would like to donate towards the Trust please either visit our website to make a donations or send it to the Treasurer, Massey Shaw Education Trust, at West India Dock, Poplar, London E14 3NU.

Donations:
http://www.masseyshaw.org/donate/

Membership:
http://www.masseyshaw.org/volunteering/membership/

To contact us or consider becoming a volunteer or alternatively becoming a member of the Society please contact us:

Email: info@masseyshaw.org
Website: www.masseyshaw.org
Twitter: @themasseyshaw
Facebook: /masseyshaw

APPENDIX III

Roll of Honour: WWII and the Blitz on London

Fireman Albert G Abrahart. London

Fireman Percy C Atchison. Beckenham

Fireman Thomas C Aldsworth. London

Fireman Edwin W Ambridge. London

Fireman Cecil R Andreazzi. London

Fireman David Appleby. London

Fireman Albert E Arber. London

Leading Watchroom Attendant Richard E Archer. London

Sub Officer Arthur Ash. West Ham

Fireman Derek E Aust. London

Fireman John A Axcell. London

Fireman Maurice C Ayers. London

Fireman Edward W Badland. West Ham

Fireman Ronald M Bailey. Beckenham

Firewoman Lilian S Baker. London

Fireman Victor Baldesarre. London

Fireman Douglas B Balbwin. London

Fireman Alan C Barber. Beckenham

Fireman John C Barrell. London

Leading Fireman Charles W Barrow. London

Firewoman Joan F Bartlett. London

Fireman Arthur E Batchelor. London

Leading Fireman Jack Bathie. London

Fireman Richard Beacon. Beckenham

Fireman Ernest R Beadle. Beckenham

Company Officer William Beard. London

Fireman George Bell. London

Fireman William F Belton. London

Fireman William T Benney. London

Fireman Joseph C Bines. London

Fireman Herbert T Blundell. London

Fireman Henry J Bouch. London

Leading Fireman George Bowen. London

Fireman Kenneth J Bowles. London

Fireman John W F Blazier. London

Fireman Christopher J Briggs. London

Fireman Henry C Brightwell. London

Fireman Albert F S Brooker. Wembley

Fireman Thomas W Brown. London

Fireman William H Brown. London

Fireman William G Brum. London

Fireman John H Burch. London

Station Officer Charles E Burden. London

Fireman Henry H Butcher. London

Fireman Richard H Butler. London

Fireman Patrick J Cambell. London

Fireman Henry J C Carden. Beckenham

Fireman Eric B Cartwright. London

Leading Fireman David J Chalmers. Beckenham

Fireman Oliver C Cheater. London

Fireman Walter H Childs. London

Fireman Benjamin E Chinnery. London

Fireman Cecil R S Chopping. London

Fireman Albert E Clark. London

Fireman David Clatworth. London

Fireman Harold G Coleridge. London

Fireman Alexander W Collins. London

Fireman Stanley T Conniff. Wembley

Fireman Herman H Conrad. London

Fireman George J Cook. London

Fireman Percy Crane. London

Fireman Frederick W Crowe. London

Fireman John Culley. London

Fireman Alfred Cumberland. West Ham

Senior Fireman Thomas W Curson. London

Fireman James Daly. London

Fireman Henry J Davidson. London

Firewoman Marjory W Davies. London

Fireman Robert J Deans. Beckenham

Fireman Frederick W Dell. West Ham

Fireman Israel Deutch. London

Fireman Hugh Dicken. West Ham

Fireman John Dilworth. London

Fireman James W N Dinwoodle. London

Fireman Henry A C Dixon. London

Fireman Bernard J Dormer. London

Fireman William Downes. London

Fireman Charles L M Drew. Beckenham

Fireman Reginald H Driver. London

Fireman Stanley G Du Vergier. London

Firewoman Hilda Dupree. London

Fireman James A C Durling. London

Fireman Edward B East. London

Fireman Cecil A Elliman. Mitcham

Fireman Herbert T W Ellis. London

Fireman Edmund F Emmett. London

Fireman Frank J Endean. Beckenham

Fireman Albert B Evans. London

Fireman Albert C Eyre. West Ham.

Fireman Cecil Farley. Beckenham

Fireman Arthur Farnin. London

Fireman Hyman Feldman. London

Messenger Percival H Field. London

Fireman Denis G Fitzgerald. Beckenham

Fireman Henry G Flegg. London

Fireman James Fletcher. London

Deputy Commandant Arthur T Ford. Barnet

Fireman Robert Forrester. London

Station Officer Thomas Forrow BEM. London

Fireman Edward Fox. London

Fireman Alfred J Francis. London

Fireman Leonard J Freeman. London

Fireman William Fuller. London

Fireman Frederick G Gage. West Ham

Fireman David W Garrick. London

Senior Fireman Albert Gentry. London

Fireman Robert W George. London

Fireman Harold C Gillard. London

Fireman Bernard J Godfrey. London

Leading Fireman Herbert B H Golden. London

Fireman George E Goldsmith. London

Leading Fireman Lionel A Gothard. London

Fireman James S Gower. London

Leading Fireman Arthur H Grant GM. London

Fireman Samuel J Gray. London

Fireman Barnet Greenburg. London

Fireman Joseph Greenbugh. London
Fireman Frank L Greenway. London
Fireman William G Grieve. London
Fireman Albert W Griffin. London

Fireman George J J Hall. London
Senior Fireman George W Hall. London
Sub Officer Henry W Halliday. London
Fireman John S Hammersley. West Ham
Fireman Bertie J F Harris. London
Section Officer James C Harris. London
Fireman Walter C W Hart. London
Fireman Christopher E Hartwell. Banstead
Fireman Alfred R Hayden. London
Fireman Frederick W Hayward. London
Fireman Leslie T Henley. Beckenham
Fireman James H Heath. London
Fireman Ernest A Hemming. London
Station Officer John W Hill. London
Fireman Sydney A Holder. London
Sub Officer Edward A Hollett. London
Fireman George H Holloway. Mitcham
Fireman Edward W Hoskins. London
Fireman Walter G Hubbard. London
Fireman Stanley R Hubbers. Beckenham
Fireman Harold Huggett. West Ham
Fireman A S Humphries. London
Fireman Frank W Hurd. London
Fireman Ernest J Hutton. London
Fireman Frances E Huxley. London
Fireman Ernest W Hyde. London
Fireman Leslie J H Hyde. London

Fireman Leslie W Issacs. London

Fireman Sydney H Jarvis. London
Fireman Harold G Jerome. Bromley

Leading Fireman James A Johnson. London
Fireman Arthur H Jones. London
Fireman Evan M Jones. London
Fireman Sidney B Jones. London
Fireman Sydney G Jones. London

Fireman Charles S Kelly. London
Fireman Robert L Kerr-Lindsey. London
Fireman Frederick G Kiefer. London
Fireman Charles T King. London
Leading Fireman David A King. London
Fireman Reginald F King. London
Fireman J D Kirkland. London
Fireman Albert V Kite. Beckenham
Station Officer Henry W Knight. London
Fireman John T Knight. London
Fireman Reginald F W J Knight. London
Fireman William F Knight. Wembley

Fireman Eric W Lambert. Bromley
Fireman Marcel Laveli. London
Fireman Charles M Layton. Bromley
Fireman Clifford M Leake. London
Fireman Thomas C Leaver. London
Fireman Victor H Legg. London
Fireman Ascher D Lettner. London
Fireman Abraham Lewis. London
Fireman Eric D Lewis. London
Fireman John J Lewis. London
Fireman John W Lewis. London
Fireman William H long. West Ham

Fireman Donald Mackenzie. London
Fireman Vincent L Mander. London
Fireman Benjamin Mansbridge. London
Fireman Harold Marriott. West Ham
Fireman Harry R Marshall. London

Fireman Richard J Martin. London

Messenger Francis P McDonough. London

Fireman Daniel B McEvoy. London

Fireman Ewen S McEwen. West Ham

Fireman Henry J Mead. London

Fireman John F Mead. London

Fireman Leslie C Medhurst. London

Fireman Victor Michaelson. London

Fireman Vernon J Middleditch. London

Fireman Arthur W Miller. London

Fireman Percy Millett. London

Leading Fireman Frank K Mills. London

Fireman Alfred E Minter. London

Fireman Frederick Mitchell. London

Section Officer G L Moore. Kingston upon Thames

Fireman Charles E Moore. London

Fireman Frederick W Moore. Beckenham

Fireman William B Moore. London

Section Officer Sydney A Morris. London

Fireman William G Morrow. London

Fireman Norman R C Mountjoy. Beckenham

Fireman John J Munday. London

Fireman C W Murphy. London

Fireman Arthur E Murray. London

Fireman Sydney J Newbold. London

Fireman Charles F Nightingale. London

Fireman George R Norris. London

Fireman Maurice P O O'Neill. London

Fireman Horace V Olney. London

Fireman Albert E Owen. London

Sub Officer Harry Page. London

Fireman Leslie J Palmer. London

Fireman Walter J Palmer. West Ham

Fireman Frederick G Parcell. Beckenham

Leading Fireman Frederick C Parfett. Beckenham

Fireman William F Parfrey. London

Fireman Harold C Parkes. Mitcham

Fireman Edward J Patterden. London

Fireman Albert E Pearton. London

Firewoman Violet I Pengelly. London

Fireman Edward E G Pepper. Mitcham

Firewoman Winifred A Peters. London

Fireman John Phelan. London

Fireman Henry Piller. London

Fireman William C Plant. Beckenham

Fireman Cyril B Porter. London

Fireman Edward Preston. London

Fireman James H Purslow. London

Fireman Frederick A Rae. London

Fireman William T Randell. London

Fireman Stanley H Randolph. London

Fireman William T Rushbrook. London

Fireman Henry C Rathbone. London

Fireman William Rawlings. Erith.

Fireman George Reardon. London

Firewoman Joan M Rudd. London

Fireman Ernest F Robinson. Mitcham

Fireman Arthur H Rogers. London

Leading Fireman Leonard Roots. Beckenham

Fireman William R Roots. London

Fireman Richard C Roullier. London

Fireman Edward Sackie. London

Section Officer Frederick C Salkeld. London

Senior Fireman Laurence W Sander. London

Fireman Stanley Sargant. London

Fireman Herbert C J Saunders. London

Fireman Albert A Saville. London

Fireman Frederick Scates. London

Fireman Ernest A Schneider. London

Fireman Arthur Seaby. London

Fireman Reginald A L Seymore. London

Fireman Benjamin J Sheldon. London

Leading Fireman Stanley Short. Beckenham

Fireman Jack A W Shrimpton. London

Section Officer James Simpson. London

Station Officer Richard W Sinstadt. London

Fireman Harry R Skinner. London

Fireman Alexander Smith. London

Fireman Edward H Smith. London

Fireman Frederick C Smith. London

Fireman Frederick J Smith. London

Fireman Thomas J Snowden. London

Fireman Romeo C Sorrenti. London

Fireman Walter J Spence. London

Leading Fireman A H Spiler. Mitcham

Fireman Harry J Stangroom. London

Fireman Oliver J Steele. London

Fireman George R Steers. London

Fireman Stanley R Stevens. London

Fireman Albert H Strange. London

Fireman Charles Strutton. London

Fireman Alfred C Sturk. London

Sub Officer Frederick C Sutherland. London

Fireman Robert Tanner. London

Leading Fireman John J Taylor. Bromley

Fireman Mervin J B Taylor. London

Fireman John Teague. London

Fireman Sidney S Tidy. London

Section Officer Frederick Tierney. London

District Officer Joseph L Tobias. London

Fireman George H Tonkin. London

Station Officer Ernest A Tooke. London

Fireman Walter Turley. London

Fireman Albert A Turner. London

Fireman Albert D Umney. London

Fireman Mathys Van Hulst. London

Fireman James Vernon. London

Fireman Harry C Vesey. London

Leading Fireman Edgar W Vick. Beckenham

Fireman Ronald V Waghorne. London

Fireman Reginald B Wakeman. London

Fireman Walter W Wallis. London

Fireman Myer Wand. London

Fireman George A Warerman. London

Fireman Frederick J Watkins. London

Fireman Henty H Wayte. London

Fireman Arthur H Wenbourne. London

Fireman William Westwood. London

Fireman Charles W Whipps. London

Fireman Frederick N Williams. London

Fireman Ronald Wilson. London

Station Officer Leslie W G Wilson BEM. London

Fireman Francis J Winfield. London

Fireman Herbert T Wolff. London

Fireman Walter H Wooder. London

Leading Fireman Walter J Woodland. Beckenham

Fireman Herbert C Wotton. Beckenham

Fireman Victor G Wratten. London

****

By the same author

Beyond the Flames

Beyond the Flames, David Pike's first book, charts his career and life in the London Fire Brigade. Published by Austin Macauley in 2013, it was shortlisted for the prestigious People's Book Prize in 2014 and was runner up in the non-fiction category. The book was also nominated for the Beryl Bainbridge Book Award and was a finalist in the Wishing Shelf Independent Book Awards 2014/15.

'A fascinating peek into the world of the London Fire Brigade. A FINALIST and highly recommended.'

The Wishing Shelf Book Awards, 2014/15

By the same author

London's Firefighters

London's Firefighters, an anthology about the London Fire Brigade edited by David C. Pike, was published by Austin Macauley in 2015. It won the Bronze Medal for the Adult non-fiction category in the Wishing Shelf Book Awards, 2015/16.

'What a superb anthology! Lots of history here including World War Two. So many heroic men and, more recently, women. Perfect for anybody interested in London life and, in particular, firefighting throughout the last century or two. Highly recommended.'

Review from the Wishing Shelf Book Awards, 2015/16